The
most
amazing
places
to walk
in Britain

PUBLISHED BY
THE READER'S DIGEST ASSOCIATION LIMITED
LONDON • NEW YORK • SYDNEY • MONTREAL

The most amazing places to walk in Britain

The most beautiful and captivating routes in England, Scotland and Wales

Contents

Introduction

Set off on foot and explore the best of Britain's landscape through its extensive network of walking routes and trails. From remote highland glens to rolling southern downs, discover the beauty and splendour of the great outdoors.

Walking is Britain's number one pastime: it's the most natural way to exercise while enjoying the pleasures of the countryside, and *The Most Amazing Places to Walk in Britain* provides a lifetime's passport to these priceless benefits. Its superb maps and easy-to-follow directions leave the walker free to enjoy the sights, the views and the unexpectedly charming corners of Britain, many of which can only be seen from footpaths and tracks.

How to use this book

The book is divided by region into six chapters. Within each chapter the walks are grouped by county, except for Wales and Scotland, which are divided into sub-regions. At the beginning of each chapter is a map of the region; within each county, numbers identify the location of the individual walks. The walks themselves are easy to follow as they are numbered stage-by-stage, both on the detailed maps and in the accompanying written instructions.

SCOTLAND
258-311

NORTHERN
ENGLAND
170-219

CENTRAL ENGLAND
114-169

WALES
220-257

SOUTHWEST ENGLAND
8-67

SOUTHEAST ENGLAND
68-113

Walkers' rights and responsibilities

Always keep to the routes described and avoid damaging the surroundings. In England and Wales it is a civil offence to wander off a path through private land. Walkers who do might be liable for any damage caused. If a right of way across farmland is muddy or obscured, walkers are not legally permitted to leave the path in order to make their own way across the field, but farmers are unlikely to object as long as crops and property are not damaged. Respect the Countryside Code - see www.countrysideaccess.gov.uk Public authorities in England and Wales are required to signpost where bridleways, paths or byways leave a road. Walkers are entitled to walk through a crop that blocks a right of way if they keep to the route of the public footpath and cause no unnecessary damage. They may also climb a locked gate across a right of way and to take the shortest

route around other obstructions. In addition, recent legislation gives open access to about 1 million hectares - nearly 2.5 million acres - of uncultivated countryside in England and Wales. In Scotland, there is a tradition of responsible access to all land unless there is a good reason for exclusion, except for areas such as railway property, quarries and airfields.

Tips and advice

Dress properly. Wear what's comfortable and never underestimate the changeability of British weather. Purpose-made walking shoes or boots are essential, as trainers or walking sandals do not give the necessary support and protection on rough ground. Dress in layers that you can peel off - specialist retailers recommend breathable materials. If the day is sunny, take a sun hat and sun cream. In cold weather, take gloves, and a hat.

Safety on the hills

Take great care when out on moorland, mountainous or hilly country. Basic safety precautions include checking the weather forecast; taking a mobile phone, map and compass; and telling someone where you are going. For further safety information, see www.country-couples.co.uk

Abbreviations

The following abbreviations are used throughout the book:
Cadw Welsh Historic Monuments, **www.cadw.wales.gov.uk**
EH English Heritage, **www.english-heritage.org.uk**
NT National Trust, **www.nationaltrust.org.uk**
NTS National Trust for Scotland, **www.nts.org.uk**
RSPB Royal Society for the Protection of Birds, **www.rspb.org.uk**
SWT Scottish Wildlife Trust, **www.swt.org.uk**

KEY TO SYMBOLS USED ON WALKS MAPS

P Car parking at start of walk
→ Walk route
. . . Detour
1 Walk instruction number

ROADS AND PATHS

Motorway
A road
B road
Minor road
Other road, drive or track
Footpath
Gradient 1 in 7 to 1 in 5
Gradient 1 in 5 and steeper
Roundabout

GENERAL FEATURES

Airport, airfield
Bridge
Car ferry
City, town or village
Isolated building
Quarry, chalk pit
Railway
Field boundary
△ Triangulation point

PHYSICAL FEATURES

Marsh
Rocky foreshore
Rocky outcrop
Sand and shingle
Sandy beach
Woodland

HEIGHT INFORMATION

Contours at 100 ft intervals above sea level

	0 - 100
	100 - 200
	200 - 300
	300 - 400
	400 - 500
	500 - 600
	600 - 700
	700 - 800
	800 - 900
	900 - 1000
	1000 - 1100
	1100 - 1200
	1200 - 1300
	1300 - 1400
	1400 - 1500
	1500 - 2000
	2000 - 2500
	2500 - 3000
	over 3000

PLACES OF INTEREST

Abbey, priory, etc
Ancient monument
Arboretum
Battle site
Cathedral
Church
Country park
Craft centre
Garden
Heritage railway
Hillfort, long barrow
House or castle in ruins
House or castle with interesting interior

Industrial feature
Lighthouse
Museum
Nature reserve
Nature trail
Picnic site
Public house or inn
Roman remains
Tourist information (open all year)
Tourist information (seasonal)
Viewpoint
Watermill
Windmill

Key

- ① Walk location
- County boundary
- Motorway
- Principal A road

(See 'How to use the book', page 6)

Ilfracombe
⑧ A39 ⑨
A361
Barnstaple
Bideford
A361
⑦
A39
A386
A377
⑬
DEVON
28-39
Bude
⑫
Okehampton A30
A39
⑥
Launceston
Dartmoor
National
Park ⑤
⑧
A30
Tavistock A386
⑦
A39 Bodmin ③ ④
Padstow ⑨ Moor
Bodmin ⑪
Newquay ⑩ Liskeard ②
CORNWALL A30 Plymouth A38
10-27 A390 A38
St Austell ①
A390
Truro Salcombe
A30
St Ives
⑤
Penzance A394 Falmouth
④
⑥ Helston
③
②

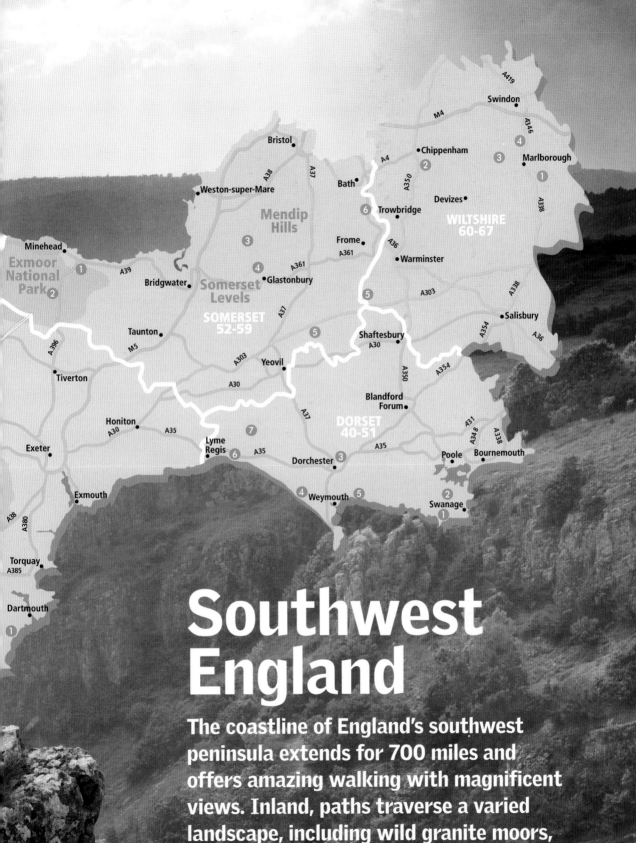

Southwest England

The coastline of England's southwest peninsula extends for 700 miles and offers amazing walking with magnificent views. Inland, paths traverse a varied landscape, including wild granite moors, wooded vales and grassy downland.

CORNWALL

Cornwall's spectacular coastline offers challenging – but rewarding – cliff paths. The pace is easier on the inland plateau, a mostly rural landscape threaded with twisting lanes that rises to the rocky dome of Bodmin Moor.

1 Talland

From open fields and glorious riverside woodland to a lively fishing port and a gorse-lined coastal path.

LENGTH **7 miles (4 hours)**

PARKING **Talland's eastern car park (opposite Smugglers Café), off A387 northeast of Polperro**

CONDITIONS **After an initial steep climb and gradual descent to the river, the walk is relatively level until the intermittent ups and downs of the coastal path**

REFRESHMENTS **Café at car park; pubs and teashops in Looe**

1 Turn right out of the car park and pass St Tallan's Church on the right. Soon turn left up a flight of steps, following a footpath sign and yellow waymark, and continue through a gate into a field. As the path rises steeply, look back for views of Talland Bay. On the right stands a landmark – one of a pair of black and white panels used by sailors for navigational purposes.

Keeping the hedge on the left, continue to the top of the field towards two gaps ahead, formed by two gates. Go through the second, waymarked, gate. As the slope eases, white cubes dotting the fields on the right mark a caravan site. Head half right for the corner of the field. Cross a stile into the caravan park, and keep straight on.

2 At the far end of the caravan site, go through a gate and continue forward onto a farm lane. A wooden gate in the hedge on the left gives a sudden vista of fields rolling down the valley and the sea glinting beyond Talland Bay. The lane meets the A387 and continues on the other side of it, rising gently past open fields on the right.

3 After levelling out, the lane bends left by a timber fence and descends towards the massed treetops of Ten Acre and Polzion woods, tucked away in the valley ahead. The lane winds down past a duck pond and the outbuildings, now holiday cottages, of Kilminorth farm on the left. About ¼ mile past the farm, turn right through a gate on a bridleway signposted to Looe.

4 Follow the waymarked bridleway towards Looe beneath a glorious canopy of beeches, oaks and other mature trees to the sound of birdsong and the murmur of streams. Soon, a viewpoint offers glimpses of West Looe river through the branches. A signpost points left down a path to the tiny hamlet of Watergate, where a former shooting lodge is now a guesthouse. Brightly coloured canoes glide up and down the river.

LOOE ISLAND, EVENING

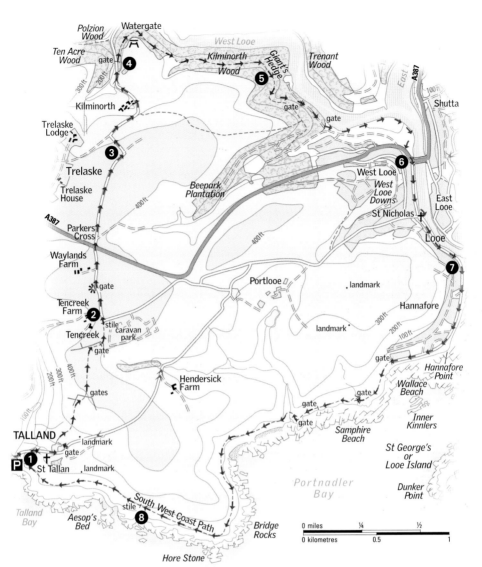

Follow the path around
a spur (ignore a waymark pointing
to a raised path on the right) and
continue for nearly ½ mile to an eroded bank
on the right, known as the Giant's Hedge. This
early medieval earthwork once ran for 5 miles
from Looe to Lerryn, south of Lostwithiel, and
may have marked the boundary of a Cornish
kingdom. Originally topped by a fence or hedge,
it still rises to 3.5m (12ft) in places.

5 The bridleway bends right, away from the
river, then back again, and descends to a metalled
riverside path by a gate. Follow this along the
bank of the river, which merges with the East
Looe river, into Looe, a bustling holiday resort
and fishing port.

6 Go past Looe Bridge, built in the mid
19th century, on the left, and follow a path to the
left of St Nicholas's Church, parts of which were
constructed from timbers recovered from
shipwrecks. Rejoin the road, which eventually
curves west to Hannafore, with its glorious
180-degree sweep of Looe Bay.

7 Head towards the small St George's Island,
also known as Looe Island, about ¼ mile
offshore. The road ends at a kissing gate, after
which a footpath leads ahead through a field to
stepping stones over a stream and another kissing
gate; continue along the path through two more
gates, over a footbridge over another stream and
up some steep steps. Bordered by swathes of
gorse, the path edges around Hore Point, passing
Hore Stone, which rises offshore.

8 Cross a stile and continue for ½ mile above
foaming, cormorant-haunted rocks before
descending into Talland. Follow the path down
to the car park and the pink- and green-hued
rocks of Talland Bay.

CORNWALL

2 Lizard

An exhilarating cliff-path walk round mainland Britain's most southerly point, visiting a beautiful cove.

LENGTH 5¼ miles (3 hours)

PARKING Beside a large green on the edge of Lizard village

CONDITIONS Fairly demanding, with some steep cliff paths

REFRESHMENTS Cafés at Kynance Cove (summer only) and at Lizard Point

1 Walk down past the block of public toilets at the edge of the green to a lane and follow the footpath sign. After a short way, fork right onto a path to Kynance Cove. Follow the path along the top of a bank between fields and through a thicket. At the end of the raised path, take the right fork. Continue across scrubland to reach a road near a pair of granite posts.

2 Turn left on the road for a few metres, then turn right onto a waymarked footpath. Continue straight ahead across the scrub until reaching a National Trust car park.

Turn right and follow the track as it winds down towards Kynance Cove, giving splendid views of the outcrops of serpentine rocks that shelter the cove from the sea. At low tide these rocks and their caves may be visited – including the Bellows, which has a spectacular blowhole when the sea surges in – but beware of the rising tide. One of the rocks, Asparagus Island, is named after the wild asparagus that grows there. Others are known as Gull Rock and the Bishop.

3 About halfway down to the cove, turn right onto the well-defined South West Coast Path, signposted to Lizard Point. Tiny orchids grow in profusion along the path, and Lizard Point, with its outlying rocks, soon comes into view. Larks sing overhead as the path dips down and rises again, leading past Caerthillian and Holseer coves.

4 Continue round Lizard Point, from where there are spectacular views back across Mount's Bay to the western tip of Cornwall and the Lizard Lighthouse. The old lifeboat station can soon be seen in the distance ahead.

Sea pinks and bladderwort line the path. Red campion, lizard plant, tormentil, tamarisk, yellow vetch, primroses and bluebells also bloom in season, and some of the cliffs and walls are smothered with the distinctive Hottentot fig. The fig was introduced to Britain in 1690, but now flourishes only near the sea in Cornwall and Devon.

5 Continue along the cliff path, round the most southerly tip of mainland Britain. The path leads on past the old lifeboat station, which closed in 1961 and is now used to store lobster pots. At the foot of the cliffs, waves crash on rocks, and seals may sometimes be seen bobbing about in the sea.

6 Follow the path past the lighthouse, which was built in 1751 to replace an early 17th-century one. Its huge foghorns can be heard 14 miles out to sea, and its light is the most powerful in Britain – in clear conditions, the beam can be seen by reflection off the sky from nearly 100 miles away.

Rounding the headland, the path curves along Housel Bay, through blackthorn bushes and past the Housel Bay Hotel. It then swings right past a bungalow, where the rocky outcrop and grassy sward of Pen Olver stretch out to sea on the right.

7 At a junction with a metalled track, Lloyds Road, before the Lloyds signal station and lookout post, turn left and follow the signposted track to Lizard. At the T-junction with the road, turn left back to the car park.

3 Loe Valley

From a former inland harbour town, round a large freshwater lake on the Penrose Estate, and along a cliff path and shingle.

LENGTH 5½ or 7 miles (3 or 4 hours)

PARKING Car park on south side of B3304 just west of Helston

CONDITIONS Easy, except for a stretch along shingle and a short climb

REFRESHMENTS Pub in Gunwalloe

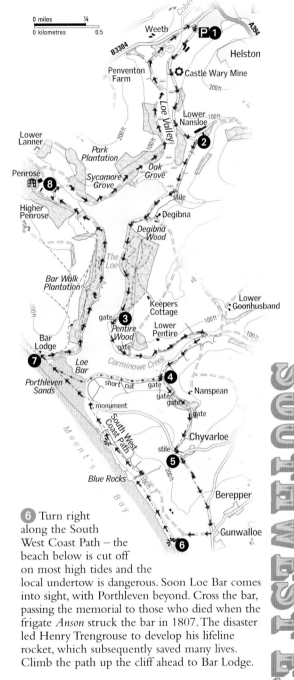

1 Turn left out of the narrow end of the car park. Turn right on the lane, passing the chimney of a disused mine, with the tiny River Cober flowing through the swamp to right. In the 13th century, before Loe Bar cut off the valley from the sea, ships sailed up the Cober to Helston.

2 At a sharp left-hand bend, turn right onto a track and follow it through trees, then through a meadow to reach a small bridge over a brook. Go over a granite stile. The Loe – a huge, sheltered freshwater lake that is a favoured spot for overwintering wildfowl – comes into sight. On its far side stands Penrose House and estate buildings. Keeping Looe Pool on the right, follow the path, marked by green arrows, through Degibna Wood and up some steps. Soon, Loe Bar can be seen through the trees.

3 After a kissing gate at the end of the wood, the path leads to Carminowe Creek. Go through another kissing gate and turn right onto a track joining from the left. At the tip of the creek turn right over a stream. Follow the path back along the other side of the creek and cross a brook.
SHORT CUT *Continue straight on to reach Loe Bar. Cross the sand to meet the South West Coast Path, rejoining the walk shortly before* **7**.

4 Turn left through a gate and bear slightly left to another gate. Follow the path, signposted to Chyvarloe, into a wood then into a field. Follow the left-hand boundary to reach a granite hedge stile. Turn right on the lane.

5 Turn left onto a track through Chyvarloe, a medieval farming settlement restored by the National Trust. Keep to left of the buildings, ignoring gates to right and left, and continue on a farm track. Continue to a lane and turn right to reach a T-junction in Gunwalloe.
Turn right and right again by a bus shelter onto a track giving fine sea views. As the track bends right, pass a concrete bench and soon after turn left downhill towards the sea.

6 Turn right along the South West Coast Path – the beach below is cut off on most high tides and the local undertow is dangerous. Soon Loe Bar comes into sight, with Porthleven beyond. Cross the bar, passing the memorial to those who died when the frigate *Anson* struck the bar in 1807. The disaster led Henry Trengrouse to develop his lifeline rocket, which subsequently saved many lives. Climb the path up the cliff ahead to Bar Lodge.

7 Turn sharp right into the Penrose Estate (NT). The track leads back along the lake through fine woodland, then curves left towards the walled kitchen garden of Penrose House.

8 Follow the track round to the right opposite the handsome stable block. At a T-junction, turn right, following the sign to Helston. Pass a lodge above a boathouse and continue along the side of the valley back to the car park.

SOUTH WEST ENGLAND

13

CORNWALL

4 Lamorna Cove

From a granite cove past old quarries, across meadows to Mousehole village, then back along the coast path.

LENGTH 4 or 4½ miles (2½ or 3 hours)

PARKING Lamorna Cove car park

CONDITIONS Steep climbs leaving Lamorna Cove, at Mousehole and on rough and rocky coast path

REFRESHMENTS Café in Lamorna Cove; pub up lane from Lamorna Cove; full range in Mousehole

1 Leave the car park and immediately turn right on a path, passing between a garden and the front of some cottages. Cross a brook and go up the side of the valley, then take the left fork into a wood. The path twists and bends as it climbs past a disused quarry, emerging into farmland. At the T-junction at the edge of Kemyel Wartha hamlet, turn right on a track through a farmyard, then bear left to a stone stile and marked footpath.

Continue on a clear path across meadows with open views of the coast ahead and to the right. At a fork, bear right and continue to a track by the hamlet of Kemyel Crease.

2 Walk through the hamlet. The track becomes a lane leading past cottages. Then fork right across a stile onto a path that passes through lovely little meadows, crosses a brook and winds through a thicket to join a track leading to the hamlet of Kemyel Drea.

Turn left just before an L-shaped barn, then turn right on a waymarked footpath, through a series of kissing gates between farm buildings. Continue across the meadows, with sea views across to St Michael's Mount and its 14th-century battlemented castle. Follow the path to the hamlet of Raginnis, crossing more stiles on the way and ignoring a path to the right. After passing a garden wall, cross a stile to a junction with a narrow road.

SHORT CUT *Turn right on the road and continue steeply down to a sharp left bend. Turn right onto the coast path and continue from* **5**.

3 Cross the narrow road and follow a track opposite towards a farm. Where the track bends left, fork right to cross a stone stile and follow the waymarked path as it descends towards Mousehole (pronounced Mowzull). The path ends at an opening in a field hedge; continue down some stone steps to meet a lane.

4 Follow the lane left, then turn immediately right onto a path that skirts a small brook before continuing into Mousehole, which the writer Dylan Thomas described as 'the loveliest village in England'. Solid, traditional cottages cluster round the small granite harbour in a jumble of alleys and passageways, and though fishing is no longer the villagers' main occupation, a few boats still put to sea in the time-honoured manner. Shark and deep-sea fishing trips start here.

Facing the harbour, turn right, then follow steep Raginnis Hill past the post office, Wesleyan chapel and Wild Bird Sanctuary, to a sharp right-hand bend.

5 At the apex of the bend, turn left onto a track to join the coastal path. To the left, across the bay, are views of Lizard Point and its lighthouse, and the satellite tracking dishes at Goonhilly. Where the path splits, fork left and cross a brook to Kemyel Crease nature reserve.

6 The path climbs steeply as it rounds the rocky headland of Carn-du, then begins its descent to the tiny harbour at Lamorna Cove. In the 19th century, ships pulled up here to load high-quality granite from nearby quarries; local stone was used to build London's Thames Embankment, as well as numerous Victorian lighthouses. Follow the path back to the car park.

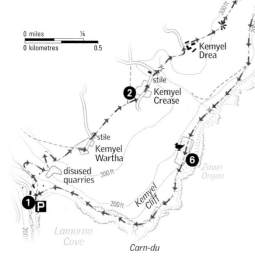

A SMALL GRANITE HARBOUR OF GREAT CHARACTER AND CHARM

MOUSEHOLE HARBOUR

CORNWALL

5 Morvah

Inland through gorse-covered moorland, past an ancient burial mound and an Iron Age fort, then along a rugged cliff path.

LENGTH 4½ or 7 miles (2½ or 3½ hours)

PARKING In village near church

CONDITIONS Mostly level paths and lanes; coast path narrow and rocky

REFRESHMENTS Tearoom in Morvah

1 From the church, return to the B3306 and walk towards Trevowhan, with the sea to the left. Where the road bends left, cross a waymarked stile to right and follow the path through fields. The path bends right, bypassing Carne Farm, to meet a tarmac lane. Turn right on the lane. At the end of the lane follow the track ahead, ignoring the next crossroads. At a fork follow the broad, grassy path left, with a stone wall to the right.

Continue ahead as the path narrows between hedges and climbs into open scrubland to reach Chûn Quoit – one of Cornwall's famous

chamber tombs, built around 4,000 years ago. Three upright stones support a massive capstone. The tomb was originally covered by earth.

2 From the chamber tomb, take the path left to Chûn Castle, a small hillfort built by a Celtic chieftain some 2,000 years ago. The superb elevated position overlooks the north coast and on a clear day also affords views south to Mount's Bay and the Lizard peninsula. Stone gateposts guard the entrance to the fort, the walls of which are still 2.4m (8ft) high in places. It is still possible to see the old well and the circular outlines of Iron Age buildings.

Leave Chûn Castle by the way you entered, then turn sharp left and continue ahead, following the path down through thick gorse to Trehyllys Farm.

3 Fork left through the farm buildings. Then follow a tarmac lane between hedges past small fields bounded by stone walls, with the ruins of a disused tin mine on the horizon; ruins of such mines dot the Cornish landscape. Where a track joins from the right, follow the lane left to a T-junction with a road.

CHÛN QUOIT BURIAL CHAMBER

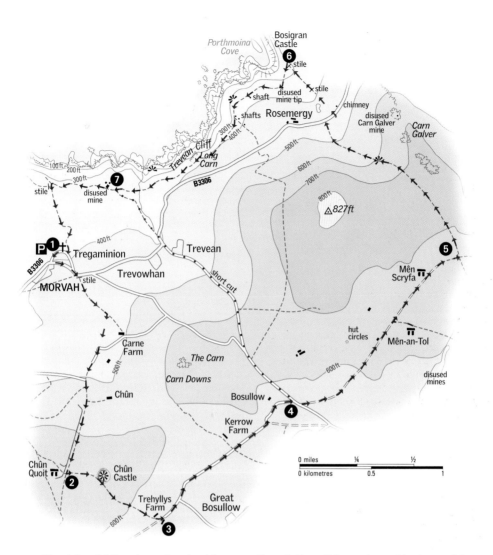

SHORT CUT *Turn left and follow the road to the right. At the B3306 go straight on to the junction with the coast path. Continue from* **7**.

4 Turn right onto the road then almost immediately left on a track, with ruins of ancient settlements and disused mines to the left and right. After about ¾ mile a path on right leads to a curious Bronze Age monument known as Mên-an-Tol, a circular flat stone with a hole in its centre standing between two uprights. Newborn babies were traditionally passed through the hole naked to receive its health-giving powers.

Continue ahead along the main track, passing Mên Scryfa standing stone in a field on the left. It bears a faint Celtic Latin inscription and may be a memorial to a warrior of the 5th or 6th century. Continue on the track to reach open moorland and a junction of paths.

5 Turn left and follow a broad grassy track as it narrows by Carn Galver rocks, home of the legendary Cornish giant Holiburn. Pass the

disused Carn Galver mine, with views of the sea and Castle Rock ahead, to a junction with the coast road.

Turn right and follow the road towards an old mine chimney. Immediately before reaching the chimney, cross the road and continue ahead on a path leading through the gorse. The path is indistinct for the first few yards, but soon becomes clear. Cross a stone stile and continue to a T-junction by another stile. Ahead is the site of Bosigran Castle, in a remarkable position overlooking the jagged rocks and spray of Porthmoina Cove.

6 Turn left on the coast path, passing disused mine tips and shafts and a turret-shaped rock formation known as Long Carn. Continue ahead until you reach a path joining from the left by a disused mine.

7 Follow the coast path across a section of boggy ground to a path on left before a descent to a stile. Turn left on this path and follow it through fields back to Morvah.

CORNWALL

6 Treen

Through fields to the coast south of
Treen, visiting two sandy beaches and
a cliffside theatre.

LENGTH 3½ or 4 miles (2½ or 3 hours)

PARKING Car park in village

CONDITIONS Steep climbs at Porthcurno;
very steep steps down from coast path to
Porthcurno beach

REFRESHMENTS Pub in Treen; pub and café
in Porthcurno

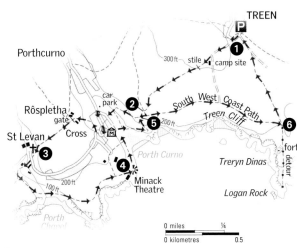

1 Walk out of the car park and turn left
onto the track opposite the shop, passing
houses with fine sea views on the left.

Where the track bears sharp left, keep ahead
into a campsite, walking between huts to a stile
in the wall. Cross the stile and follow the path
through fields and along a hedge, over a
succession of stiles, to meet a track running
between blackthorns towards the sea. Continue
ahead for a few metres to a junction of paths.

2 Turn right and follow the path descending
to a T-junction, ignoring other paths to left and
right. Turn right towards a car park, then turn
left onto a tarmac lane signposted to Minack
Theatre and St Levan.

The lane climbs steeply, giving good views of
Porthcurno beach and Logan Rock. At a sharp
bend, turn right past a newly built block of flats,
then take the narrow tarmac lane to the hamlet
of Rôspletha. After the last house on left, turn
left through a kissing gate by a gateway and
follow the broad grassy path across a field, passing
a Celtic cross, to St Levan's Church.

3 Go into the churchyard and follow the path
left around the church, then cross the lane and
continue ahead on a footpath signposted to
Porthgwarra Cove.

Soon after crossing a brook, at a fork in the
path, bear left above the sandy beach at Porth
Chapel cove. Ahead, the Lizard peninsula
stretches out into the sea. Follow the coast path
for about ¼ mile to the open-air Minack
Theatre, carved dramatically into the cliffs, and
its visitor centre. The theatre was built in 1933.
Plays are performed here on summer evenings.

4 Continue on the coast path to steep steps
down to Porth Curno beach. Alternatively, to
avoid the steps, turn left onto a track and walk
past Minack House, then turn right onto a lane
past the Mariners Lodge Hotel, and right again
to the beach.

From the bottom of the steps, continue along the
side of the beach past the Museum of Submarine
Telegraphy (limited opening), marking the point
where undersea cables fanned out across the
world during the Second World War. Tours are
given of the tunnels that were built to protect
the telegraph system.

Turn right on the path to climb back up the
low, lumpy cliffs on the other side of the bay.
The path bears left to a T-junction with the
long-distance South West Coast Path. The slope
is covered with wind-sculpted blackthorns and
gorse brush, while the rocks are heavily
weathered with cracks and fissures reminiscent
of elephant hide.

5 Turn right on the path, retracing a small
section walked earlier. Continue ahead, with
impressive views of the jagged promontory of
Treryn Dinas. Pass between two Second World
War pillboxes and continue ahead along the coast
path to a National Trust collection stone and a
junction of paths.

DETOUR *Turn right on a path to Logan Rock on the
Treryn Dinas headland, passing the remains of a large
Iron Age promontory fort. The nearby Logan Rock is a
huge boulder that could be rocked by hand, providing
a lucrative visitor attraction, until it was toppled from
the cliffs in 1824 by a Lieutenant Goldsmith and his
crew. The Admiralty made him return the boulder to
its original position, a task demanding considerable
ingenuity and expense, but it can no longer be rocked.*

6 Turn left on the path, climbing gently across
fields to meet a farm track. Follow the track to
the left into Treen and the car park.

7 Pentireglaze

An invigorating coastal walk round Pentire Point to the Rumps, a dramatically sited Iron Age fort.

LENGTH 3½ or 4 miles (2 or 2½ hours)

PARKING Old Lead Mine car park

CONDITIONS Some fairly steep slopes and stony paths; walking boots recommended

REFRESHMENTS None on walk

1 From the car park exit, turn left and follow a track between farmhouses, then go down a lane to the right of the barns. At the bridleway signpost, where the lane rounds a corner, turn right through a gate. Follow the track, with a view ahead to Gulland Rock across Padstow Bay, across fields and through three more gates. Where the South West Coast Path from New Polzeath joins from the left, turn right to Pentireglaze Haven, then follow the path across the grass behind the sands.

2 At the far end of the cove, go through a National Trust gate and climb the steps. The path rounds the point then drops down to a small inlet, where a path from Pentire Farm joins from the right. Cross a footbridge over a stream, and climb once more, looking back for a superb view over Polzeath surfing beach. Continue round a second point with stunning views ahead of rugged cliffs. Continue as the path drops again towards flat rock beds then climbs to Pentire Point.

3 At Pentire Point enjoy the views of Newland Rock ahead. On Stepper Point, to the southwest on the other side of the Camel estuary, is the

Daymark, a lookout tower and navigation point. Follow the path as it curves right.

The whole of Pentire Point is a working farm, producing corn, cattle and sheep. The National Trust manages the coastal region without the use of chemicals, so encouraging a thriving community of wildlife. The rough grass is kept at bay by winter-grazing hill sheep, allowing a profusion of wild flowers to flourish. Kidney vetch, sea campions, sea pinks or thrift, stonecrop and thyme line the clifftops and are enjoyed by an abundance of butterflies. Many species of seabird breed along this stretch of coast. Among them is the fulmar, which can often be spotted swirling gracefully on the air currents.

4 Once round the point, look ahead for a view of the Rumps, a small peninsula with Iron Age defences. Inland are views across farmland to Polzeath. A bench has been erected here on the cliffs, in front of which is a plaque, set in the rock, with a dedication to the poet Laurence Binyon (1869-1943). It is inscribed with one of his poems, *For the Fallen*, which was written nearby. Continue on the coast path, going through a gate in a splendid traditional wall of local stone, filled in with soil for hedging.

5 Continue past a gated path on the right. The views of Rumps Point and its Iron Age fort get more dramatic as you approach. Three ramparts across the narrow neck of the peninsula are clearly visible, defending the pair of conical grassy mounds round which the sea swirls and crashes. Continue to where path forks.
DETOUR *Take the left fork onto the lower path to explore the site of the fort.*

6 Fork right onto the upper path. Continue round the peninsula and go through a gate. Follow the path up, then down and up again round a gully, with a wall on the right. Go through a gap in the wall and turn left through a gate, onto the path with the wall on left. Go through another gap in the wall, follow the edge of the field, then go through another gate to Com Head.

7 Leave the cliff edge to follow the path up through gorse. Above Pengirt Cove, go through a gate and follow the path round a small cove, close to the cliff edge. Just before the slate stile, take the path through a gate to the right, signposted to the Lead Mine car park, and head diagonally right across a field to a gorse-covered knoll, behind which is the car park.

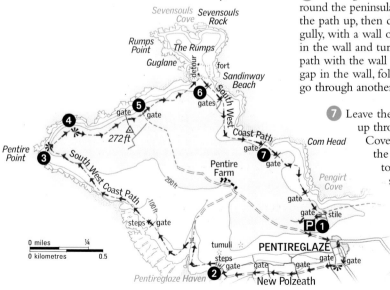

CORNWALL

8 Boscastle

Through a tranquil, wooded valley, to a church set in ancient woodland and Boscastle's unique harbour.

LENGTH 3½ or 5½ miles (2 or 3 hours)

PARKING Car park on B3263

CONDITIONS One gentle and one slightly steeper climb

REFRESHMENTS Full range in Boscastle

1 From the far end of the car park, follow the path through a gate, passing finger posts to Newmills and St Juliot's. Follow the track across the meadow. Evidence of the scouring out of the landscape caused by a massive flood in 2004 is clear all along Valency Fields and Valley.

Continue along the path through Minster Wood, keeping the Valency river on the right, to a wooden footbridge and finger post.
DETOUR Go straight ahead through woods with the river close by. At Rose Cottage, which was once a National Trust ranger's house, the path widens; continue ahead through a kissing gate. Where a road joins from the left, continue ahead and go through a gate to a house called Elm Cottage. Behind the house take the footpath left, following the sign for St Juliot's Church. The narrow path climbs up fairly steeply through woods and fields to the church, the graveyard of which includes some Celtic crosses. In 1870 Thomas Hardy, who was by training an architect, visited St Juliot's to prepare for the church's restoration.

2 Turn right to cross a wooden footbridge, then climb, fairly steeply in places, up through woodland for about ½ mile. Where the path forks, bear right on the path to Minster Church. The graveyard is now maintained as a nature reserve. The church, built on the site of an old monastery, lies below the level of the land, hidden from the road.

3 Leave the churchyard through a gate and turn right onto a lane. After about ¾ mile, at a sharp bend left, follow a fingerpost to climb steps ahead and cross a stile into a field. Follow the path down into the Jordan Valley, with views ahead to Forrabury Church and the white tower – an old coastguard station – on the Willapark headland beyond. Follow the path and sign to Old Village. This leads to a pretty spot by a stream in front of an old cottage. Follow the track through a gate and uphill to a junction with a road. Turn right on the road and continue steeply downhill, passing a shop on the right.

4 Where the road forks, go left to climb uphill. At the T-junction at the top of the hill, turn left and immediately right up Forrabury Hill, and soon take a footpath on the right signposted to the coast path. Follow the path across Forrabury Common which, by ancient custom, is common grazing land between November and February. Keep right of Forrabury Church, walking past the ancient strip-field system, known as 'stitches'.

5 At a meeting of paths, turn right towards Willapark headland, the site of a prehistoric settlement. Beyond the headland, follow the path along the cliff edge, then down to Boscastle Harbour with its quays and fishermen's homes.

Shortly before low tide, the blowhole at Penally Point can be seen and heard in action. From time to time, the pressure of the sea as it is forced through this hole creates a spectacular spray across the harbour entrance. So narrow is the entrance to this once-important harbour that, when seas were high, ships had to be towed in with ropes braced round posts on the shore. The 16th-century Harbour Lights building, which was completely destroyed in the flood of 2004, was rebuilt in 2006.

6 At end of the harbour, join the main road through the village. Bear left and cross the road to return to the car park.

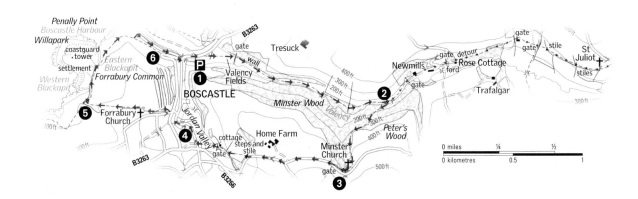

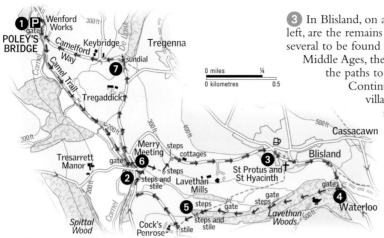

3 In Blisland, on a small patch of grass on the left, are the remains of a wayside cross, one of several to be found in the area. Dating from the Middle Ages, these granite crosses marked the paths to nearby churches.

Continue to the large, tree-shaded village green, surrounded by fine stone buildings, including the Coach House and the Blisland Inn at the western end and, facing you at the far end of the green, the Mansion House.

Turn right along the southern side of the green, past the Old School House and the church of St Protus and St Hyacinth. Continue along a lane signposted to Bodmin, as it bends round to right and descends, with a well-preserved wayside cross on the left.

Continue to cross over a narrow stone bridge spanning a stream and, immediately beyond, go through a kissing gate on right into Lavethan Woods, a Woodland Trust nature reserve.

4 Follow the path through trees with a stream below. Where the path divides, bear right and continue through beech, birch and holly trees, drawing nearer to the stream. Ignore a wooden gate leading into a field and turn left, up steps in the bank and round to the right to continue through the wood, parallel to the edge of the field, then bend left uphill and down to a metal gate. Go through the gate into the fields below Lavethan buildings, keeping close to the wood on the left and looking out for wooden ladder-type steps leading back to the wood. Climb these steps and follow the woodland path to some stone steps and a wooden stile.

5 Cross the stile into a field, then bear right across the field to a stone stile in the hedge. Go over the stile and turn right onto a lane that leads downhill. Where a road joins from the left, go right, round a bend, to return to the road junction at Merry Meeting.

6 Stay on the St Breward road, ignoring a side turn on the left signposted to St Mabyn and a right fork signposted to Blisland. After a gentle climb, the lane drops steeply down to where a stone bridge crosses the De Lank river. In the centre of the bridge is the remains of a sundial.

7 Continue to a stone-built farmhouse just beyond the bridge, where the lane bends right towards St Breward. Go straight ahead, on a lane signposted to St Tudy, the Camelford Way, leading back to Poley's Bridge.

9 Poley's Bridge

To the idyllic stone village of Blisland and its stunning church, followed by a stretch of woodland.

LENGTH **4 miles (2 hours)**

PARKING **Camel Trail car park, opposite Wenford clay works, off the road from Blisland to Penpont at Keybridge**

CONDITIONS **One gentle climb. Lavethan Woods very muddy after rain**

REFRESHMENTS **Shop and pub in Blisland**

1 From the south side of the car park, beside a notice board, take the Camel Trail, a walk and cycleway on the former trackbed of a railway; until 1983 it carried clay for export from the Wenford works to Boscarne Junction, near Wadebridge. Follow the Trail for ¾ mile, with the river on right. Go through a second gate to meet a road, then turn left and immediately meet another road. This is Merry Meeting.

2 Cross the road and take the signposted path over some stone steps, bear right and go over a wooden stile. Climb the field diagonally to the right and turn right over an elaborate wooden stile. Keep close to the hedge on the left until you reach the old stone steps at the end of the hedge. Turn left at the steps and, with another hedge on the left, head for some more stone steps in the bank at the top left corner of the field.

Climb these steps and turn right on the lane towards Blisland. The high roadside banks are full of hazel, honeysuckle and wild flowers growing out from between the double stone walls. In spring, primroses, violets and bluebells jostle for position. There are views on the right through gateways, over the stone buildings of Lavethan Mills to a wood on the far side of the valley.

CORNWALL

10 Lanhydrock

Follow peaceful paths winding through woods and along a rushing river in a National Trust country estate.

LENGTH 3½ miles (2½ hours)

PARKING National Trust car park at Lanhydrock House, off B3268 south of Bodmin

CONDITIONS A level riverside path leads to a steepish climb through Great Wood towards the end. Woodland paths may be muddy after rain

REFRESHMENTS Café at Lanhydrock House

1 From the back of the car park go through the gate and follow the waymarked path, keeping the cricket ground to the right and an adventure playground to the left. The path ends at a minor road. Turn left to meet a T-junction.

2 Cross the road and take the track ahead. Soon, where tracks meet, bear right through a gate on a waymarked path. The wood is largely coniferous, with some areas of mature oak. Follow a broad stony track for about 200m and, ignoring other paths, turn right at a yellow waymark on a footpath guarded on both sides by silver birches. The path descends through woodland. Beyond a waymark, where another path joins from left, it skirts the fields of Cutmadoc Farm on the right.

Soon after the path starts to descend more steeply, bear right at a fork, following a waymark. Towards the bottom of the hill, a path joins from the left. You will hear the chattering of a brook, also on the left.

3 Go through a gate and turn left on a road, then immediately go through a gate on the right and turn right, along Station Drive. The drive was built in the mid 19th century to link Lanhydrock with the Great Western Railway at Bodmin Road station (now Bodmin Parkway), and was later lined with exotic trees, including a giant redwood. Station Drive ends at a gate beside a house called Station Lodge.

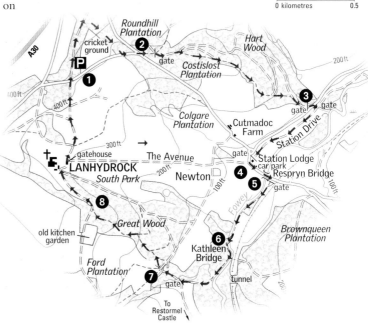

BEECH WOODLAND NEAR LANHYDROCK

4 Beyond the lodge turn left on a road, passing a car park on the left, and cross Respryn Bridge, whose central arch dates from the 15th century. During the Civil War, after Royalist forces had seized Lanhydrock, King Charles I crossed the bridge to stop his men from pillaging the house. The word 'respryn' is generally thought to mean 'the crow's ford'.

5 At the far side of the bridge, turn right through a gate and fork right to the banks of the Fowey. Follow the path along the edge of the river, where an otter may occasionally be spotted in the clear shallow waters.

6 Cross Kathleen Bridge, a stout wooden structure erected in 1992 with the help of the Royal Engineers. Turn sharp left and continue along the path beside the river bank.
Less than ¼ mile from the bridge the path rises away from the river. It then goes through a gate, passing immediately on the left another gate that marks the start of a footpath to Restormel Castle. At this point, the wood seems to whisper with water from myriad streams.

Carry on ahead, keeping left at a fork soon after, to a T-junction with a farm track.

7 Cross the track and climb up stone steps in the wall opposite into Great Wood. Stately Scots pine, beech and oak stand shoulder to shoulder with sweet chestnut and sycamore. As the path ascends to the top of Great Wood, it is met at intervals by paths from the right. Ignore them, keeping straight on. Towards the top, the walls of the old kitchen gardens can be glimpsed to the left. The gardens, which once supplied fruit and vegetables to the big house, now grow plants for National Trust properties in Cornwall.

8 At the top of the hill, the path curves right and merges with a gravel track, passing between rhododendrons and camellias. The track slopes down to a gate and Lanhydrock House. Follow the road to the front of the house and the 17th-century gatehouse. Leading away from the gatehouse is a spectacular avenue of beeches. Continue to the entrance kiosk, where tickets can be bought to visit the house and gardens. Follow the minor road back to the car park.

CORNWALL

11 Minions

An exploration of the archaeology of Bodmin Moor, from the Bronze Age to the early 20th century.

LENGTH 6 miles (3½ hours)

PARKING Car park just east of village

CONDITIONS Mostly firm paths and roads; some open moorland; steep scramble to the Cheesewring

REFRESHMENTS Pubs in Minions, the Crow's Nest

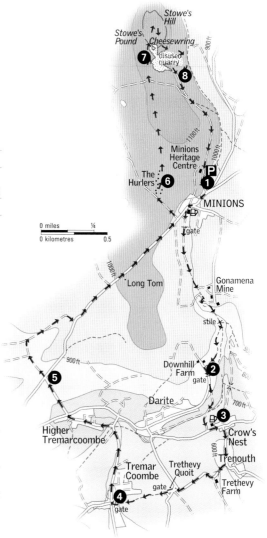

1 From the car park, turn right along the road through Minions. Just beyond the Cheesewring pub, turn left down a footpath, following an old trackbed that served the local mines. Passing through the derelict site of the Gonamena Mine, the path descends through a cutting, diverting briefly to cross a modern track. Return to the path through the cutting, cross a stile, then bear right at a waymark, climbing up through spoil heaps of rock and soil. At Downhill Farm the path becomes a metalled track.

2 Bear left as the track emerges onto a lane. Continue ahead then, as the lane swings to the right beside a bungalow, fork left down a bridleway. At a road turn left, passing the Crow's Nest pub.

3 Turn right at the junction to follow a narrow lane beside a stream. At the next junction bear right, and where the lane reaches a farm road bear right again. The lane climbs to a road junction. Cross the junction and go through a kissing gate ahead to Trethevy Quoit, a megalithic burial chamber. Return through the kissing gate and turn right to follow the signposted narrow bridleway, and continue downhill.

4 Go through the gate at the bottom of the hill and turn right on the road through Tremar Coombe, climbing from the village onto common land. After ½ mile turn left just before a roadside bench. Follow the lane over the crossroads to a junction with the Minions road.

5 Continue ahead, following the lane when it bends right. Turn left on the road to Minions and continue across the moor, passing Long Tom, a standing stone inscribed with a Christian cross. At the Minions village sign, turn left up the track signed to the Hurlers. Pass the car park, then turn right across open moor to the stone circles. The largest is 41m (135ft) in diameter.

6 Cross the moor towards the granite outcrop of the Cheesewring. Aim to the left of the quarry ahead. There are no formal rights of way across

the moor, but walkers are allowed as long as they behave responsibly and keep dogs under control. Within ½ mile, cross a grassy track and continue briefly on the path up the flank of the hill. Turn right immediately under the Cheesewring and follow the quarry fence up the rough, steep path.

7 Bear left towards the summit of the hill, crossing the massive stone rampart of Stowe's Pound. The Bronze Age hillfort encloses strange rock formations, and dramatic views stretch from it across the moor. Beyond lies a second enclosure containing the remains of a settlement. Returning from the summit, keep the Cheesewring to the right and follow the quarry fence to the left.

8 At the foot of the hill bear right along the track into a disused quarry. Its granite rockface is a popular challenge for climbers. Beyond the quarry, the track passes the Minions Heritage Centre, in a restored mine building. Continue along the track to return to the car park.

12 Bude Canal

From invigorating clifftops to inland fields, returning along a tranquil towpath past a marshy haven for birds.

LENGTH 5½ miles (2½ hours)

PARKING Car park by tourist information office

CONDITIONS Easy, on paths and turf, but cliff edges are dangerously unstable

REFRESHMENTS Pubs and restaurants in Bude

1 Facing the Falcon Hotel, cross the road and follow the right bank of the canal towards the sea, passing the museum. Cross the canal at the lock gates and turn right to the lifeboat station, established by William IV in 1837.

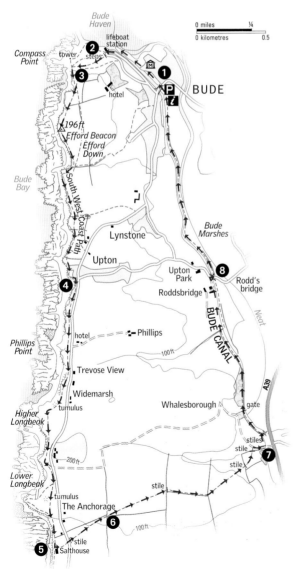

2 Turn left up the steps and follow signs to the South West Coast Path. Continue upwards and turn right on the coast path, which climbs to the clifftop. Follow footpath signs across the turf, passing Compass Point tower – built in the 1830s as an ornamental feature and a shelter for coastguards.

3 Continue along the clifftop, which offers fine views of the contorted rock formations of the cliffs, sedimentary layers of sandstone and dark shale that are more than 300 million years old. The path dips and climbs across turf for nearly a mile. It then descends behind some houses, and bends left to the approach road that joins Bude and Widemouth.

4 Just before the road, follow the path to the right and continue between the road and the cliff. On the shore, some 60m (200ft) below, jagged spines of stone, the eroded strata of old cliffs, extend into the sea. As the broad golden sweep of Widemouth sands appears ahead, the path drops down towards a clifftop cottage.

5 Before reaching the cottage, turn left up a track, cross the road and climb a stile. The path beyond continues through a cultivated field, heading for its top left corner, where four fields meet and a farm track joins from the left.

6 Cross the track into the field ahead on the left. There is little sign of a path, but eventually a stile comes into view ahead. Climb the stile and follow a wall of smooth sea pebbles on the right and go through a gap in the field boundary ahead. Bearing slightly to the left of Marhamchurch, now visible across the valley, descend through another field and climb a stile. Follow the path as it swings left, climb another stile and turn right for a short way down a concrete farm track.

7 Turn left over a stile just before a small bridge, then turn left over another stile onto a broad footpath. Beyond a gate, the path follows the towpath of Bude Canal.

When it opened in 1835, the canal stretched for 35 miles to Launceston, and an ingenious system of ramps and pulleys enabled boats to negotiate gradients. This stretch of the waterway is long overgrown, and now only fishermen and wildfowl frequent its peaceful banks.

8 Cross the bridge and turn left through a gate to continue along the right bank of the canal, which from here to Bude and the sea remains a navigable waterway. Bude Marshes on the right are a wetland reserve that attracts swallows, willow warblers, kingfishers and snipe. Just before the bridge, turn right to return to the car park.

CORNWALL

13 Morwenstow

Dramatic scenery on an energetic walk, that includes three steep climbs across undulating cliffs and coombs.

LENGTH	5 or 6 miles (4½ or 5 hours)
PARKING	Car park above churchyard gate
CONDITIONS	Arduous clifftop walk, with steep climbs and descents
REFRESHMENTS	Pub in Crosstown

1 Go into the churchyard, where a figurehead of a kilted highlander marks the grave of the crew and captain of the *Caledonia*, wrecked in 1843. Walk towards the converted barn next to the vicarage. Cross a stile between the barn and wall, and follow a lane into a wooded coomb that runs steeply down to a stream. Cross the stream and climb up to fields. Continue straight ahead along the field boundary and go through a gate. Turn right through a second gate and follow the track into the farmyard. On the far side bear left; when the track bends right, go straight on through a gate, heading towards a farmhouse. Cross a stile and go through a gate into a lane between hedges, and turn left at a tarmac lane.

2 At Cornakey Farm, turn right into the farmyard and onto a track. Pass through two gates and into a field, then take a footpath diagonally left across two fields towards Marsland Manor. Climb a stile and follow the path as it descends steeply into a wooded gorge and crosses a stream. Climb out of the gorge and continue onto a track, following it round the left side of the manor (whose massive chimney indicates the Elizabethan origins of the building), then across the gravel yard to a tarmac lane.

3 Turn left. As the lane bends right, continue ahead on a track signed to the coast path. Soon the track becomes a sunken lane; where it bends to the right around a house, take the footpath to the left. Follow this through a hazel coppice, forking right where the path divides. From high above the coomb, the path looks down on a canopy of woodland. Keep to the high ground, ignoring the paths down into the valley, as the cliffs and shale beach appear up ahead.

4 At the coast path (denoted by an acorn sign) turn left up to the top of the cliff high above Gull Rock. Here, a bench provides a chance to rest, admire the view and watch the seabirds wheeling with raucous shrieks round the foaming, jagged rocks below. Continue along the coast path. The route is arduous, but the scenery and solitude are compensation. The path drops almost to sea level in a wild coomb of scrub and bracken, then climbs upwards again. Above Cornakey Cliff, level fields grazed by sheep and cattle are followed by another descent and climb.

5 Continue upwards to walk along the top of Henna Cliff. Then, ignoring a path on the left, descend steeply to a rocky cove below Morwenstow. Climb the farther slope to a footpath on the left, just before a gate. SHORT CUT *Turn left to return to Morwenstow church.*

6 Continue along the coast path and climb over a stile. The path drops steeply into another coomb. Shortly before reaching a stream, turn left and follow the stream up the valley along the gentle incline of a woodland path. Ignore paths to the right and keep to the left bank of the stream, following waymarks.

Turn left up steps and cross a gate into a field. Cross the field and go over another gate to a path leading beside the Bush Inn. Turn left on the tarmac lane in front of the inn and follow it back to Morwenstow church.

Map labels: West Mill, Old Mill Leat, Marsland Water, Marsland Beach, Gull Rock, Litter Mouth, stile, Marsland Cliff, 300 ft, 200 ft, gate, Marsland Manor, 400 ft, stile, stile, Lower Cory, Cornakey Cliff, Yeol Mouth, 400 ft, Cornakey Woods, Cornakey Farm, gates, gate, Yeolmouth Cliff, Yeolmouth, stile, Henna Cliff, 469ft, gate, Westcott Farm, gates, 400 ft, 200 ft, 300 ft, Cotton Beach, short cut, lych gate, stile, MORWENSTOW, gate, stile, Crosstown, gates, Tidna Shute, 200 ft, 300 ft, The Tidna, Tidnacott, Tonacombe, Higher Sharpnose Point, South West Coast Path

0 miles ¼ / 0 kilometres 0.5

THE COAST PATH NEAR MORWENSTOW

DEVON

Best known for Dartmoor's rugged moorland trails, Devon has plenty of gentle walking, too, mainly through lush, rolling countryside and along the beautiful north and south coastlines.

1 Slapton Ley

A fascinating nature trail beside a reedy freshwater lake, which is separated from the sea by a narrow shingle bank.

LENGTH 2 or 2½ miles (1½ or 2 hours)

PARKING Car park halfway along Slapton Sands, on A379 1 mile north of Torcross

CONDITIONS Easy, but boardwalk across swampy section of nature reserve slippery after rain

REFRESHMENTS Pub in Slapton

① Cross the road from the northern end of the car park. The entire village was evacuated during the Second World War, when the area was commandeered for battle practice by the US Army. A nearby obelisk on the shingle was erected by the Americans in gratitude.

② Go over Slapton Bridge, from where there are good views of both parts of Slapton Ley (pronounced Lee), the largest freshwater lake in southwest England, separated from the sea by no more than a shingle ridge. This strange natural phenomenon was formed at the end of the last Ice Age, when melting ice caused the sea level to rise, and shingle built up between the headlands to north and south. Just beyond the bridge, turn left through a gate to a boathouse, which marks the start of a waymarked nature trail.

③ Follow the edge of Lower Ley, an open expanse where mallards, moorhens and many other waterbirds feed and breed. (The Higher Ley, to the north, is now almost obliterated by reedbeds.) Open water gives way to reedy marsh, where trees growing in the shallows create the feel of a miniature mangrove swamp. The Ley is a site of special scientific interest, supporting an increasingly rare community of interdependent plants and animals.

④ The path emerges onto a patch of open ground. To the left is a reedy section out of bounds to visitors. The vegetation here has been allowed to return to a wild state to attract the more timid wetland creatures such as buntings and warblers.

Cross the open ground and take the path that leads to the left of a rustic seat, into the trees, and follow it as it bears right.

⑤ At the gate to South Grounds Farm take the path leading left down three steps to the start of a stretch of boardwalk. The boardwalk winds across a swampy section of the reserve. Here reeds, bulrushes and, in summer, flag irises, watermint flowers and purple loose-strife – in places shoulder-high – sparkle with the blues and greens of dragonflies, while frogs splash and call all around.

Beyond the reeds, on the open water to the left of the boardwalk, cormorants can often be seen perching on the stumps and branches of dead waterlogged trees to dry their outspread wings. DETOUR *At the end of the boardwalk follow the path ahead to Deer Bridge through a wilder part of the reserve. For much of its way the path is protected from the waters of the Ley by an ancient dyke. Beyond it stretches a patchwork of alders and reeds where birds such as herons, kingfishers, reed buntings and reed warblers can be seen. From the low stone bridge, retrace your route to the boardwalk.*

⑥ Turn right at the end of the boardwalk, leaving the nature reserve, and follow the signpost to Slapton, passing a small sewage works on the right. Gradually Slapton comes into view, an up-and-down village of stone cottages, many colourwashed in white or pink. There is an ancient church, St James's, and a dramatic ruined medieval tower.

⑦ Turn right onto the lane, which passes Slapton Ley Field Centre (which manages the reserve) before leading back to the car park.

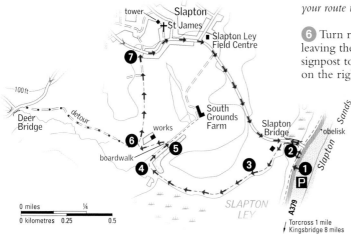

2 Harford Moor

An exploration of southern Dartmoor, crossing old parish boundaries and the track of an old tramway.

LENGTH 5 miles (3½ hours)

PARKING Car park at Harford Moor Gate, east of Harford

CONDITIONS Even on sunny days, low cloud or mist can swathe parts of Dartmoor in minutes; take a compass, and do not attempt the walk if the cloud is low or if rain is forecast

REFRESHMENTS None on walk

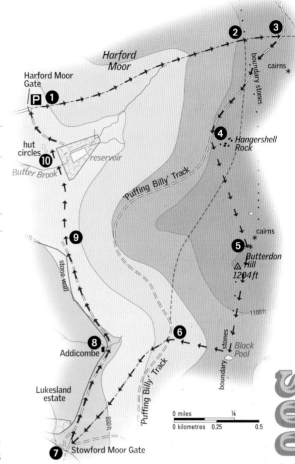

1 A semicircular grassy bank edges one side of the car park. From the centre of the bank's rim, walk straight ahead across the moor, with a coniferous plantation immediately on the right and Hangershell Rock visible slightly to the right in the distance. This was a medieval route across the moor, but there is no obvious path now. Climb gently towards the head of a broad, shallow valley, gradually shifting direction slightly to the left (northwards). There are scattered rocks to the left. When you see a distinctive grassy cairn on the horizon, aim slightly to the left of it, with Hangershell Rock still to the right.

2 Some ¾ mile from the start of the walk, a row of stone markers (an old parish boundary) stretches away to the right and left. One stone, about 75cm (2ft 6in) high, is much more prominent than the rest. Walk due east behind this stone, keeping the grassy cairn on the right, until you meet a broad stony track. Ahead, beyond the brow of a hill, is Spurrell's Cross, a medieval stone waymarker.

3 Turn right on the track. Pass the grassy cairn on the left and cross the line of stone markers again. The track follows the route of the Red Lake Tramway (known locally as the 'Puffing Billy' track) which, until 1932, carried china clay from workings near central Dartmoor to Ivybridge. As the track comes level with Hangershell Rock, leave the track and walk up to the tor.

4 From Hangershell Rock head south to Butterdon Hill, making for the second from the left of three cairns on the horizon.

5 The summit of Butterdon Hill – at 367m (1,204ft) the walk's highest point – offers glorious views of the moor to the east, west and north, and southwards to the sea. From the trig point, take the good track ahead to Black Pool, heading south downhill, then turn right to rejoin the 'Puffing Billy' track.

6 Continue ahead on an unsigned path that leads to Stowford Moor Gate. Down to the right is the long wall of the private Lukesland estate and a ruined tin-miner's cottage at Addicombe.

7 At Stowford Moor Gate, where the path leaves the moor at a wide gate set in stone walls, turn sharp right and follow the stone wall of Lukesland estate to the cottage at Addicombe. The path leads across a stream whose bank is dug with small channels once used for washing tin ore.

8 From Addicombe follow the wall for a further ½ mile until it veers left. At this point keep straight ahead, making for the rocky outcrop ¼ mile away on the skyline.

9 Head towards the left of a reservoir hidden in the conifers ahead. This is Dartmoor's smallest reservoir. Cross a small stream on stepping stones.

10 Keeping the trees and reservoir to the right, you will see ahead several rings of stone – the remains of Bronze Age huts. Pass through these stone circles and go straight on up to a gravel track. Turn left to return to the car park.

DEVON

3 Merrivale

Some of Dartmoor's most spectacular granite tors pepper this atmospheric, windswept stretch of moorland.

LENGTH 6 miles (3½ hours)

PARKING Car park ¼ mile east of Merrivale on B3357, about 7 miles east of Tavistock

CONDITIONS Firm paths; some rougher stretches over moor, including a steep climb from Ward Bridge out of valley

REFRESHMENTS Pub in Merrivale

1 Turn left out of the car park and follow the road downhill past the Dartmoor Inn. Just before the road swings to right by the quarry entrance, turn left along a path, walking between a high drystone wall and a leat, or manmade watercourse, with moorland on one side and cultivated fields on the other. Dartmoor ponies, descended from the wild horses that roamed the moorland more than 1,000 years ago, graze by the leat. Continue alongside the wall past Vixen Tor – at 27m (90ft) the highest of Dartmoor's spectacular granite tors.

2 Still following the moorland wall, cross a stream on stepping stones. The route continues up the shoulder of Pew Tor past a disused quarry, where blocks of half-dressed granite lie scattered in the heather.

Dartmoor's granite quarries were developed in the 19th century, and were the source of building stone for many Victorian bridges, harbours and naval installations. Follow the clear, firm track as the route diverges slightly from the wall to Pewtor Cottage. Keep to left of the cottage and follow a gravel drive to a junction with a minor road.

3 Cross the road and go straight ahead over a triangle of grass, then follow the minor road, bearing right then left past 14th-century Sampford Spiney church. The village includes a Tudor manor house.

4 Where the road swings right ¼ mile beyond the church, continue straight ahead down an ancient track between high banks. Bear left at another minor road, descending to Ward Bridge, where trees and rhododendrons shade the tumbling waters of the River Walkham. Follow the road on a steep climb out of the valley.

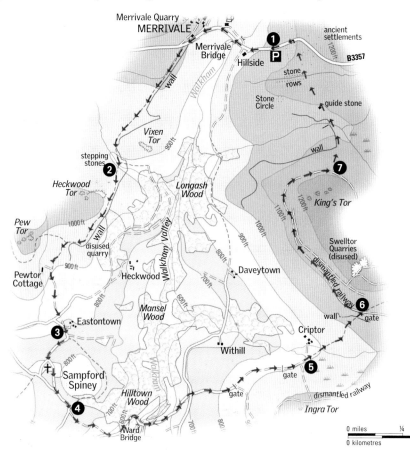

At a crossroad continue straight ahead up the dead-end lane towards Criptor. Beyond a gate, the lane becomes a track across the moor, then passes through a second gate.

5 The track bends to the left before a stream and becomes a private driveway; after the stream turn right on a signposted path scarcely distinguishable through the gorse and moor stone. Waymarks indicate the route. Jump over a stream and climb the left side of the valley towards a communications mast on the horizon. The path becomes more clearly defined as it passes through an old stone wall and climbs steeply to a gate.

6 Go through the gate and turn left along the trackbed of the old Princetown railway, first built as a horse-drawn tramway in the 1820s.

There are fine views to left across wooded Walkham valley as the track curves round the rock-strewn slopes of King's Tor. Beyond a shallow cutting, a farm and the communications mast come into view ahead, with a moorland wall downhill to left.

7 As the track swings to the right, the wall turns sharply in the opposite direction. Turn left off the track towards a wall and follow it to a stream. Jump over the stream and head uphill to an 18th-century guide stone visible on the skyline. From the guide stone, go straight on, with the quarry face at Merrivale ahead and slightly to the left.

Before reaching the main road, the route passes through one of Dartmoor's best-preserved prehistoric landscapes, a unique assembly of aligned stones, monoliths, enclosures and hut circles dating from the Bronze Age, when the moor was still well-populated farmland. On reaching the main road, turn left to return to the car park.

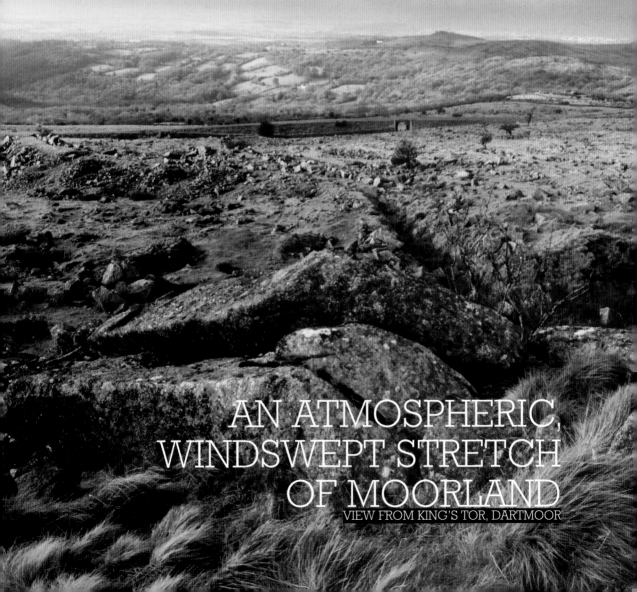

AN ATMOSPHERIC, WINDSWEPT STRETCH OF MOORLAND
VIEW FROM KING'S TOR, DARTMOOR

DEVON

4 Bellever

By the East Dart river, among sighing firs and over wind-scraped rocks on a climb from forest to moor.

LENGTH 4½ miles (2½ hours)

PARKING Forest car park, Bellever

CONDITIONS Fairly level, along high forest and moorland tracks

REFRESHMENTS None on walk

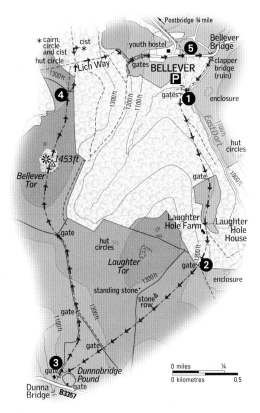

① Turn right at the entrance to the car park and follow a forest track past a picnic site and a signposted forest walk, both on the right, to a gate. Go through the gate. Soon, where the track divides, fork right, signposted to Laughter Hole Farm. Continue along the track for about ⅓ mile to another gate. Beyond the gate, walk past Laughter Hole Farm to where the track divides. Fork right and follow a woodland track signposted to the B3357. Continue up the gentle slope to a gate on the forest boundary.

② Go through the gate and follow the track ahead, signposted to Dunnabridge Pound. After ¼ mile, to the right is a stone row (a common feature on Dartmoor, probably associated with early astronomical observations, such as the position of the Sun and Moon on the summer and winter solstices) and beyond it a 2.75m (9ft) high standing stone. The track continues across moorland, through a gate to Dunnabridge Pound, a large circular enclosure. Dartmoor ponies are driven into the pound each September, to be counted and selected for the sale ring. At the side of the pound is an ancient, covered stone bench, brought here from nearby Crockern Tor.

Continue to a signposted footpath on the right, immediately in front of a gate that leads onto the road.

③ Turn right and follow the footpath sign, alongside a stone wall, towards Bellever Tor – the rocky high point immediately ahead. Continue beside the wall to a gate, beyond which a wide path leads uphill to the tor. Buzzards can often be seen in the sky above this stretch of the moor. The large birds of prey, distinguished by their broad straight wings and lazy, wheeling flight, gather in pairs or larger groups, searching the ground for prey or carrion. Frequently it is noisy groups of mobbing crows, flapping round the buzzards, that first draw the walker's attention to them.

The view from Bellever Tor stretches beyond Postbridge across the barren, rock-strewn expanses of Dartmoor National Park. From the tor, continue ahead in the same direction, downhill through a gap in an old stone wall, to a red marker post on the edge of forest. Walk ahead on the track from the marker post to a major junction of tracks a little farther on.

④ Carry straight on for a further 100m to a path on the right. Turn right to the remains of a cist – a stone burial chamber originally covered by a mound of earth.

Retrace your steps to the junction of tracks and turn left, signposted to Bellever. This stretch of the path follows the Lich Way, a medieval route linking the villages of Postbridge and Lydford – centre of one of the biggest parishes in England. In the past the path was used by bearers carrying coffins for burial to St Petrock's Church in Lydford.

Join a minor road leading into Bellever and continue to a turning on the left immediately beyond the youth hostel.

⑤ Turn left and continue straight ahead, passing a track on the right that leads to the car park. Continue to the edge of the East Dart, then turn right on a path that runs beside the river. Carry straight on, passing the remains of a medieval clapper bridge – much less complete than the one a short distance upstream at Postbridge. About 200m farther along the riverbank turn right on a gravel path leading to the car park.

5 Manaton

An up-and-down route combining village greens, a tree-shaded torrent and wild high country peppered with granite outcrops.

LENGTH 6 miles (3 hours)

PARKING Car park in village centre

CONDITIONS Varied, challenging walk, climbing from wooded valley to high tor

REFRESHMENTS Café and shop at Becka Falls

1 Turn left out of the car park and follow the road across the village green to where it forks. Take the right-hand fork, past the parish hall, to a bridleway on the right, signposted to the village of Water. Follow the bridleway for ½ mile to a track junction.

Turn right and continue through woodland to another junction immediately before a thatched farmhouse on the edge of Water.

2 Turn right and follow the path signposted 'Manaton Direct'. It skirts around the side of a thatched farmhouse to reach a driveway. Walk along the drive, away from the gate to the farmyard, into the village of Water.

The lane goes past cottages, grouped around a tiny green and the old village pump, before reaching a T-junction. Turn left, signposted to Trendlebere Down.

The surfaced lane peters out into a rough track after ⅓ mile. Follow the track, which bends sharp right and reaches a gate on the perimeter of Houndtor Wood. Go through the gate and follow the track into the wood for a few yards, where it divides into two paths.

3 Fork right, signposted to Becka Falls, and carry on straight ahead, crossing a stile into woodland inhabited by otters and wild minks.

Free public access to the woodland is restricted to the path, so ignore side paths to the left – one leads down steps to a footbridge downstream from the falls, a second to a main footbridge immediately below the falls. Ignore right turns beyond the path to a bridge beside the falls and continue to a crossing of paths beside a trail post numbered 'A7'. Turn left to a minor road.

4 Turn right on the road then take the first turning to the left, signposted to Beckaford. The road goes uphill and over a cattle grid on the edge of the open moorland. Immediately beyond the cattle grid turn right and follow the track through a gate leading off the moor. Continue to a fork in the track and keep left to a second gate leading back onto the moor. The path arrives at a signpost for Hound Tor.

Turn right towards the tor and cross a granite footbridge over Becka Brook. The path climbs past a small fir plantation to a gate.

5 Go through the gate and continue to Hound Tor, passing through the ruined medieval village of Hundatona. Beyond the tor the path descends to a minor crossroads at Swallerton Gate. Take the road signposted to Manaton, then turn right immediately on an unmarked road. Continue ahead to a gate.

6 Immediately beyond the gate turn right on a moorland path that heads between two groups of rocks on Hayne Down. Ignore a left fork after 50m. To the left is the outcrop of Bowerman's Nose. Go through a gate onto a driveway, following it for 200m to a stile on the left.

7 Cross the stile and follow the path across a field to another stile leading onto a minor road. Turn left on the road, past Mill Farm, and follow it uphill to Manaton crossroads.

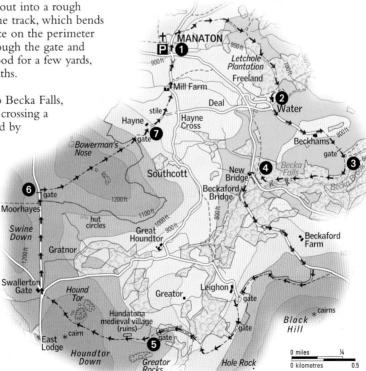

33

DEVON

6 Scorhill

Across open moorland and over medieval granite bridges, passing ancient standing stones, beneath a vast, dome-like sky.

LENGTH 4½ miles (2½ hours)

PARKING Car park at end of road through Gidleigh and Berrydown

CONDITIONS High moorland walk that should not be attempted in misty weather; take a compass and wear walking boots

REFRESHMENTS None on walk; full range in Chagford

① Go through the gate at the end of the road leading from the car park and follow the left of two stone walls. Where the path divides at a corner of the wall, continue straight ahead, away from the wall and across open moorland. From the top of a low rise, Scorhill Circle – a group of 23 standing stones erected in the Bronze Age – can be seen. Head towards it, over open ground.

② Turn left at Scorhill Circle, on a well-defined path that winds downhill across several granite-slab bridges. Immediately before the second of these, Wallabrook Bridge, turn right on a path to Teign Tolmen – a huge, pierced boulder, about 100m downstream, which has been shaped over thousands of years by water erosion. Local folklore held that anyone who slid through the hole and stood on the ledge beneath would be cured of whooping cough and rheumatism.

Return to the bridge, cross it and take the path going downhill and over the North Teign river via the Teign-e-ver clapper bridge. On the far bank of the river, follow the path uphill, alongside a stone wall bounding some fir trees. Continue along the wall until it turns a corner.

③ Turn half right, away from the wall, and continue for about 200m to a pair of stone rows, which only become apparent as the path draws closer to them. The high, craggy point of Kestor Rock is now visible about ¼ mile away to the left across Shovel Down. Continue from the stone rows to Long Stone – a 3m (10ft) high standing stone, carved with letters relating to its use in recent centuries as a parish boundary marker. Turn left and walk over the open moor towards Kestor Rock – there is no clear path.

Pass to the right of the top of Kestor Rock, enjoying a view down the valley of the Teign to Chagford. Just beyond an outcrop, turn left on a grassy path, marked by a row of rocks, partly overgrown with turf. Continue downhill to an unfenced lane leading from Batworthy farm.

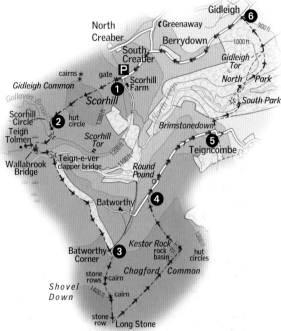

CLAPPER BRIDGE, SCORHILL

④ Turn right and go along the lane, which leads past the side of Round Pound, an animal enclosure that dates back to the Iron Age. Cross the cattle grid where the lane leaves the open moor, and continue ahead for almost ¼ mile to reach a sharp right-hand bend, where a track branches off to the left.

⑤ Turn left along the track, which descends into woodland. Turn right at the first junction along a path and left at the next one – both turnings are signposted as footpaths.

Continue downhill to the North Teign river, encountered earlier on the walk, and cross a footbridge to the far bank. The path climbs a wooded slope, before bending to the right and continuing parallel to the river. After a short distance, the path divides. Take the left fork, going uphill along the edge of mixed woodland to reach a minor road.

⑥ Turn left on the road. The tiny hamlet of Gidleigh, which lies in the other direction, is worth visiting on the return drive for its ruined castle and Holy Trinity Church.

Continue along the road. Behind and to the left, small fields fall away to steep, wooded valleys. Ahead, cultivated slopes merge into the moorland of Gidleigh Common. Carry on through the hamlet of Berrydown to reach the car park.

DEVON

7 Stoke

Sheltered coombs and scenic cliffs, an unexpected waterfall cascading down to a pebbly beach, and woodland gardens.

LENGTH 4½ or 5 miles (2 or 2½ hours)

PARKING Car park by church

CONDITIONS Good paths and fairly easy climbs; keep away from unstable cliff edge

REFRESHMENTS Inn at Hartland Quay, café at Docton Mill (March to October)

1 From the car park, turn right on the lane towards Hartland Quay. Just after the last cottage on the right, turn right through a gate to a path. Facing a fine sea view, the path drops down through the coomb. Despite the shelter of the valley, many of the trees have been wind-swept into weird, contorted forms.

2 At a fork, ignore a path to the right that leads over a stone bridge, and instead bear left. Climb

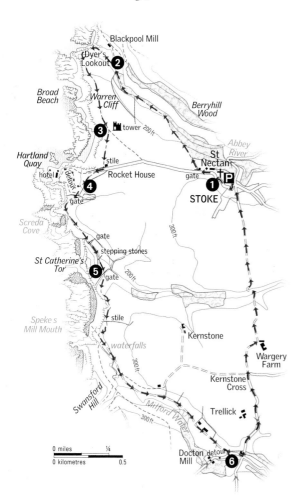

a wild, uncultivated slope to a viewpoint known as Dyer's Lookout. In August 1868 the schooner *Saltash* came to grief on the jagged rocks below the lookout, with the loss of all her crew. Continue left along the clifftop, staying back from the edge.

3 About ½ mile farther on, pass the crumbling ruins of a 17th-century tower. Continue along the clifftop to reach the Rocket House at the side of a lane. Now a private home, Rocket House was built in 1890 to house the rocket-launching apparatus of Hartland Quay's coastguards.

Climb a stile and turn right on the footpath, which leads beside a lane before joining it for a short distance.

DETOUR *Follow the lane round a right hairpin bend down to Hartland Quay, where the harbour buildings house a pub and museum of local history.*

4 Continue straight ahead on the path leading through gorse and heather to a breathtaking panorama of the cliffs. Steps cut into the turf lead down to a gate. Follow the path through another gate and into a peaceful hidden valley beneath the strange eroded pyramid of St Catherine's Tor. In medieval times the valley was the swannery of nearby Hartland Abbey. Stepping stones take the path across a stream and up through a gate in a stone wall.

5 Follow the path to the right, up to clifftop fields. After crossing a stone wall, the path descends to Speke's Mill Mouth, passing a line of pits that were used for storing sea sand before the days of artificial fertilisers. Flag irises now bloom in their rich soil and wild flowers grow along the banks of Milford Water, a burbling stream that plummets unexpectedly into a deep, sheer-sided gorge. Famous for its geological interest, the waterfall is also exceptional for its beauty.

Remaining on the left side of the stream, follow the track up the valley, ignoring a path that forks left. Continue to a junction with a lane.

DETOUR *Turn right to Docton Mill and its gardens, planted around ponds and streams.*

6 Turn left, walk up to a crossroads and turn left uphill. At the next crossroads continue straight on along a lane marked 'unsuitable for motors'. The lane passes Wargery Farm, becoming a track. Follow the track for ¾ mile towards the tower of Stoke's St Nectan's Church. Turn left at the road junction in the village and go through the lych gate into the churchyard.

St Nectan's Church, largely 14th century, has a fine interior, with a 'Pope's Chamber' containing local relics. The tower may have been built as a landmark for seafarers. Leave the churchyard by the south gate to return to the car park.

8 Hunter's Inn

A secluded inn, exhilarating clifftops, woods of ancient oaks, mosses and ferns, and the earthworks of a Roman fortlet.

LENGTH **7 miles (4 hours)**

PARKING **Car park opposite National Trust shop**

CONDITIONS **Some moderately steep climbs; stepping stones at Heddon's Mouth may not be passable after wet weather**

REFRESHMENTS **Hunter's Inn and NT café**

1 Turn left out of the car park and follow the road to the left of Hunter's Inn. Cross the bridge and turn right on a track into the densely wooded coomb beside the lively Heddon river. Fork right, following the signpost to Woody Bay. Beyond a gate, the track leads across an open hillside, beneath steep slopes of scree to reach a footbridge on the right.
SHORT CUT *Turn right over the footbridge, then right again to join the path a short distance before* **3**.

2 Do not cross the bridge, but continue ahead to Heddon's Mouth, where a limekiln stands above the pebble beach. If the water is shallow enough, cross the stream by the stepping stones and turn right to follow the left bank back up the coomb, otherwise return to the footbridge and follow the short cut.

3 Turn sharp left to follow the signposted South West Coast Path and Tarka Trail. The path climbs above the tree line to round a headland, passing to the right of Highveer Point and revealing

breathtaking views along the coast. On a clear day, Wales is visible across the Bristol Channel and coastal freighters out to sea appear like tiny toys.

4 Continue along the coast path. Guillemots nest on rocky ledges far below, and in summer the slopes are ablaze with gorse, bell heather and ling. With little shelter from the sun, in summer the heat can be ferocious before the path dips down into a cleft in the cliffs, where a refreshing plume of water cascades into a pool.

5 Beyond the waterfall, a stile across a wall soon leads into established oak woods. The ancient sessile oaks, on a floor of grasses, ferns and moss, create an ideal environment for woodland butterflies and birds.

As the path swings right, there are glimpses through the trees of Woody Bay. In the 1960s this was one of the first pieces of land bought by the National Trust in its campaign to save unspoilt stretches of coastline.

6 Go through a gate to reach a track. In the early 20th century, when there were plans to develop the cove into a holiday resort, the track wound down to a pier, but storms destroyed the pier and the scheme foundered. At a fork bear right on a track, uphill through woods. On reaching a road turn sharp right, passing a car park on the left.

7 At a hairpin bend, continue straight on through a gate to a track. Views of the sea can be seen over treetops before the track leads through another gate to an open hillside. After 3/4 mile, turn left to a fortlet, where Roman legionaries were stationed in about AD 60. The earthworks are slight but the panoramic views stretch for many miles.

8 Return to the track and turn left towards Hunter's Inn. The track runs above precipitous escarpments and is lined with strong retaining walls. A spring-fed trough beside the path once provided welcome refreshment for horses that toiled up from the inn. As the track turns inland up the valley, a dense canopy of trees comes into view. The track descends gently through these woods, then emerges to the left of Hunter's Inn, with the car park 100m ahead.

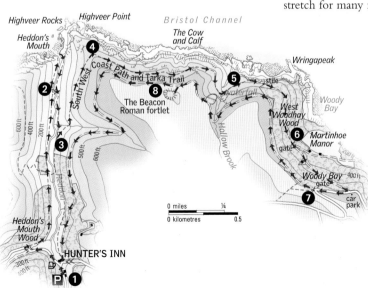

DEVON

9 Malmsmead

Across Exmoor's farmland, woods and barren moor – the bleak, wild landscape linked with the fictional Doone family.

LENGTH 7 miles (3½ hours)

PARKING Car park in Malmsmead

CONDITIONS Generally firm tracks, but some rough moorland; do not attempt the walk in misty or snowy conditions

REFRESHMENTS Café at car park; teas at Cloud Farm

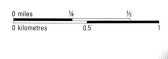

① Turn left out of the car park and then left again at the road junction, passing around Lorna Doone Farm. Cross the packhorse bridge beside the ford, which marks the border of Devon and Somerset. After about 100m, turn right up a lane leading to Cloud Farm, which is signposted to Doone Valley. Just beyond a gate, the lane passes through woods, with patches of rhododendrons beside Badgworthy Water.

② At Cloud Farm, turn right and follow the path across a footbridge. Upstream, a little waterfall tumbles past the piers of an old bridge.
    At a T-junction, turn left up a bridleway to follow the stream towards moorland slopes. A memorial beside the path commemorates R.D. Blackmore, who used this valley as a setting for his novel *Lorna Doone* (1869). The path climbs through oak woods to a gate, leading into the ancient wood of Badgworthy, recorded in the Domesday Book more than 900 years ago.

③ Ignore a path on the right, which follows the bottom of Lank Combe, and cross the footbridge ahead over Lankcombe Water, a rivulet of tumbling rills and shady pools. The path runs past rhododendron thickets, but soon the route becomes much wilder, as it climbs towards the head of the valley. As the path swings

to the right, it passes some old stone walls and moss-covered boulders, lying in the bracken. These are the remains of the medieval settlement of Bicheordin, which was established before the Domesday Book and has been deserted since the 14th century. In *Lorna Doone* these ruins are inhabited by brigands.

④ Follow the path as it bends to the right up Hoccombe Combe, past the ruins of a shepherd's cottage, ignoring a path on the left that leads down to the stream. At first, the route is well defined, passing between hedges of beech along drystone walls, but as it rises onto moorland, it can barely be seen. Soon, however, a gate comes into view ahead and slightly to the right.

38

VIEW OVER MALMSMEAD

5 Go through the gate and bear slightly to the left, along an ill-defined bridleway that leads out across the moor. This is Exmoor's harshest face – a bleak and boggy landscape, more than 305m (1,000ft) above sea level.

The path starts to become clearer as it dips down towards a ford in Lank Combe. Ford the stream and continue to follow the path, which bends to the right, to reach a signpost. Here a broad, clear track crosses the path.

6 Turn right along the track. Within ¼ mile, as clear views towards the distant coast begin to open up on the left, the track swings to the right, with a less distinct path forking up to the left. Take this left-hand fork and follow it,

as it passes through grassland and heather. Large herds of Exmoor ponies can often be seen grazing on this part of the moor.

The path drops down into a coomb and passes across a rivulet to meet a clearer track. Turn right onto this track and continue for about ½ mile to reach a lane.

7 Turn right along the lane. After crossing a cattle grid, the lane drops steeply down from the moor, offering excellent views of the valleys, woods and ridges that give north Exmoor its distinctive character.

Continue along the lane, which swings to the left, into Malmsmead, passing Lorna Doone Farm on the right to return to the car park.

DORSET

Astonishingly unspoilt and with an impressive variety of scenery, Dorset is a great destination for walkers. Its wild chalk downs, pretty valleys and lowland heaths offer some of the south's best walking paths.

1 Worth Matravers

A fine coastal walk offering a challenging descent followed by a climb to an unusual medieval clifftop chapel.

LENGTH 4 miles (3 hours)

PARKING Car park by Renscombe Farm, west of village

CONDITIONS Steep in parts

REFRESHMENTS Tearoom and pubs in Worth Matravers

1 Leave the car park by the kissing gate at its far end and take the path diagonally right across a field with views over to a cleft in the coast. Go over a stile, and cross the next field and stile.

2 Turn left on the South West Coast Path with fine views across to Portland harbour and, just ahead, a steep descent to the sea at Chapman's Pool. Follow the coast path; a short distance further along is a memorial garden on left, dedicated to all Marines killed in action between 1945 and 1990. Just beyond the memorial garden cross a stile where four headlands come into view to the right. To the left is St Aldhelm's Head Quarry and ahead in the distance are old whitewashed coastguard cottages.

3 On reaching a flight of stairs, take the steps down, descending nearly 60m (200ft) with a handrail most of the way. Climb back up the other side and continue on the coast path; just beyond is a stone bench from where St Aldhelm's Chapel can be seen ahead.

The path passes close to the tiny stone chapel, which was built in 1140, according to legend, by a heartbroken father in loving memory of his newlywed daughter and husband who drowned when their boat capsized. The chapel is an unusual example of Norman ecclesiastical architecture: the corners of the square building are aligned with the points of the compass, whereas most church buildings of the period are rectangular and the walls themselves are oriented. Inside, fine 12th-century vaulting from a central pillar supports the roof.

4 At a lookout post for the National Coastwatch Institution, the path rounds the point and starts to descend steeply. Continue along the cliffs as the path dips and rises for nearly a mile with exciting craggy views. Eventually the path starts to cut inland around the top of the disused Winspit Quarry. Descend a flight of steps; the ledges and caves of the old quarry works can be explored, with caution, down a path to the right.

5 From the steps, take the track on left leading up towards Worth Matravers. To left and right, the striations of strip lynchets – medieval terracing – can be seen running horizontally along the grassy hills.

6 Where the track meets a small sewage works, fork left then right over a stone stile where the track begins to climb steadily back to the road. At the road turn left to Weston Farm. Where the road curves right past the farm, take the track to the left beside a wooden post marked St Aldhelm's Head. Afer a short distance take the path on the right, through a gate, which leads back across the field to the car park.

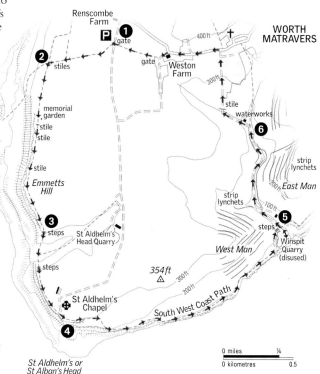

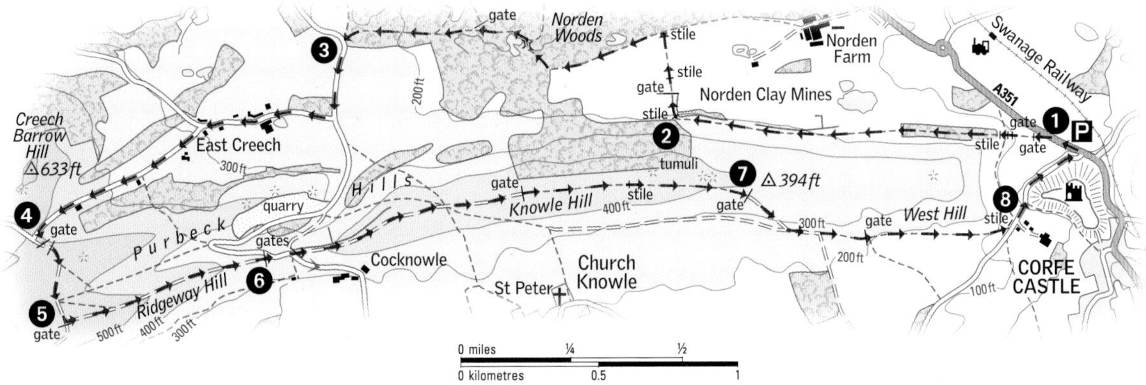

2 Corfe Castle

From woods with tranquil pools, along the crest of a hill and back to the spectacular ruins of Corfe Castle.

LENGTH 5½ miles (3 hours)

PARKING Corfe Castle car park on A351

CONDITIONS Very muddy in parts after rain

REFRESHMENTS Pub and tearoom in village

1 Turn right out of the car park and follow the verge for a short distance. At a speed restriction sign, cross the road, go through a kissing gate and take the path diagonally right over the field, through another gate and over a crossing of paths. Continue over a stile and follow the path with the hill to left through woods. From a clearing the view extends north across heathland to Poole Harbour. The path opens out, curves right through bracken, passes beside a gate on right and re-enters woodland with a wire fence on the right. The Norden Clay Mines buildings may be glimpsed through the trees – clay has been mined here since the 19th century.

2 Where the track ends at a gate and stile, turn right down a field, following yellow waymarks through another gate and over a stile, and cross the field with wire fence to left. Enter Norden Woods and turn left along a pretty woodland way where birch trees overhang a water-filled claypit to the right. At the end of a field on the left, bear right and cross two wooden bridges by a pond and then turn left at signpost for East Creech. At a fork bear left with a stream to the left, past boundary stones marked 'AP', to a minor road.

3 Turn left on the road and after ¼ mile turn right on another minor road, which gently rises with Creech Barrow Hill ahead. Pass through a farm beside a roadside duckpond to the four or five old houses that make up East Creech.

Turn left opposite a phone box and follow the road on a long gradual climb with glorious views back over to the blue waters of Poole Harbour. Hang-gliders and buzzards may be glimpsed above Creech Barrow Hill to right.

4 At the top of the hill, where the road bends sharply right, take the first track left and continue through a gate into Stonehill Down nature reserve. After a further short climb, with tumuli to the left, the long grassy curve of the Purbeck Hills is seen snaking away to left.

5 At the top, immediately in front of a gate, turn left along the crest of Ridgeway Hill. The view to left ahead extends over quarries to Poole Harbour; to right is Church Knowle, with Kingston farther along the horizon.

6 Go through a gate and join the road for a few metres, then go through a small gate onto a track climbing back to the top of the ridge.

The views to the left now extend farther west, towards Lulworth Heath. Pass a memorial stone and look down over Church Knowle and its square church tower on the right. The tall chimneys of Bucknowle House can be seen to the right; ahead is Corfe Common and the long stone strip of Corfe Castle village. After some tumuli on the left, follow the path down diagonally right, leaving the crest, and follow the sign for Corfe.

7 Go through a gate and at the track ahead turn left, with the gorse-covered slope of the ridge to left and farmland to right. Soon the keep of Corfe Castle (NT) can be seen. On entering National Trust land keep straight on along the base of the hill, following the sign 'Corfe ½ mile'.

8 Go through a gate to join a path just before the stream. Follow the sign to the car park. To visit the castle, go over the wooden bridge and cross the road, and take a path running between the castle and the stream. From the village square turn into the castle entrance on the left.

SOUTH WEST ENGLAND

DORSET

3 Higher Bockhampton

Paths through heath and forest to Thomas Hardy's cottage and across the Wessex countryside that features in his novels.

LENGTH 1½ or 5½ miles (1 or 3 hours)

PARKING Thorncombe Wood car park

CONDITIONS Paths through forest, heath and undulating farmland

REFRESHMENTS Hotel at Lower Bockhampton

1 Leave the car park by Post 1 of the Thorncombe Wood Trail and follow the nature-trail arrow markers from Post 1 to Post 11.

At Post 11, leave the marked trail by going straight ahead on a wide path, avoiding Post 12. Continue past Post 18, then follow the path to the right through an iron fence and onto heathland. Black Heath forms part of Thomas Hardy's fictitious Egdon Heath, much of which is now forest and farmland. The heath supports diverse wildlife, including common lizards, slow-worms, adders and roe deer. Large natural hollows, known as swallet holes, can be seen here and in the forest.

2 Fork left past Rushy Pond (at Post 14), which attracts newts, dragonflies and damselflies, then turn left downhill to Hardy's Cottage (NT), birthplace of the novelist in 1840 and his home until the age of 34.

SHORT CUT *To return to the car park, turn left on a track signposted to Higher Bockhampton.*

3 From Hardy's Cottage, turn right on a track signposted to Puddletown. Continue straight on at a crossing of tracks. Ignore a track joining from the left and a narrow path on the right, and continue to a five-way junction.

4 Turn sharp right on a track that runs along the edge of Puddletown Forest on the left and wooded heathland on the right. Ignore any left turns. In places, rhododendrons grow along the track. At one point, a view suddenly opens out between the trees on the left to the Purbeck Hills. After a level ½ mile, the path drops steeply and then rises slightly.

5 At a sharp left bend, as the path begins to descend again, continue straight on along the path ahead and climb over two stiles into a field. Cross to another stile, to the left of a house in the far corner of the field. Go over the stile, cross a road and take the farm track ahead. After a short distance, fork right before some barns, following a yellow waymark. Cross the first field, on the side of the Frome Valley, diagonally to a stile in the right-hand fence, just above the bottom corner. Frome Valley was the Valley of the Great Dairies in Hardy's *Tess of the D'Urbervilles*. It is where Tess worked as a dairymaid. Go over the stile.

6 Cross the next field to another stile to the right of some farm buildings. Climb over the stile, cross a farm track and the next small field, then go over a footbridge and follow the left edges of the fields to reach a house. Follow the path past the house to a gravel drive leading between

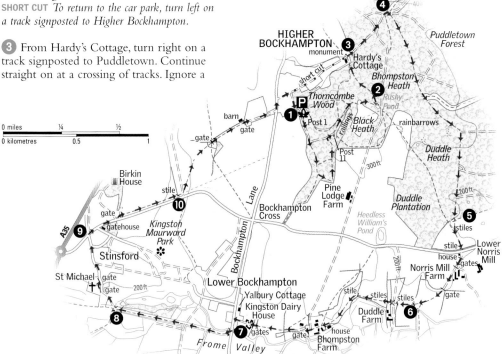

some buildings. Where the drive bends to the right, keep straight on, passing through a gate, on a path signposted to Lower Bockhampton.

Just beyond a farmhouse turn left, go through a gate and cross the fields and stiles ahead to a gate in front of the red-roofed buildings of Kingston Dairy House. Go through the farmyard and follow the lane beyond. Turn left at the road T-junction at Lower Bockhampton and cross the river.

7 Turn right and follow the riverside path. In Hardy's *Under the Greenwood Tree*, Mellstock choir members walked this way. After ¾ mile, cross a low bridge over some water.

8 Turn right along a path that joins the lane to Stinsford. Turn left into St Michael's churchyard, where the poet Cecil Day Lewis is buried, as is the heart of Thomas Hardy, whose ashes are in Poets' Corner at Westminster Abbey in London. Leave the churchyard by the top gate and continue along the lane past the agricultural college buildings on the right.

9 At a T-junction, turn right past the gatehouse of Kingston Maurward Park on the right. Just past the stone pillars of the entrance to Birkin House on the left, turn left on a path that runs parallel to the road.

10 Beyond a stile, turn left on a track, then turn diagonally right by a signpost and walk up to a gate. Go through the gate and follow the field edge past a barn, go through another gate and walk along the track past a house. Turn left on the road, then turn right back to the car park.

HARDY'S COTTAGE

DORSET

4 Abbotsbury

A climb to the top of an escarpment with fine views over Chesil Beach, and a visit to a 14th-century chapel.

LENGTH 8 or 9 miles (4 or 4½ hours)

PARKING Main car park off B3157

CONDITIONS Steep climb to top of escarpment

REFRESHMENTS Pub and tearooms in Abbotsbury; pub in Portesham; café at Swannery car park

1 Turn left out of the car park and follow the road round to the right. Opposite the post office, turn right into Back Street. After 150m, turn left on a track before Spring Cottage, then soon fork left and follow the path uphill through a gate. Continue up, ignoring a path on the right, to Lime Kiln car park and go through the gates to a limestone bank. The path rises diagonally to the right, giving a sweeping view of Chesil Beach.

2 At a junction, turn right through the left of two gates, signed for the South West Coast Path. Go through another gate and, after 100m, keep straight on as the fence bends to the right. Continue for ⅓ mile to a signpost, where the path bends left towards a road. Turn left on the road and, after 50m, turn right on a path, leading along the top of a gorse-covered hillside.

3 At the next signpost, leave the coast path on the left and go straight on to Portesham (pronounced Possum), descending along the edge of the escarpment. Where the slope steepens, by a waymark and a gate on the left, zigzag to the right, then go left along the valley bottom and pass through a gate to the left into woodland.

At the end of the wood, take the left of two gates and follow the edge of a field. Cross a farm track and continue into Portesham, where Admiral Hardy (1769-1839), who served with Nelson at Trafalgar, lived. Turn right on the road.

4 Turn left onto Church Lane, then left through St Peter's churchyard. On the far side of the churchyard, turn right on a road then, just beyond Blagdon House, No. 16, turn left on a path.

Enter the sports field ahead, beside some modern houses, and turn right past a playground to join a path at the far left corner. Cross the left edge of the next field and take the drive to the right of the former Portesham railway station (now a private house) to reach a road.

5 Turn right on the road. After 100m, just beyond a farm, turn left on a track. Avoiding a right fork to a caravan site, take the next right fork. After 20m, cross a single plank on the left, leading to a woodland path. Go through a waymarked gate and follow the top edge of two fields. Turn right on a track at East Elworth Farm, then go right at a T-junction with a road.

6 At the next farm, take the track to the left by the thatched Old Farm House. After 200m, turn left through a waymarked gate on a rising track that passes between hedges and is overgrown in parts. Emerge onto downland and, at a meeting of paths, turn right over a stile and follow the acorn markers and yellow arrows of the coast path for 1¼ miles along the crest of the hill, eventually dropping down to a road. Chapel Hill, topped by St Catherine's Chapel, is ahead. Its

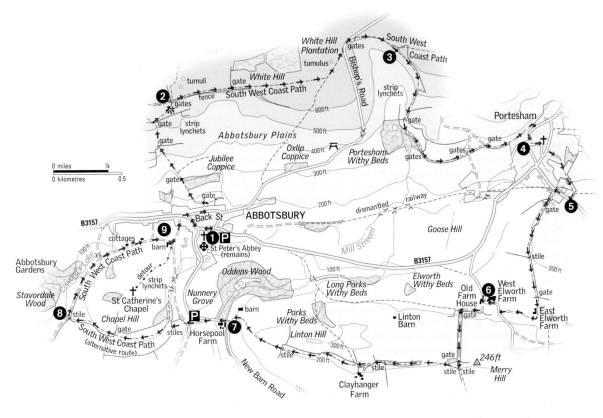

slopes are prominently striped with lynchets, the remains of Saxon terraced field systems.

7 Turn right on the road, then fork left past a car park to a toilet block. A road to the left leads to the Swannery. Follow the road to the right and immediately climb over a stile on the left, signposted to the Tropical Gardens. Beyond the next stile, continue straight on at a signpost, skirting Chapel Hill and passing two Second World War pillboxes, to reach a T-junction.

8 Turn right on the track towards Abbotsbury, keeping right at the next two junctions. Continue to a stone barn on the right.

DETOUR *Turn right, go around the barn and climb the hill to St Catherine's Chapel, which was built in the late 14th century by the Abbey of Abbotsbury.*

9 Continue on the main track into Abbotsbury. At the road, turn right past the post office and follow the road as it bends to the left, back to the car park.

ST CATHERINE'S CHAPEL ON CHAPEL HILL, OVERLOOKING CHESIL BEACH

DORSET

5 Osmington

A chalk-hill figure carved in the 19th century, a prehistoric hillfort and magnificent downland and coastal views.

LENGTH 5½ or 6 miles (2½ or 3 hours)

PARKING Church Lane, Osmington

CONDITIONS Mostly on grass and along good paths, with one climb; can be muddy

REFRESHMENTS Pubs in Osmington, Sutton Poyntz

1 With St Osmond's Church on your left, walk along Church Lane. In 1816, the artist John Constable sketched and painted Osmington and nearby Weymouth when he spent his honeymoon there at the vicarage. Behind the churchyard lie the ruins of 17th-century Osmington Manor. Continue past Village Street, which joins from the right, and follow the road out of the village.

2 By an old water pump turn left onto a track signposted to Sutton Poyntz. Pass a caravan site on the right, go through a gate and cross a field to another gate ahead. Cut into White Horse Hill, on the right, is a chalk figure of King George III on a horse. Continue diagonally across the next field to its far right corner, then follow the edges of the next two fields.

3 At a junction of tracks, continue ahead and go over a stream, then turn left before a gate, as waymarked, into Sutton Poyntz. Turn right on the road past a watermill. Just before the duckpond, cross the footbridge on the left and turn left along the millstream and behind the watermill. Turn left on the road then right into

Puddledock Lane. Just after the lane bends right by Old Dairyhouse, ignore a first right turn and take the next right, a signposted footpath.

4 Enter a field and follow the rising track ahead. Above is Chalbury, an Iron Age hillfort. Follow the track as it bends round to the right then, at the end of the next field, left up the edge of another field. Go through a gate and head along the grassy track towards some power lines. Continue to two stiles by a road. Climb the right-hand stile, not joining the road but almost doubling back, following the fence on the right.

5 Where the fence bends left, walk across a grassy terrace, part of an old quarry. The fence then drops away to the right; do not descend, but walk up the terrace to cross a dilapidated stone wall. Continue over the stile ahead. There are glorious views to the Isle of Portland, whose limestone quarries have supplied pale yellow Portland stone for facing great buildings, such as St Paul's Cathedral and Buckingham Palace.

At a road, turn left. Soon, turn right on an inland section of the South West Coast Path, which runs for ¾ mile along high ground near the edge of the slope, with glorious views.

6 Turn left on a signposted path to a track by ruined barns. Turn right on the track; ignore a first track to the right, then at a fork bear right. After a short way, a path on the right leads down to the white horse – just to the left – but it is difficult to make out at such close range.

7 Keep forward along the coast path, go through a gate and fork right, following a signpost to Osmington. On joining a lane, continue ahead back to the village.

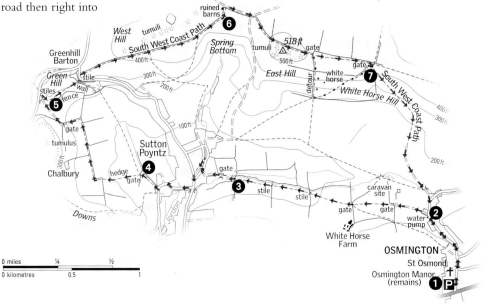

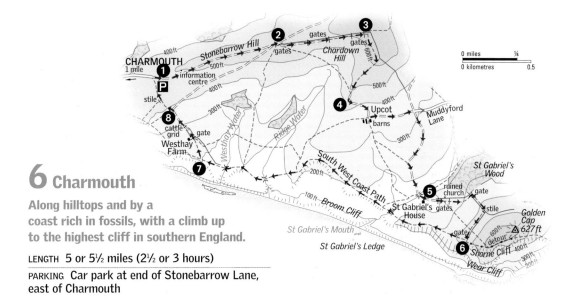

6 Charmouth

Along hilltops and by a coast rich in fossils, with a climb up to the highest cliff in southern England.

LENGTH 5 or 5½ miles (2½ or 3 hours)

PARKING Car park at end of Stonebarrow Lane, east of Charmouth

CONDITIONS One steep climb, to Golden Cap

REFRESHMENTS None on walk; pubs in Charmouth

1 Turn right out of the car park, past the NT information centre on the left. The path follows the line of Stonebarrow Hill, a haunt of kestrels, merlins, hobbies, buzzards and peregrines. In the distance to the right is the summit of Golden Cap, which will be passed later in the walk. Continue on the path for ½ mile to reach gates.

2 Go through the right-hand pair of gates, signposted to St Gabriel's and Golden Cap, then immediately fork left, signposted to Chardown Hill. The path runs alongside a fence on the left, through several gates, and above the head of a deep valley immediately on the right.

3 Just after the valley head, and after a bench, turn right at the fence corner, signposted to Upcot. The path follows the fence. At the next fence corner, bear half-right, signposted to Upcot and St Gabriel's, and follow the path downhill to meet a track at the bottom of the slope.

4 Turn left on the track, which passes between houses at Upcot (NT), a farm run using traditional farming methods. In front of farm barns, turn left, signposted to St Gabriel's. At the next junction turn right, again signposted to St Gabriel's. A 'private access' sign farther along the track refers to vehicles; walkers are welcome.

5 At a thatched former farmhouse, turn left, signposted to Golden Cap. Go through a gate and follow the track to the right of the ruined St Gabriel's Church. This and the thatched farmhouse are all that remain of the village of Stanton St Gabriel's, which was abandoned when the old Dorchester road was moved in 1825 to

the route of the present A35. The church dates from at least 1240, and possibly from Saxon times. In the early 19th century smugglers used the building to store brandy.

Follow the track through a gate and along the bottom of a field and through another gate. Turn right at a signpost along a field edge to a stile on the right, signposted to coast path. Turn right to cross the stile back into a field and follow the field edge to a gate and coast path signpost.
DETOUR *Turn left to climb up to the 191m (627ft) summit of Golden Cap, the highest point on England's south coast, giving views from the Isle of Portland in the east to Start Point and Dartmoor in the west. A horizontal layer of resistant sandstone gives the cliff its level 'cap'. The cliff is just a tiny part of the vast Golden Cap Estate (NT), which includes 6 miles of coastline with 20 miles of public paths.*

6 Turn right, just in from the cliff edge, on the coast path, which is unclear at first on the ground. Do not go too close to the crumbly cliff edge – it can be dangerous. Cross a footbridge, and after ½ mile ignore a path leading inland, signposted to Stonebarrow Hill and Morcombelake. Continue on the coast path, crossing a second footbridge. Be careful to avoid walking on the landslips, as they can be unstable.

7 About 150m after a third footbridge, turn right at a signpost for Westhay and Stonebarrow, making for a gate to the right of Westhay farmhouse. Go through the gate and follow the path, which merges with a concrete track from the farm and crosses a cattle grid.

8 After 120m, where the track bends right, bear half-left on a rising bridleway, signposted to Stonebarrow. Ignore all right turns and a stile on the left. Continue to the car park.

SOUTH WEST ENGLAND

A STRETCH OF THE RIDGEWAY IN WILTSHIRE

The old roads of the west

Southwest England is scored with ancient tracks, used by travellers, traders and drovers for millennia.

The old road snakes away up the slope of the ground between two cornfields, an undulating ribbon of white in a deeply grooved bed of chalk and flint, typical of so many of the downland tracks of southern England.

At the crest of the ridge, five lanes meet in a dusty circle trodden out over uncounted centuries by the feet of drovers and the hooves of flocks and herds. Here, a great swathe of northern Hampshire comes into view. On the map, the old road crosses from edge to edge in a purposeful westward run under various titles: White Hill and Ford Lane, Pack Lane and Harroway – ancient names all. It was Saxon

travellers who styled the stony track Harroway or Hoary Way – the 'Old Road', a highway across the chalk landscape that must have seemed ancient to those fighters and farmers from the Low Countries when they arrived to settle southern England 1,500 years ago and found it already cutting through the forests and hurdling the open hills.

Not far off, outlined against the sky and half-obliterated by the plough, rises the grassy dome of a Bronze Age burial mound, symbol of the power and dignity of the one whose bones lie within – perhaps a warrior chief interred with sword and treasures after battle, maybe a

trodden out into grooves by the passing feet of men and beasts, were an ideal matrix for the creation of permanent paths – small sections of way frequently travelled by large numbers. These paths, for example between a sizeable settlement and the nearest river ford, joined up over time and developed into through routes.

Such ancient trackways had certain characteristics in common. They tended to keep to the high ground, away from the dangers of the thickly forested, swampy valley floors, descending only to cross streams and rivers at dependable, firm-bottomed fording places. They kept just off the crest of the hill or ridge, so as to be sheltered from the worst of the weather, and also to allow those who travelled them to have a grandstand view of any approaching strangers without themselves being silhouetted on the skyline.

As the tracks matured, they developed thick margins of woody tree species – more like linear sections of forest than hedges – which afforded protection from wind and rain, offered fruits and nuts in autumn, and helped keep driven animals to the straight and narrow path. They also avoided settlements – or the settlements avoided them, for who would want travelling traders, beggars, brigands or even armies marching past their front yard?

A sense of place

The place names along the old roads are a treasury of history and romance. Along the Hampshire section of the Harroway, for example, is the hamlet of Well, where fresh water springs; the meeting places of Four Lanes End and Five Lanes End; Dirty ('Didicoy') Corner where the didicoy, or gypsies, would gather; Chapmansford where chapmen, or pedlars, plied their trade with passers-by – all these names encapsulate millennia of itinerant life along the ancient highway. And the routes that the trackways follow, tucked away in the folds of the hills, hidden in the woods, slinking through the skirts of towns disguised as Packhorse Road, The Drove or Green Lane, seem to add to their mystery and magic.

The great Ridgeway National Trail that runs from Avebury through Wiltshire, Berkshire and Oxfordshire is the best known of the old roads of southern Britain. But there are many others: the Lun Way, the Ox Drove, the Icknield Way, the West Wiltshire Ridgeway – not to mention the most venerable of all, the Harroway itself. For five thousand years these hollow ways were the most important trading and travelling routes in these islands, helping to bolster and shape the societies they served. Today they lie mostly forgotten, like tarnished old lamps waiting only for some fortunate Aladdin of a walker to rub up against them by luck.

noblewoman among jewelled necklaces and decorated pots, who last walked these rollercoaster downs four millennia ago. Yet the track was already ancient then, a hollow way that had been in use for at least two thousand years by the time the tomb at the crest of the hill was built.

The Harroway stretches in one mighty, unbroken curve of some 300 miles across the whole expanse of southern Britain, a great concave arc from the Kentish shore near Dover (where nowadays it's known as the North Downs Way) by way of the high country of Kent and Hampshire, by Stonehenge and the Wiltshire and Dorset downs to the Devon coast at Seaton.

Ancient highways

The Anglo-Saxon kingdom of Wessex was founded on the great chalk lands of southern England, the region that we think of today as comprising South Somerset and Dorset, Hampshire and Wiltshire. The soft chalk and clay, so easily

DORSET

7 Netherbury

Along a river valley where flax mills once operated and through fields past a Tudor manor.

LENGTH 7 miles (4 hours)

PARKING In village hall car park

CONDITIONS No steep climbs; one steady ascent on quiet lane, and one muddy descent

REFRESHMENTS Pub at Melplash

1 Turn right out of the car park, then left at the road junction by a bus shelter. After a stream appears to left of road, turn right at the next junction on an unsurfaced track. Continue ahead, with the River Brit to right, for about ¼ mile.

2 At the end of the track go through the left-hand gate and continue ahead, following a blue waymark; ignore the waymarked path to the left. At the end of the field, go through a gate to the left of an electric power post. Follow another blue waymark, joining a hedgerow on the right. Go through a gate and continue on a concrete track past houses at Oxbridge to a T-junction with a minor road.

3 Turn left on the road. Where the road bends sharp right, turn left onto a concrete track, then immediately cross the stile on the right. Turn left along the field edge and go through a waymarked gate near a barn. Go through another gate, keeping to the right of a brick lean-to by the barn, and cross a stile. Continue along the field beside a conifer hedge.

At the top of the field turn left, then turn right over a stile next to a wooden gate. Walk along the edge of the field and cross a stile into woodland. After about 30m, fork right to the far edge of woodland, and continue into a field.

4 Cross straight over the field to a gate visible on the opposite side. Go through the gate and follow the track to a junction with the A3066. Cross over to the minor road opposite, signposted to Mapperton, and continue ahead on this road, avoiding side turns. After 1½ miles, pass a

NETHERBURY VILLAGE

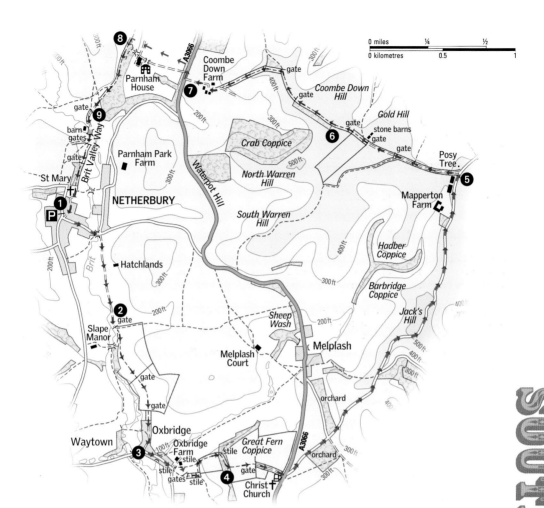

farmhouse and barn on the left to reach a junction with a bridleway on the left.

The Posy Tree at this junction was a meeting point for survivors of the Great Plague of the 1340s, which ravaged Mapperton; only a large stump remains to mark the spot. The church burial ground at Netherbury was barred to plague victims, who were buried on nearby Warren Hill.

5 Turn left on the bridleway, between hedges. At the next junction, go straight on through a gate and follow the fence to another gate. Continue ahead past stone barns on the right to a third gate and follow the track ahead.

6 Keep forward with a wire fence on the left until the path descends to a blue-waymarked gate. Go through the gate and follow the waymarked path to right of the field fence. At the next path junction, ignore a gate ahead and turn left. Continue gently downhill to a farm road, turning right in front of Coombe Down Farm to meet the A3066.

7 Turn right for a short distance on the A3066, passing on the left the driveway to Parnham House, a Tudor mansion. Parnham House is privately owned and is not open to visitors. Turn left onto a waymarked bridleway and continue ahead, with Parnham House on the left, across a deer park. Follow posts with white top markings, then blue waymarks to a junction of paths at the edge of woodland.

8 At the junction turn left. Where the woodland ends, keep straight on, following a dragonfly sign that denotes the Brit Valley Way, which runs beside the River Brit from Bridport to Beaminster. The valley's flax mills once supplied the Bridport fishing net industry.

9 After about 150m turn right through a gate, then left in front of a barn and through another gate. Go ahead through yet another gate and along the edge of a field, following yellow waymarks. Go through a gate and woods to St Mary's Church, with its 15th-century tower. Follow the track back to the car park.

SOMERSET

Exmoor's stream-filled combes, the Quantock Hills, the limestone Mendips and Cheddar Gorge are this county's main delights. Walkers with a head for heights can also enjoy its fine coastline with dizzying cliffs.

1 Dunster

A gentle walk through grassland to a castle, an ancient earthwork, and back to a historic town.

LENGTH 3 or 4 miles (2 or 3 hours)
PARKING Park Street, off West Street
CONDITIONS Easy paths and moderate climbs
REFRESHMENTS Teashops in Dunster

1 Turn left from the car park to the River Avill and cross the two-arched packhorse bridge, known as Gallox Bridge. Ignore a path to the right and keep straight on. At the next junction turn sharp left, signposted to Carhampton and Withycombe. Go through a gate and follow the footpath left, signposted to Carhampton.

Continue uphill across open sheep-grazed grassland, with the woods of the former deer park to right, and to left an ever-improving view of Dunster Castle and the sea beyond. Walk up a broad grassy track, cross a stream bed and go through a wooden gate. Continue up towards the horizon, with a conifer copse on the left.

2 At the top of the hill, go through Carhampton Gate and turn right to follow a wide stony track that continues to climb, with

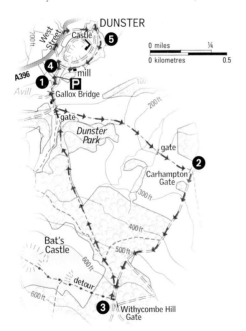

woods on the right and arable fields on the left. The views to the left extend over Carhampton to Dunster Beach and the Bristol Channel. Steam trains of the West Somerset Railway puff to and from Minehead, along the edge of the shore.

The path becomes steeper as it enters the woods. Ignoring a path on left, continue uphill and turn right through Withycombe Hill Gate. DETOUR *Keep forward on a broad path into the open; humps and bumps indicate that a Roman camp, known as Bat's Castle, perched on this mound. Ahead, on a twin mound, was an ancient British camp.*

3 Follow the broad gravel track signposted to Dunster downhill through conifers and beeches, with glimpses through the trees of the ancient earthworks. Continue to a major junction of paths and tracks. Fork right, following the blue marker on a tree. After about ½ mile, ignore a path on the left, curve right through the gate crossed earlier in the walk. Return over the packhorse bridge to the car park.

4 To visit Dunster Castle and gardens (NT), go forward through the barriers into Mill Garden. Turn left to West Street, where many of the cottages were once the homes of woollen workers. Turn right and walk to the castle entrance on right. Ahead, on left, is St George's Church, noted for its exceptionally long rood screen. A monastic tithe barn and circular 13th-century dovecote stand behind the church. Beyond is the High Street, with its eight-sided yarn market, built in 1609 as an outlet for Dunster cloth, and a building known as the Old Nunnery, put up by monks for the use of their guests.

5 Turn right through the castle entrance. Surrounded by beautiful terraced gardens and a large park, this mighty stronghold was home to the Luttrells for 600 years before it was passed on to the National Trust. Follow waymarked paths through the grounds to a river walk alongside the Avill. A map of the castle and gardens is available from the ticket office.

The walk ends at a stone gateway beside the 17th-century watermill. The mill's two overshot water wheels are just inside the gateway. The mill behind has been restored to full working order and produces stone-ground flour commercially, available with other products from the mill shop.

Walk past the mill along Mill Lane. A mill-leat runs along the right side of the lane. Turn left between bollards into the pleasant Mill Garden to return to the car park.

2 Winsford

From peaceful woodland to exhilarating moors with the chance to see wild ponies and deer.

LENGTH 5 miles (3 hours)

PARKING Car park opposite garage

CONDITIONS Moderately easy, with one steep downhill stretch and some shallow stream crossings by stepping stones; wear walking boots

REFRESHMENTS Tea garden, café and pub in Winsford

❶ From the car park, cross the road, passing the memorial cross on the right, and bend left uphill past the Royal Oak inn.

❷ Just before the road bends right turn left on Yellowcombe Lane, signposted to Winsford Hill. Climb the stone-surfaced lane between banks with overhanging holly, soon gaining good views over Winsford. At the top, keep to the track as it bends right through a beech wood, following the right side of a valley above a stream, then descends to a gate by the stream.

❸ Go through the gate (ignoring the stile and bridge on left) and follow the path past Yellowcombe Cottage, then cross the stream. Walk up the left side of the valley, with the fence and stream on right. Climbing gently, the path passes Halse Farm on the far side of the stream. Keep to the path as it leaves the stream to the right and continues uphill to emerge from the wood. Cross an expanse of open bracken-covered moor to reach a gate.

❹ Go through the gate and turn left on the path. Follow the wall to the Caratacus Stone, under its shelter. The stone bears the inscription 'caratici nepus', which means nephew or kinsman of Caratacus, the leader of the Welsh Silurian tribe at the time of the Roman invasion.
Turn right towards the crossroads, then turn right again onto the B3223, signposted to Simonsbath and Exford. Walk along the right-hand side of the road for ½ mile, with stunning views over the moors.

❺ At a wooden signpost, bear half-right from the road, following the directions to Withycombe. A grassy track starts a few metres beyond the signpost. Keep forward at a crossing of paths to the edge of the Punchbowl, a steep-sided, U-shaped valley. The moors can be seen dipping sharply on both sides to form the 61m (200ft) deep hollow, backed by a patchwork of fields. Walk to the left, round the Punchbowl's rim. A farm can be seen at the bottom. Keep right at a meeting of paths and descend to some trees and a gate with a blue waymark.

❻ Go through the gate, keeping the fence and trees on the right. Continue downhill, following the fence and line of trees. After a few hundred yards, turn right at a post with a blue waymark and follow the path to right of the trees.
At the signpost to Withycombe, pass through a gate and continue downhill through the field to another gate onto a farm track, which bends down to the left across a stream. Go between and then round the back of the farm buildings, following the path signposted to Winsford.

❼ At the farm entrance, where the surfaced track goes uphill to the left, follow the Winsford sign to right, along the edge of a field. Keeping the hedge on the right, continue through several yellow waymarked gates and over fields grazed by sheep and cattle. To the right is Burrow Wood and ahead Winsford church tower appears over the hill.

❽ As the path narrows between hedges, go through a wooden gate. Continue over three stiles, to a lane. Turn right into Winsford, passing the turning to St Mary Magdalene's Church. Cross the ford, pass a memorial on the right and turn left to the car park.

SOMERSET

3 Cheddar Gorge

Spectacular views of the deep, often densely wooded, limestone gorge and a scenic walk through a nature reserve.

LENGTH	4 miles (3 hours)

PARKING Layby off B3135, near tourist information centre

CONDITIONS Steep in places; muddy and slippery after rain; wear shoes with ankle protection

REFRESHMENTS Restaurants and cafés in Cheddar

1 From the parking place, walk downhill along the road to the information centre. A few metres beyond it, turn right on a waymarked track next to the Toy Museum. Follow the track for 200m as it gets steeper then levels out. Reaching the side of a house, follow the path until it comes level with the top of another house on the left.

2 Turn sharp right, following a green Gorge Walk waymark, fixed to a tree. The route enters a wood, then becomes steeper and overhung by hawthorn. As the wood thins out, there is a good view back to Cheddar. Go through a gate and continue on the path to a stile. Cross the stile and follow the path as it bears right, walking uphill with a fence on the left. Where the fence ends, continue ahead to a break in a low stone wall on the right.

3 Turn right through a gap in the wall by a yellow waymark post. Take the path on the far right, following a NT waymark on a wooden post. At a clearing and crossing of paths, a post points left to Black Rock and Gorge Walk. *DETOUR For a view deep into the crevice of the gorge, go straight ahead downhill. Take great care, as the steps are very steep and there is no handrail.*

4 Turn left and follow the path through a waymarked gate by the side of a wall. For ¼ mile the route is undulating and slightly rocky underfoot, with views to the right over the cliffs at Horseshoe Bend. Buzzards may be spotted overhead. Cross a stile by the side of a gate and continue along the descending path.

5 Go down wooden steps at the steepest point and continue straight on, across the steps over the stone wall ahead. The path slopes up through a field, taking you into Black Rock Nature Reserve. Cross a stile as the path slopes down into a wooded area, continuing ahead to a track at the bottom.

6 Turn sharp right onto the track, passing a notice board on the left giving details of trails through the Black Rock and Velvet Bottom reserves. Follow a yellow waymark over a stile and continue along the track through a gate to the road. Cross the road to take a path ahead, slightly to the right. The ascent through the woods gets steeper, with a long climb through the inspiring scenery.

At the top, go through a yellow-waymarked gate. Where the path divides, a short distance farther on, fork right, following a blue-waymarked bridleway, ignoring a yellow waymark to the left, and continue ahead to a stile.

7 Cross the stile, then bear left at a fork. The path opens out and views towards Cheddar Reservoir emerge ahead. To the right, rocks known as The Pinnacles jut into the gorge like fingers. Follow the path as it slopes down and away from the gorge, ignoring any paths to the right. The route broadens, with scatterings of hawthorn, gorse, brambles and bracken, then narrows and becomes increasingly rocky; take care on the stones.

Fields open up to the left, as you reach Jacob's Ladder on the right – these steps go all the way to the bottom of the gorge. A little farther along, on the right, is Pavey's Tower, which can be climbed to enjoy the far-reaching views from the top.

8 Continue ahead through a wooded area to a lane. Turn right at the lane, then turn right on the road and walk past the shops to the parking place.

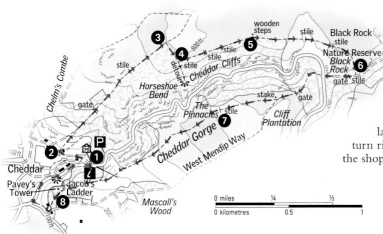

CHEDDAR GORGE

SOMERSET

4 Meare

A route revealing the hidden charms of the
Somerset Levels wetlands, with riversides
and marshes vibrant with birdlife.

LENGTH 6½ miles (3 hours)

PARKING On lane near Abbot's Fish House

CONDITIONS Flat terrain with marshes; fields are
crossed by irrigation channels, or rhynes,
passable only in certain places

REFRESHMENTS Pub in Meare

1 From Abbot's Fish House – used in medieval
times to store fish for the monks of Glastonbury
– follow the lane to the river and cross a bridge
by River House. There is a view to the right of
Glastonbury Tor. Turn left along the banks of
the River Brue, which can be muddy in places.
Pass a stone bridge on the left, ignoring the path
from Meare Farm, then continue ahead through
a gate and keep straight on. On the other side
of the river is a field of willows, and herons can
be seen along the banks. Beyond a large single
willow clump and a metal trough on the right,
the route meets a rhyne on the right. The flat
lands of the Somerset Levels are prone to
flooding – 8,000 years ago much of the region
was an inlet of the sea.

2 As you approach two metal gates, turn sharp
right by a line of hawthorns alongside a rhyne.
At a junction of rhynes, go through a gate and
turn half-right alongside another rhyne heading
towards a wooden bridge.

3 On reaching a broad channel, White's river,
cross the footbridge to the far bank, where a
Second World War pillbox can be seen on the
left. Head diagonally left across the field (the
path is indistinct at first) towards a barn. Just
before the barn, cross a bridge over a rhyne,
and continue alongside the much larger Decoy
Rhyne to the barn. Here turn left over the gated
bridge onto a well-defined farm track. After
500m go through a metal gate and continue
towards a wooded area, passing under power
cables. After a second metal gate, bear right,
ignoring a track from the left, and walk to a
metalled road.

4 Turn right on the road, then immediately
left along London Drove. To the right are long
peat-cutting channels; on both sides there are
waterlands where reed warblers can often be
heard. An information board for Westhay Moor
National Nature Reserve, run by Somerset
Wildlife Trust, details the vast array of wildlife.

Wicker-and-wooden hides at intervals on both
sides provide opportunities to observe, listen to
and photograph the many birds in the area. Otter
and mink can also sometimes be seen here in
summer. Continue along London Drove to a
junction with a road.

5 Turn right. At the next junction turn right
onto Dagg's Lane Drove. Expanses of water are
soon visible to the right. Again, hides to the left
and right are ideal for birdwatching. Turn right
into Westhay Moor reserve some 300m before
the drove reaches the road and a car park.

6 Follow the broad grassy track to the junction
with London Drove. Turn left and retrace your
steps to Meare.

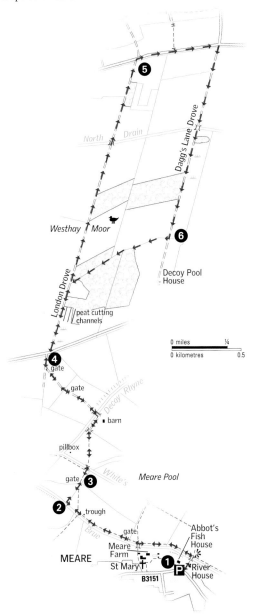

5 South Cadbury

Downland ridges with beautiful views, and through valley pastures to the earthworks of an ancient fort.

LENGTH 5½ miles (3½ hours)

PARKING Car park just south of church

CONDITIONS Easy; one climb to Cadbury Castle

REFRESHMENTS Pubs in South Cadbury and Corton Denham

① From the car park turn left. Soon after the junction with Crangs Lane, turn left over a stile signposted to Sigwells. Cross a stream and follow the left-hand edge of a field, to a track. Cross a waymarked stile in the hedge on the right, then turn immediately left along the edge of a field. Continue to a gate. Go through the gate and follow the field edge for about ⅓ mile.

② At the end of the field turn right and follow the path down through trees. Cross a ford and continue on a broad track past farm buildings and through Whitcombe to a road junction. Bear left uphill. At the brow of the hill turn left up some steps and over a stile, signposted to Corton Denham. Turn right and follow the path along the lower slopes of the hill for about ½ mile. The tower of St Andrew's Church at Corton Denham comes into view ahead. Follow the path downhill through a metal gate to a road.

③ Turn left to enter Corton Denham. Opposite St Andrew's Church turn right on Middle Ridge Lane. Where the lane bends left, turn right over a stile. Cross two more stiles in quick succession, bearing right across a field past barns and cottages. At the end of the field cross a double stile and a footbridge and skirt the next field to a gate. Turn left uphill on Ridge Lane, climbing gently over Corton Ridge. Beyond the brow of the ridge, the track ends at two waymarked gates.

④ Go through the right-hand gate, turn right and follow the grassy path for ¾ mile, with fine views to the left and ahead. Where the path divides, fork left downhill to a blue waymark, through a gate and down a lane to a road.

⑤ Follow the road ahead, signposted to South Cadbury. Where a lane joins from the left, turn left over a series of stiles and go diagonally left across a field. Cross a stile leading to a road and continue on the path opposite to another road. Turn right. About 60m past Village End – the last house in the village – turn right up a short narrow path to a field. Turn right along the field

edge for 40m then right over a stile. Follow the path slightly uphill with a wire fence on the left, turning left with the fence at a corner. About 100m beyond the corner, turn right uphill to a stile at the edge of a walled wood.

⑥ Follow the path through the wood, then climb steeply to the edge of one of Cadbury Castle's lower defensive banks. Turn left up a grassy slope through a gap in the earthworks. The hillfort, built around the 3rd century BC, was refortified by the Britons in the late 5th and early 6th centuries AD as a defence against the Saxons. This was the time of King Arthur, and Cadbury Castle is one of the legendary sites of Camelot. A timber feasting hall has been one of the discoveries on the site.

Turn right across the top of the fort towards a solitary thorn tree at a break in the earthworks above South Cadbury. Pass the tree on the left and go downhill to a path just below. Turn left; at a T-junction turn right on Castle Lane and descend to the road. Turn left to visit tiny St Thomas à Becket Church, with its medieval wallpainting said to represent the murdered archbishop, or right to the car park.

SOMERSET

6 Hinton Charterhouse

Past an old priory to a pair of monumental viaducts that once carried railway lines, then along an old canal towpath.

LENGTH 7½ miles (4 hours)

PARKING Near St John the Baptist Church

CONDITIONS Mostly easy going, but with one steep, rough section; boots needed

REFRESHMENTS Pubs at Hinton Charterhouse, Midford and Combe Hay

1 Enter the churchyard and turn right on the footpath. Continue through a gate under trees and over a stile, and follow the path across parkland studded with oak, beech and pine trees; 18th-century Hinton House can be seen on the left. Beyond a prominent group of pines, cross a stile, go over the field and through the gate onto a road.

2 Cross over a stile opposite and follow the path half right across the field. Continue past Hinton Abbey and the remains of the priory on the right, noting the gabled tower that was the chapter house, with a library above and dovecote at the top. Cross a stile and bear slightly right to cross a second stile. Follow the path for ¾ mile over fields. At Pipehouse village, cross a broad track and stiles to join a narrow path beside a hedge, and meet a road.

3 Turn left. Where the road becomes a marked byway, continue ahead on a broad track between tall mature hedges. Where the path divides, fork left down a rough, rocky path through a tunnel of branches. To the right are glimpses of 18th-century Midford Castle, now a private house.

4 At the foot of the hill, turn left on the road and immediately right, taking great care when crossing the road, and go over a footbridge across a stream by an old watermill. Follow the raised path across a field. Cross a stile and go under a railway viaduct that once carried the Somerset and Dorset line and crosses a lower viaduct built for the Great Western branch line; both are now disused.

5 Turn right on a minor road, then right at a main road 200m ahead. Opposite the Hope and

MIDFORD CASTLE

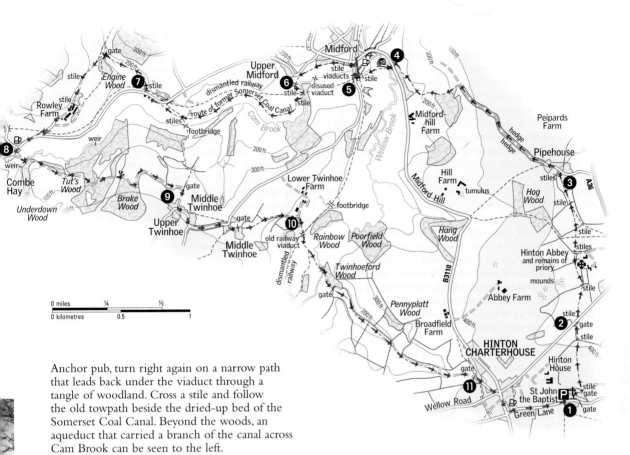

Anchor pub, turn right again on a narrow path that leads back under the viaduct through a tangle of woodland. Cross a stile and follow the old towpath beside the dried-up bed of the Somerset Coal Canal. Beyond the woods, an aqueduct that carried a branch of the canal across Cam Brook can be seen to the left.

6 Just beyond a canal bridge, cross a stile and turn left. Continue to a stream, turn right under the viaduct and then left over a stile to rejoin the towpath, which leads towards the end of the valley. Cross two stiles 10m apart and continue to farm buildings. Cross the road and follow the path under the viaduct.

7 Cross a stile. To the left is the first of many lock chambers that once formed a watery staircase taking boats up and down the hill. At the head of the valley, where paths cross, turn left in front of a gate, cross a bridge and take the path that climbs through trees. At the top of the hill turn left. Cross a stile, turn right on a farm track and continue up the field beside the fence. At the top cross a stile, turn left and go through Rowley Farm. Continue ahead on the road, under the viaduct, to a T-junction. Turn right.

8 Just beyond the Wheatsheaf inn, turn sharp left after a telephone box onto a bridleway. The track crosses Cam Brook, with an impressive weir to the right. Beyond the trees the track climbs gently. With woods to the left, continue round the curve of the hill. After a stretch in scrubby woodland, the path leads along the side of a wood with farmland to the left. Where the woodland ends follow the path to the left and skirt a field with a hedge to the right. At the end of the field go through a gate and turn right on a farm track, to meet a road.

9 Turn left; the road soon divides. Turn left again between banks and hedgerows. Where the road bears left past Leeson's Cottage, turn right on a concrete drive. Just before a converted barn, fork left through a gate onto a grassy path, and continue downhill along edges of fields.

10 Where the path meets a track by a house, turn right downhill and go under the viaduct. Cross a metal footbridge and immediately turn left over a wooden footbridge. Turn right to follow the path by a stream. Leave the woodland by a gate, and follow the path as it swings left around a bracken-covered hill. With the stream on the left, the path climbs gently through fields.

11 Go through a gate and follow the path between houses onto a lane leading up to Hinton Charterhouse. Turn right on the main road, then turn left by the pub to return to the parking place.

WILTSHIRE

Walks in this county cross some of Britain's finest rolling downland, skirting prehistoric monuments and pretty, historic villages. But the region is also known for its fine vistas and charming river valleys.

1 Great Bedwyn

Along a canal towpath to a pumping station housing one of the world's oldest working steam engines.

LENGTH 4½ or 5 miles (2 or 2½ hours)

PARKING At or near Great Bedwyn station

CONDITIONS Easy going on good paths

REFRESHMENTS Pub in Great Bedwyn and Wilton

1 From the station, take the road leading across the railway and the Kennet and Avon Canal. Now used mainly by pleasure craft, the canal was built to provide a link between Bristol and the Thames. It opened in 1810.

2 Beyond the canal, turn right at the wharf and follow the towpath for 2 miles. The canal climbs through a series of locks, which lift it out of the Kennet valley at Hungerford to a summit level a mile from Crofton, before descending to the Avon valley. Each boat crossing the summit drains away 454,600 litres (100,000 gallons) of water, which has to be replaced by the pumping station. DETOUR *Cross the canal at the bottom lock gates, go under the railway and climb steps to Crofton Pumping Station, open in summer; the oldest of the two steam engines began work in 1812. The canal summit is still 1 mile away, so water has to be pumped uphill.*

3 From the lock near the pumping station, cross the footbridge by the sluice gates at the head of Wilton Water, a reservoir created when springs that fed into the canal were dammed. Continue on the path beside the water.

4 At a road turn left into Wilton, a village of thatch and timber. Continue down the main street. At a junction follow the road round to the left towards Great Bedwyn, climbing gently between banks ablaze with wild flowers in season.

5 Beyond a couple of cottages, Wilton Windmill comes into view to the right. At a road junction turn right and continue ahead.

6 Where the road to Hungerford joins from the right, turn left on the byway. Ignore a farm track that swings left, and continue ahead on the path.

7 Where the path emerges from the trees, turn right between two ponds – they may be overgrown – and cross an open space to an uphill track. Just beyond a sign pointing back to the windmill, take a forest track signposted left to Great Bedwyn. With pine to one side and silver birch on the other, the track leads through a clearing to another area of mixed woodland.

8 Where paths cross, follow the signpost ahead to Great Bedwyn. Where the gravel track ends, follow a grassy path across a clearing and back into woodland. Continue on the path into a little glade with an imposing oak at its centre, and go straight on through an area of dense conifers to the end of the woodland.

9 Turn right and then left to go round two sides of a field, heading for a gap in the hedge at the bottom right-hand corner. Go through the gap and follow the path down the left side of the field. At the bottom go through a gap in the hedge on right.

10 Turn left on the road to Great Bedwyn. Cross the canal and the railway to return to the station.

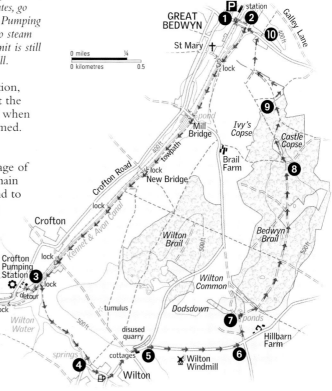

2 Lacock

A saunter along field paths that includes a converted abbey and views over the Avon valley.

LENGTH 6 miles (3 hours)

PARKING National Trust car park by abbey

CONDITIONS Easy

REFRESHMENTS Pubs and tearoom in Lacock

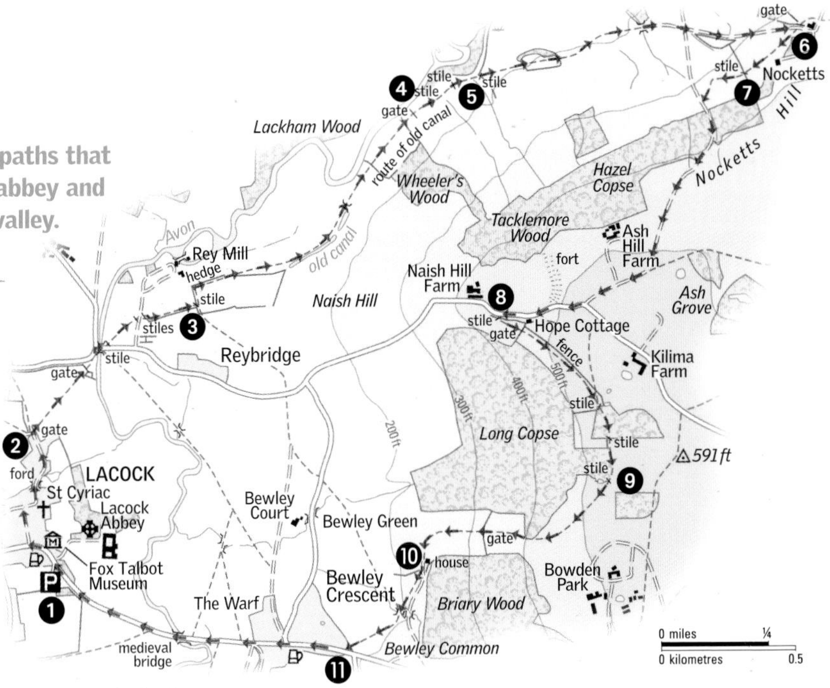

1 From the car park, follow footpath signs to the village and turn right on a street opposite the Red Lion. Turn right again to the 15th-century Church of St Cyriac and, at church gateway, turn left. Cross an old packhorse bridge and continue up the road.

2 At a T-junction turn right through a gate on a surfaced path across a field, then down to a road. Cross a bridge over the Avon then turn left over a stile by a footpath sign. Cross the field and go over a stile where a wall joins a fence. Cross a road and a second stile, and take the path ahead.

3 At the next stile turn left and follow the edge of a field round to the right. Go through the nearest gap in the hedge and continue ahead to a raised bank and through a gap in bushes to an old canal towpath. Follow this through scrubby woodland. The Avon is soon seen again below to the left, winding through open countryside.

4 Beyond an old bridge to the right follow the path into scrub and out again. Continue along the old canal towpath. From a rise in the next field, a stile at the edge of a wood comes into view.

5 Go over the stile onto a path bearing right. Head over pasture and fields, first towards a house on the horizon, and then towards the right-hand edge of a line of prominent trees. The path widens to a farm track; continue ahead.

6 At the top of a hill, just before a farm, turn sharp right. Follow the footpath through a gap in a hedge and cross a stile opposite.

7 Soon turn left along a surfaced road that leads through woods. Continue along a track and turn right on a road, noting faint traces of ancient defensive earthworks in a field on the right.

8 Beyond Hope Cottage on the left cross a stile in the hedge on the left. Turn sharp left, and at a fence go through the right-hand gate. The path leads along the steep, wooded flank of a valley. Continue into woodland ahead, pass to the right of tall pine trees to a junction of paths and turn right to leave the woods. Continue on the path towards the next tall group of pine trees.

9 Where woodland on the right ends, cross a stile onto a yellow-waymarked path. Cut through parkland to the right of the most prominent clump of beech, and a large single oak. Turn right along a track towards a gap in the woods. Gradually the grand house of Bowden Park comes into view to the left. Passing between two patches of woodland, go downhill to a gate. After a second gate, turn left then right to follow the edge of a field, and head steadily downhill.

10 By a stone house at the corner of the woods, turn left on a broad track. Go through a gap in a hedge to where park gates can be seen on the left. Bear right over the common towards a road.

11 Turn right on the road. Pass the Bell Inn on the left and cross the river valley by a medieval stone causeway and bridge. At the road junction by Lacock Abbey, turn left to return to the car park.

The abbey (NT), founded in 1232, was dissolved in the 16th century and converted into a private house, modified later in the Gothic style. The pioneering photographer William Henry Fox Talbot lived here in the late 19th century, and a medieval barn beside the abbey houses a museum of photographic history.

WILTSHIRE

3 Avebury

To the spectacular prehistoric sites of
Avebury stone circle, West Kennett long
barrow and Silbury Hill.

LENGTH 5 or 7 miles (3 or 4 hours)

PARKING National Trust car park at Avebury

CONDITIONS Easy going on good tracks and paths.
The exposed downs offer no shelter if the
weather turns bad

REFRESHMENTS Pub and restaurant in Avebury

1 In the far right-hand corner of the car park
from the entrance take the path signposted to
the stone circle. Just beyond a sports field the
great bank of the henge appears. Avebury, the
largest stone circle in Europe, was created some
4,000 years ago. The stone circle was originally a
ring of 98 stones with two smaller rings set inside
it; the bank, originally in dazzling white chalk,
was formed from excavated material when the
circular ditch, once 9m (30ft deep), was first dug.

Enter the circle by a gate next to the Henge
Shop and follow the circle round to the right.
Cross the road and follow the bank and ditch
to a gate by the next road.

2 Turn right on the road, an ancient track that
was a main route from London to Bath until the
18th century. Where paths cross, beyond farm
buildings on the right, continue ahead on a chalky
track, signposted to Ridgeway and Rockley.

Traffic noise gives way to the song of the
skylark and meadow pipit as the path climbs
steadily but gently through downland. The
chalky path becomes a grassy track that leads
up a short steep rise, giving a fine view back
over Avebury, with the tall Cherhill monument
in the distance.

DETOUR *At the top of the hill go straight ahead
through a gate to Fyfield Down, scattered with sarsen
stones similar to those at Avebury. About ¾ mile down
path, humps and hollows in the ground mark the
fallen hut walls of an Iron Age village.*

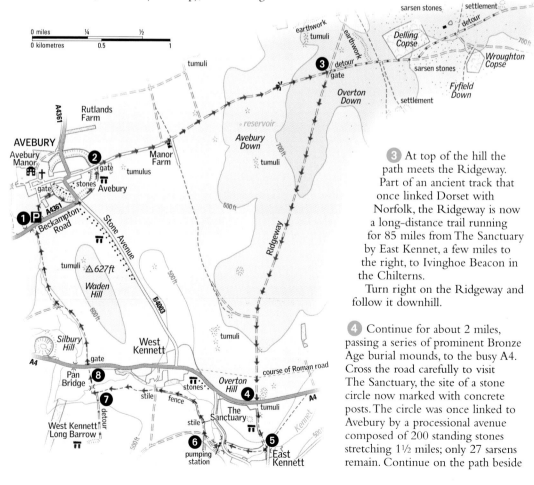

3 At top of the hill the
path meets the Ridgeway.
Part of an ancient track that
once linked Dorset with
Norfolk, the Ridgeway is now
a long-distance trail running
for 85 miles from The Sanctuary
by East Kennet, a few miles to
the right, to Ivinghoe Beacon in
the Chilterns.

Turn right on the Ridgeway and
follow it downhill.

4 Continue for about 2 miles,
passing a series of prominent Bronze
Age burial mounds, to the busy A4.
Cross the road carefully to visit
The Sanctuary, the site of a stone
circle now marked with concrete
posts. The circle was once linked to
Avebury by a processional avenue
composed of 200 standing stones
stretching 1½ miles; only 27 sarsens
remain. Continue on the path beside

The Sanctuary, past another round barrow to the left. Here in the valley there is richer soil, and a more regular pattern of fields divided by mature hedgerows.

5 At the foot of the hill, just before a bridge over a stream, turn right on a broad path along the edge of a field. The village of East Kennett is to the left. On meeting a road, turn left and immediately right on a track past the little pumping station, ignoring a track on the left.

6 Beyond a hedge, turn right on a narrow path overhung by trees. Where the leafy tunnel ends, cross a stile and continue with a fence on the left. Silbury Hill, Europe's largest prehistoric mound, built around 2000 BC on a spur of natural chalk, looms ahead.

Follow the fence as it swings left on a grassy path through fields. Cross a stile, go over a farm road and continue on a path at the side of a field to a surfaced track joining from the left.
DETOUR *Turn left to West Kennett Long Barrow, a Neolithic burial site constructed at least 4,000 years ago, and one of the largest and most accessible Neolithic chambered tombs in Britiain.*

7 Follow the path, which soon swings right over the Kennet before continuing to the A4.

8 Cross the road carefully to a wooden gate, and join the path to right of the Kennet, still a small stream as it skirts Silbury Hill. The path continues beside a fence and then follows the curve of the river towards Avebury. Cross the road and turn right to the car park.

WINTER SUNRISE, AVEBURY STONE CIRCLE

WILTSHIRE

4 Ogbourne St George

An exhilarating walk over rough downland and along part of the ancient Ridgeway, by a 6th-century BC hillfort.

LENGTH 6½ or 8 miles (3½ or 4½ hours)

PARKING In village, where road is widest

CONDITIONS Good going on tracks and paths, but can be very muddy in wet weather; boots or stout shoes recommended

REFRESHMENTS Range in Ogbourne St George

1 Follow the main street up then down to the bottom of the hill. Turn right onto Church Lane and walk to St George's Church. The church was built between the 12th and 15th centuries; its oldest surviving part is the arcade in the nave with its plain, robust Norman pillars. Go through the churchyard to a stile in a high beech hedge behind and to the left of the church. Cross the stile and follow the path along the hedge line and across a meadow beside a line of young trees. Cross a further three stiles and go through a narrow gap in the hedge to a road.

2 Cross the road to the bridleway opposite, part of the Ridgeway, which soon becomes a rough track climbing steadily between hedges.

3 Where the hedges end, go through a gate, ignoring a fork to the right. The track becomes a hollow way through the grassy downland and, as it climbs, forms a natural boundary between sheep pasture to the left and arable fields to the right.

From higher on the ridge, superb views extend to the right across a great plain towards Oxford, and to the left down into a sinuous

THE RIDGEWAY TOWARDS BARBURY CASTLE

valley. The path dips and climbs
for 2½ miles before it reaches a
wooden gate near a group of farm
buildings. Go through the gate.

DETOUR *Following the Ridgeway signs, turn right on
an unmade road, then left through a gate on a tree-
shaded path opposite Upper Herdswick Farm. This
leads past a car park and picnic site to Barbury Castle,
a hillfort built around the 6th century* BC.

4 Turn left on a broad track, marked as a
byway, leading down through arable and grazing
land. In season, wild flowers such as Oxford
ragwort and bird's-foot trefoil line the path.

5 Continue on the track, keeping to the right
of some woodland, which includes beech, oak
and pine. The ground begins to level out and is
bordered on the right by long grassy gallops.
Ogbourne St Andrew is to the left ahead.

6 Near the head of one of the gallops, where
the track divides, fork left on a track marked as a
byway, which climbs to a large barn. Follow the
track leading straight ahead, passing the barn on
your immediate left, and continue between two
areas of gallops. A patchy hawthorn hedge comes
into view; keep this to your left.

7 Where the hedge ends, turn left across the
gallops. Continue down a track with open fields
on either side, and at a T-junction turn left. At
the end of the track, go through an iron gate on
the right into a field. At the bottom of the field
go through another iron gate by a solitary large
beech tree, and turn right onto a track.

8 Continue on the track, which swings to the
right. It becomes a quiet country lane, leading
past houses and a huge converted barn, to
Ogbourne St Andrew.

9 Turn left at the T-junction beyond St Andrew's
Church. Where the road bends sharply right,
turn left on a byway first bordered by high
hedges but later by rolling farmland. The hamlet
of Southend, with its mixture of timber-framing,
brick, stone and thatch, appears on the right.

10 Where tracks meet, go straight on. The
byway becomes a leafy tunnel, emerging onto
a bend in the road into Ogbourne St George.
Turn right into the village.

SOUTHWEST ENGLAND

WILTSHIRE

5 Stourhead

Through a breathtaking landscape of woodland, valleys and sculptured gardens crammed with handsome monuments.

LENGTH 5 miles (2½ hours)

PARKING In NT Stourhead car park at edge of Stourton village

CONDITIONS Easy, along estate tracks and field paths

REFRESHMENTS Pub and café at Stourton

1 Walk through the NT reception centre. Entry tickets are not required for the walk, but tickets are needed if you wish to visit Stourhead House or its gardens, at the start or the end of the walk.

Follow the zigzag path as it leads down to the road and turn left, passing the Spread Eagle Inn and St Peter's Church. To the right stands the 15th-century spire-like Bristol Cross, a tribute to the monarchs who helped Bristol; it was moved from the city to Stourhead in 1765.

Visible on the far side of Stourhead Lake is the Pantheon, built in 1753 to house classical statues. It is one of the Greek and Roman-inspired monuments built around the lake in the 18th century by the architect Henry Flitcroft for the banker Henry Hoare II, the creator of the gardens at Stourhead. The lake, constructed from a series of medieval fishponds, is 1¼ miles round.

Keep to the path, continuing on past the Temple of Apollo, high up on the left, to reach a rough stone arch.

2 Just beyond the arch, turn right on a track, signposted to Alfred's Tower, passing on the left a smaller lake, with a cascade and a water wheel, and a pump-house built in the 1920s to pump water to a nearby reservoir. Cross a cattle grid and follow the track as it bends to the right, slightly uphill through pasture, passing a tree-crowned knoll – Top Wood – to the left and Beech Cottage and woodland to the right. At the brow of a hill, Alfred's Tower appears on the skyline. Continue to a stile and a gate.

3 Cross the stile and follow the track ahead, with woods on the right and pasture and more woods on the left. After 100m, where a stony track bears left, go straight on through a gate and up a grassy track, signposted to Alfred's Tower. Soon the ruins of Tucking Mill appear in a field on the left. Keep to the track, heading for a stile and a gate in the corner of the field.

4 Cross the stile into coniferous woodland, planted in the 1930s, which includes Douglas fir, larch, Sitka spruce, and western hemlock. Stay on the track, ignoring turnings to the left and right. Eventually the track starts to climb up to reach a grassy glade at the crest of the hill. Turn left to Alfred's Tower, a 49m (160ft) high, three-sided folly built in 1772 by Henry Hoare II. It is said to mark the spot where, in AD 879, Alfred the Great rallied men to repel the invading Danes, who were then defeated at nearby Edington.

5 Retrace your steps to the head of the forest track and continue ahead for about 100m, then turn right on another track, with a field on the left and a wood on the right. Continue into the wood, ignoring a right turning signposted to Park Hill. Descend through the woods to reach a stile and a gate, that opens onto the grassy vale of Six Wells Bottom. To the left is St Peter's Pump, which dates from 1474. It was removed from Bristol in 1766 and erected here in 1768. The hexagonal structure, which is

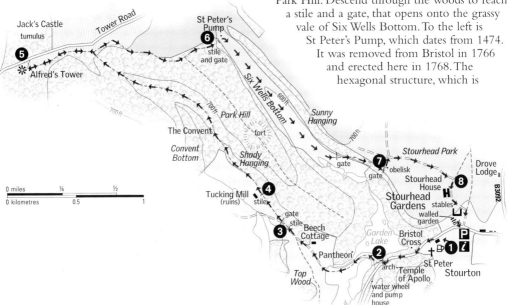

STOURHEAD GARDENS IN SPRING

decorated with weather-worn ecclesiastical figures, collects the springs at the headwaters of the River Stour to feed the estate's lakes.

6 Beyond the gate, turn right and follow the broad, grassy valley downhill for ¾ mile. Where the valley narrows, with woods closing in on both sides, are three medieval ponds. At the head of the first pond, by a large oak tree, bear left up the side of the valley to a gate. Go through the gate and follow the sign to Stourhead House (NT), with the ponds and several oak trees below to the right. Go through another gate to reach the obelisk, built in 1839-40 from Bath stone.

7 Turn immediately left, past the obelisk, to meet a crossing farm track. Turn right along the track, across pasture, towards Stourhead House, designed in 1721-5 by the architect Colen Campbell, for the banker Henry Hoare I.

8 Turn right and follow the path around the front of the house and past the stables. Just after the stables and before the entrance gate, fork right into a walled garden. The 19th-century red-brick terraces were built to supply flowers, fruit and vegetables for Stourhead House. Follow the left wall of the garden and turn left over a bridge to the reception building and car park.

Southeast England

Forests and hills are separated by a patchwork of fields in England's 'garden'. To the south and northwest of London, the paths of the North Downs and Chilterns give wonderful views over a well-ordered landscape.

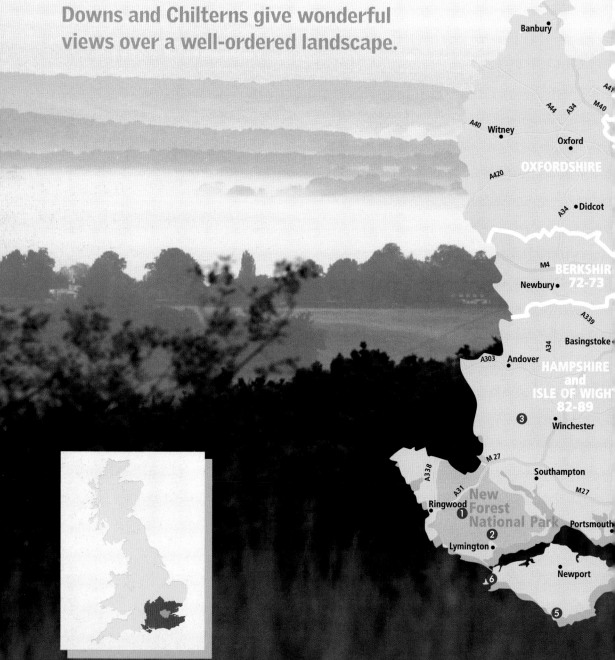

Banbury

A44 A34 M40

A40 Witney

Oxford

OXFORDSHIRE

A420

A34 Didcot

M4 **BERKSHIRE 72-73**

Newbury

A339

A34 Basingstoke

A303 Andover

HAMPSHIRE and ISLE OF WIGHT 82-89

③ Winchester

M 27

A338 A31

Southampton

M27

New Forest National Park

Ringwood ①

② Portsmouth

Lymington

⑥

Newport

⑤

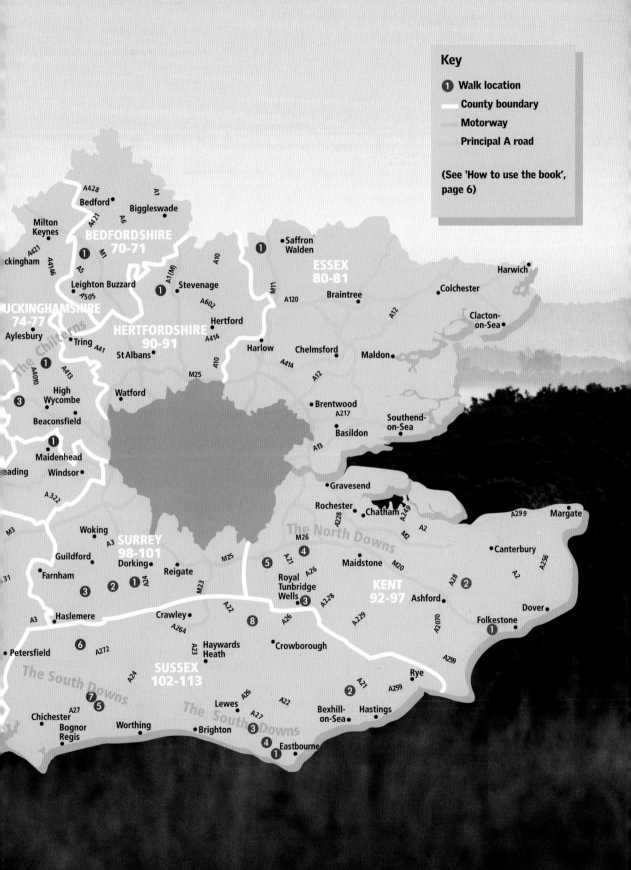

Key

● Walk location

County boundary

Motorway

Principal A road

(See 'How to use the book', page 6)

A428
Bedford
Biggleswade
A1
Milton Keynes
A421
A421
A6
ckingham
A4146
A5
M1
BEDFORDSHIRE 70-71 ●
A10
● Saffron Walden
Leighton Buzzard
A505
A1(M)
Stevenage ●
A602
M11
ESSEX 80-81
Braintree ●
Harwich ●
Colchester ●
A120
A12
Clacton-on-Sea ●
UCKINGHAMSHIRE 74-77 ●
Hertford ●
A414
Hertfordshire
Aylesbury ●
The Chilterns
Tring ●
A41
HERTFORDSHIRE 90-91
St Albans ●
A10
Harlow ●
Chelmsford ●
Maldon ●
A414
A12
A4010
A413
● High Wycombe
M25
Watford ●
A12
❸
Beaconsfield ●
Brentwood ●
A217
Southend-on-Sea
Basildon ●
● Maidenhead
A13
● Gravesend
eading
Maidenhead
Windsor ●
Rochester ●
A228
Chatham ●
A249
Margate ●
A299
A322
The North Downs
M2
A2
M3
Woking ●
M26
❹
Canterbury ●
A256
Guildford ●
A3
SURREY 98-101
Dorking ●
Reigate ●
M25
❺
A21
Maidstone ●
M20
A2
Farnham ●
A24
❷
❶
A26
KENT 92-97
A28
❷
31
❸
Royal Tunbridge Wells
A128
Ashford ●
Dover ●
A2070
Haslemere ●
Crawley ●
A22
❸
A229
Folkestone ●
A3
A264
❽
A26
A259
❶
❻
A272
Haywards Heath
A23
Crowborough ●
Rye ●
SUSSEX 102-113
A24
The South Downs
Lewes
A26
A22
❷ A21
A259
Hastings ●
❼
❺
A27
The South Downs
A27
Bexhill-on-Sea ●
Petersfield ●
Chichester ●
Worthing ●
❸
Bognor Regis
● Brighton
❹
❶ Eastbourne

BEDFORDSHIRE

Walkers in Bedfordshire often make for the greensand ridge starting near Leighton Buzzard, which forms part of the gentle route in this county. Ridge-top paths give glorious views over woodland, lakes and parkland.

1 Woburn

Wild woodland contrasting with the beautifully manicured grounds of one of Britain's great stately homes.

LENGTH 6 miles (3½ hours)

PARKING Beside Bedford Hotel in Park Street

CONDITIONS Easy, with only slight gradients

REFRESHMENTS Full range in Woburn

1 Walk along Park Street to the crossroads in the village centre and turn right into Bedford Street. At the junction with Caswell Lane, a gravel track, turn left and go through a gate, following the signs for Woburn Walks. The track meets Timber Lane, a minor road through a housing estate. Turn left to reach a T-junction, then turn right and follow the road to a footpath on the left, signposted to Greensand Ridge Walk and waymarked with a muntjac deer emblem.

2 Turn left on the path, which climbs across fields to a grassy ridge at the head of Wayn Close – a broad tree-lined avenue. Continue

down the avenue to a gate leading onto London Road (the A4012). Turn right. After a short distance turn left through Ivy Lodge gate, following the signs for the Greensand and Circular walks. The fenced path arrives at an iron gate.

3 Go through the gate. The path immediately divides into three. Turn right, following waymarks across a wide expanse of parkland where herds of deer are a common sight. Walk along the side of Basin Pond, and turn right in front of the ornately designed Basin Bridge.

The path passes to the right of more ornamental ponds and an ancient ice house before crossing a small footbridge over a stream. Continue to Paris House, built for the 1878 Paris Exhibition and later reconstructed in the park.

4 Go through the gate at the side of Paris House and turn left along the outside of the estate wall. The waymarked trail passes copses and fields before plunging into Milton Wood – strikingly wild in contrast to the neat lawns and parkland around Woburn Abbey. Rabbits scatter ahead, and an occasional muntjac deer bounds off with its strange, lolloping gait. The path emerges onto open ground beyond the wood

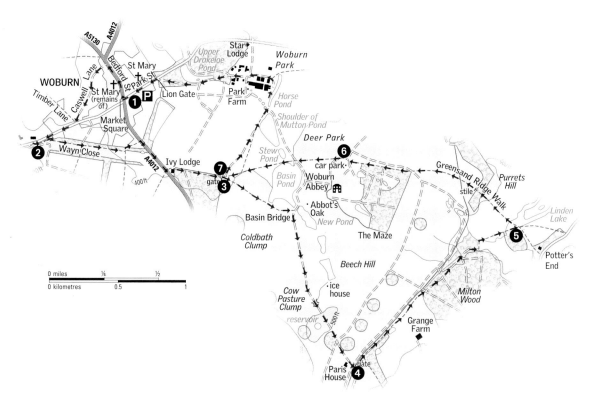

and leads towards the bamboo-lined fringes of Linden Lake, arriving at a junction of paths before it reaches the side of the lake.

5 Turn left on the Greensand Ridge Walk and climb across a broad meadow to a dark strip of fir trees. Go through a stile at the far boundary of the firs and climb a rounded summit, from which there are views over the park to more distant wooded hills. Continue from the hilltop to a tree-crowned ridge where the abbey and its surrounding grounds come into view. Follow the path downhill to a fence separating part of the abbey gardens from the parkland. Walk alongside the fence to reach the visitors' car park.

6 Continue past the car park, on the left, still following signs for the Greensand Ridge Walk. Cross the parkland in front of the stately home – an 18th-century palace built on the site of a medieval Cistercian abbey. The path leads between Basin and Stew ponds to the iron gate where you entered the grounds of the park.

7 Turn right in front of the gate and follow the track past two more ponds, on the right, to some estate workers' houses and offices. At the end of the buildings turn left and walk along the estate drive, passing Upper Drakeloe Pond on the right. Go through Lion Gate into Park Street and turn left to return to the car park.

WOBURN ABBEY PARKLAND

BERKSHIRE

The Thames grows into a mature river on its way through Berkshire, with charming towns and villages on its banks. One of the most delightful is Cookham, where this county's route begins and ends.

1 Cookham

Along and off the Thames, an ever-changing scene of pleasure craft, motor launches, barges, rowers and waterbirds.

LENGTH 5 miles (2½ hours)

PARKING NT car park at Cookham Moor, on western outskirts of Cookham village

CONDITIONS Easy going, mostly along towpaths

REFRESHMENTS Pubs in Cookham; café beyond railway bridge opposite Bourne End

1 From the car park take the path leading towards Cookham and signposted to Cock Marsh. Ignore a left turn to Cock Marsh a little farther on, and continue across Cookham Moor,

parallel to the main road, to join the high street (the B4447). Follow the high street to the left, passing a house called Fernlea, the birthplace in 1891 of the artist Stanley Spencer. On the left is the 15th-century half-timbered Bel and the Dragon pub, next to a cottage with a sign reading: 'All fighting to be over by 10pm'. This dates back to the sport of cockfighting, which was prohibited in 1849.

Just before the junction with the A4094 is the Stanley Spencer Gallery, which houses artefacts of the artist and many of his paintings and drawings. The gallery occupies a former Victorian Methodist chapel, which Spencer attended as a boy. Spencer spent most of his life in and around Cookham – for him 'the scene of heavenly visitations'. He portrayed many scenes of village life, such as *Swan Upping at Cookham* (1915-19, now part of the Tate collection); set against the

THE THAMES TOWPATH BY COOKHAM

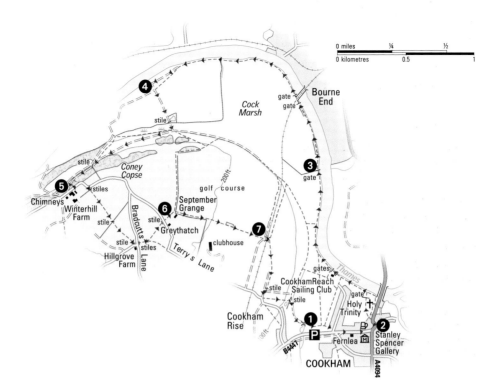

backdrop of Cookham Bridge, it shows boats involved in the annual July ritual of the marking of swans' beaks to record ownership of the birds.

2 At the T-junction turn left and left again, bearing immediately right to Holy Trinity Church, with its 12th-century nave and 15th-century tower. Follow the churchyard path (indicated by footpath signs), which passes Spencer's grave, to a metal gate and a path leading to the Thames. Turn left on the towpath, beside graceful willows arching over the riverbank. At Cookham Reach Sailing Club go through two metal gates. Beyond the club, where a yellow arrow points left towards a golf course, go straight on along the river to a kissing gate.

3 Pass through the kissing gate onto the flat ground of Cock Marsh, once an island and a source of willow used in basket-making. It is now a haven for birds such as redshanks, mallards and coots. The path becomes wooded as it approaches a railway bridge across the Thames. Go under the bridge, through a kissing gate, passing houses, onto an open, quiet stretch of towpath, curving with the river. Pass behind a cottage on the right, bearing left away from the river.

4 Turn left on a wide signposted track across a field to a stile in the corner. Ignoring paths to the right and left, cross the stile and go ahead to another sign, showing routes to the left and right. Turn right along the climbing track, which

becomes more wooded as it rises, with wide views to the right over the river. Continue over a stile to reach a road, opposite a house called Chimneys.

5 Turn left on the road. After 100m, turn right over a stile beside a gate leading to Winterhill Farm. Go ahead and then over a second stile onto a path fenced in on both sides. After 300m, cross a third stile and follow the path as it drops down to a fourth stile at a junction with a road opposite a white house. Bear half-left over the road and a stone stile and follow the grassy path. Cross a stile and turn left, heading across a field towards a stile at a junction with a road.

6 Cross the stile and road and take the signposted path to the left of September Grange and Greythatch houses on the right. Follow the path to a gap in a hedge at the field corner. Turn right, following the hedge. Where the hedge ends, keep ahead to cross a golf course, with the clubhouse and car park on the right. Go straight on, passing a shed and cypress trees, to a small bridge over the railway.

7 Beyond the railway, turn right along a clearly defined path, with the Thames below to the left. Cross a stile onto a gravelled area with a few houses. Keep left and turn sharp left onto a signposted path that runs between houses to a stile. Cross the stile and turn right, following the path across a field and over a small footbridge to a corner of the Cookham Moor car park.

BUCKINGHAMSHIRE

With an abundance of well-maintained footpaths, the Chiltern Hills offer some of the best walking in Buckinghamshire. Trails skirt tracts of airy beechwood, cross rich pasture and follow the county's green lanes.

1 Coombe Hill

Along the ancient Ridgeway, through Chequers estate to the highest viewpoint in the Chilterns.

LENGTH 5 miles (3 hours)

PARKING National Trust car park at Low Scrubs, off B4009 at Butler's Cross

CONDITIONS Steep in places

REFRESHMENTS Pub in Ellesborough

1 Facing the road, go through the gate in the right-hand corner of the car park. Take the left of three footpaths advancing towards the gorse and silver birches of the plateau, then turn left through a kissing gate marked 'Ridgeway Path'.

2 At the road turn right, then left through a kissing gate and stile into a beech wood. Keep ahead over several path crossings; at the remains of a stile on the right go through a gap in the fence, clearly marked with the Ridgeway Path sign. Eventually you emerge from the trees to views of wide, spacious fields and the wooded hills of the Vale of Aylesbury. The rutted path runs steeply down past a logging mill to a minor road.

3 Cross the road and go through a waymarked kissing gate into the Chequers estate. The 16th-century house has ornamented chimneys and mullioned windows, and in its time was a prison for Lady Jane Grey's sister and the home of descendants of Oliver Cromwell.

In 1917 Chequers was presented to the nation by Lord Lee of Fareham as a place where prime ministers might rest and recuperate. Follow the path between fields and across Victory Drive, lined with beeches planted by Sir Winston Churchill. Go through two kissing gates and ascend meadows beyond, then walk right along the edge of Maple Wood, with a good view of Chequers.

4 At the next meeting of paths go through a kissing gate and turn right, along the edge of Whorley Wood. Go through a gate to a crossing of paths and follow ahead around the side of Beacon Hill, partly on steps cut into the chalk as it enters Ellesborough Warren. A stile takes the path into the open, then over the shoulder of Beacon Hill. Ahead is the tower of the church of St Peter and St Paul at Ellesborough; to the left is a wooded mound concealing the remains of Cymbeline's Castle. Legend has it that this was where the forces of Cymbeline, the local British king, stood against the Romans in AD 43.

Cross another stile and walk diagonally to the right across a cultivated field in the direction of Ellesborough church.

5 At a road go through a kissing gate, turn right, then almost immediately right again on a footpath by Dame Isabella Dodds' Almshouse. Turn left through a gap in the hedge, following yellow waymarks along the chalky path.

6 At the road, turn right then left onto a signposted bridleway just past Coombe Hill Farm. At a gate behind the farm, turn left along the bridleway that skirts the foot of Coombe Hill, with a golf course on the left.

7 Just before a gate at the end of the golf course turn sharp right to climb to the summit and the monument. It commemorates the men of Buckinghamshire who died in the South African War of 1899-1902. An indicator points out the sights from Chequers to Brill Hill, the Vale of Aylesbury and the Cotswolds beyond Oxford. Most of the route that has just been walked can also be seen.

Continue across the plateau, following the path to the car park.

2 Brill

From a windmill perched high on a hill to a medieval fortified tower and an 18th-century duck decoy.

LENGTH 6 miles (3 hours)

PARKING Car park by windmill

CONDITIONS Muddy in places

REFRESHMENTS Pubs in Brill

3 Fork right across a field towards a gap in the hedge opposite, and continue through a gateway to climb a stile on the left into a coppice. Cross a stile into a field and continue ahead.

4 Cross stiles through trees at a corner of a field and take the track ahead. A clump of trees and shrubs on the right conceals the remains of a medieval moat. Cross a stile and turn right on the minor road to Boarstall village. Much of the village was destroyed during the Civil War, when Boarstall Tower (NT) was besieged by Parliamentary troops. Continue on the road to Manor Farm.

5 Turn left after the farmhouse onto a footpath to Boarstall Decoy Nature Reserve. The 18th-century duck decoy is a channel covered by netting, running off a small lake, into which ducks are driven by Dutch spaniels, bred especially for the purpose. Originally the birds were destined for the table; now they are ringed and returned to the wild. There are demonstrations at weekends during summer, as well as a nature trail and exhibition hall.

Return to the road and turn left. At a T-junction turn left again.

6 After about ¼ mile, cross over to a road sign on other side of the road and follow a trail up Muswell Hill, climbing the pastures. The trail follows the border between Oxfordshire and Buckinghamshire. Cross a road at the summit, go through a gate and take the asphalt path opposite. The ground falls away, giving magnificent views towards the Cotswolds.

1 With your back to the windmill, turn right on South Hills Road, following a yellow waymark. At a junction fork left, then turn right to cross a stile between a house and outbuildings. Cross three more stiles and walk diagonally across a field, aiming to the left of the red house ahead. Climb a stile and turn right on the road.

2 Take the second footpath on the right, opposite a marked bridleway, with fine views. Where the track turns right to a farm entrance, continue ahead on the track to cross a wooden walkway over a stream. Follow the main track, ignoring other paths, downhill to the B4011.

Turn right on the busy road, crossing it with care, and after a cottage on the left, cross a stile waymarked 'Circular Walk'. Follow the path around the edge of Boarstall Wood to a waymarked post in the fence.

7 Before the path becomes the driveway to a farm ahead, turn right to a gate ahead marked 'Keep dogs on leads' and walk diagonally over the brow of the hill back to the road. Turn left towards Brill and continue ahead to the car park. The land by the roadside beneath the windmill is pitted and bumped from ancient clay diggings. Pots were made in the village as long as 800 years ago, and its bricks were used to build nearby Waddesdon Manor and Thame Grammar School.

BUCKINGHAMSHIRE

3 Southend

A figure-of-eight walk embracing low,
thickly wooded hills, open fields, narrow
lanes and quiet Chiltern villages.

LENGTH 6 miles (3½ hours)

PARKING At north end of village green

CONDITIONS A few steady climbs

REFRESHMENTS Pubs in Fingest and Turville

1 With the north side of the village green on the
right, walk ahead on the concrete road towards
Southend Farm. Cross a stile on the left, just before
Southend Cottage, into a field. Turn half-left
towards Summerheath Wood ahead, then bear right
to a stile. Cross the stile and, ignoring a path to
the left, continue ahead, dropping steeply over an
open field. At the end of the field, cross a stile to
meet a road. Cross the road and then a stile, then
follow a fence uphill to a stile and gate by a road.

2 Turn right on the road and then left on a
track into Churchfield Wood. Just inside the wood,
turn right on a track running near the edge of
the wood. The track narrows as it descends,
bearing left to cross the wood, and eventually
reaches a stile at the edge of the wood. Cross
the stile into a large field, turn right and follow the
field edge. At the end of the field, go through an
opening onto a short track that leads to a
junction with a road.

3 Turn right on the road and continue into
Turville, where weathered brick cottages are
grouped along the roadside, opposite the squat
tower of flint-built St Mary's Church, dating
from the 14th century. In the porch is a list of
the vicars of St Mary's, dating back to 1228.

Pass to the left of the church and, opposite a
telephone box, turn left between the cottages to
reach a gate. Do not take the path ahead, which
climbs towards the windmill visible on the
hilltop, but turn right through a gate and follow
the path gradually uphill to a stile. Cross the stile

THE ROLLING CHILTERN HILLS

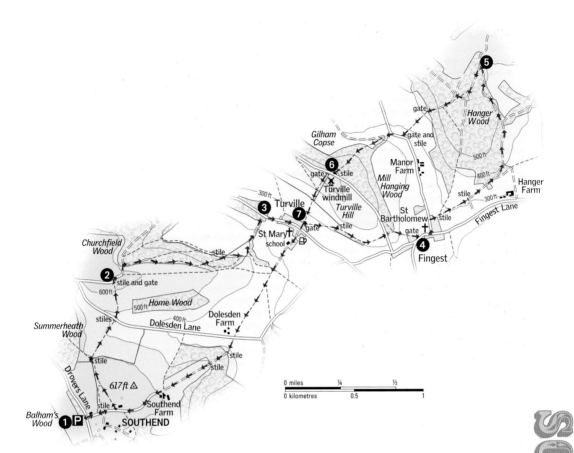

and go along a tree-lined path to reach a road. Cross the road and the gate ahead, and follow the path ahead. This soon bears right to emerge onto a road in Fingest by St Bartholomew's Church. The church dates from the 12th century and has a double-roofed tower that dwarfs the nave.

4 Turn left into Fingest, with its flint, brick and timber-framed houses, then turn left past the church along Chequers Lane. Just beyond Church Cottage, turn right on a path with a slightly hidden signpost. Follow the path between the houses to a stile at the edge of a field. Do not cross this stile, but take the narrow path to the right to reach another stile. Cross the stile and continue along the field edge over another stile to join a stony track. Turn left uphill and follow the track to Hanger Wood. Where the track divides, take the left fork, which continues to climb along the edge of the wood. Follow the track until just before it emerges from the wood.

5 Turn sharp left, going gradually uphill, and follow the woodland track to a crossing of tracks. Just beyond the crossing, at some rough wooden signs, turn right along a clear path and then left down a wide grassy track. Continue ahead, over a crossing of tracks, as the track descends more

steeply to reach a gate. Go through the gate and follow the fence downhill to another gate and a stile, to a road.

Turn right on the road. After 50m, turn left into an open area on the edge of a wood. Follow the track ahead, then soon turn left on a path winding up through trees. Continue uphill to a stile by a road opposite the privately owned Turville windmill, dating from the early 19th century and in use until 1912. It was featured in the 1968 film *Chitty Chitty Bang Bang*.

6 Cross the stile and turn right on the road. Just past the windmill, turn left through a gate into a field. Follow the left edge of the field on a path that drops steeply towards Turville.

7 On reaching the road at Turville, cross the road and take the lane ahead, which leads past a school on the right and then between houses. Beyond the houses, follow the tree-lined path to an open field. Go straight over the field to Dolesden Farm, then cross a gate onto a road. Cross the road onto the path ahead. After 60m, cross a stile and continue ahead uphill on a wide track that leads to Southend Farm. Take the concrete road to the right of the farm and follow it to the village green at Southend.

Stranger than fiction

Curious experiences await the inquisitive walker on the fringes of the Greater London sprawl.

The margins of London have an amazingly deadbeat reputation. For those who have never ventured out along its footpaths and bridleways, the wheel of countryside that lies with London at its hub seems cast under a pall of mediocrity. Often, it is thought not to be worth any walker's while to go exploring in the tame Home Counties, when the Cotswolds, the paths of the south coast, the dales and heights of the Peak District and the Welsh mountains lie just a few hours down the motorway.

But a train journey of an hour, or even less, from central London can lead to a cornucopia of weird and wonderful places, all waiting to be tasted by anyone who can follow an Ordnance Survey map. The country stations immediately outside the capital are gateways to forgotten antiquities, seldom-visited churches sheltering sublime works of art, ancient woods, special wildlife sites, hauntings and spooky tales.

Rare treasures

Circling round London, and beginning in the southeast with Kent, not half a mile from Eynsford station at Lullingstone, is one of the ugliest buildings in the county, an unsightly concrete shell. But on view inside is the county's loveliest piece of Roman art – a wonderful mosaic pavement, depicting, among sea monsters and winged horses, a graceful and naked Europa being carried off by Jupiter in the shape of a bull. This was once the dining room floor of a fine villa, the early Christian frescoes of which are on display at the British Museum.

A few miles east at All Saint's Church, Hollingbourne, another masterpiece resides under lock and key. This is the Culpeper Cloth, a remarkable 1.8m (6ft) long embroidered altar cloth, or perhaps funeral pall, created in the mid-17th century by the four Culpeper sisters. It has a border of angels and of Kentish fruit – quinces, mulberries, pears and peaches, pomegranates, cobnuts and grapes – all exquisitely worked.

Even in the seemingly bland Surrey commuter-belt strange things can thrive. One of the strangest is the massive, ancient yew tree that dominates St George's churchyard at Crowhurst, a couple of miles across the fields from Godstone station. The venerable tree, completely hollow, was fitted with a door and an internal bench in

THE FANTASY OF THE HELLFIRE CAVES HAS LONG OUTSTRIPPED REALITY

HELLFIRE CAVES, WEST WYCOMBE

1820. How old the yew may be is a matter of conjecture. It must be at least 1,500 years old, far older than the church it stands beside.

Moving west along the line of the North Downs, there is a poignant legend, dating back to 1193, to be pondered beside the Silent Pool, which lies equidistant from Gomshall and Chilworth stations. It tells how Prince John (later to be King) was spying on the beautiful Emma, a woodcutter's daughter, as she bathed naked in the spring-fed pool. Emma waded deep into the water, to escape the peeping prince, and was drowned. Her brother, leaping in to save her, perished too. It is said that Emma may still be seen on moonlit nights, slipping beneath the haunted waters.

Farther west, a most remarkable transformation has taken place at Greenham Common in Berkshire, just over a mile from Newbury station. Here, the former USAF airbase, famous for the women's peace camps set up outside its perimeter fence throughout the 1980s, has been returned to nature. Anyone who knew Greenham Common then would hardly recognise the place. Runways are blanketed in grass and wild flowers, fuel tanks are now dragonfly ponds and cattle graze where nuclear bombs once trundled. A few of the old army buildings remain – the control tower, the base of a weather recording station, fire hydrants and fuel tanks – their quiet decay a contrast to the vigour of the natural world.

Caves of hell

To the northwest of London, 3 miles from High Wycombe station in Buckinghamshire, a bizarre sight greets the walker on top of the hill above West Wycombe. The Church of St Lawrence that stands there has a huge golden ball – big enough to accommodate two people – moored to the top of its tower. Below the church is a hollow, hexagonal structure of flint, embellished with grotesque carvings and a line of funerary urns. The golden ball was used as a morse signalling post for members of the so-called 'Hellfire Club', an irreverent society of hedonists founded in the 1740s by local baronet Sir Francis Dashwood. The flint hexagon was the club's mausoleum; its urns were intended to house the hearts of its members after their deaths.

Some 90m (300ft) below the church and mausoleum are the Hellfire Caves, where Dashwood and his chums are said to have 'entertained' ladies of a certain demeanour. How much is true and how much hokum is anyone's guess. Dashwood certainly ordered the construction of the hand-dug caves – by local workers after a poor harvest – but the popular fantasy of the Hellfire Club and its antics has long outstripped reality. Today the caves, complete with cavernous banqueting room, inner temple and grotesque carvings, continue to play to the myth.

ESSEX

The gentle, undulating landscape of Essex makes for easy walking. Dotted with woods and sleepy villages, the single route in this section begins and ends at the charming 15th-century village of Clavering.

1 Clavering

Over fields and down lanes, from one peaceful ancient village to another, past a tiny house and woods with medieval names.

LENGTH **6 miles (3 hours)**

PARKING **In layby off B1038, on western outskirts of the village**

CONDITIONS **Some paths may be overgrown in spring and summer**

REFRESHMENTS **Pubs in Clavering and Arkesden**

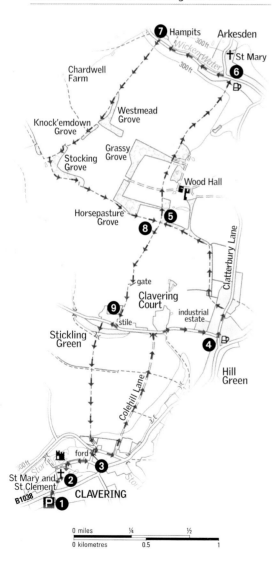

1 Cross the road and walk down the lane signposted to Clavering Church, towards a handsome group of buildings: the private Old House, the Guildhall and St Mary's and St Clement's Church.

2 Follow the path to the right around the church and turn right along railings, behind which lie the remains of a castle moat and millpond. Continue with a holly hedge to the left to a cluster of cottages dressed in pastel plaster and thatch. Turn left on a short street.

3 Cross the bridge by the ford. On the other side of the minor road is the smallest house in Essex, 3m (10ft) square and once a ford-keeper's lodge. Turn right on the road, with the stream to the right. Turn left at Colehills Close and immediately left into a lane, with branches arching overhead. On reaching open fields, follow the path to a road. Turn right and continue past Victorian Clavering Court and a small industrial estate.

4 At the sharp bend right in the road before the Cricketers inn, turn left on Arkesden Road (Clatterbury Lane); after 50m, opposite a thatched cottage, take the narrow unmarked footpath on the left and continue ahead through a gap in the hedge into a field. Turn right on the path and follow it through one field into the next, then bear left along the edge of a coppice.

5 At a crossing of paths, turn right to follow the line of trees passing the entrance to private 17th-century Wood Hall on the right. All around is a wide expanse of farmland dotted with woods. Go straight on along a narrow grassy path. Arkesden church is seen above the trees ahead.

6 At a junction with a minor road, with the 17th-century Axe and Compasses pub to the right, turn left on the road into Arkesden, a cluster of colour-washed and white-weatherboarded houses, many with individual bridges over the little Wicken Water. St Mary's Church, high on its knoll, contains some fine monuments, including one to the Elizabethan Richard Cutte and his wife with their children kneeling about them. From Arkesden, follow the road for about 1/3 mile into Hampits, a hamlet that includes a Victorian chapel and a former inn called Ancient Shepherd.

7 Just beyond Hampits take the marked footpath to the left. Follow it beside a line of trees to Knock'emdown Grove, passing a track

on the right to Chardwell Farm. Many of these woods have names dating back to the Middle Ages. At a yellow waymark sign, turn left along the edge of a wood, noting a fishpond ahead.

8 After about ½ mile, at the end of Horsepasture Grove, turn right at the junction encountered earlier down a path signposted to Stickling Green. Where the track bends sharp right, continue ahead on a grassy path. Where this path bends sharp

right on the edge of trees, turn left through a gap in the hedge, crossing over some planks over a ditch, and continue, with a hedge on the right, alongside a paddock to a gate with stile.

9 Cross the stile and continue along the edge of a field with hedge on the right. At the minor road turn right into Stickling Green, a pasture since the 14th century, now surrounded by large houses. Cross the green and take the marked footpath leading left between two hedges, then go over a footbridge. Follow the path below power lines until they diverge on the hill crest. Go through a gap in the hedge and down a field path towards Clavering. Cross stiles at each end of a paddock. Continue over the footbridge to cottages by the ford. Turn right between houses onto a holly-hedged path to the churchyard and back to the layby.

CHURCH OF ST MARY, ARKESDEN

HAMPSHIRE & ISLE OF WIGHT

Lying within reach of the capital, Northern and central Hampshire offer excellent walking on the chalk downs. Southern Hampshire's New Forest and the Isle of Wight are a step removed – little worlds of their own.

1 Burley

Easy going across the open heath of the New Forest, which attracts an abundance of wildlife.

LENGTH 4½ miles (2½ hours)

PARKING Car park opposite playing fields on south of road just outside village

CONDITIONS Easy walking, but ground may be wet and boggy in places

REFRESHMENTS Full range in Burley

1 With the road on your left, take the gravel path leading away from the wood, parallel to the road, across the heath with its covering of heather dotted with gorse. The area is rich in flora and fauna, including orchids, rare little Dartford warblers, sand lizards and the even rarer smooth snake. The path follows a gravel ridge, with fine views in every direction, then dips to a raised causeway through a boggy valley cloaked in bilberry bushes. As the path begins to drop, Sway Tower, built as a folly in 1879, is visible on the horizon. Beyond the bog, the path crosses an old railway cutting on what was, until 1964, a branch line from Brockenhurst to Ringwood.

2 Where the track divides at the top of a rise, fork right. Follow the path as it bends right towards old gravel workings on the left, then curves left to follow a fence round the gravel pit. The path then broadens out as it heads along a sandy ridge with splendid panoramic views.

3 Where the path divides, bear right with a conifer plantation stretching along the horizon ahead. Continue downhill to Whitten Pond, a favourite grazing ground and watering hole for cattle and ponies. Keep the pond on the right.

4 Beyond the pond, bear right to the Forestry Commission notice board. Fork right towards the woodland. At a second path division, fork left and continue to the junction with a road.

5 Turn right on the road, then cross an old railway bridge and turn half-left onto a path that goes under telephone wires towards a wood. Follow the path through heather, past a tree-shaded pond on the left. In summer look out for marsh fritillary butterflies with orange-red and yellowish wing markings.

6 Beyond the pond, bear right along tracks with clumps of gorse, birch and pine to the left. Continue on open heath. Pass through a line of pine and birch to more open heath, with wooded hillside and a white house to right.

7 Where the path divides just before telephone wires, turn right to climb to the top of Castle Hill, with views backwards to the distant towers of Bournemouth and, on a clear day, Purbeck Ridge. At the top of the hill follow left to the earthworks of the Iron Age fort of Castle Hill.

8 Go through the low ramparts of the fort and turn right onto a gravel driveway leading along the brow of a hill. Just beyond some houses, turn left and cross a stile into the woods then down to the road.

9 Turn right and take the footpath opposite, signposted to Burley, walking to the left of the road alongside fields grazed by ponies and donkeys, and eventually emerging at the village.

10 In Burley, turn right at the war memorial, then left by the garage onto a path through the wood, which leads back to the car park.

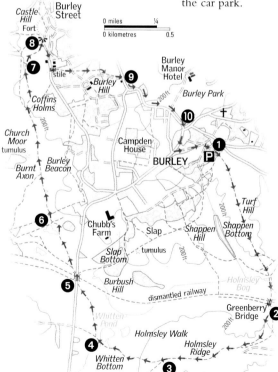

2 Rhinefield

Heathland, mature open woodland, a plantation of majestic, exotic conifers and an extravagant Victorian building.

LENGTH 4½ miles (3 hours)

PARKING Whitefield Moor car park, on road northeast of Brockenhurst

CONDITIONS Easy walking, but ground likely to be boggy in parts; waterproof footwear essential to cross ford

REFRESHMENTS Hotel at Rhinefield House

1 In the car park, walk past the toilet block and turn right along a grassy path, with heather to the left and trees and shrubs to the right.

2 Turn left onto a gravel path towards mixed woodland dominated by conifers, oak and beech. At the entrance to the wood, cross a footbridge and continue straight on, over two crossings, along the track to where the wood ends. The glade opposite, with a lookout tower at its centre, is a deer conservation area.

3 Follow the path left along the edge of the wood, crossing another footbridge, round a clearing: it is unwise to cut across this clearing as the ground is usually very boggy. Locate the fence and follow it to the right to a second clearing, then to a broad stream with a stile just in front of it.

4 Cross the stile and follow the path beside the stream. On reaching a broad gravel track, turn right and, if the water is up, wade through the ford. Keep to the path, which continues down an avenue of tall conifers.

5 At a meeting of five tracks, go straight on. Continue over two minor crossings to a junction where the track bends sharply right.

6 Turn left, then at another junction turn left near a red marker post onto a path that leads down to Rhinefield Ornamental Drive.

The drive is bordered by grand, exotic trees, with great clumps of rhododendrons in between. The trees, mainly rare conifers, were planted in 1859 to line the approach to a lodge, built in the reign of Charles II but later demolished. The most impressive are the Wellingtonia redwoods, one of which is 50m (165ft) tall, with a girth of 8m (26ft).

At Black Water car park, the path meets the ornamental drive. Turn left on the drive and continue ahead.

7 As the drive swings left at the entrance to Rhinefield House, turn right on a forest track to follow a fence round the perimeter of the estate, passing the estate lodge, a grand house with a charming cupola.

Beyond the lodge is Rhinefield House, a magnificent example of late Victorian extravagance, built mainly in Tudor style and now a hotel. Continue past formal terraced lawns, then go straight across a small clearing to a gate.

8 Go through the gate and follow the path through woodland. After a second gate, cross an area of heather and bilberry to a footbridge over a stream. Follow the path past a stand of tall conifers to open heathland with extensive views. Take the wide, sandy path across the heath and up a slope to the top of the ridge.

9 Where paths meet at the top of the ridge turn left, then immediately take the left fork to follow the path along the uphill side of a line of pines, to a footbridge over a stream. The path passes through a vast expanse of ling, flowering in July and August.

10 At a junction just beyond the footbridge, turn left. Cross a second footbridge, then where path divides fork left. At a second fork bear right to return to the car park.

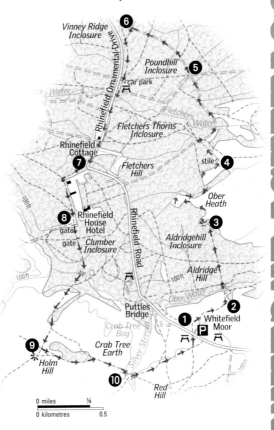

HAMPSHIRE & ISLE OF WIGHT

3 King's Somborne

A walk that links some of the most attractive villages in west Hampshire's beautiful Test valley.

LENGTH 8½ miles (4 hours)

PARKING By village hall and playing fields

CONDITIONS Easy

REFRESHMENTS Pubs in King's Somborne and Horsebridge

1 Turn right from the car park and walk along the A3057 towards Stockbridge, passing the Church of St Peter and St Paul on the right and the Crown inn opposite. Turn left up Cow Drove Hill. Just past the last house, climb steps on the left and turn right along the edge of the field to a junction with a broad road. Turn left. Where the road bends right, continue ahead on a marked track to the Clarendon Way. Go down the gravel track, crossing the Test Way, then go over Park Stream and on to the River Test.

2 Cross the bridge and follow the path to a junction with a road. Beyond a gate turn right into Houghton. At the village hall cross the road and turn left up Stevens Drove. After a telephone kiosk turn right and follow the narrow path between the playing field and a private track. Cross two drives to meet a path.

Turn left. Go through a gate; after a second gate turn right, follow the edge of the field to its corner, then turn left. Just after some power lines, the path meets a concrete track.

3 Continue ahead on the concrete track as far as Eveley Farm drive. Then keep straight on along a path at the field's edge. Go through a large gap in the hedge and turn left. Walk along the field edge, then cross a stile in the hedge and turn right on a track, which meets a wider track at an old bench. Turn left. After ½ mile, turn right on the Clarendon Way. Follow waymarks to a stile.

4 Cross the stile and go past Rookery Farm. After 250m turn left onto a track, leaving the Clarendon Way, to a road. Turn right, crossing a stream, and at Broughton's main street turn right. Opposite the post office turn left onto a footpath. After about 60m, turn left on a path that winds alongside paddocks linked by gates and stiles. Where the gravel track swings left between houses, keep straight on to cross a stile. Beyond the stables of a stud farm on the left, cross a broad track and continue alongside more fields.

Cross two stiles, then where two paths meet, turn right over the stile and walk diagonally left across the field to a double stile. Cross both stiles, keep straight on across the corner of the field to a stile in a tall hedge. Go over the stile and turn right on a track.

5 Where the track splits into three, fork left and walk to the top of Honeycomb Wood. At a road turn left and continue for about a mile. At the foot of the hill turn right and continue to a T-junction. Turn right past the gatehouses of Bossington House, and a stone church on the left. Opposite Bossington Farm turn left, cross the River Test and continue to a second river.

6 Cross the bridge and a stile, and follow the path diagonally across a field towards a line of trees, to cross another stile. Turn left, skirting Horsebridge railway station, now a restaurant. Walk past the bridge to the station entrance and turn right, heading for the John of Gaunt inn. Turn right at the inn, following the road as it curves left. Pass a house and turn left over a stile into a field. Keep to the right-hand side of the field, passing under power lines. The final mile of the walk, marked by yellow arrows and peppered with gates, leads through gardens and fields behind a row of houses, before meeting the A3057.

Cross the road and take the footpath ahead. At a kissing gate turn left onto the playing field and continue back to the car park by the village hall.

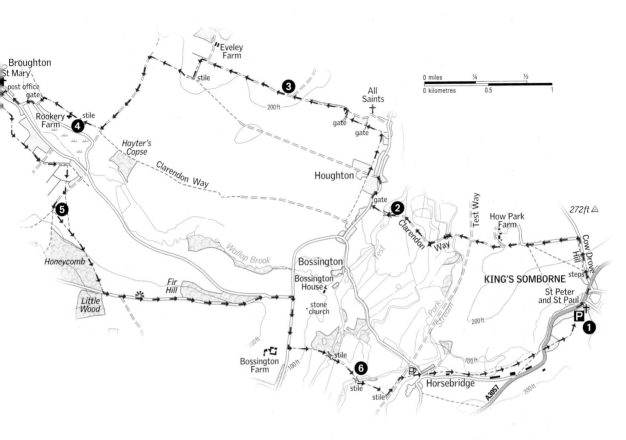

Broughton
St Mary
post office
gate
Rookery **4**
Farm stile

Eveley
Farm
stile **3**
200ft
All
Saints
gate
gate
Houghton

Hayter's
Copse
Clarendon Way

5

Honeycomb
Fir
Hill
Little
Wood

Wallop Brook

Bossington
Bossington
House
stone
church

gate
2
Clarendon
Way

Test Way
How Park
Farm

272ft △

Cow Drove
Hill
steps

KING'S SOMBORNE
St Peter
and St Paul

200ft
P **1**

Park
Stream

Bossington
Farm
100ft
stile
6
stile
stile
P
Horsebridge
100ft
200ft
A3057

0 miles ¼ ½
0 kilometres 0.5 1

VIEW OVER KING'S SOMBORNE

HAMPSHIRE & ISLE OF WIGHT

4 Selborne

An exploration of the woodlands and rolling countryside loved by 18th-century naturalist Gilbert White.

LENGTH 4 or 4½ miles (2½ or 3 hours)

PARKING Car park behind Selborne Arms

CONDITIONS One steep uphill climb; may be muddy in parts; descend Zigzag with caution

REFRESHMENTS Pub in Selborne

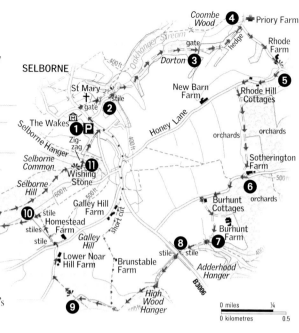

① From the car park turn left on the main village street, passing the Wakes, the former home of the naturalist Gilbert White and now a museum. White was born in Selborne in 1720, and spent most of his life in the village as a clergyman. On the village green is St Mary's Church – White's grave is on the north side of the church, and inside the church two stained-glass windows honour him.

At the church, turn right on a path signposted first as Hangers Way to Alton and then to Long Lythe. Cross the churchyard and go through the gate into Church Meadow (Glebe Field). Turn right across the field and cross a stile in the hedge to join a tarmac lane.

② Turn left on the lane, which becomes an ancient cobbled path that once linked the village with a priory. Pass water-treatment works and a house on the left, then continue through an ancient beech wood for about ½ mile to a gate at the edge of the wood.

③ Go through the gate and follow the top edge of fields. Priory Farm is visible ahead, while the wooded slopes of Long Lythe rise beyond the water meadows to the left.

④ At the entrance to Priory Farm turn right along the lane to a T-junction with Honey Lane. On left is the Oakhanger Stream valley and the giant radar domes at Oakhanger village.

⑤ Turn right on Honey Lane to climb past Rhode Hill. Beyond Rhode Hill Cottages, turn left into a leafy tunnel and follow the track. On the right, through trees, is the slope of Selborne Hanger. Continue to a farm at a T-junction.

⑥ Turn right on a sunken, tree-lined road and continue to a footpath signpost at Burhunt Cottages. Turn left and follow the track for about ½ mile. Directly ahead are the oasthouses of

Burhunt Farm. Where the track bends left, turn right on a narrow grassy path alongside farm buildings. Follow the path to a footpath signpost.

⑦ Turn right and cross a footbridge, which may be partly hidden by brambles, then climb to emerge on a broad slope of open grass, bracken, nettles and brambles. On the far side of the slope a stile leads to the B3006.

⑧ Cross the road, go over a stile and follow a path ahead through trees between fields and up a slope to High Wood Hanger. Turn right on a bridleway and go on to the edge of a wood. **SHORT CUT** *About ½ mile along the bridleway a signposted footpath to the right leads back to Selborne.*

⑨ At the edge of the wood, turn right on a stony track and continue downhill with views of Selborne Hill ahead. At a junction with a tarmac lane, turn right. Cross a minor road, go over a stile and follow the footpath sign to Hanger's Way. Continue through fields towards the woods of Selborne Hill, crossing two stiles.

⑩ At the entrance to the wood, cross a stile and turn left, climbing gently to meet a broad, grassy ride. Turn right, almost doubling back, and follow the path to the Wishing Stone, a legacy of Gilbert White, and a viewpoint bench.

⑪ Take steps to the Zigzag, a path of hairpin bends built by White in 1753 to give access to the woods of Selborne Hanger. Follow it down to join a path leading back to Selborne.

5 Niton

Past lighthouse towers and golden sandstone cliffs, with sweeping views over the Isle of Wight from high downs.

LENGTH 4 or 5½ miles (2 or 2½ hours)

PARKING On roadside in centre of village, near church; alternatively, in car park about 1½ miles west of Niton on A3055 and start walk at point 5

CONDITIONS Two climbs and a clifftop path; some paths are numbered

REFRESHMENTS Pub in Niton

1 From the road in front of St John the Baptist Church take Pan Lane to right of the lych gate. Ignore the first right turn to Ladyacre Farm, and keep forward past houses on the right to climb Bury Lane.

2 After about ½ mile, where the view opens out, turn left at the T-junction and ignore a stile on the right. Go through the next gate into a field. Keep ahead on a well-defined grass track to a gate and cattle grid, following a blue waymark, and continue over the ridge to cross a gate in the fence ahead.

[Map showing: Hoy Monument, St Catherine's Down, detour, Hoy Monument, gate, gate, stile, gate, 2, St Catherine's Hill, St Catherine's Oratory, mast, mast, stile, Niton Down, car park, 3, 4, 5, 500ft, 700ft, 600ft, 400ft, Bury Lane, Ladyacre Farm, Pan Lane, St John, 1, P, NITON, 7, A3055, gate, 6, mast, West Cliff, 300ft, Blackgang Road, Coastal path, Gore Cliff, Undercliff, 0 miles ¼, 0 kilometres 0.5]

DETOUR *Go through a wooden gate to the right, signposted Hoy Monument. Turn right along St Catherine's Down. The lofty ridge offers views towards the western and eastern extremities of the Isle of Wight, and the view southeast highlights the rolling, patchwork landscape characteristic of the island. Continue ahead to Hoy Monument. The 22m (72ft) stone pillar was erected by a merchant, Michael Hoy, to mark a visit to the island by Tsar Alexander I of Russia in 1814. Later, a plaque was added on the north face of the pillar's base to commemorate the British soldiers who died in the Crimean War.*

3 Turn left after the gate and continue uphill, following a path with a fence on the left, to St Catherine's Oratory (EH).

Nicknamed the Pepper Pot, the oratory was built in the early 14th century as a penance by a local landowner, Walter de Godeton, after his servants looted a ship that had been carrying wine from a Picardy monastery but was wrecked in Chale Bay. The oratory was demolished in the 16th century, but the 10.5m (35ft) tall tower was retained as a navigational aid for mariners.

4 Past St Catherine's Oratory, continue on the path downhill, towards the sea, and cross a stile into a field. Go ahead downhill, bearing slightly left, towards the curved ridge on the right. Keep ahead across the field to a footpath sign and steps down to the A3055.

5 Cross the road, walk through the car park and take the path signposted to the coastal path. Go up the steps and continue ahead to the cliff edge, then turn left.

Running down to the sea, below Gore Cliff, is the Undercliff, an area of deep, narrow clefts, or chines. Follow the coastal path, ignoring all paths to the left and right. St Catherine's Lighthouse rises from the foot of the Undercliff at St Catherine's Point. After about ¾ mile the path passes a radio mast to the left, then follows a field edge. Pass through a swing gate and descend through a copse to a junction with the A3055.

6 Cross the road to the pavement then turn right and immediately left on a driveway, signposted 'Coastal Path NT31 Ventnor 4'. Soon, at a fork, bear left on a lane signed 'Public Bridleway NT26 Niton Village', and continue to the next junction of paths.

7 Turn sharp left to return to Niton village past the primary school. Turn right on the main road, then left at the pub and right into Star Inn Road, signposted to Newport. At the T-junction turn left back to the church.

HAMPSHIRE & ISLE OF WIGHT

6 Alum Bay

Following in the footsteps of Lord Tennyson, above multicoloured cliffs and the Isle of Wight's dramatic Needles.

LENGTH 4½ or 6 miles (2½ or 3 hours)

PARKING Car park by the Needles Pleasure Park

CONDITIONS Some strenuous climbs; some paths are numbered

REFRESHMENTS Café in leisure park

❶ At the north end of the car park is a monument to Guglielmo Marconi, who carried out radio experiments here from 1897 to 1900. Take the small road, closed to motor vehicles, to the left of the car park paybooth. It soon bends right, signposted to the coastal path, with a good view of the multicoloured cliffs of Alum Bay, named after the alum that was mined there.

After about ½ mile, ignore a flight of steps up to the left of the coastal path and continue ahead to Needles Old Battery (NT), built in 1862 as part of the Solent defences to counter threats of a French invasion.

TENNYSON DEEMED THE AIR NEAR ALUM BAY TO BE 'WORTH SIXPENCE A PINT'

VIEW FROM HEADON WARREN TOWARDS THE NEEDLES

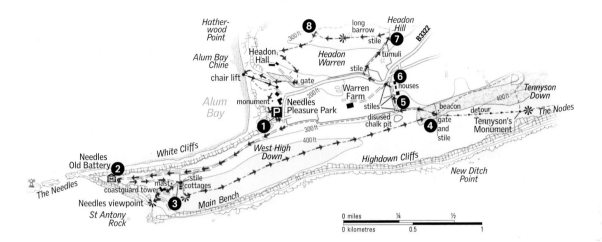

2 Immediately in front of Needles Battery, climb a flight of concrete steps on the left. At a concrete track, by a mast, turn right past a coastguard tower, signposted 'Rocket Testing Site, Needles View Point', then right again on a path to the Needles viewpoint.

The Needles, tooth-like pinnacles of a chalk down, are the remnants of a ridge that once reached the mainland and has gradually been eroded by the sea. A slender 36m (120ft) stack known as Lot's Wife fell in 1764 with a crash that was said to have been heard on the mainland. The Needles lighthouse at the end of the ridge was erected in 1859. Retrace your steps along the concrete track.

3 Where the track bends sharp left below some cottages, cross a stile ahead and fork right on the coastal path, past the corner of a fence and on to the top of West High Down. When the sea comes into view ahead, turn left along the ridge and follow the path for 1¼ miles to reach a gate and stile.

DETOUR *Go through the gate and past a fire beacon. Turn half-right and continue for ¼ mile to Tennyson's Monument, a huge granite cross that crowns the 130m (482ft) summit of Tennyson Down and is maintained as a navigational aid.*

The poet Lord Tennyson, who lived nearby at Farringford House (now a hotel), walked here regularly, declaring the air to be 'worth sixpence a pint'; the local views inspired his Idylls of the King. *Chalk grassland lichens and orchids grow on the two ridges of Tennyson Down and West High Down, from where there are panoramas of much of the island and views of Hurst Castle (EH), a fort on the nearest part of the mainland that dates from Tudor times.*

4 At the gate turn sharp left. Continue downhill on the well-defined grass track to a stile, with a disused chalk pit on the left.

5 Cross the stile and continue along the path to just before a T-junction. Cross the stile on the left for a short diversion along a field edge and cross the next stile to rejoin the path and reach the junction with the B3322.

6 Turn left on the road for 170m, then cross a stile on the right (signposted T16, to Headon Warren). Head past a tree ahead to a fence. Turn right along the field boundary, with the fence on the left, uphill to a stile. On the right is a fenced-off tumulus, an ancient burial mound.

7 Go over a stile by a National Trust sign into Headon Warren, the largest area of heathland on the Isle of Wight. Follow the path for a short distance, then turn sharp left just before the crest of the rise and a three-way path junction. Continue ahead to pass a fenced-off Bronze Age burial mound on the right. From here there are views of the chalk cliffs sweeping down to The Needles. Continue ahead on the path, ignoring a path running uphill on the right, to reach a bench, slightly obscured to right.

8 Beyond the bench follow the coast path descending to the left and at a fork bear right. The scant remains of Hatherwood Point Battery, used for searchlight experiments between 1889 and 1897, come into view. Turn sharp left onto a grass and gravel track. Ignore a track on the left and continue round a bend right, then at a fork ignore the path right and continue downhill to a zig-zag gate, passing Headon Hall away to the right. Cross a driveway near Alum Bay Tea Rooms and take the signposted woodland path half right to Alum Bay Chine. From the beach either ascend to the car park by the chair lift (March to September only) or go up the steps back to the path, then take the steps up to the right under the chair lift and to the leisure park.

HERTFORDSHIRE

The county's landscape is agreeably rural, encompassing fine estates and grand houses. The featured walk is long but undemanding, meandering through pretty lanes, fields and lovely landscaped gardens.

1 St Paul's Walden

Through woodland and along sleepy byways and green gallops to the fairytale towers of a grandly eccentric house.

LENGTH 7 miles (4½ hours)

PARKING Near gates of All Saints Church

CONDITIONS An unchallenging walk on quiet roads, green lanes and wide gallops

REFRESHMENTS Pub in St Paul's Walden and Langley

1 Go through the church gates and follow a signposted footpath to reach a lane beyond the churchyard. Turn left on the lane for a short distance, then turn right along a narrow path, passing a house and garden. Walk across the fields to emerge on the B651. Go over a stile on the opposite side of the road and then follow the waymarkers, passing to the left of a solitary tree in the middle of the field. The path converges

with the field boundary and follows it to a stile. Cross the stile into another field and continue past Little Easthall Farm to emerge onto a lane.

2 Turn left on the lane, then a little farther on cross a stile on the right leading to a footpath, which goes across fields to a minor road junction near Middle Easthall Farm. From here, follow the fenced road signposted to Langley, turning right into Langley Lane just beyond the driveway that leads to Shilley Green Farm.

Continue walking along Langley Lane – a quiet road despite the close proximity of the tower blocks of Stevenage, which are clearly visible on the horizon – to reach the B656.

3 Take the lane on the opposite side of the road into Langley. This bends to the right by a pub in the hamlet and peters out into a footpath going straight ahead. Continue on through a narrow belt of woodland and down into a valley. Follow the path as it bends sharply to the right, then turn left immediately onto a side path leading uphill to a gate, where the path divides.

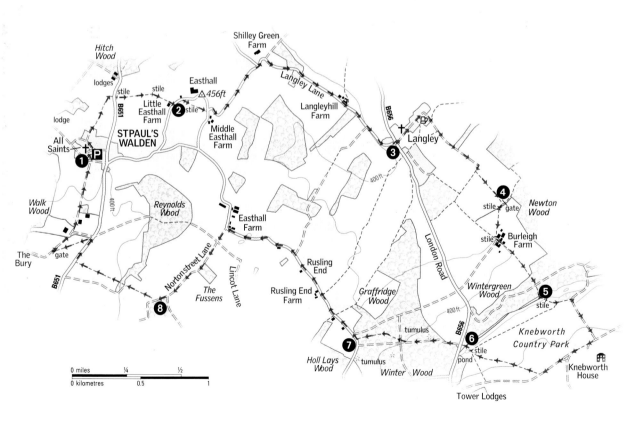

4 Turn right in front of the gate and follow the fence for about 35m to reach a stile on the left. Cross the stile and aim for the right-hand side of the outbuildings at Burleigh Farm. Cross another stile and follow a permissive path around the farmhouse into some fields. Walk down the slope into Wintergreen Wood. A ladder stile over a deer fence marks the far edge of the woodland.

5 Cross the ladder stile and turn left along a gravel path that skirts a small, tree-lined lake, to reach the end of an avenue of lime trees. Walk up the avenue, towards Knebworth House, the seat of the Lytton family since 1492. The building was transformed into today's turreted, Gothic structure by the 1st Baron Lytton, Sir Edward Bulwer-Lytton (1803-73), a popular Victorian novelist, playwright and politician.

At the top of the avenue of trees turn right, passing through the car park at Knebworth Barns, and continue along a track that leads to a group of horse chestnut trees. Fork right along a footpath by the trees, then walk across the grass and down the side of a gentle valley. Pass to the left of an area of bushes and rough vegetation towards a small, shallow pond, where there is a ladder stile over a fence.

6 Cross over the stile and walk past a gate to reach the side of the B656. Take the path on the far side of the road and go along it into Winter Wood. The path widens out into a broad, green gallop, passing between some fir trees. At a junction of tracks, turn half right, following waymarks to reach a minor road.

7 Turn right on the road and continue along it for nearly a mile, past Rusling End Farm, to reach a sharp right-hand bend. Fork left at the bend onto Nortonstreet Lane, an unsurfaced byway. Follow it to the point where a wide, tree-lined gallop joins it from the right.

8 Turn right and walk along the gallop. The Georgian house now visible ahead is The Bury. It was one of the childhood homes of the late Queen Mother and is particularly noted for its magnificent 24ha (60 acre) garden.

The B651 cuts across the gallop. Turn right on the road, then after a short distance turn left onto a signposted path that eventually rejoins the avenue of trees.

Go through a kissing gate and turn right onto the driveway that leads from The Bury. Follow the driveway as it goes downhill to a right-hand bend, then branch off to the left on a track that follows the line of a beech hedge. Keep on the track, passing to the left of a house with unusual windows, to return to the gates of All Saints Church, which can be seen ahead.

THE BURY

KENT

The picturesque woods and fields of the Weald in rural Kent offer gentle routes that can be enjoyed all year round. By contrast, the North Downs are the perfect place for bracing, hill-top walking.

1 Hythe

From the Cinque Port of Hythe through woods, past a castle and scattered farms to the Royal Military Canal.

LENGTH 6½ miles (4 hours)

PARKING Car park on Military Road, near Red Lion Square in town centre

CONDITIONS Two steady uphill sections

REFRESHMENTS Full range in Hythe

1 From the High Street, face the town hall and clock, and take the covered alley called Market Hill. At the T-junction turn left then right to part-Norman St Leonard's Church. Cross the churchyard, with a wide sea view behind, and turn right on North Road. Continue across two junctions and follow the road ahead uphill. After a sharp bend left at Blackhouse Hill, continue to a marked track on the left.

2 Follow the track into a field, then along a wide track that leads past Saltwood Castle. The castle, mentioned in the Domesday Book and enlarged in the 12th and 13th centuries, is not open to visitors. Continue to the end of the drive.

3 Turn right on the road then left into a farmyard and through a gate ahead. Cross the small field to the Church of St Peter and St Paul. Follow the path through the churchyard, then turn right on the lane and follow it round a sharp bend right. Just past a house called The Field, bear left onto a bridleway.

4 Follow the path to a waymarked division at the start of a wood. Turn left, following yellow Saxon Shore Way waymarks. The path drops to a footbridge across a shallow stream to a road.

5 Take the waymarked path almost opposite and continue along the edge of a field. Go through a gate at edge of a wood and follow the path to a bridge across a shallow stream, then to a junction with a broad grassy path. Continue ahead on the Saxon Shore Way, and sharp left uphill through a gate into a field. Cross the field to a gate to the left of a group of buildings, one of which has a cross on its roof, to meet a road.

6 Cross the road to a track by the bus stop, passing a pond on the left, then follow the Saxon Shore Way across fields for ¾ mile to a road.

7 Turn right, then left at a side road signed to West Hythe. Just before the bridge over the Royal Military Canal, turn left onto a bridleway.

8 Follow the leafy canalside footpath ahead to Hythe. The canal was built in the early 19th century as a defensive measure against a threatened Napoleonic invasion; today rowing boats can be hired at several points.

9 On reaching residential Green Lane in Hythe, continue to the junction with the main road, then ahead back to the car park.

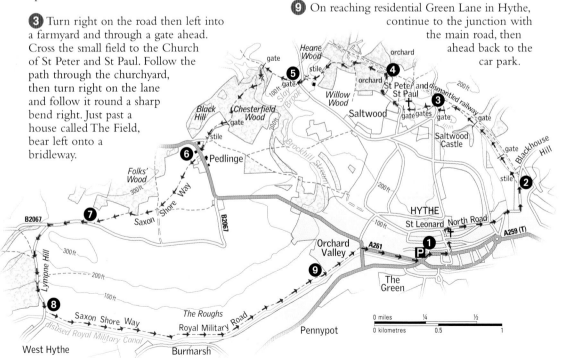

2 Wye Downs

Sweeping views from the heights of the Wye Downs, and woodland paths through a gentle valley.

LENGTH 5 miles (3 hours)

PARKING Car parks on either side of road about midway between Hastingleigh and Wye

CONDITIONS Good, clear paths throughout; two fairly steep sections in second half of walk

REFRESHMENTS Restaurant near car park

① From the road, face the Devil's Kneading Trough restaurant and turn left, then turn right onto a tarmac track. Descend through open countryside to a signposted grassy track on the right at the entrance to Coombe Manor.

② Turn right and continue to go through a gate on the left, then continue ahead. The path winds along the edge of woodland and through open country for about 3/4 mile, to a junction with a wide, stony farm track.

③ Continue on the path opposite into a field then follow the right-hand side of the field to a gate. Cross another field and another gate then after about 10m, at the start of a clearing, turn left on a path into woodland. The turn is easy to miss but the path soon becomes clear.
  Follow the path through the woods into a field. Continue ahead, with woodland on the right and hedge on the left, to the end of the hedge, then turn left downhill on a grassy track to meet another track. Turn right and follow the tree-lined field edges to a gate. A side path on the right leads steeply up to Crundale church.

④ Continue ahead a few metres to a waymarked junction and turn left, passing a cottage on the right, to a concrete farm track. Follow the track gently uphill, crossing a junction with another concrete track. The track narrows to a waymarked path between overgrown hedges, then enters Warren Wood where it widens into a track again. Continue ahead, ignoring side paths to the left and right, as the track winds through the wood, emerging to open views of rolling fields at a narrow road.

⑤ Turn left and follow the road to a sharp bend right. Take the narrow footpath on the left, entering Warren Wood once more.
  The path climbs uphill quite steeply then levels out and winds through the wood. Just after a sharp bend left, the path enters a clearing and meets a waymarked junction of paths and tracks.

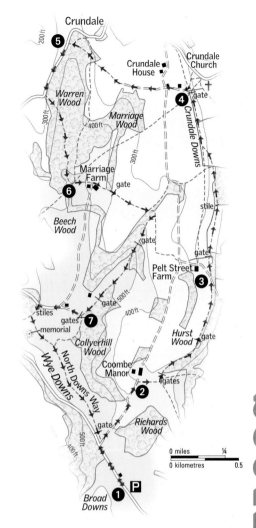

⑥ Continue on the track ahead past Marriage Farm buildings on the right, then follow it down through a gate and into open country. At a strip of woodland, follow the path ahead through the trees as it bears right, then go right at a fork.
  The path leads uphill again through woodland, then levels out and crosses a field. Continue ahead as the path narrows, to a gate across the path and another one on the right.

⑦ Turn right through the gate and follow the track to a tarmac lane, then continue ahead for 100m to a footpath on the left marked North Downs Way. Follow the grassy path to a ridge, where the view opens up. Follow the North Downs Way to the left. Downhill, not visible from the path, is the Crown memorial; the large outline can be seen only by walking onto the grassland. The path ahead keeps to the ridge with vast views to the right of a patchwork quilt of fields and woodland. After 1/2 mile, the path goes through a gate and drops down to meet the road. Turn left to the car parks.

KENT

3 Lamberhurst

Through glorious estate grounds to a romantic garden beside castle ruins and on across woods, fields and streams.

LENGTH 6 or 6½ miles (3½ or 4 hours)

PARKING Car park by St Mary's Church, off B2162 north of Lamberhurst

CONDITIONS Gentle slopes through parkland and woodland; route through fields at end of walk not always obvious

REFRESHMENTS Pub at Kilndown

1 Go into the churchyard of St Mary's, a medieval church with a fine nave and carved pulpit made in 1630, memorials to the Hussey family of Scotney Castle, and a blue stained-glass window by John Piper.

Pass the church tower and turn left past the porch, on a path that veers right out of the churchyard. Go through a gap in the fence, to the left of the manicured lawn of a golf course. Walk along the right-hand side of the field and cross a footbridge over the River Teise. Walk along the left-hand side of the next field, then turn left on the track to cross the small bridge over the A21.

Continue up the track to the gates of Pierce Barn, then follow a yellow marker right into a field and walk along its left-hand side.

2 Cross a stile into Scotney Castle Estate and proceed to a stile on the left. Climb the stile and turn right, crossing parkland. Keep to the right of a brick building to cross a stile. Ignore a track to the right and keep to the path ahead, signposted to Kilndown, climbing through woodland. Just before the path reaches the main driveway to Scotney Castle (NT), there is a small tree-encircled lake behind trees to the right.

To the left, down the drive, is old Scotney Castle, a medieval ruin with a moat, set in a romantic landscaped garden. The newer, 19th-century castle is a private home.

3 Cross the drive and take the footpath ahead, signposted to Kilndown, which leads down a grassy path across parkland with old trees to footbridges and stone parapets, crossing Sweet Bourne and the River Bewl. Continue straight ahead, climbing up towards Kilndown Wood.

4 Enter the wood and continue ahead. At a junction with a track, turn left and keep straight ahead at the left bend, following a yellow waymark onto a gently climbing stony track through woodland. After a house on the left, fork left onto a path signposted to Kilndown. The

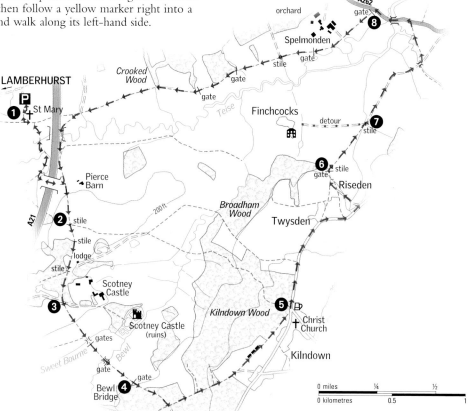

path leads through a large clearing edged by vast trees whose branches arch gracefully overhead, then back through woodland. It eventually ends at a junction in the village of Kilndown, which has a few houses, a pub and 19th-century Christ Church, whose interior reflects the Gothic Revival style of the Victorian age.

5 From Kilndown continue down the quiet country road. After pantile-hung Hillside Cottage on the left, the road bends right then left. After the left bend turn left along a track. Continue ahead, with paths joining from the left, to a gate.

6 Go through the gate and immediately go half right over a stile and continue diagonally over parkland. From the path there is a fine view of Finchcocks, a large red-brick Georgian mansion. At the far corner of the field, cross a stile onto the driveway to the house.
DETOUR *Turn left along the driveway to visit Finchcocks (limited opening), which houses a unique collection of historic keyboard instruments, including chamber organs, harpsichords, virginals, spinets and pianos.*

7 Turn right, away from the house, and follow the drive for about ½ mile. Just after a small bridge with a brick parapet, fork left and continue to meet the A262. Turn left and follow the road along its grass verge, passing a watermill on the left and crossing the river.

8 Some 200m after crossing the River Teise, turn left through double gates and onto a concrete track across a hop garden. As the track bends right to Spelmonden farm (with brick buildings to the left) go into a field and straight ahead to leave by the left-hand gate. Proceed in the same direction, continuing along the edges of a succession of fields through gates and over stiles, keeping parallel with, but one field above, the river.

Past Crooked Wood go ahead through a hop garden, then forward on a field path, heading for the tower of St Mary's Church in Lamberhurst. At the fence by the A21, turn left and follow the path to the small bridge over the road. Cross the bridge and walk down to the field, then turn right and return to St Mary's Church and the car park.

SCOTNEY CASTLE

KENT

4 Knole Park

A circular walk through Knole Park, ending with splendid views of the Medway Valley from One Tree Hill.

LENGTH 4 miles (2½ hours)

PARKING One Tree Hill car park, west of Bitchet Green

CONDITIONS Easy walking, almost all on the flat

REFRESHMENTS Teashop at Knole

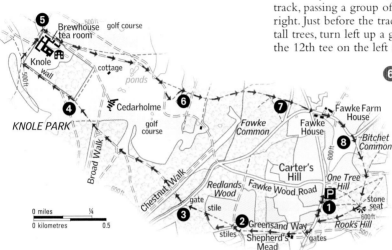

1 With your back to the car park, turn left downhill and take the gravelled path on the right to a house called Shepherd's Mead. Just before the gates to the house, turn sharp right on the narrow waymarked Greensand Way, which emerges from woodland to give pleasant views over a patchwork of fields and hedgerows.

2 Where the path meets a broad track, turn right and immediately left over a stile. Go round the left-hand edge of a field towards a stile into woodland. Cross the stile and continue on a well-trodden path to a road.

3 Cross the road and go through the left of two gates opposite into the deer park surrounding Knole (NT). Thomas Bourchier, the Archbishop of Canterbury, built Knole in 1454 as a residence for himself and future archbishops. It passed from the Church to Henry VIII in 1538 and then from the Crown into private ownership when Elizabeth I gave it to the Sackville family in 1566. It houses fine collections of furniture, tapestries and portraits.

Follow the broad path straight ahead, across metalled Chestnut Walk, which is lined with ancient trees. Cross Broad Walk and continue towards Knole.

4 Follow a sandy track round to the left of a house, skirting its massive stone garden walls and two stretches of wrought-iron railings through which the house can be glimpsed. At the end of the wall turn right along a grassy track which leads into a sweeping gravelled drive past the great Knole gatehouse.

5 Beyond the house, turn right on an estate drive below a battlemented stone wall. Just before the drive becomes an avenue lined with tall beech trees, turn half left on a grassy track to the golf course. By the 14th tee, fork right on a metalled track, passing a group of raised ponds on the right. Just before the track swings right towards tall trees, turn left up a gentle grassy slope, with the 12th tee on the left and a green on the right.

6 At the edge of the golf course, go straight ahead, crossing a wide grass track, and continue downhill with a pine wood on the left. At the bottom of the hill, follow the more prominent grassy path through woodland to a metal gate out of Knole Park. From the gate, follow the path uphill through woodland, crossing a stony path. The path narrows, ending at a road.

7 Cross the road and continue ahead on a path, then ahead over crossroads along the road signposted to Stone Street and Ightham, passing Fawke House on the right and Fawke Farm House on the left. The road descends steeply before bending left at the bottom of hill.

8 At the bend, go into the clearing on the right of the road and take the path ahead, which climbs steeply through woodland and is joined at the top of the hill by another path from the left.

At the next junction of paths, just beyond a sign for One Tree Hill, turn right for a few metres alongside a single-rail fence and, at a sharp right bend, duck under the fence and continue for about 100m to a wide grassy clearing. Climb the earth bank on the far side of the clearing to a granite seat commanding splendid views over the fields, copses and farmhouses of the Medway Valley.

With your back to the views, take the signposted Greensand Way path on the left. At a path junction bear right and continue to the road and car park to the right.

5 Chartwell

Rolling parkland, dappled woods and quiet paths in an area rich in historic houses, including Winston Churchill's home.

LENGTH 4½ miles (3 hours)

PARKING Darent car park, off A25 east of Westerham

CONDITIONS Easy; potentially muddy patches

REFRESHMENTS Range in Westerham

1 Follow the signs for the town centre, through the churchyard and to Westerham Green. Cross the road at a point about halfway between Wolfe's statue on the right and Churchill's on the left. Go up the steps opposite and up narrow Water Lane, then through a kissing gate into a field.

2 Turn right onto the marked Greensand Way link path and cross over the River Darent, a shallow stream at this point. Turn left on a cul-de-sac road, which leads to a gate.

3 Take the narrow waymarked Greensand Way just to the right of the gate, climbing quite steeply to the left of woodland, and continue

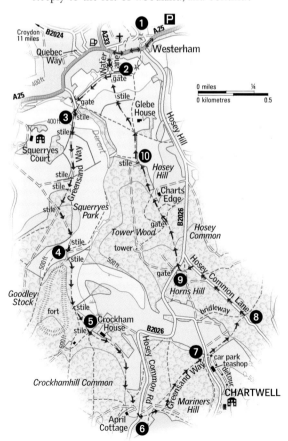

over a stile. The path levels and widens as it cuts through farmland. Go over two stiles and continue through a small copse to cross yet another stile onto a gravelled track. Turn left on the track and descend gently into a wooded valley.

4 At the bottom of the hill ignore the track and stile on the left and continue straight ahead. Cross a waymarked stile into a field and, with woodland on the right, follow the level path as it broadens. At the next stile ignore a path to the right beside a wood and take the path forking left across a field, from where Crockham House, a private home, comes into view.

5 Cross a stile beside the house and, following a boundary fence to the left, continue for about ½ mile to meet the B2026.

6 Cross the road and follow the marked path, which climbs steeply but briefly around the edge of Mariners Hill. Just past where a path merges from the right, turn left and follow Greensand Way signs through woodland to a road.
DETOUR *Go ahead on the driveway to visit Chartwell (NT). Sir Winston Churchill lived in the house from 1924 until his death in 1965. The house and garden are open to the public between March and November.*

7 Cross the road and take the narrow path, waymarked Weardale Walk, just left of the entrance to Chartwell car park. The path climbs steeply, on the fringe of light woodland, with occasional views of Chartwell's parkland. Continue to a lane.

8 Turn left and continue for ⅓ mile, passing a broad track on the left and a footpath on the right. Take the next marked footpath on the left, which crosses a short stretch of woodland to meet the B2026.

9 Cross the road towards a gate straight ahead. Turn right just before a gate onto a path through Tower Wood, which still bears the scars of the great gale of 1987. At a crossing of paths, go straight ahead, following the sign 'FP 352' posted on a tree beside a gate. After a few metres, go through a waymarked gap in the fence and turn right on a path that leads past the lovely gardens of Charts Edge. Turn right where paths meet and continue to the edge of the wood.

10 Cross a stile into a field and immediately turn right off the path running along the edge of the wood. Continue up the field alongside a fence for 50m. As Westerham comes into view at the top of the ridge, bear half left on an indistinct path. Head just left of Westerham's steepled church and cross a stile onto a steep path, which leads down to Westerham Green.

SURREY

The county of Surrey has two special treasures: its commons, many in National Trust ownership, and its woodland. More than a tenth of Surrey is wooded, and its walking trails cross many lovely heaths and glades.

1 Friday Street

From a remote hamlet by an ancient estate, through woods and past Wealden villages with beautiful churches.

LENGTH 6 miles (3 hours)

PARKING In car park at top of hill above village

CONDITIONS Easy; some muddy bridleways

REFRESHMENTS Pubs in Friday Street, Abinger Common and Wotton

❶ From the car park walk left along a footpath skirting a quiet lane. After ⅓ mile, cross the lane to a bridleway into woods. At the junction with Hollow Lane turn right then turn left to pass Old Rectory and keep on steeply uphill to the hamlet of Abinger Common. Turn right to the beautiful Norman church of St James.

❷ Cross the churchyard and bear right then left to skirt the garden of private Abinger Manor. In the garden is a tree-covered motte, a Norman fortified mound. Continue across fields, with views towards the North Downs, to Raikes Farm.

❸ Go between farm buildings and across the lane to a track leading half right over a field, then go forward along a narrow bridleway. Keep right to reach Paddington Farm, then go between farm buildings to the busy A25.

❹ Cross the A25 and take the track ahead to Broomy Downs, passing a giant oak tree on the left with seven separate trunks, and the top of the rise. Relics more than 8,000 years old have been found in this area.

❺ At the top of the rise bear right, following blue arrows, soon with views of the North Downs hills. Continue ahead to a large granite cross commemorating Samuel Wilberforce (a son of the slavery abolitionist William Wilberforce), Bishop of Winchester, who fell from his horse and died here in 1873. At the road ahead turn left then right onto the second bridleway to skirt woods on the right. Go between the buildings of Park Farm. Then cross a lane and take the path to the right to the partly Saxon St John's Church, which contains the tomb of the 17th-century diarist John Evelyn. Follow the lane to the A25.

❻ Cross the A25. Walk through the pub car park and bear half right to the corner of the field, then continue ahead, with Wotton House on the right. The house has been in the hands of the Evelyn family since the 16th century. Follow the path across a footbridge and on into Damphurst Wood. Take a track between barbed wire fences and then down to join a broad track. Turn left following a stream, dammed into ponds separated by weirs, to a pond at Friday Street. The water was once used to power the bellows and forge hammers of a 17th-century ironworks. At the pond, turn right onto a lane and walk uphill to the car park.

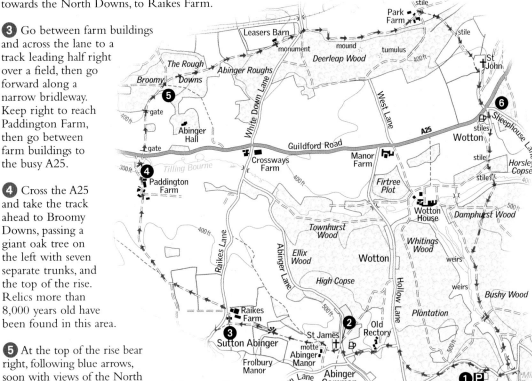

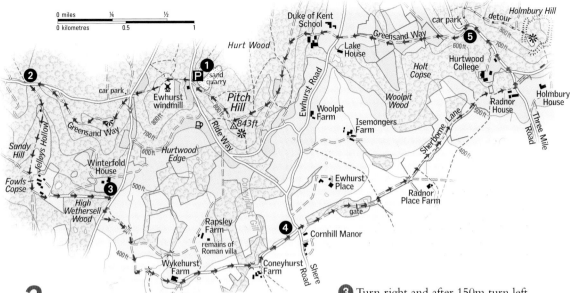

2 Pitch Hill

Along thickly wooded ridges with superb views and across farmland to an Iron Age hillfort.

LENGTH 6 or 7 miles (3 or 3½ hours)

PARKING Car park near top of Pitch Hill (north of Ewhurst), on right

CONDITIONS Two steep climbs

REFRESHMENTS Restaurant near car park

1 From the car park cross the road and walk a few metres up the drive of Mill Cottage to a post with a GW waymark. The letters denote the Greensand Way, which runs for 105 miles along the greensand hills (coloured dark green by the mineral glauconite) of Surrey and Kent from Haslemere to Hamstreet. Follow the steep path to cross a tarmac drive at the top. Bear left past houses, one of which is Ewhurst windmill, a large tower mill. By the windmill bear left at a division of tracks and follow the track downhill to a tarmac lane.

Cross the lane and take the path to the left, marked GW, following the contours of the land. Follow the path as it drops away, ignoring side paths to the right, to where it ends at a tarmac road.

2 Turn sharp left on a roughly surfaced drive running steeply downhill beside a ravine on the right called Jelleys Hollow. At the gates of a house with this name turn left along a narrow bridleway to a farm and cottages at the bottom of the hill. Follow the path as it becomes a tarmac lane, eventually passing Winterfold House with gardens on the left. On the right is High Wethersell Wood. Follow the lane to a road.

3 Turn right and after 150m turn left along a bridleway between high banks with overarching trees. After the track crosses a stream, ignore a footpath on the left and follow on to a division of paths with a small pond on the left. Continue forward uphill, eventually passing Wykehurst Farm, where the track becomes a tarmac lane. At Rapsley Farm to the left, a Roman courtyard villa of the 2nd century AD was excavated in the 1960s. Follow the lane over Coneyhurst Gill to a junction with Shere Road.

4 Take the tarmac bridleway opposite to a farm gate. Go forward on the waymarked path, ignoring a stile and side path on the left. Continue alongside a boundary hedge, later with fields on both sides. The path starts to climb the ridge and ends at Three Mile Road. Turn left and continue for ¼ mile to a car park on the right.
DETOUR *Turn right on the car park access track then right again, up to the Iron Age hillfort on Holmbury Hill. The massive defensive embankment and ditch are easily traceable. From the 261m (857ft) summit there is a huge panorama south across the Weald to the South Downs.*

5 Turn sharp left on the Greensand Way to a junction of paths. Turn right and at a farm gate follow the path left between fields. Continue downhill to a junction with Ewhurst Road.

Cross the road and go up the drive of the Duke of Kent School. Keep on the path that swings to the left behind the school buildings and climbs steeply uphill. Continue along the upper edge of the escarpment and follow the GW waymarks up to Pitch Hill. Here views stretch over the Weald and to the South Downs, and along the greensand escarpment.

From the summit of Pitch Hill follow the path downhill, passing a sand quarry, back to the car park.

SURREY

3 Hambledon

Beautiful Surrey villages, a magical
arboretum and a detour to the summit
of Hydon's Ball.

LENGTH 7½ or 8 miles (3½ or 4 hours)

PARKING Opposite St Peter's churchyard

CONDITIONS Mostly sandy paths

REFRESHMENTS Pub at Hascombe, café at
Winkworth Arboretum

1 With St Peter's Church to the left, take the
Greensand Way track, marked 'GW', rising to
the right of the parking area, with farmland
opening out to the left. Pass a reservoir on the
right and continue to a junction.

2 Turn sharp right on the lane, then left at a
bridleway sign on a rising path. Follow the path
beside the lane; at a fork bear right and continue
on the path, with the lane on the right. The path
rises gradually, first through woodland, then with
woodland on the left and fields on the right.
There are far-reaching views across to Black
Down and, on a clear day, as far as the South
Downs. The path descends gradually to the
level of the fields on the right, then goes
back into woodland. Ignore a footpath
on the right and go straight on to
reach Markwick Lane.

3 Turn left and after 100m
turn right on a deeply banked
path. Go through a metal gate
onto a sandy path into the heath
and woodland of the Hurtwood.
At the top of the rise, the path
becomes a sandy track,
continuing over an open area
of ferns and clumps of trees.
Continue ahead, ignoring a
right fork, two crossing
tracks and another
right fork.

4 At the next meeting of paths, turn sharp
right to follow the yellow GW arrow. Then turn
left onto a steep downhill path, following
another GW arrow. After 100m, ignore a steep
path on the left with a GW arrow and continue
ahead on the path curving left. After 20m turn
left downhill, soon meeting up again with the
Greensand Way. Go through a gate and down the
right edge of a field, then through another gate
and over a stile. Continue through the next field
to the White Horse pub at Hascombe.

5 Take Church Road on the left to St Peter's
Church, and follow it to reach a private drive. Turn
left in front of the cottage onto a path. Ignore a
stile on the right by a field, and continue to the
right on a wide track, through a gate and ahead
past some sheds to a junction. Turn left between
fences to reach another gate and a road.

Turn right to reach 16th-century Winkworth
Farm and its exquisite formal garden. Beyond the
farm, turn right onto a lane to the car park for
Winkworth Arboretum (NT), first planted in
1937 by Dr Wilfrid Fox and containing more
than 1,000 species of tree and shrub.

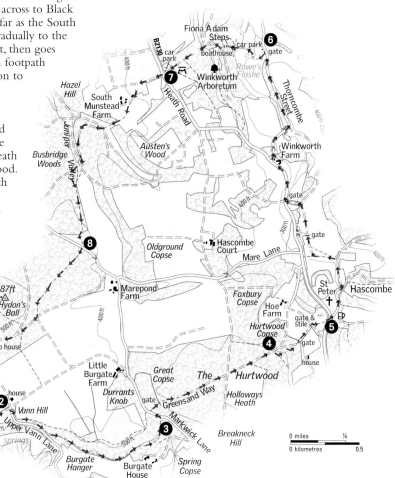

WINKWORTH ARBORETUM

6 Before the car park, go through a gate on the left and continue on a signed grass track, which soon becomes a sandy path, past the end of the lake. At a junction, with a boathouse on the left, turn right to and up the Fiona Adam steps. Take the left of two parallel paths ahead and continue to a crossing of paths. Turn left at a five-trunked tree onto a track to the café and car park.

7 Go through the car park, keeping left, and cross the road onto a lane signposted to South Munstead Farm. Fork left towards the farm; where the drive bears right, continue ahead on a path towards woodland. The path climbs gradually and soon Juniper Valley is seen below. Continue ahead, ignoring a track that merges from the right and a bridleway off to the left; follow the path on the left, which soon climbs steeply uphill, then

levels out again. After about ¼ mile, the path turns right then left, and soon reaches a road.

8 Follow the woodland path opposite, ignoring side turnings, until fields come into view. At a path junction with blue waymarks and a small pond opposite in the corner of a field, turn right onto a wide track and continue to a meeting of paths with a pump house to the left.
DETOUR *Turn sharp right on the steep path to grand views from the 181m (593ft) summit of Hydon's Ball, a hill dedicated to Octavia Hill, co-founder of the National Trust in 1894.*

9 Continue on the sandy path ahead. At a barn, bear left and continue to a gate at Hambledon's St Peter's churchyard. Opposite is a limekiln, last used in the 19th century.

SUSSEX

Beyond high coastal cliffs, river valleys penetrate the 80-mile chalk ridge of the South Downs, the top of its hills linked by a network of tracks commanding superb views over beechwoods and coombs.

1 East Dean

Easy paths across grassy hillsides and along the rollercoaster ridge of the mighty Seven Sisters, with views to Beachy Head.

LENGTH 4 or 6 miles (2 or 3 hours)

PARKING Village car park by Tiger Inn

CONDITIONS Some steep climbs and descents

REFRESHMENTS Pub and tearoom at East Dean; hotel at Birling Gap

1 Go into the village centre and, with the pub behind you, walk across the green to its top right-hand corner. Turn right on the road. After 30m, where the road bends right, turn left on a rising concrete track. Continue up to a gate and uphill across a field to St Mary's Church in Friston. Its earliest remains are 11th century, and the roof dates from about 1450; it contains an alabaster tomb to Thomas Selwyn, who died in 1613, and his wife. Go through the churchyard and turn left on a track to Crowlink.

2 After the last house in Crowlink, follow the field path, with a fence on the right. Where the path forks, go straight ahead and proceed towards the cliff edge – but keep well away from the edge: the cliff is very unstable.

3 Turn left along the top of Seven Sisters – in fact, eight chalk bluffs that resemble a giant natural rollercoaster. Viper's bugloss, a spectacular downland plant, grows on the turf. Continue to a signpost at the top of the last of the Sisters before Birling Gap. At this signpost keep right towards the houses, and go through a gate to a T-junction of paths.

4 For the short route, turn left in the direction of East Dean and follow instructions from **6**. For the full route, turn right and descend to Birling Gap. Steps lead down to the shore at this break in the cliffs. Take the rising path opposite the hotel, to the left of the telephone box and cottages, and continue along the clifftop. Pass to the left of disused Belle Tout lighthouse, built in 1834. An Iron Age embankment is visible on the cliff. Beyond the lighthouse the view extends to the lighthouse at the foot of Beachy Head. Continue to a bend in the road.

5 Turn sharp left onto a broad grassy path, running close to the road on its seaward side, returning to Birling Gap. Retrace your steps up the stony track to the right of the hotel. Past the last house, the track narrows and bends right.

6 Ignore the South Downs Way to the left and keep on up to a gate by the sign for Crowlink. Continue uphill. Go through the next gate, signposted to East Dean. Midway across the field, leave the main track and pass to the right of a prominent stone barn. Some 300m beyond the barn, fork right onto a path descending to East Dean; this path is easily missed, but it is obvious once you are on it. (If you reach a kissing gate in trees at the end of the field, you have overshot the path by about 200m.) At the bottom of the slope pass immediately to the left of the garden wall of the first house, go through a gate and follow the lane back into East Dean.

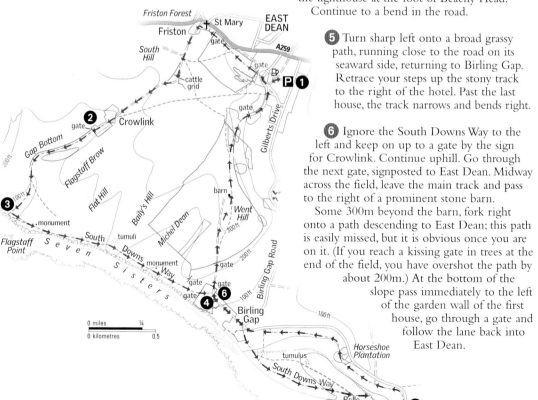

2 Battle

Past the site of the Battle of Hastings through woodland and past a lake, with the option of a detour into a nature reserve.

LENGTH	4½ or 6 miles (2½ or 3 hours)
PARKING	Public car park at Budgens supermarket
CONDITIONS	Easy
REFRESHMENTS	Full range in Battle

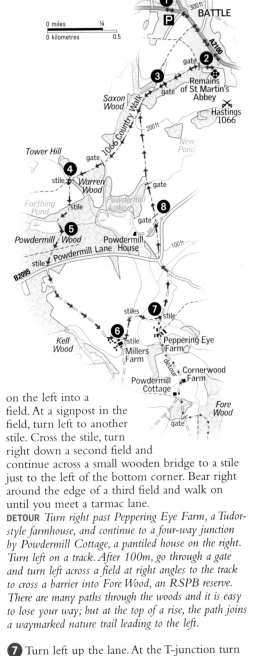

❶ Turn right down High Street. On the right after the roundabout is the Almonry and Town Model, which gives a history of the town. Continue to the abbey, built by William the Conqueror to fulfil a vow he took before his victory at the Battle of Hastings. It stands on the ridge where King Harold of England and his troops were drawn up before the battle. Its altar marks the spot where Harold was killed.

❷ Take the road between the abbey gateway and Pilgrim's Rest, a half-timbered 14th-century building, passing toilets and a car park on the left, where the road becomes a stony track. The route now follows the waymarked 1066 Country Walk, a 131-mile trail from Pevensey Castle to Rye. The track soon enters a field and continues along its left edge.

❸ Fork right at a bridleway signpost, following the 1066 Country Walk, to join a well-trodden path across a field past Saxon Wood on the right. Continue on the bridleway through a gate, passing through mixed woodland.

❹ Just beyond a footbridge across a stream, where the woods on the left end, turn left over a stile onto a path across a field. Cross a stile into the nature reserve in Powdermill Wood.
 At a fork of paths keep right. The path skirts the edge of Farthing Pond, a lovely stretch of water with water lilies and rushes. Fishermen can often be seen along its tree-lined banks.

❺ At the far end of the pond take the right fork over a footbridge across a stream and keep straight on, climbing steeply. At the top of the slope continue ahead to meet busy Powdermill Lane. Cross the road carefully and take the concrete and grass track straight ahead, which leads downhill to Millers Farm. The group of farm buildings includes an oast-house.

❻ Immediately after passing the farm on the right, just beyond a driveway leading to a brick house on the left called Badger's Keep and before reaching a group of barns, take a signposted stile on the left into a field. At a signpost in the field, turn left to another stile. Cross the stile, turn right down a second field and continue across a small wooden bridge to a stile just to the left of the bottom corner. Bear right around the edge of a third field and walk on until you meet a tarmac lane.

DETOUR *Turn right past Peppering Eye Farm, a Tudor-style farmhouse, and continue to a four-way junction by Powdermill Cottage, a pantiled house on the right. Turn left on a track. After 100m, go through a gate and turn left across a field at right angles to the track to cross a barrier into Fore Wood, an RSPB reserve. There are many paths through the woods and it is easy to lose your way; but at the top of a rise, the path joins a waymarked nature trail leading to the left.*

❼ Turn left up the lane. At the T-junction turn left and, at the next road junction, go up the bank opposite and turn right onto a field path running beside a hedge alongside Powdermill Lane.

❽ At the top of the hill, where the road bends right, continue on a path that leads through a farmyard and becomes a wide lane with a metalled centre and grass on either side. At the signpost passed earlier in the walk, turn right onto the path back into Battle.

SUSSEX

3 West Firle

Quiet villages of the South Downs, exhilarating coastal views, and a country retreat for artists and writers.

LENGTH 7 miles (3½ hours)

PARKING Village car park at West Firle (signposted to Firle)

CONDITIONS Easy going, with one steep ascent of about 158m (520ft)

REFRESHMENTS Pubs in West Firle and Alciston

1 Leave the car park by the main entrance, and turn left on the village street. This bends right by the Ram Inn and passes a left turn to St Peter's Church, which has a stained-glass window of 1985 by John Piper.

2 Beyond the turn to the church, go forward on an unmade bridleway past barns. Just after a wall begins on the left, follow a farm track around to the left along the bottom of a field.

3 At the end of the field, pass a belt of trees, turn right up the edge of the next field and follow the path through a gate up to the crest of the South Downs. As you climb, Firle Tower, now a private house, is prominent in the valley below.

4 Turn left on the South Downs Way, heading for the gate on the skyline. The long-distance path, waymarked with acorn motifs, passes several Bronze Age burial mounds. The view from Firle Beacon at 217m (712ft) encompasses the cliffs of Seaford Head and, farther east, the Seven Sisters; to the north lies the Weald.

5 At a meeting of four tracks and a tarmac lane joining from the left, keep on the South Downs Way, on the left-hand track leading straight ahead.

6 Where the fence on the right swings away turn left, following the sign for the bridleway and the blue arrow across the grass to a stile, with Alciston visible below. Bear left and follow the path downhill. Cross another stile, turn right and continue down to a T-junction with a track. Turn right, then left into Alciston, which has relics of a monastic grange owned by Battle Abbey before the Reformation: a huge flint-walled tithe barn, a former fishpond and a ruined 14th-century dovecote.

7 Pass the Rose Cottage pub on the left. Opposite a brick cottage (No. 53), go through a gate into a field and go forward to another two gates at the far end. In the second field, ignore a gate to the left and go forward to leave the field at its far right-hand corner. Follow the right edge of the third field.

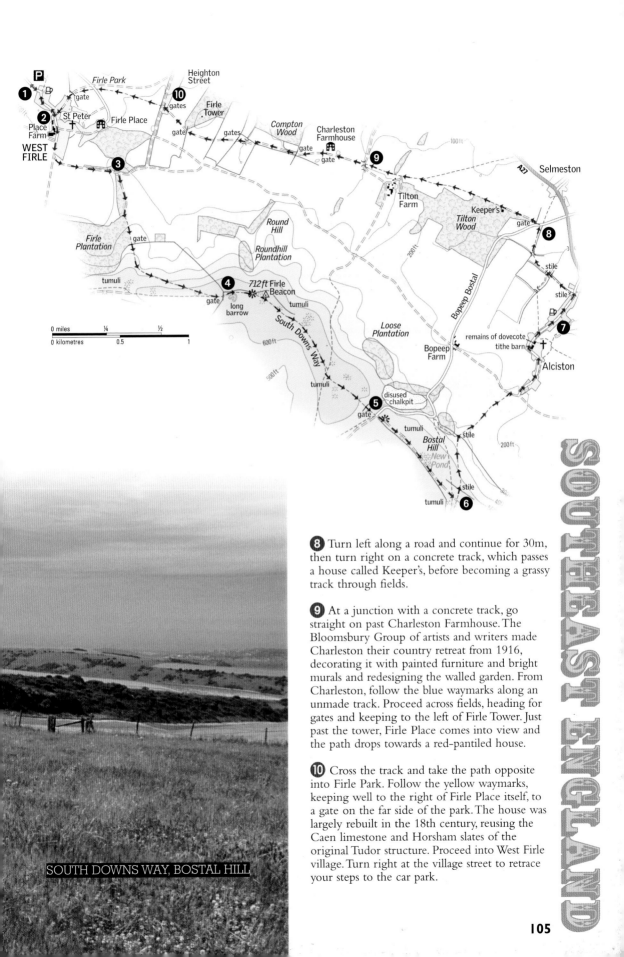

Map labels:

P
1
2
Place Farm
WEST FIRLE
St Peter
Firle Place
Firle Park
gate
Heighton Street
10
gates
Firle Tower
gate
gates
Compton Wood
gate
Charleston Farmhouse
gate
9
100 ft
A27
Selmeston
3
Tilton Farm
Keeper's
Tilton Wood
gate
8
Round Hill
Firle Plantation
gate
Roundhill Plantation
200 ft
stile
stile
tumuli
4
712 ft Firle Beacon
long barrow
tumuli
South Downs Way
Loose Plantation
Bopeep Bostal
remains of dovecote
tithe barn
7
600 ft
Bopeep Farm
Alciston
500 ft
tumuli
5
gate
disused chalkpit
tumuli
stile
200 ft
Bostal Hill
New Pond
tumuli
stile
6

0 miles   ¼   ½
0 kilometres   0.5   1

SOUTH DOWNS WAY, BOSTAL HILL

8 Turn left along a road and continue for 30m, then turn right on a concrete track, which passes a house called Keeper's, before becoming a grassy track through fields.

9 At a junction with a concrete track, go straight on past Charleston Farmhouse. The Bloomsbury Group of artists and writers made Charleston their country retreat from 1916, decorating it with painted furniture and bright murals and redesigning the walled garden. From Charleston, follow the blue waymarks along an unmade track. Proceed across fields, heading for gates and keeping to the left of Firle Tower. Just past the tower, Firle Place comes into view and the path drops towards a red-pantiled house.

10 Cross the track and take the path opposite into Firle Park. Follow the yellow waymarks, keeping well to the right of Firle Place itself, to a gate on the far side of the park. The house was largely rebuilt in the 18th century, reusing the Caen limestone and Horsham slates of the original Tudor structure. Proceed into West Firle village. Turn right at the village street to retrace your steps to the car park.

SOUTH-EAST ENGLAND

SUSSEX

4 Alfriston

From 'the cathedral of the downs' to the
National Nature Reserve at Lullington Heath
and the Long Man of Wilmington.

LENGTH	6 miles (3 hours)
PARKING	The Willows car park north of village
CONDITIONS	Gentle uphill gradients; one steep descent
REFRESHMENTS	Pub at Alfriston

1 Turn left out of the car park, passing an old
market cross and the Star Inn. Turn left on the
path by the United Reformed Church, and keep
slightly to the left, down a walled path. Cross the
White Bridge over the Cuckmere river, and
follow the surfaced path ahead.

2 Turn right on the road by Plonk Barn, then
immediately bear left on a path signposted to
Lullington Church; ignore another path to the
left. The main path follows a field edge and then
leads through woodland to the church, which
is signposted on the left.

THE LONG MAN OF WILMINGTON

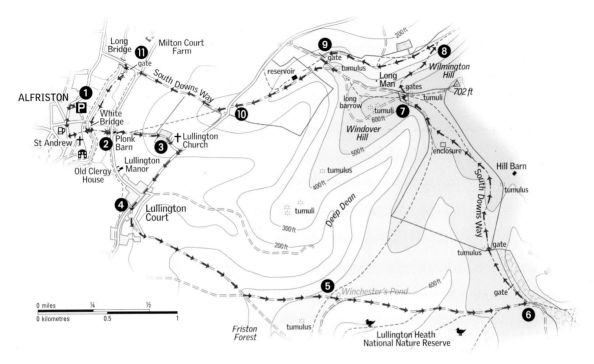

3 Lullington Church, a 13th-century building measuring 5m (16ft) square, is among the smallest churches in Britain. Part of the chancel is all that remains of the original building, although there are traces of the nave in the churchyard. Rejoin the main path, turning right on reaching a road. Go straight on at the next road junction, towards Litlington.

4 About 100m beyond the junction, take the rising track on the left, just past Litlington Court, signposted to Jevington. Follow the path as it slopes gently upwards for ¾ mile. At a four-way meeting of tracks turn left, proceeding with a fence on the left.

5 At the next meeting of tracks, go straight ahead into Lullington Heath National Nature Reserve, which occupies one of England's largest areas of chalk heath. To the left of the track lies Winchester's Pond, a 19th-century dewpond whose vegetation attracts dragonflies, birds and mammals. Go forward, ignoring side turnings; eventually the path starts to climb.

6 After a mile, when the track starts to descend, turn left at a four-way junction, following a path through bushes to a gate. This is the South Downs Way, marked with acorn motifs. Go straight on along a field to the next gate. The path continues ahead, parallel to the right field edge. It eventually veers left, passing to the right of a small enclosure and joining a fence on the left before leading across the head of a dramatic valley.

7 Do not follow the South Downs Way through the next gate at the corner of the fence, but instead turn right for 50m, go left through another gate and, bearing slightly to the left, follow the waymarked bridleway signposted to Wilmington and Folkington, that leads down the escarpment; it soon bends right and drops steeply.

8 At the foot of the escarpment turn left, then fork left just before a group of trees, to pass the base of the Long Man of Wilmington. The origins of this chalk-hill carving are obscure. No known record of the 'long man' predates a drawing of 1710, but he is thought to be much older. He has been explained variously as a fertility symbol, a god, a folly, or a carving by a monk from Wilmington Priory, visible to the north.

Continue on a gently rising chalky path that is later joined by a fence on the right.

9 Go through a gate and turn left uphill for 100m, then turn sharp right down a track that leads past a concrete building – a covered reservoir – to the road.

10 Cross the road and take the bridleway opposite. Ignore a stile on the left and descend to the next road. Go forward towards Alfriston.

11 Just before the river bridge go through a kissing gate on the left and follow the river back to the White Bridge at Alfriston. Retrace your steps to the car park.

SUSSEX

5 Amberley

The alluring flood meadows of Amberley Wildbrooks, and a museum laid out in an old chalkpit.

LENGTH 3½, 6 or 6½ miles (2, 3 or 3½ hours)

PARKING Near church

CONDITIONS Easy

REFRESHMENTS Pub, shop in Amberley; tearoom near Amberley station

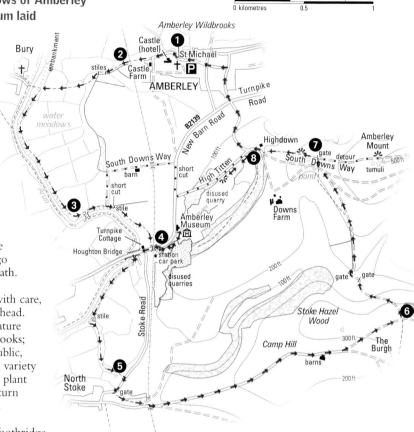

1 Follow the cul-de-sac past St Michael's Church on the left and along the curtain wall of Amberley Castle. Where the track bends left to a farm, go straight ahead on a grassy path.

2 Cross the railway line with care, then follow the field path ahead. Wide views embrace the nature reserve of Amberley Wildbrooks; the reserve, closed to the public, provides habitats for a huge variety of birds and more than 150 plant species. At the River Arun turn left along the embankment.

3 Do not cross the next footbridge but go on along the embankment, soon passing a caravan site. Continue to the B2139.

SHORT CUT *About 200m beyond the footbridge, turn left through a gate onto the South Downs Way. Follow the track over a railway bridge. Turn right on the B2139, then next left. Rejoin the main route at* **8**.

4 Turn left on the B2139 and then right into the station car park to Amberley Museum, laid out in an old chalk quarry. Its exhibits include a blacksmith's shop, a pottery, a printing works, a narrow-gauge railway and steam road vehicles.

Return to the road and turn left, towards the river, passing a former turnpike cottage. In the middle of the bridge take the path on the left onto an island. Cross another bridge and follow the embankment for more than ¼ mile. Just after crossing a stile, turn left on a path leading along the edge of a copse to a surfaced lane.

5 Turn right on the lane, then left through a gate after 150m. Go up a short slope on the right to join a bridleway and where the path emerges from bushes at a meeting of tracks, go straight

on, following a signpost. Continue for 1 mile along a gently rising lane. About 100m past a group of barns called Canada, fork left uphill by a road sign barring vehicles except for access.

6 At a four-way crossing of tracks, turn left downhill. From the bottom of the hill, the track bends right through a gate and ascends. Continue uphill with a fence on the left. The valley to the right, which is largely untouched by modern agriculture, has traces of medieval field systems.

DETOUR *At a junction with the South Downs Way, turn right and continue for ¼ mile to the viewpoint of Amberley Mount.*

7 Turn left on the South Downs Way; there are fine views of Amberley village, castle and the Wildbrooks reserve. Continue between fences and descend to a lane. Turn right on the lane.

8 At the next road junction turn left on High Titten to a viewpoint on the left. Return to the junction and turn left to Amberley.

6 Lurgashall

Woods, farmland and coppicing, ancient paths and a climb onto Black Down for fabulous views.

LENGTH 5½ miles (3 hours)

PARKING By village green

CONDITIONS Mainly well-defined, with some steep paths and lanes

REFRESHMENTS Pub in Lurgashall

1 Facing the Noah's Ark pub, turn right to cross the lane and enter the churchyard through a gate. St Laurence Church has a huge 16th-century portico, formerly used as a meeting place and the village school. About 30m beyond the gate and before the church, head half-left, following a line of yew trees towards a footpath sign. Cross two dilapidated stiles and head for a gate in the field. Go through the gate, cross the gravelled drive and turn right onto a second drive marked by a yellow arrow and leading between ponds. Continue ahead on the path through a small field and over a stile by a gate, turning right onto a wide gravelled track. Ahead conifers along the crest of Black Down come into view.

2 After about ⅓ mile and just after the track bears right and crosses a small stream, cross a stile on the left into a field. Follow fingerposts across two other fields, then turn left below the garden fence of Shopp Hill Farm and follow the bottom edge to a stile. Cross this into and then out of woodland, then bear right in front of some cottages to reach a junction with Jobson's Lane.

3 Turn left on the lane and after ¼ mile turn sharp right up the steep slope of Quell Lane. The lane winds through Quellwood Common, an area of mixed woodland that includes beech, oak and ash, and is full of wild flowers.

4 After ½ mile, towards the top of Quell Lane, where it swings right, take the broad track ahead along an ancient green lane. The track becomes a metalled driveway and ends at a tarmac lane. Turn left and follow the lane to the gate piers of Blackdown Park on the left.

5 Continue on the lane to a small grassy layby on the right, with a NT sign for Black Down. Take the steep track leading towards the 280m (917ft) summit of Black Down. Keep ahead to a fenced area and go through the NT gate. When the path levels out to a junction, continue ahead on a narrower track to a viewpoint, known as

the Temple of the Winds, with panoramic views to south and east from a large semicircular stone seat. Return to the gate piers of Blackdown Park and turn right over a stone stile onto a drive. Down a slope on the right is the private Blackdown House, a stone mansion with mullions and tall chimneys. It dates from 1640 but was enlarged in the 1840s by the architect Anthony Salvin. Where the drive bears right to the house, keep ahead through a gate by a cattle grid towards Blackdown Farm. Where the track bears left to farm buildings, follow the footpath sign through a gate into a field. Keep to the grassy track past farm buildings on the left, to another gate.

6 Go through the gate to a crossing of paths. Continue ahead on a downhill track with fields on both sides, then Windfall Wood on the left. The track passes a lodge on the left and enters the wood, then meets a road.

7 Turn left. After 100m turn right on a tarmac path (Courts Yard) signposted to Guardian Cottage, with wide grass verges and trees on either side. Just before the tarmac ends at a builder's yard, bear left on a muddy track into woodland, with a small field, sometimes filled with holiday caravans, on the right.

8 A few metres after the field on the left ends, cross over to a narrower path on the left through a gap in the trees. Follow the path slightly uphill through a chestnut coppice. On reaching the end of the woodland, cross the first of several stiles on the edge of fields, then continue on a grassy path between an orchard on the left and a thorny hedge on the right. At the end of the orchard, cross several more stiles in fields and onto Lurgashall village green.

SUSSEX

7 Bignor Hill

A gentle walk across unspoilt downland and along the Roman embankment of Stane Street, and up to a touching memorial.

LENGTH 4 or 5½ miles (2 or 3½ hours)

PARKING NT car park on Bignor Hill, south of Sutton

CONDITIONS Easy paths and route-finding; can be very muddy after rain

REFRESHMENTS None on walk; pub in Bignor

1 From the car park take the hard track leading past the 'No cars' sign towards radio masts, joining the South Downs Way. After 200m, just beyond an information board about Stane Street, a Roman road, turn left along the raised embankment of Stane Street itself.

As the path stretches straight ahead and leads gently downhill towards the sea, visible in the distance, it is easy to imagine being a Roman legionary marching from London to Chichester. Here and there along the path the flint core – *stane* is Anglo-Saxon for 'stone' – shows through where it has been disturbed by tree roots or eroded by herds of sheep. Where the fence on the right swings away farther to the right, continue along the embankment.

2 At the next junction of paths, climb a stile and continue along Stane Street. The route runs through part of the Slindon estate (NT), where traditional husbandry is promoted; sheep grazing encourages the growth of downland flora such as common orchids that cannot survive in invasive scrub. The windmill visible ahead on 128m (420ft) Halnaker Hill is a tower mill of about 1750, immortalised in Hilaire Belloc's poem 'Ha'nacker Mill': 'Sally is gone that was so kindly, / Sally is gone from Ha'nacker Hill / And the Briar grows ever since then so blindly; / And ever since then the clapper is still... / And the sweeps have fallen from Ha'nacker Mill.'

Carry on along the edge of the field, ignoring side paths and passing a track down to Gumber Farm, which offers accommodation for walkers and riders on the South Downs Way. Beyond a gate, the path leads between hedgerow trees.

3 At the edge of North Wood, turn sharp right at a meeting of seven tracks and paths, and follow the path signposted to Upwaltham steadily uphill for ¾ mile.

4 On reaching the top of the hill, turn right and continue ahead, ignoring side turns to the left and right.

5 Some 150m after leaving the forest, fork left at a field corner, and follow the track along the edge of a copse towards the masts seen earlier in the walk, which now come into view again.

6 At the next junction, turn left and immediately right, and follow the South Downs Way back to the car park. The track leads past the remnants of Iron Age cross-dykes, built as defences. Another track, leading south from the car park, leads to the site of a Neolithic camp with a causeway built between 5,000 and 6,000 years ago.

DETOUR *To climb to the summit of Bignor Hill, continue from the car park along the South Downs Way, on a track to the right of the road, and walk gently uphill for ½ mile. The summit of Bignor Hill offers a breathtaking panorama. Nearby is Toby's Stone, a memorial, in the form of a mounting block, to James Wentworth-Fitzwilliam (Toby), 1888-1955, the honorary secretary of the Cowdray Hunt in the 1920s. It is inscribed 'Here he lies where he longed to be' – and few final resting-places can have had a more spectacular outlook.*

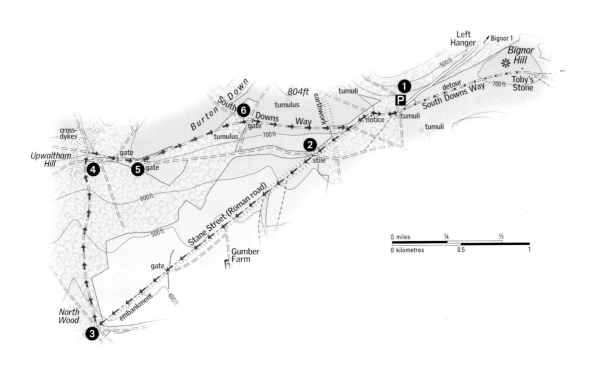

Left
Hanger
Bignor 1
Bignor
Hill
* Toby's
Stone
South Downs Way
detour
700ft
500ft
400ft
1
P
tumuli
notice
tumuli
South Down
Burton
804ft
tumulus
earthwork
tumuli
Downs Way
6
gate
700ft
2
tumulus
stile
cross-
dykes
gate
tumulus
Upwaltham
Hill
4
5 gate
600ft
Stane Street (Roman road)
500ft
Gumber
Farm
gate
North
Wood
embankment
400ft
3

0 miles		¼		½	
0 kilometres			0.5		1

VIEW FROM TOBY'S STONE, BIGNOR HILL

SUSSEX

8 Ashdown Forest

The exhilarating expanses of Ashdown Forest, as immortalised in the adventures of Winnie the Pooh.

LENGTH 6 miles (3 hours)

PARKING Gills Lap car park, off B2026 south of Hartfield

CONDITIONS No daunting hills, but sturdy footwear needed to cope with muddy patches

REFRESHMENTS None on walk

1 Facing away from the road junction, cross the grassy expanse behind the car park and walk uphill along a broad track to a round clump of Scots pines on Gills Lap, one of the highest points of Ashdown Forest. Continue past a trig point and a disused quarry to the right, to the Enchanted Place viewpoint on the left.

The viewpoint has a memorial to A.A. Milne and E.H. Shepard, the author and illustrator of the Winnie the Pooh stories. It bears the inscription 'And by and by they came to an enchanted place on the very top of the Forest called Galleons Leap'. Beyond this point the track is badly eroded and drops steeply for about ½ mile. About 150m ahead the track swings right and becomes less clear, as it passes through scrubby woodland to meet the B2026.

2 Cross the road and take the bridleway opposite, marked 'Horse Route', that winds through mixed woodland of silver birch and beech and eventually downhill to a shallow stream at the valley bottom. Cross the stream and continue on the track uphill.

Bear right on a broad track that climbs steadily, with views of coniferous woodland below and a tree-dotted skyline on the right. Where the roofs of Wren's Warren become visible through the trees to the right, turn left on a track that climbs through woodland.

3 At a junction of tracks turn right, following a 'WW' waymark – the long-distance Weald Way. Continue climbing steadily for about a mile across open heathland of gorse and heather with a belt of trees on the left, following the waymarks for the Weald Way.

THE HEATH AND WOODLAND OF ASHDOWN FOREST

4 Where the track meets the B2026, cross the road and, keeping a small circular car park to the left, take the lane marked 'Private Road to Old Lodge' downhill past a tile-hung lodge. Continue down the drive for ½ mile, passing a small nature reserve on the right.

5 By a metal gate across the drive, go through the wooden gate on the left and follow the footpath diversion signs. This path, which is marked by occasional signs, leads down the right-hand edge of several fields. At an area of fenced-off woodland, turn right, going over a bridge and a stile, then continue ahead, with the fence on your right, for about 150m.

6 Pass through a gate into woods and take the narrow path winding downhill through the trees. Cross a wooden bridge over a stream and follow the narrow path uphill to the left, as it winds through more trees, to reach a broad track. Go left downhill and continue to a stream on the left.

7 With a pond on your right, cross this stream, whose water is often bright orange because of the iron deposits in the soil – an iron industry

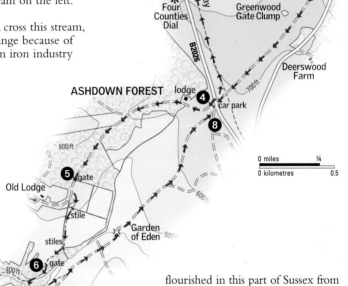

flourished in this part of Sussex from Tudor times to the 17th century. The trees of Ashdown Forest provided charcoal to power the furnaces of the ironworks.

Beyond the stream, continue on a broad track running parallel to the main stream, with views of open heathland to the right. After ½ mile, the track crosses the stream by a wide footbridge at a point called the Garden of Eden, and continues uphill for another ½ mile to the B2026 and the small circular car park passed earlier.

8 Cross the road and follow the Weald Way sign across heathland for a short distance. Turn left and follow the broad rutted track parallel to the road, which leads back to Gills Lap car park, with its panoramic views over the forest and the countryside beyond.

Peak
District
National
Park
7
6

Buxton
5
3
4
1
2
A619
A623
A53
A6
A61
M1
A619
Worksop
A1(M)
A631
A57
A614
A156
A1
Scunthorpe
A18
M180
A15

Chesterfield
Matlock
Mansfield
A617
Newark-
on-Trent
A46
A1
Lincol
A1

Leek
A523
...SHIRE
18-127
NOTTINGHAMSHIRE
A17

Whitchurch
Stoke-
on-Trent
Stone
A50
A515
Ashbourne
A52
Derby A52
Nottingham
A46
A17
Granthan
2
A1

Oswestry
A49
A53
A41
STAFFORDSHIRE
156-157
A518
Stafford
2
A51
Burton-
upon-Trent
A38
A50
A606
A607
Loughborough
A1
A46

Shrewsbury
A5
M6
Cannock
Lichfield
Tamworth
Walsall
A5
A444
LEICESTERSHIRE
Leicester
M69
M1
A6
Oakham
A47
Stamfo
Melton
Mowbray

Telford
3
M54
Wolverhampton
M6Toll
M42
Nuneaton
M1
Market
Harborough
A47
Stamfo

SHROPSHIRE
152-155
2
1
A49
A458
Bridgnorth
Birmingham
1
WARWICKSHIRE
166-167
M6
A421
Corby

Ludlow
A456
Kidderminster
A449
Bromsgrove
Redditch
Coventry
A45
Rugby
A14
Kettering
NORTHAMPTONSHIRE
150-151
A508
A509
A45

Leominster
2 A44
A49
WORCESTERSHIRE
168-169
Warwick
M40
A46
Stratford-
upon-Avon
A429
M1
Daventry
1
A5
A43
Northampton

HEREFORDSHIRE
136-137
A438
Worcester
Great
Malvern
Evesham
2
1
A44

Hereford
A438
A465
A9
1
M50
2
Tewkesbury
Ross-
on-Wye
A417
2
Stow-on-
the-Wold
5

Gloucester
Cheltenham
A40
Forest
of Dean
1
GLOUCESTERSHIRE
128-133
3
Cotswold
Hills
Cirencester
4
A48
M5
A46
M4

Key

1 **Walk location**

━━ **County boundary**

━━ **Motorway**

Principal A road

(See 'How to use the book',
page 6)

Central England

Grimsby

The Wolds

A16

A158

A1028

NCOLNSHIRE 138-141

Skegness

A452

Boston

A52

A16 · A17

Spalding

Wisbech

A47

Peterborough

A141

A1(M)

A14

CAMBRIDGESHIRE 116-117

Ely

Huntingdon

A10

A142

St Neots

A428

A7 · A14

Cambridge

A10 · M11 · A11

A505

Hunstanton

A148

Fakenham

King's Lynn

A47

Downham Market

A1122 · A1101 · A10 · A134 · A1065

East Dereham

Swaffham

NORFOLK 142-149

A11

A140

Cromer

A149

The Broads

A140

Norwich

AA7 · A146

Great Yarmouth

Lowestoft

Thetford A1066

A143

A11 · A143

Southwold

A12

Newmarket

A14

Bury St Edmunds

A14

A134

Stowmarket

SUFFOLK 158-165

Aldeburgh

Sudbury

A12

Ipswich

A14

Felixstowe

The heartland of England combines rich farmland with a glorious industrial past. Relics of old trades, rugged moorland and lush valleys characterise a region that offers walks to suit all tastes.

CAMBRIDGESHIRE

The woods, farmland and marshes of Cambridgeshire provide easy walking and fine views. Ramblers may catch glimpses of the cathedral city of Ely, which rises from the fenlands on its ancient island dome.

1 Great Chishill

Breathtaking views along the ancient Icknield Way and Heydon Ditch, and on to an 18th-century windmill.

LENGTH 5 miles (2½ hours)

PARKING In Heydon Road near telephone kiosk

CONDITIONS Steeper paths slippery after rain

REFRESHMENTS Pubs in Great Chishill and Heydon

1 Cross the road and turn right along the pavement by the Rectory Farmhouse towards the Pheasant inn. Continue across New Road, noting the early 19th-century lockup – the little village jail – on the right.

2 Just beyond Lime Farm Barn turn left on a marked path towards Icknield Way.

The path, a tunnel of overhanging branches, descends to become a narrow, hedged way between wide, curving fields whose verges in summer are a tangle of marguerites, scabious and morning glory. The hillside on the right is marked by strip lynchets, the remains of medieval agricultural terraces.

Shortly after walking past the strip lynchets, where the hedges end, at a point more than 90m above sea level, a huge panorama opens out towards the Gog Magog Hills. To the right the view encompasses the spires and towers of Cambridge and to the right of the city, on a very clear day, you might get a distant glimpse of Ely Cathedral; while to the left the view reaches into Bedfordshire.

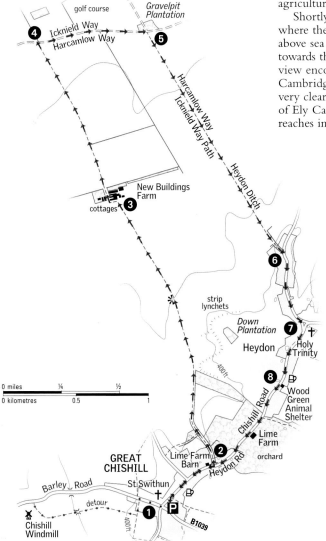

3 The path follows a power line down to New Buildings Farm. The farmyard contains a private collection of locomotives that can be seen from the path as it swings left along a flint wall then right past cottages to rejoin the waymarked track. As the path climbs, the views over prairie-like fields become ever more expansive. In the mid distance light aircraft may be seen near an old hangar, a vestige of a Second World War airbase. The base was one of several satellite stations of Duxford Airfield to the north.

4 The path reaches a T-junction with the Icknield Way. Turn right and walk along the remains of this broad trade route that once ran from The Wash to Salisbury Plain, and was already ancient when Queen Boudicca brought her chariots through. To the left is a golf course with a vast medieval barn as its clubhouse and, ahead, a clump of trees.

5 At the centre of the clump, turn right on a waymarked trail. This path, part of the Harcamlow Way, is Heydon Ditch, a defensive earthwork or dyke built in about AD 500 running from the ridge ahead to the marshes of Fowlmere. Follow Heydon Ditch as it climbs. At the summit it goes through thick hedges to emerge on Fowlmere Road, Heydon.

6 Turn right through the village centre, which is a mix of converted flint barns and thatched and tiled cottages.

Beside Heydon's triangular village green is Holy Trinity Church. Although the 13th-century building was badly damaged in air raids during the 1940 Battle of Britain, it was skilfully restored in 1956; only the brickwork of the tower conflicts with the flint of the original.

7 Facing away from the church entrance, turn left by a flint wall along Chishill Road, passing the old school house of 1846 and the late Georgian Heydon Place. Farther along the road is the William IV pub, which contains a fascinating display of old agricultural implements.

8 Almost next door to the pub is the Wood Green Animal Shelter. A blue plaque reveals that this was the home of Arthur, the catfood star of TV fame. The village of Heydon ends at the entrance sign to Great Chishill. Continue past New Road, back to the telephone kiosk and parking place.

DETOUR *The 18th-century post mill on the Barley Road can be reached by a path from the centre of Chishill just below St Swithun's Church.*

CHISHILL WINDMILL

DERBYSHIRE

All the walks in this section are in the beautiful high moorland and dales of the Peak District. This dramatic landscape has drawn walkers for hundreds of years. It became England's first National Park in 1951.

1 Beresford Dale

Easy paths through varied dales bordered by limestone crags, and along the banks of the tranquil River Dove.

LENGTH **5 miles (2½ hours)**

PARKING **At side of road on the approach to Beresford Dale, off B5054 west of Hartington**

CONDITIONS **Paths can be muddy after rain**

REFRESHMENTS **Full range in Hartington**

1 Walk to the road's end, where a pool on the Dove is shaded by beech trees. Take the woodland path to the left of the footbridge and stepping stones, beside the river and between precipitous slopes.

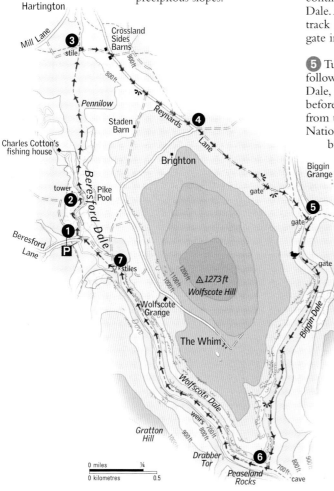

2 Just before the next footbridge is Pike Pool, with its spike of limestone. The path then crosses to the far bank. After ¼ mile, glimpsed through trees on the left, are the ruins of the fishing house built by Charles Cotton, a close friend of the poet and writer Izaak Walton, author of *The Compleat Angler* (1653). A stile set in a drystone wall marks the end of Beresford Dale; the valley opens out and the path wends across fields round the foot of Pennilow hill, towards Hartington.

3 At a junction of paths cross the stile and turn right up a stony track between drystone walls to some barns. Where the path meets Reynards Lane turn right and continue ahead between fields for ½ mile, ignoring a right turn.

4 At a four-way meeting of lanes and tracks, continue straight ahead, signposted to Biggin Dale. After a level stretch, and beside a barn, the track narrows and descends steeply through a gate into a dry valley.

5 Turn right at the foot of the valley and follow signs for a bridleway through Biggin Dale, swinging left through a gate by a dewpond before turning sharp right as another path joins from the left. This part of the Derbyshire Dales National Nature Reserve is known for its butterflies, wild flowers and plants, including red hemp nettle and Western gorse. The valley becomes increasingly narrow and sheer-sided, with limestone boulders littering the path. Enter the National Trust's South Peak estate; nearly a mile farther on, the dramatic outcrops of Peaseland Rocks appear ahead.

6 At the river turn right along Wolfscote Dale and continue for just over a mile, with the river on the left. Limestone crags give way to high grassy banks, then reappear farther on. The river tumbles downstream over weirs, while ducks dip and dive among the rushes.

7 By a footbridge, go through two stiles at the end of Wolfscote Dale and continue across the wide meadow ahead to the footbridge at the head of Beresford Dale, that was passed at the start of the walk. Cross the bridge to the parking place.

2 Stanton Moor

High moorland, Bronze Age remains, and an extraordinary tunnelled and carved gritstone outcrop.

LENGTH 4½ miles (2½ hours)

PARKING Birchover Road, 1 mile south of Stanton in Peak, by wide path marked by oblong boulder

CONDITIONS Easy; short climb at end

REFRESHMENTS Pubs in Birchover

1 Take the wide path near the parking place and cross the stile visible ahead onto Stanton Moor, a gritstone plateau rising to 323m (1,060ft) above the rolling limestone countryside. In the Bronze Age the area was used extensively as a burial ground and as a place of worship; it contains 70 stone cairns, several stone circles, ring cairns, and a standing stone, Cork Stone, which soon appears on left.

2 At a junction of paths turn left past a circular burial mound, and follow the path for ½ mile through heather moorland to a copse of silver birch. In a glade to the left is the mysterious Nine Ladies Stone Circle, and some metres to its southwest stands the solitary King Stone. The stones are thought to have formed part of a Bronze Age ritual complex.

3 Just beyond the stone circle fork right onto a path that leads towards woodland with a fence stile visible ahead. Cross the stile, keep right and continue to a curious isolated tower rising out of the birch and bracken. The tower was built by the local Thornhill family to celebrate the enactment of Earl Grey's parliamentary reforms of 1832. Ignore a stile to the right and continue on the path ahead along the edge of Stanton Moor, with dramatic views to the left over Darley Dale and a large lead reclamation works. Fork left to see the Cat Stone, so called because it loosely resembles a feline head. Rejoin the main path and continue with a fence on the right past scattered burial mounds and disused quarries to reach a stile on right beside a large cairn.

4 Cross the stile and when the path beyond reaches the junction and circular burial mound passed earlier, turn left and descend to a lane at the southern edge of the moor. Turn right on the road and after 50m take the path on the left to Barn Farm, which leads into the farmyard.

Do not turn immediately right in the farmyard but continue half left to skirt the barn ahead, leaving it on right. A short distance beyond the farm a signpost by a wall points in four directions.

Keeping the wall on the right, take the path ahead through an iron gate and continue through two fields to a junction with a farm track running between stone walls.

5 Turn right along the track, passing Ivy House and Cowley Knoll Farm, and continue to a lane. Turn left on the lane, then immediately right on a path that leads through meadows alongside Birchover Wood, with dramatic views of Cratcliff Tor and the twin tors of Robin Hood's Stride ahead. Follow the path past Rocking Stone Farm, so called because one of the huge gritstone rocks above it moved naturally on a sandstone pivot until it was vandalised in 1799. The path bears right round the hill through several stiles and gates and on downhill towards Birchover.

6 Continue past the vicarage, where the path becomes a lane. Just before the Druid Inn, a footpath to left winds up to Rowtor (rough tor) Rocks, a remarkable jumble of gritstone blocks. A local vicar, Rev Thomas Eyre (d.1717), had them tunnelled and carved into walkways, rooms, alcoves and seats for friends and family, and also created a study within the rocks. The strange area was once thought to have been the haunt of Druids.

7 Cross the road by the inn and take the path ahead, which climbs through woodland to a quarry on the Birchover to Stanton road. Turn left along the road to the parking place.

CENTRAL ENGLAND

DERBYSHIRE

3 Miller's Dale

Towering railway viaducts, a wooded vale and a historic village high above the Wye's rippling falls.

LENGTH 4½ or 6 miles (3 or 4 hours)

PARKING Miller's Dale railway station

CONDITIONS A couple of steep climbs; rocky path in Monk's Dale usually wet and slippery

REFRESHMENTS Pub by river in Miller's Dale

1 Go through the gate on the left of the station buildings. Turn left on the Monsal Trail, following the route of a dismantled railway over a viaduct with dramatic views to the River Wye below. To the right of the path are four old limekilns, once used to convert local stone into quicklime.

2 Where a path leads to the right to Miller's Dale Quarry, turn left down a steep path opposite, across a wooden footbridge and a smaller concrete bridge. Bear left on the path, then turn left on the road that soon joins the main road through Miller's Dale.

3 Cross the road to St Anne's Church, and follow the sign for Monk's Dale up a narrow passage to the left of the church. The path leads through into the dale, a National Nature Reserve with an abundance of wild flowers and butterflies in summer. Do not fork left, but go straight up the rocky path, which soon descends, with hawthorn and wild rose trees on the left and the start of the valley on the right.

4 Cross the footbridge over the brook at the bottom of the valley, and follow the path through light woodland. Where the trees end, continue along the craggy hillside. The path dips and climbs, drops steeply towards the brook, and enters a leafy jungle of hawthorn, hazel, wild rose, birch and moss-covered walls, where tree roots curl like claws around firmly bedded limestone rocks.

5 Beyond the woodland, pass through a small clearing and between sheer rock faces. Cross a field towards a stile onto the road, but do not go over the stile. Instead, turn left along the edge of the field for a short distance and, at a second stile in the wall, turn left onto a steep path that leads up the hill away from the road.

Towards the top of the field, with magnificent views of pastures crossed by drystone walls, the path merges with the Pennine Bridleway at a gate, becoming a passage between stone walls.

6 Follow the walled passage as it curves right and, just after passing through a gate, go immediately left over a stile. Walk beside the wall before entering another walled passage. Where this passage ends, walk straight on to the sign and gate, from where there is a good view of Wormhill ahead. Walk towards the village down the long field and turn left at the field's end, then turn right onto a track.

7 Just past ivy-clad Holly House on the right, the path meets a road from Wormhill, which leads up to St Margaret's Church. Although the present building is Victorian,

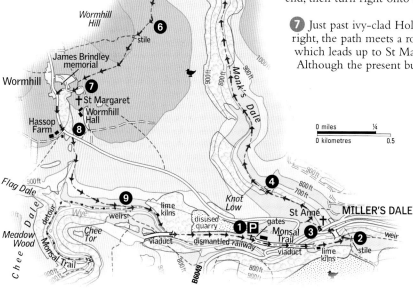

AUTUMN AT CHEE TOR AND RIVER WYE, CHEE DALE

a church is known to have existed here since the 13th century, and the community – with its manor, foresters, verderers and wolf hunters – was mentioned in the Domesday Book.

Turn right into the village, where to the right is a well and a memorial above it to James Brindley, born within Wormhill parish. The 18th-century engineer, who never learnt to read or write, built more than 365 miles of canals.

Turn left down the road, passing Hassop Farm and the Elizabethan Wormhill Hall, the ancestral home of the Bagshawe family.

8 After a bend in the road, take the footpath on the right signposted to Chee Dale and Blackwell. Keep to the left around the hillside, ignoring paths that drop to the right. The rocky path descends to a footbridge over the Wye.

DETOUR *Just before the bridge, turn right and walk along the river, which gurgles over rippling falls, to where springs and the rocky face of Chee Tor announce the entrance to Chee Dale. Continue through this spectacular gorge, walking over large stepping stones in the river, to a wooden footbridge, and return.*

9 Do not cross the bridge, but continue on the path with the river on the right towards Miller's Dale station, climbing the steep embankment beside a viaduct to return to the Monsal Trail. Turn left past some limekilns, which can be visited. Leave the trail and go through a gate into the station car park.

DERBYSHIRE

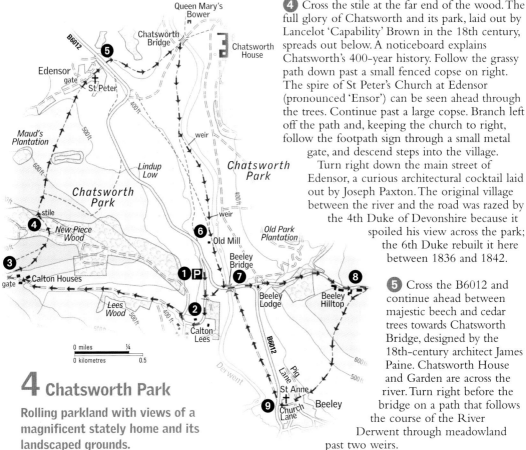

4 Cross the stile at the far end of the wood. The full glory of Chatsworth and its park, laid out by Lancelot 'Capability' Brown in the 18th century, spreads out below. A noticeboard explains Chatsworth's 400-year history. Follow the grassy path down past a small fenced copse on right. The spire of St Peter's Church at Edensor (pronounced 'Ensor') can be seen ahead through the trees. Continue past a large copse. Branch left off the path and, keeping the church to right, follow the footpath sign through a small metal gate, and descend steps into the village.

Turn right down the main street of Edensor, a curious architectural cocktail laid out by Joseph Paxton. The original village between the river and the road was razed by the 4th Duke of Devonshire because it spoiled his view across the park; the 6th Duke rebuilt it here between 1836 and 1842.

5 Cross the B6012 and continue ahead between majestic beech and cedar trees towards Chatsworth Bridge, designed by the 18th-century architect James Paine. Chatsworth House and Garden are across the river. Turn right before the bridge on a path that follows the course of the River Derwent through meadowland past two weirs.

4 Chatsworth Park

Rolling parkland with views of a magnificent stately home and its landscaped grounds.

LENGTH 6 miles (3 hours)

PARKING Calton Lees car park, off B6012 about 1½ miles north of Beeley

CONDITIONS Mainly gentle gradients

REFRESHMENTS Pub in Beeley, restaurants at Chatsworth House and Garden Centre

1 Go to the far end of the car park and follow the lane past Chatsworth Garden Centre to the village of Calton Lees and a small T-junction.

2 Where the lane bends sharply left, follow the footpath sign straight ahead through a gateway onto a track. Continue for ¾ mile up a gentle incline, with a stream to left and steep meadows to the right.

3 At the hamlet of Calton Houses, look back for a magnificent view over the valley and parkland. Walk on between houses, go through a gate and take the path on the right. It leads beside a stone wall to a wide meadow with a barn and cottage to the right, before entering a narrow strip of woodland.

6 After the second weir, the ruins of the Old Mill appear. Built by James Paine, the mill was used until 1952. In 1962 it was badly damaged by falling trees, but its fine proportions still provide an enchanting focus for the park's southern edge. The path meets the B6012 by Beeley Bridge, also designed by Paine.

7 Turn left on the road, cross the bridge and continue towards Beeley, another well-preserved estate village. Fork left by Beeley Lodge up a steep narrow lane to the cluster of buildings and farm called Beeley Hilltop.

8 Soon after the lane becomes a track, take the path on right just beyond the last farm building. The path leads diagonally across the farmyard and out at the far right-hand corner, then passes to the right of a stone wall and continues down through meadows to the village of Beeley and its largely Norman church of St Anne.

9 Cross the B6012 and take the path ahead back to Beeley Bridge. Cross the bridge and turn left on the path to return to the car park.

5 Gradbach

Across an open hillside along a gritstone ridge, through a quiet valley and over moorland to a spectacular 'secret' gorge.

LENGTH 5 or 6 miles (3 or 3½ hours)

PARKING Peak National Park car park by River Dane, about 2½ miles west of Flash

CONDITIONS Muddy in parts; one steep climb

REFRESHMENTS Gradbach Mill (weekends)

1 Turn right out of the car park, passing a driveway on the right to Gradbach Youth Hostel, a converted 18th-century flax mill. Where the road forks, with the chapel of the Buxton and District Boy Scout campsite on the left, continue down the narrow road, ignoring a marked path to the right, and walk left up through two styles bordering a farmyard. Take the waymarked path onto Gradbach Hill, a craggy gritstone ridge topped by wind-sculpted tors. Follow a rough waymarked path for about ¾ mile along the lower edge of the fields just below the ridge on the left. To the right a wood, then a patchwork of smaller fields, descend to Black Brook.

2 Follow the path diagonally left through a gap in the tumbledown wall ahead. Continue half left across the field, heading towards a wall leading over the brow of the hill. Go through a gate stile onto the waymarked path leading uphill over peaty moorland, with striking views to the right across the valley. Beyond the brow of the hill, continue to follow the waymarked path. Go over a stile next to a gate and on down a grassy track.

3 Just before a road, pass a farm entrance and take the footpath on right signposted to Roach End. Keep to the left of a solitary stone gatepost. Pass through a narrow stile ahead and turn immediately right through a gap in a broken-down wall. Continue on the path to another stile and head down the next field path running above Black Brook from Goldsitch House on the left.

4 Turn right and go over a stile in the wall, down a short field to another stone stile leading to the water's edge. The path follows Black Brook, then climbs above it to a four-way signpost before dropping sharply through a stile, across a footbridge and up through thigh-high heather on the other side. At the top of the hill, continue past a large stone house and on up a track.

DETOUR *To see dramatic jagged gritstone rock formations, continue on the track to a road. Turn left and immediately right up stone steps, where Bearstone Rock looms to the right, and follow the path for ½ mile towards The Roaches. From the trig point, 505m (1,657ft) above sea level, there are tremendous views over three counties – Derbyshire, Staffordshire and Cheshire.*

5 Follow the path on the right near the top of the track over a stile in a wall and turn sharp right down to Back Forest, a mature wood of birch, oak, spruce and larch, carpeted with heather, bracken and bilberry.

6 Just inside the wood, fork left towards Lud's Church, a dramatic gorge where 13th-century Lollards, rebel Church reformers, are said to have worshipped. Keep following signs for the gorge; heeding the erosion warning, bear left to the top of the gorge then descend steps on the right and walk between the sheer faces of the rock fissure.

7 At the far end of the gorge, climb up and turn left down a path. At a rocky outcrop turn sharp right, following a sign for Gradbach. At a second fingerpost head down the stone steps towards the River Dane. At a footbridge over Black Brook, turn right up the track and left over a stone stile onto a path close to the river. Bear right past the youth hostel and continue to the road. Turn left to the car park.

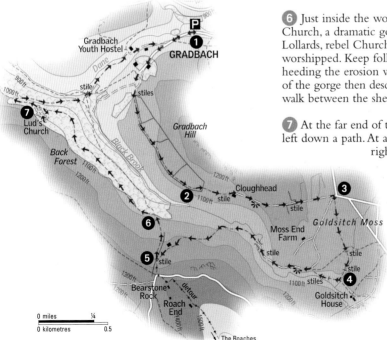

DERBYSHIRE

6 Mam Tor

A steep climb to the ridge of the Shivering Mountain and its Bronze Age hillfort, and on through a dale with a Norman ruin.

LENGTH 5½ miles (3½ hours)

PARKING Car park in Castleton, off A625

CONDITIONS Demanding; steep section to the ridge has deep ruts and becomes very slippery in wet weather; walking boots essential

REFRESHMENTS Full range in Castleton

1 With your back to the main road, take the footpath running along the right edge of the car park to Hollowford Road and turn left, signposted to Hollins Cross and Edale. After 100m, turn left on an unmarked track overhung with trees, beside a stream. The track emerges from the trees into fields, with a view to the left of the high cliff of Mam Tor. Continue over a series of stiles to Dunscar Farm – the cluster of buildings among trees ahead.

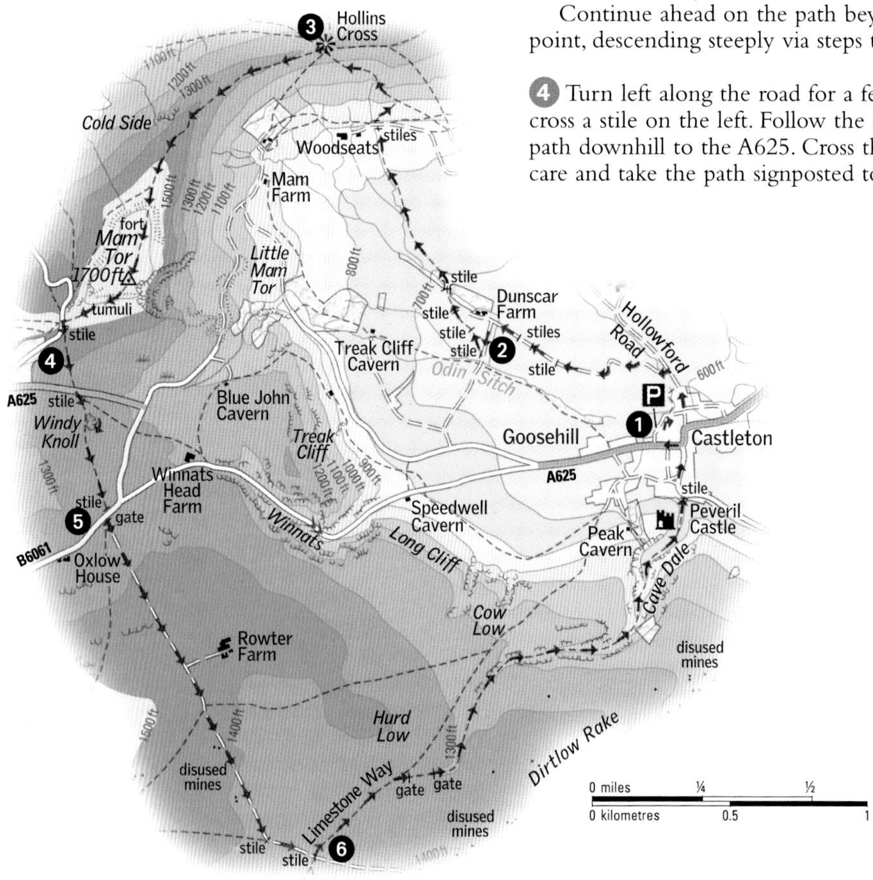

2 At Dunscar Farm, turn left down the drive for a short distance to a stile on the right. Leave the drive and cross the stile into the fields. Proceed over more stiles to a footbridge over a brook. Beyond the footbridge, the path bends left to follow the brook up a gentle slope to the base of Hollins Cross – the steep hill ahead. Cross the two stiles close together at the foot of the hill. Follow the zigzag route to a cairn on the summit, where a number of ancient bridleways from Hope and Castleton to Edale meet.

3 With your back to the path you came up, turn sharp left at Hollins Cross summit and follow the path along the ridge for ¾ mile to Mam Tor. There are stunning views to the right across Edale to Kinder Scout, and on the left to the high country beyond Castleton.

Follow the wide, paved path to the trig point at the 518m (1,700ft) summit of Mam Tor – the site of a Bronze Age hillfort, whose huge rampart is enclosed by a single ditch 2m (7ft) deep; large quantities of jewellery, pottery and weapons, up to 4,000 years old, were excavated there in the 1960s. Known locally as Shivering Mountain, Mam Tor has an unstable shale face, and landslips have carried away sections of the hillfort.

Continue ahead on the path beyond the trig point, descending steeply via steps to a road.

4 Turn left along the road for a few yards, then cross a stile on the left. Follow the signposted path downhill to the A625. Cross the road with care and take the path signposted to Windy

Knoll, a shallow cavern to the side of the path, where more than 6,500 animal bones, dating from the Stone Age, were discovered in 1875. The cave was once a waterhole where grizzly bears, sabre-toothed tigers, bison, wolves and reindeer stopped to drink. Cross a stile at the top of the field onto the B6061.

5 Cross the road and go through a gate just to the right, then follow a surfaced drive leading to Rowter Farm. Walk along the drive until it bends sharp left into the farmyard, then go straight ahead on a rough track across upland pasture. Ignore a footpath to left signposted to Castleton, and continue to a T-junction. Turn left to meet the signposted Limestone Way at a stile.

6 Cross the stile and turn left on the Limestone Way towards Castleton, passing old mine workings on the right. Where the path divides a short distance farther on, fork right and continue downhill, through rolling turf-covered terrain. Go through a couple of metal gates across the track to arrive in the upper reaches of Cave Dale. This deep ravine was probably formed at the end of the last Ice Age, when water from melting glaciers eroded the porous limestone.

As the path drops deeper into the gorge, there is a dramatic view on left of the Norman keep of Peveril Castle, perched above pale limestone bluffs and protected on three sides by natural fortifications. The castle was begun by William Peveril, one of William the Conqueror's knights, and completed by Henry II.

Cross a stile at end of the path to reach the edge of Castleton. The car park is a few minutes' walk away, across Market Place and down cottage-lined Castle Street.

AN EERIE NORMAN RUIN
PEVERIL CASTLE AND VIEW DOWN CAVE DALE

DERBYSHIRE

7 Edale

A challenging walk in the highest reaches of the Peak District, taking in part of the Pennine Way.

LENGTH 7 miles (5 hours)

PARKING Edale car park

CONDITIONS A challenging walk that should be attempted only when the weather is fine and the forecast good, and not after heavy rain or snow; wear walking boots and take a compass, waterproofs and warm clothing

REFRESHMENTS None on walk; pubs in Edale

1 Go down the steps from the car park and turn right to follow the lane north through Edale village and Grindsbrook Booth, beyond which it becomes an unsurfaced track. Where the track divides, fork right through a narrow wooden gate. Cross a footbridge over Grinds Brook and a stile beyond.

2 Climb the stile and follow a path paved with squares of natural stone over open pasture, with the brook sheltered by trees on the left. After a short distance the path divides. Fork left, towards the head of the valley, and continue through a small copse with a stile on its far boundary.

3 Cross a stile and footbridge just beyond it to emerge into open country of heather, bracken,

peat and rock, where the silence is punctuated only by the bleating of sheep and the chatter of streams. Beyond a small waterfall on Grinds Brook, the path becomes steeper, winding beside and crossing the boulder-edged brook. Not far below the summit, the main stream curves away round a bend to the right, and a tributary joins from the left.

4 Turn left and follow the course of the tributary, scrambling up a staircase of boulders to a cairn, where the path divides.

With your back to the path you walked up, turn half left at the cairn – southwest, if you are using a compass – and follow a poorly defined path across level ground for about 250m to a rocky outcrop, which is not immediately visible from the cairn.

5 Beyond the outcrop, take the well-worn path skirting the edge of the escarpment. There are fine views to the left across the Vale of Edale to Mam Tor and Hollins Cross. To the right is Kinder Scout, the Dark Peak's highest point, and close to the scene in 1932 of a mass trespass by people campaigning for freer access to the countryside.

Continue along the path to Crowden Clough, then up to Crowden Tower, perched above the deep cleft of the clough.

6 From here the path links a number of eroded rock formations – the Wool Packs, Pym Chair and Noe Stool – before bending left and

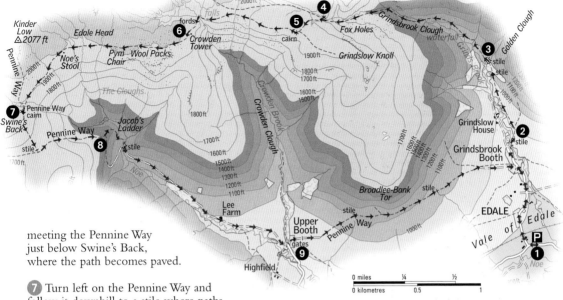

meeting the Pennine Way
just below Swine's Back,
where the path becomes paved.

7 Turn left on the Pennine Way and
follow it downhill to a stile where paths
cross. Cross the stile and turn sharp left, still
on the Pennine Way, which descends to the
head of a gorge.

8 Fork left, down a paved, stepped section
of the path known as Jacob's Ladder. From
the bottom of the steps continue across a
stone bridge over the Noe and go over a stile
beyond it. The path follows the left side of a
valley to merge with a track from Lee Farm
to Upper Booth.

9 Turn left by the phone kiosk and follow
Pennine Way signs through a farmyard bounded
on both sides by stiles. Turn right at the second
gate to follow a waymarked path.

The final stretch of the walk, signposted to
Grindsbrook Booth and Edale, follows a path
uphill across fields to the base of the escarpment.
Walk ahead on a straight, gentle downhill path
to the lane at Grindsbrook Booth. Turn right to
return to the car park.

OPEN COUNTRY OF
HEATHER, BRACKEN,
PEAT AND ROCK
GRINDSBROOK AND GRINDSLOW KNOLL, ABOVE EDALE

GLOUCESTERSHIRE

The ancient Forest of Dean to the west of Gloucestershire is one of the county's major attractions. To the east, the 102-mile Cotswold Way traces the Cotswold escarpment and forms part of the featured walk from Winchcombe.

1 Forest of Dean

A walk along forest tracks that takes in traces of old mines and a modern sculpture trail.

LENGTH 6½ miles (4 hours)

PARKING Cannop Ponds car park, off B4226 east of Broadwell

CONDITIONS Clear paths and tracks; one steep but short climb

REFRESHMENTS Kiosk at Cannop Ponds; café at Beechenhurst Lodge

1 Follow the tarmac road beyond the car park, by the end of a first pond, to a gate across the cycle track. Immediately past the gate, turn right to follow the path along a second pond. Both ponds were once reservoirs feeding a water wheel for ironworks at Parkend. At the end of the pond, turn left on the footpath and bear left across the cycle track, which runs on the bed of the former Severn and Wye Railway. Go through a swing gate, joining the 100-mile Gloucestershire Way, to a junction with a broad track.

2 Turn left on the track and continue ahead, ignoring paths on the left. At a junction, where the Gloucestershire Way goes right, continue ahead to a junction with the B4226.

3 Cross the road and turn right, then bear left into Beechenhurst Lodge picnic site. Beyond the

lodge, follow the signposted Sculpture Trail uphill to a large log chair and a viewpoint.

4 Turn left and follow the track downhill. Where the track bends right, continue forward on a narrower path, passing the Heart of Stone sculpture in a clearing on the left then descending to a gate. Cross a cycle track, climb the stile and continue over a bridge across Cannop Brook. Cross a road and take the path ahead through an oak wood. At a crossing track continue ahead on he uphill path to meet a broad track.

5 Take the narrow path ahead, bearing left on reaching a grass track. Keep ahead on the forest path, rising steeply. Where the slope eases, at a track junction, there are good forest views. Continue ahead uphill; the path soon levels, then drops to another broad track.

6 Cross the track and continue ahead on the uphill path, with conifers on the left. Continue to a T-junction with a broad track, ignoring crossing paths.

7 Turn right. After 175m, at a track junction, turn left onto a narrow footpath through conifers. Fork left, then bear right onto a broad track.

8 Turn left onto a stony downhill path. At a junction turn right onto the path down Wimberry Slade, on an old tram road. Continue past a working coal mine on the left to a track crossing. Turn left and then, just past an information board, turn right on a downhill track through conifers, which bends left to pass a council depot. This was once Cannop Colliery. At a tarmac road turn right, past a cycle centre, down to the B4234.

9 Cross the road and bear right onto the cycle track. Cross another road and continue along the cycle track onto the ponds' access road. After 70m, turn right onto a footpath back to the car park.

2 Winchcombe

Wide-ranging views along the Cotswold Way and from the outstanding prehistoric burial mound of Belas Knap.

LENGTH 5 or 6 miles (2½ or 3 hours)

PARKING In Vineyard Street

CONDITIONS One moderate climb

REFRESHMENTS Range in Winchcombe

1 Walk towards Sudeley Castle along Vineyard Street – formerly called Duck Street, as it led to a ducking stool in the River Isbourne. Cross the bridge over the river, then turn right opposite Almsbury Farm through a kissing gate by a signpost for the Cotswold Way. Cross the field to a gate opposite and go over the brow of the hill. Follow the path to a meeting with a road.

2 Turn left and walk along the road. After about ¼ mile turn right through the entrance to Corndean Hall, signposted Cotswold Way.

3 Where the drive meets a path fork left, cross a kissing gate and head uphill, following waymarks to the right of the first oak tree. Climb over the stone stile at the top of the hill by a road junction, or go through the kissing gate. Continue on the road ahead for 100m to a stile on the right.

4 Turn right over the stile and continue up through woodland, following signs to Belas Knap. The path soon climbs steadily, arriving at a kissing gate where commanding views of Winchcombe and Sudeley Castle reward the walker's effort. Continue along the path to a stone stile, beyond which is the burial mound. Built in about 2000 BC and measuring 54m (178ft) long by 5.5m (18ft) wide, Belas Knap long barrow lay undisturbed for almost 4,000 years. Excavations in the mid-19th century revealed remains of 38 skeletons in four separate burial chambers.

5 Retrace your steps to the road, with views over Cleeve Common to the left. Turn right onto the road and continue along it for about ⅓ mile. The road is narrow and well used by vehicles, so exercise caution.

6 Turn sharp left down a track signposted as a public footpath, which leads past the remains of a Roman villa on the left. All that can be seen is a stone-wall enclosure, planted with pine trees; there is no public access to the villa remains.

7 Keeping farm buildings on the left, continue on a path, edged first by hedges on both sides and then by a fence and a hedge, past Wadfield Farm with its large stone gateposts. The name Wadfield derives from the word 'woad', a plant yielding blue dye used by ancient Britons and once grown in the area.

There are striking views of Sudeley Castle and the surrounding countryside as the path descends gently through farmland. Climb a stile and continue along the field boundary as it curves round, past a gate, to reach a stile in the hedge on the right.

8 Cross the stile and turn left along the edge of a field. Bear left over a narrow wooden bridge, then cross two fields, linked by another bridge, on a well-worn, often muddy, track, heading towards the tower of St Peter's Church in Winchcombe. Cross a slab bridge and a stile to enter a third field, aiming for a marker on the telegraph pole, then for a gate. At the lane turn left and continue to the gatehouse entrance to Sudeley Castle.

DETOUR *Turn right through the gates. A chestnut avenue leads through rolling parkland, passing a ruined tithe barn, to the castle and its splendid gardens. Sudeley Castle (NT) was largely rebuilt in the 19th century, and the ruins of the 15th-century banqueting hall are the only remnants of a building that was demolished in 1649.*

9 From the castle gates follow Vineyard Street past a row of almshouses on the right back to the parking place.

WINCHCOMBE B4632 gate Isbourne detour gate Beesmoor Brook stile Sudeley Castle Wadfield Grove stile stile Corndean Lane gate Cotswold Way stile Wadfield Farm stiles remains of Roman villa gate Belas Knap stile long barrow

0 miles ¼
0 kilometres 0.5

GLOUCESTERSHIRE

3 Haresfield Beacon

Through beech woodland and pasture to magnificent views from the crest of the western Cotswolds.

LENGTH 4½ or 6 miles (2½ or 3½ hours)

PARKING Shortwood car park

CONDITIONS Generally firm paths

REFRESHMENTS None on walk; pub in Edge

1 Turn right out of the car park, cross a stile and take the path leading through a wood. Continue along the edge of fields with a wood on the right (where roe deer can sometimes be seen) for about ½ mile, passing a small tumulus on the left. Cross a stile to meet a road, and turn left along the road to a T-junction signposted to Haresfield Edge.

2 Turn left, and just beyond, turn right between Stoneridge Farm and Harefield Farm onto a track that descends gently. Cross a stile and turn left on an indistinct path beside a wire-fenced area on the left, walking over pasture to Pitchcombe Wood. From here there are fine views of the Painswick Valley. Cross over a stone stile and turn right, keeping the wood to the right. Then follow signs to the left, along an indistinct path, to a stile by a road.

3 Cross the stile, turn right and immediately left over another stile into woodland. Almost immediately turn right along a bridleway and continue ahead to meet the road again.

Cross the stile and road, heading to the right, and take the path on the left. Walk past the grassy mounds of disused quarries, bearing right towards a drystone wall, then downhill with Painswick church spire visible ahead, ignoring a path to the left.

SNOWFALL IN THE COTSWOLD HILLS AT HARESFIELD BEACON

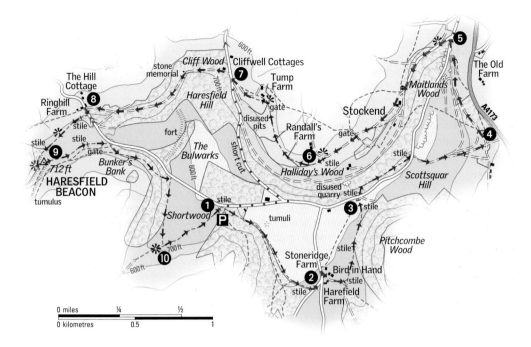

4 At a crossing of tracks, turn left onto a path running parallel to the A4173. Follow the path through woodland and at the minor road beyond it, turn right and continue ahead for 100m.

5 Turn sharp left onto a metalled track, with Haresfield Hill and Cliff Wood ahead. Increasingly fine views extend to the right beyond lush rolling pasture towards the Vale of Gloucester. At a fork, bear right and continue on the metalled track for about ½ mile to the entrance to Randall's Farm.

6 Go through a gate onto a metalled drive with Halliday's Wood to the left. Just beyond a horse training area on the right, leave the metalled track, which bears right to the farm, and cross a stile. Follow the path over several fields, with views of Gloucester Cathedral and Robins Wood Hill to the right.

Eventually the path descends slightly and bends left between thorn trees and past craters of disused pits on the left, then broadens and winds through woodland to a metalled road. SHORT CUT *Turn left onto the road and follow it as it skirts the edge of Halliday's Wood. At a T-junction turn sharp right and continue ahead to return to the car park.*

7 Turn right on the road and soon take a path forking to the left, with a blue Cotswold Way mark on a post, past a cottage and into Cliff Wood. Where the path bends left, a stone memorial commemorates the ending of the Siege of Gloucester by Royalist troops in 1643.

Follow the broad path through the wood for about a mile, crossing a track before you reach a metalled road.

8 Turn left up the road and soon turn right on a path signposted to Haresfield Beacon. Pass stables, cross a stile and follow the broad track uphill with views to the Forest of Dean and Malvern Hills. At a farm gate the path narrows, climbing between a barbed-wire fence and trees. Cross a waymarked stile and follow the grassy path ahead up to Haresfield Beacon, 217m (712ft) above sea level, and crowned by Iron Age earthworks with spectacular views.

9 To descend, face the radio transmitter tower visible on the skyline, walk down a very short distance and turn left on a path. Go through a gate and follow the path as it dips and climbs, keeping a wire fence on the left. Go through a waymarked squeeze stile and a gate, and continue along the edge of the hill.

At the road, turn right down steps, signposted Cotswold Way, and follow the path along the edge of a wood. Go through a gate and climb through woodland. Follow the waymark sign to the right across pasture to the topograph, a circular, three-dimensional map of the local countryside cast in bronze, showing the landmarks of the panoramic view.

10 From the topograph, continue in the direction of the radio transmitter tower on the skyline, and turn left on a well-trodden narrow path back to the car park.

GLOUCESTERSHIRE

4 Peaked Down

Over Cam Long Down to an Iron Age fort, with a detour to Owlpen Manor within a restored Tudor estate.

LENGTH 5½ miles (3 hours)

PARKING Car park by Peaked Down, off road from Cam to Ashmead Green

CONDITIONS Generally easy

REFRESHMENTS Pub in Uley

1 From the car park take the right-hand track uphill, then bear right up the steep grassy path with Peaked Down on the right. Follow the path to the left over the crest, bearing left downhill. At a junction of several paths, follow the blue arrow and acorn sign ahead up a steep rutted track to the top of Cam Long Down.

Magnificent views stretch in all directions. In the foreground to the right, the isolated hill topped with a clump of trees is Downham Hill, also known as Smallpox Hill, the site of an 18th-century isolation hospital for smallpox victims: food was left at the base of the hill for collection.

Continue ahead and descend Cam Long Down on a gravelly track towards a farm. Go over a waymarked stile, continue to the right of the farm buildings and onto a metalled lane. Turn left at the T-junction and continue past Hodgecombe Farm and along the steep gravel track ahead, marked Cotswolds Way, to the top of the hill and a layby beside a road.

2 Turn right onto a bridleway through a gap next to a gate, forking away from the road. At a junction turn left along a well-trodden path, with the Iron Age fort of Uley Bury on the right. At a fork, take the bridleway to the left downhill. At a path junction, go through a gate into woodland and continue straight ahead down to a gate with views over Uley and beyond.

Go through the gate and continue ahead downhill across pasture, towards the church tower and through a kissing gate. Continue ahead on a narrow path between gardens to the churchyard. At the T-junction turn left beside the wall around the churchyard to a road.

3 Cross over and bear left past 17th-century Old Crown inn, then turn right down Fiery Lane and continue ahead to Owlpen. In the hamlet is Owlpen Manor, on a restored Tudor estate, and the Victorian Church of the Holy Cross which contains unusual Pre-Raphaelite mosaics.

Where the road bends to the right, turn right over a stile on a path that skirts the fields beside the River Ewelme, crossing several stiles to reach a path junction. Turn right onto a path over a bridge and up a metalled road to a T-junction. Turn left and after 60m turn right onto a metalled path between gardens. At the T-junction turn left past a school to reach a lane. Turn right and follow the lane to Uley's main street.

4 Turn right and just past the post office turn left on an uphill track. At the top turn left through a kissing gate. Go through another kissing gate and take the grassy path towards Uley Bury, following it to the left between wire fencing. Cross a stile on the right onto a path up a field and into woods and follow the waymarked path bending left uphill. Near the top turn right onto a path uphill and then left at a wooden gate. The path bends right, crossing several other paths, with a disused quarry on right. Follow the track downhill, passing exposed tree roots clinging to the sheer limestone beneath them.

5 At a road junction continue ahead past Hydegate Kennels. After 100m fork right onto a narrow hedged path. Turn right at a junction of tracks and follow a broad stony track uphill towards Cam Long Down. Where the main track bends right, fork left on a hedged track uphill through a gate. At a five-path signpost, bear left towards Peaked Down then immediately right, back to the car park.

132

5 Bourton-on-the-Water

Quiet strolls beside trout streams, across fields and down country lanes, passing mellow Cotswold villages.

LENGTH 6 miles (3 hours)

PARKING Car park near Birdland

CONDITIONS Easy going

REFRESHMENTS Tearooms and pubs in Bourton; tearoom at mill and hotel in Lower Slaughter; hotel in Upper Slaughter

1 Walk along the main street to St Lawrence's Church on the right. Turn right on a footpath beside the church to a crossing of paths, then turn left behind the houses and continue to an enclosed path. When this turns right, go up and over the disused railway line, then follow the path through fields to reach the main road, the Foss Way.

Cross the road and climb a stile into a field. Go to a marker post in the hedge opposite and cross a footbridge over a stream, leading to a stile into the next field. Follow the blue arrow on a slight diagonal to the right. The view opens out over gently undulating hills, patched with woodland. Climb a stile onto a lane and turn right.

2 Follow the lane as it swings left, then turn right through a gate and follow an enclosed bridleway through fields. At a crossing, continue ahead to the village of Lower Slaughter. The River Eye runs beside the track, tumbling over small weirs. Turn left at the village road then cross the road ahead, past stone cottages with slate roofs, and along the riverside path past the mill.

3 Turn left at a signpost to Wardens Way and continue through gates to a tranquil riverside walk. When the path reaches a gate, turn away from the river and head across a field then cross parkland dotted with giant oaks, past an Elizabethan manor on the left. Cross a footbridge over the river and follow the path to a road leading to Upper Slaughter.

4 Turn left into the village. A chapel in St Peter's Church is dedicated to Francis Witts (1783-1854), rector and lord of the manor, whose *Diary of a Cotswold Parson* described the life of the area. With the church to the right, continue to the left of an island of trees, out of the village. At a T-junction go straight ahead on a path that climbs to a wood. Before reaching the wood turn right on a track. Go through a gate and continue ahead, veering slightly left up a slope, through several more gates, to a road.

5 Turn left and walk past Manor Farm and the manor itself, hidden behind an immense yew hedge. Continue for ½ mile and look out for a small layby on the right, then take the bridleway leading off it, to a signpost on the right.

6 Turn left onto an enclosed bridleway and follow this to a signposted right turn. Go down to a gate and continue with the hedge on the right, then pass through a gate and along an enclosed bridleway to a bridge over the River Windrush. Cross the road onto the riverside road opposite. Immediately beyond the first house on the right, turn right onto a path. Cross a footbridge and walk along the other side of the river, over a stream and on to a gate in the far corner of a field. Go through the gate onto a narrow path. At a road, turn left to the crossroads, then turn right to return to the car park.

(map)

St Peter

Upper Slaughter

parkland

gate

gate

gates   gate

Eye

5

Manor Farm

St Mary

gates

3

Wagborough Bush

Pennshill

Lower Slaughter

disused quarry

Springhill Barn

wall

Wall

disused quarry

600 ft

gate

2   gate

500 ft

stile

Foss Way

gate

mill

6   500 ft

Slaughter Farm

stile

playing fields

dismantled railway

stile

BOURTON-ON-THE-WATER

Windrush

gate   gate

St Lawrence

gate

0 miles   ¼

0 kilometres   0.5

1 P

Birdland

Inner city rambles

Birmingham's historic network of canal paths flow deep
into the Midlands' industrial heartland.

The year 1769 was a seminal one for walking in the Midlands, though not for immediately obvious reasons. That year, pioneer canal engineer and untutored genius James Brindley brought his Birmingham Canal Navigation into the city centre from the coalfields of Wednesbury, 9 miles away to the northwest in the Black Country. The brass-workers, ironmasters and toolmakers of Birmingham had become desperate for cheap coal and were sick of the delays caused by horse-drawn consignments bumping slowly over bad roads. As soon as the canal opened, the precious black fuel came pouring in and its price plummeted.

Brindley, the semi-literate innovator, had introduced a transport system that was to catapult the city of Birmingham to the peak of its 19th-century prosperity. In the process, he laid the foundations for some of the best walking in England's grey industrial heartlands, which today still lend an extra dimension to the Midland routes in this guide. The towpaths alongside Birmingham's canal system, redundant for decades as commercial thoroughfares, offer the urban walker a remarkable network of waterside routes through the heart of England's second city. And the canals stretching beyond the city boundary offer further easy walking to anyone who can follow a basic large-scale map.

James Brindley would gasp in astonishment at Gas Street Basin in Birmingham's city centre today. Up to 9m (30ft) above canal level, the scene looks not unlike that which the great engineer would have known: red-brick tollhouses and whitewashed canal-company offices, a stumpy factory chimney and lines of moored narrowboats. But behind and above all of these, tower the architectural grandiosities of the late 20th century: smooth-faced giants of tinted glass and concrete, so out of proportion to what surrounds them that the eye tends to discard them in favour of detail of a more human dimension – lunchtime drinkers, two men eating sandwiches, a dog barking at a swan.

Linking city to country

Where Brindley had shown the way by water into Birmingham, others were not slow to follow. By 1792 the Worcester & Birmingham Canal Company had begun to dig southwards from Gas Street Basin to create a route to the River Severn and the Bristol Channel via the city of Worcester – a good 29-mile trek from Birmingham, mostly along towpaths but occasionally using other paths to circumvent tunnels. Its great highlight is the descent of the spectacular flight of 30 locks at Tardebigge, but much of it makes good country walking. The best sections are between Tibberton and Stoke Prior (which includes the flight of locks) and between Stoke Prior and Wast Hills.

By the 1850s there were 160 miles of canals in the Birmingham area. 'More canals than Venice' was the boast of the locals, who soon began referring to their city – with more dark humour than discernment – as the 'Venice of the North'.

Crossing Broad Street and the windy prairie of Centenary Square from Gas Street Basin, walkers get a real sense of the energy and optimism of Victorian Birmingham. Matthew Boulton, James Watts and William Murdoch, three great entrepreneurial heroes of the Industrial

Revolution, stand grave on a common plinth, their capable hands full of plans for the future. Nearby, a complicated modern sculpture shows massed ranks of joyful citizenry, striding towards the technological future from the smoke-belching factories of the past.

Waterside walkways

Beyond Centenary Square, walkways drop to reach the towpath of the Birmingham & Fazeley Canal. Here are the arteries of water that lie – largely unseen – below the city. The Birmingham & Fazeley, engineered by the brilliant Scotsman John Smeaton and opened in 1789, was always a problem to operate around the 13 busy locks at Farmer's Bridge, where round-the-clock traffic jams built up as the barge skippers jostled, manoeuvred and sometimes fought for entry to the locks. Halfway down the lock flight, it used to be possible to climb up to Newhall Street and

visit Birmingham's splendid Museum of Science and Industry. But this treasure house of beam engines, bottling machines, hydraulic pumps, pistons and flywheels closed in 1997 and, since then, the city has lacked a dedicated science museum.

Back up the lock-flight slope, walkers will find themselves at Deep Cutting Junction. England's vast canal system describes a giant figure-of-eight, with its centre right here, at this spot in the heart of Birmingham, where three canals meet – the Birmingham Canal Navigation, the Worcester & Birmingham and the Birmingham & Fazeley. This is where narrowboat skippers and towpath walkers pause at the start or the end of their journey. Looking over towards Birmingham's heartland, beyond the futuristic glass towers, low brick archways lead the eye beneath humpbacked canal bridges more than two centuries old, to where treacle-black water reflects the city's enterprising past.

BOULTON, WATTS AND MURDOCH; BROAD STREET, BIRMINGHAM

HEREFORDSHIRE

An unspoilt, sparsely populated county, known for its fruit farms, cider and Herefordshire cattle. On its western border with Wales are rolling hills with good walking trails that offer far-reaching views.

1 Black Hill

An exhilarating ridge-top walk, giving panoramas over moor, remote valley and gentle farmland.

LENGTH 5 miles (3 hours)

PARKING Black Hill picnic site, signposted from Llanveynoe, north of Longtown

CONDITIONS Steep climb at start; some rough paths

REFRESHMENTS None on walk; nearest pub in Longtown

1 From the top of the car park and picnic area, cross the stile to the left of a gate. Avoid the level track to the right and take the path that rises straight up onto the ridge of Black Hill – Crib y Garth. The hill was the setting for Bruce Chatwin's novel *On the Black Hill*, published in 1982. The story is about twin brothers who grow up through the 20th century on a farm called the

Vision, after a farm in the Vale of Ewyas. The fictional local market town of Rhulen is based on nearby Hay-on-Wye.

Follow the path along the knife-edge ridge. A magnificent panorama spreads out over the Olchon Valley on the left, and the gentle folds of the Monnow, Escley and Golden valleys to the Malvern Hills on the right.

As the ridge widens, the path follows its right-hand side. Continue to the triangulation pillar at the 640m (2,100ft) summit. The Black Hill is unique among the Black Mountains in that it lies in England and is therefore outside the Brecon Beacons National Park.

2 Keep to the main path, which leads back towards the middle of the ridge, and the head of the Olchon Valley comes into view on the left. The moors on the summit are alive with skylarks, and buzzards are very likely to be seen. Another regular bird is the merlin, close to its southerly limit in Britain. Welsh mountain ponies also graze the hills.

Continue for nearly a mile, then keep a look out on the left for a little path through the heather, which leads down into the head of the Olchon Valley.

3 Turn sharp left on the path, leaving the main route, which continues along the ridge to join Offa's Dyke Path. The way down into the Olchon Valley becomes clearer, passing a roofless stone ruin on the right and a stream in a gorge, bounded by craggy slopes. High on top of the ridge on the right, the English-Welsh border accompanies Offa's Dyke Path.

4 Where a fence joins on the right, continue on the uneven path down to a track leading between banks to a lane.

5 Turn left on the lane, with views between ash, beech and oak trees over the lower Olchon Valley on the right.

6 After about a mile, turn left at a road junction back to the car park.

Map labels: Darren, stone ruin, 2000ft, 1900ft, 1800ft, 1700ft, 1600ft, 1500ft, 1400ft, Black Hill, 2100ft, Crib y Garth, Upper Blaen, gate, Town House, Firs Farm, The Place, Blaen, Penywyrlod, 1200ft, 1100ft, 1000ft, Olchon Brook, Olchon Valley, Sunny Bank, gate and stile

0 miles ¼ ½

0 kilometres 0.5 1

2 Kington

A glorious walk for views, including glimpses of the Brecon Beacons and the Malvern Hills.

LENGTH 6 miles (3 hours)

PARKING Car park behind Burton Hotel

CONDITIONS Straightforward; two gentle slopes

REFRESHMENTS Hotel in Kington

1 Leave the car park on the path signposted to the High Street. Turn left towards the clock tower, then right to follow the road uphill. At the Swan Hotel turn right into The Square, then left into a second square. Continue past Walnut Gardens, then bear right downhill. You have now joined the long-distance Offa's Dyke Path, which is waymarked with acorn symbols. At a junction go straight down Crooked Well to a footbridge over a stream.

2 Go over the bridge, then cross the A44 with care and follow the lane opposite. Where the lane bends left, turn right, signposted to Offa's Dyke Path. Follow the path through a gate and across a field, to cross another gate by the cottages of Bradnor Green hamlet.

3 Continue to a signpost 50m ahead, then turn left on a track that rises gently and splits into three by the corner of a wall. Take the middle track, which passes close to the bottom of a common. On the distant left is the long whaleback hill known as Hergest Ridge. Beyond are the flat-topped Black Mountains and twin summits of the Brecon Beacons. Continue to where the track divides just before Bank House, on the left.

Keep right and go downhill past an old water pump in trees on the right. Keep to the right of the Croftlands driveway, on a track along the left edge of a large field.

4 At the end of the field go through a gate and follow the track through a conifer plantation. At the end of the plantation, go through a gate and cross the field to a stile. Over the stile follow a path that runs alongside woodland, with farm buildings a short way off on the left, then cross a stile on the left into a field. Follow the waymark arrow on the stile to join a track near the bottom left corner of the field. Follow the track through more fields to a stone ruin on the left.

5 Beyond the ruin turn left and cross a stile into a field. After a second stile bear right to a signpost on the shoulder of Herrock Hill. Turn right onto Offa's Dyke Path and follow the acorn symbols. The path now follows a section of the great earthwork built for Offa in the 9th century to mark the western boundary of his kingdom of Mercia. Views on the left extend to the Titterstone Clee Hill in Shropshire, and ahead to the jagged outline of the Malvern Hills. After the path bends right at a signpost on the flat top of Rushock Hill, continue to the next signpost.

6 Turn right to leave the dyke and, following the direction of a sign, cross the field and a stile to the diagonal line of trees in the next field. Cross the field to a stile at an Offa's Dyke waymark. Beyond the stile follow waymarks across fields to red-roofed Quarry House.

7 Pass to the right of Quarry House to join the driveway, then cross a narrow road. Go half left down through the golf course to a signpost at Bradnor Green, and retrace your steps back to Kington.

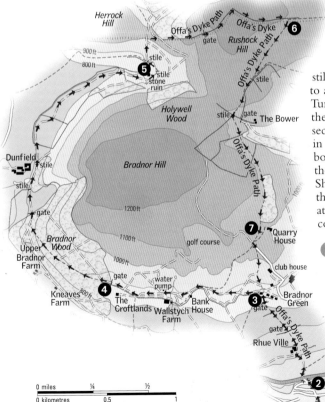

LINCOLNSHIRE

This county's best walking is on the deeply rural, sparsely populated Wolds, a range of open chalk hills and lush valleys. An area of outstanding natural beauty, paradoxically it is one of the least visited parts of England.

1 Walesby

A breezy stride along the Viking Way to a church with a special appeal for all ramblers and country lovers.

LENGTH 4½ or 5 miles (2½ or 3 hours)

PARKING Village hall car park in Otby Lane

CONDITIONS Easy, with two gradual climbs

REFRESHMENTS Tearoom in Tealby

1 Turn right up Otby Lane. Opposite the rectory turn left to a gate, then along the field edge towards the slate-roofed Mill House Farm with the green slope of the Wolds behind it. Turn right at a path junction, passing to the left of the house. Cross a footbridge on the left and follow a bridleway sign ahead up through a gate, keeping a hedge and fence on the left.

2 Nearing the crest of the hill, go ahead through a gate and then in about 100m look for a gate in the hedgerow. Go through it and turn

RAMBLERS' (ALL SAINTS') CHURCH, WALESBY

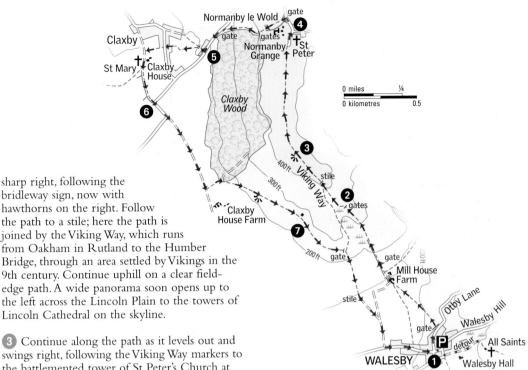

sharp right, following the bridleway sign, now with hawthorns on the right. Follow the path to a stile; here the path is joined by the Viking Way, which runs from Oakham in Rutland to the Humber Bridge, through an area settled by Vikings in the 9th century. Continue uphill on a clear field-edge path. A wide panorama soon opens up to the left across the Lincoln Plain to the towers of Lincoln Cathedral on the skyline.

3 Continue along the path as it levels out and swings right, following the Viking Way markers to the battlemented tower of St Peter's Church at Normanby le Wold among trees ahead. Normanby means 'Norsemen's village', reflecting local Viking influence. Across a valley the huge 'golf ball' of Claxby Radar Station can be seen. St Peter's Church, dating from the 13th century, is built in red-brown ironstone; inside, the pillars bear unusual carvings such as a ram's horn curlicue and a man apparently afflicted with toothache.

4 From the church follow the lane round to the left. At a farm entrance, turn left through a gate into a field and follow the boundary of Normanby Grange down through two more gates. Continue downhill round the edge of Claxby Wood between green mounds, where rabbits abound, to a gate onto the road into Claxby. Turn left on the road.

5 Beyond a house named Rowan Cottage, turn right onto a tarmac drive then take the left path through a lawned area beside a garden. Aim for the bottom left corner, through a gap into a second lawned area. Now keep to the right. As the path bends the Three Sisters vineyard, planted in 2002, is visible to the right. Cross a road in Claxby where a plaque on the right marks the site of an ancient smithy. Follow the path ahead, then turn left at the road to pass St Mary's church, which has more grimacing heads carved on the pillars.

Beyond the church, take a permissive path by the edge of a field to meet another road. A mound in the field on the left is said to have been a Georgian ice house for the former Claxby Manor.

6 Follow the road ahead for 100m, then bear left up a narrow hedged lane leading to Claxby House Farm. Just before the farm buildings, turn left on a track round the tip of woods. Ignore a fork to the left and keep ahead, passing to the right of a conifer plantation. This gently rising track commands another good panorama across the Lincoln Plain.

7 At the crest of the hill, the tower of the Ramblers' Church – All Saints – in its isolated hilltop setting above Walesby comes into view, before the path descends a grassy slope to rejoin the Viking Way. Pass through a gate, then cross a stile beside a cattle grid shortly after and follow a broad farm track to a road. Turn left to return to the car park.

DETOUR *To visit the Ramblers' Church, instead of turning to the car park, continue to the main road and turn right to find a footpath sign on left to Ramblers' Church. Follow the path to All Saints' Church. It is called the Ramblers' Church after a window given by the Grimsby and District Wayfarers' Association in 1950 that shows Christ blessing ramblers and cyclists. In the unadorned interior even walkers' muddy boots do not seem out of place – though there is a warning against letting sheep stray in. Sturdy Norman arches stand out against white walls and screen, and the bench seats are set casually on a rough stone floor. Neglected by Victorian restorers, the church preserves a charming medieval simplicity.*

LINCOLNSHIRE

2 Woolsthorpe

A relaxing stroll beside a meandering river to a canal towpath and gentle wooded hills in the heart of England.

LENGTH 5 miles (2½ hours)

PARKING In centre of village

CONDITIONS Undemanding, but paths can be muddy after rain

REFRESHMENTS Canalside pub at halfway point of walk

① From the village centre walk along Main Street to the crossroads at the north edge of the village, then go straight ahead on Sedgebrook Road. Continue past the Belvoir Hunt stables to reach a signposted footpath on the left, just before the end of the houses.

② Go down the steps and turn left along the path, which leads across fields to a farm track from Grange Farm, on the right. Do not go over the bridge but continue straight over the track to reach the side of the meandering, willow-lined River Devon. Follow the path along the riverbank to a footbridge. Cross the bridge and turn right along the opposite bank, over a series of stiles, to reach a minor road.

③ Turn right on the road. Cross the bridge over the river and continue straight on past a right turning, the end of Sedgebrook Road. On the far side of the bridge over the Grantham Canal (Stenwith Bridge), turn right down a flight of steps to join the towpath, with the canal on your right-hand side. The canal, closed to commercial traffic since the 1930s, connects Grantham with West Bridgford, a distance of 33 miles.

Follow the towpath for about ½ mile, to Woolsthorpe Bridge. (If you wish to visit the Rutland Arms pub, cross this bridge and walk back along the opposite bank.) At the bridge, continue along the towpath; beyond a flight of restored locks, the canal bends sharp left through a shallow cut in the disused railway embankment. Follow the canal to a short distance before Longmoor Bridge, where a path veers off to the left.

④ Turn left onto the path then immediately right over the bridge, and continue straight on uphill between overgrown hedges of blackthorn and ash. This section of track, part of Sewstern Lane, an old drovers' road, is followed by the Viking Way long-distance footpath. Continue straight on between the brick abutments of a dismantled rail bridge, beyond which the going becomes steeper. Pass two other tracks joining from the left to reach a signposted junction.

⑤ Fork right at the signpost through a gap in the hedge, then turn left and continue straight across the field to another gap leading onto a minor road. Cross the road and continue ahead between a fence and a hedge, then follow the woodland track to a stile.

⑥ Cross the stile and immediately turn right, down a slope flanked by woodland to the right and an open slope ahead and the to left – revealing a fine view of Belvoir Castle and the Vale of Belvoir. Cross a stile into a cricket field and continue straight ahead towards two benches at the left-hand corner of the field. This leads into the car park of Woolsthorpe's Checkers pub and into Main Street.

To reach Belvoir Castle by foot, turn right opposite the telephone kiosk into Belvoir Lane, then follow the Jubilee Way signs; on reaching the road, turn left and look for the entrance signs. By car, turn left at the crossroads by the Belvoir Hunt stables and follow the road to the entrance.

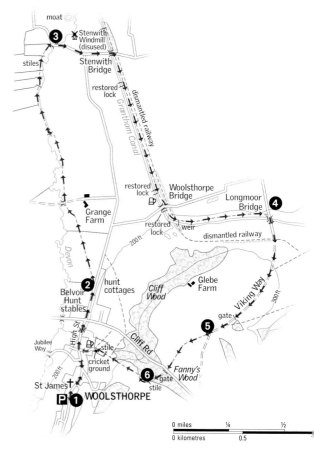

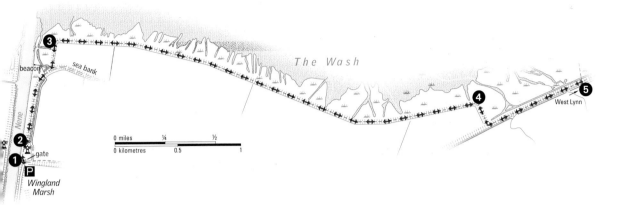

3 The Wash

To a remote sea bank and back, with
wonderful views across saltmarshes –
a haven for wildfowl and waders.

LENGTH 7 miles (3½ hours)

PARKING At East Bank car park beside River
Nene, north of Sutton Bridge

CONDITIONS Easy going on flat, grassy paths

REFRESHMENTS None on walk

1 Walk from the car park back to the road.
With the River Nene on the left, go through a
gate ahead and continue past a lighthouse on the
right, the pair to another on the opposite bank
of the river. The lighthouses were built between
1829 and 1834, not as guides to shipping, but to
commemorate the opening of the new River
Nene outfall. Originally the lighthouses were at
the very edge of the coast, but the land beyond
has since been reclaimed from the sea, a practice
that has been discontinued because of the
importance of this coast as a wildlife sanctuary.

The lighthouse on this bank of the River
Nene was the home, intermittently, from 1933 to
1939 of Sir Peter Scott, the pioneering naturalist
and artist. When he lived here the lighthouse was
surrounded by water on three sides at high tide,
with the last sea bank only 20m away.

2 Climb up onto the embankment, between
the Nene on the left and a ditch on the right.
Follow the embankment ahead towards The
Wash, passing on the right a bank that was the
limit of the sea in 1953.

3 Follow the embankment as it curves right
into the sea bank, built in 1974 to protect newly
reclaimed land from the sea. The bank stretches
to the estuary of the Great Ouse and continues

beside the river to West Lynn, a distance of some
10 miles. From the bank, the west and east coasts
of The Wash can be easily seen on clear days,
while inland are vast cultivated fields bounded
by ditches.

The Wash once stretched inland almost to
Suffolk but has slowly silted up over the
centuries. The fenland to its south and west has
been reclaimed from the sea, most effectively in
the 17th century by the Dutch engineer
Cornelius Vermuyden. What was once a land
of water and islands, mist and huge flocks of
birds, is now some of the most productive arable
land in Britain.

4 After about 2½ miles, follow the bank as
it bends briefly inland to meet another bank
coming in from the right. Turn left and continue
ahead with The Wash to the left. The immense
expanse of mudflats – marsh, giving way to sand,
and then shallow sea – is an important winter
feeding ground for wildfowl and wading birds,
such as grey plovers, curlews, oystercatchers,
godwits, dunlins, brent and pink-footed geese,
wigeon, eider and shelduck.

Many of these birds return to their Arctic
breeding grounds in summer, so the walk is
of most interest to an ornithologist in spring,
autumn and winter. There is, however, a rather
mournful solitude and beauty to the area at
all times. The Wash sand banks are home also
to one of the largest colonies of common seals
in Europe.

5 Out to sea is a man-made island, built in
the 1970s and now a bird reserve. Do not
venture off the sea bank and onto the marsh,
where there is a risk of being cut off by the
tides. Retrace your steps along the sea bank or
continue farther towards the Great Ouse estuary.

141

NORFOLK

The level expanse of Norfolk's countryside offers easy walking beneath big skies. Inland, paths traverse fields and forests; on the coast they cross dunes and saltmarshes rich in birdlife.

1 Castle Acre

An amble through the gentle west Norfolk countryside, taking in a Norman castle and medieval priory.

LENGTH 6 miles (3 hours)

PARKING In car park of Ostrich Inn (or beside Stock Green in village centre)

CONDITIONS Easy going; some paths are narrow and uneven

REFRESHMENTS Pubs and tearooms in Castle Acre

① Turn left from the pub car park onto the High Street. Pass the Bailey Gate, the old entry to Castle Acre Castle (EH), on the right. At the end of the High Street, fork right down Pye's Lane, signposted 'Castle', to reach the flint remains of the 11th-century motte and bailey stronghold, built by William de Warenne, the husband of William the Conqueror's daughter Gundrada.

Retrace your steps along the High Street and pass the 15th-century Church of St James the Great. Just beyond the entrance to the Old Vicarage on the right, turn left on South Acre, which leads gently downhill. The ruins of Castle Acre priory can be seen through the trees to the

RIVER NAR NEAR CASTLE ACRE

right. At the bottom of the valley runs the River Nar, little more than a stream, and the lane swings round to the right.

2 Cross the bridge over the river by a ford. This peaceful spot is on the route of the Peddars Way, an ancient track leading from Knettishall Heath in Suffolk to the north Norfolk coast at Holme next the Sea. Follow the lane as it climbs away from the ford and levels out between hedgerows, bending left round Church Farm. To the right is the flint and brick South Acre rectory, with the Church of St George visible in the trees beyond. At a crossroads continue straight ahead on a road.

3 Where the road bends left, do not follow the Peddars Way sign but go straight ahead on a rising track, crossing broad fields. The track then descends between hedgerows past Herrington's Pit, an old gravel pit. At a crossroads of tracks by Bartholomew's Hills Plantation turn right gently uphill, with a hedge on the right and a large field on the left. The track descends to another crossing of paths, then rises again past a mixed plantation on the left to reach a crossing of paths with a brick barn seen across the field to the right.

4 Continue ahead on a bridleway, passing the Three-cocked-hat Plantation of trees on the right, to reach a large, double-trunk oak tree. Turn right on another bridleway and continue past an open iron barn to a road.

5 Go straight over the road onto the bridleway ahead to meet a track leading left to West Acre. The ruins of an Augustinian priory can be glimpsed through the trees to the left, although little is left apart from the 14th-century gatehouse. Turn left on the track, then after a few metres turn right on a path leading through a delightful clearing in the woods, passing a private bird reserve and Warren Farm on the left.

6 At a ford, turn right on a lane and then turn left on a path leading to a footbridge over the Nar, past Mill House, and over another footbridge. Follow the path across a water meadow and through a gate. Continue through woods for some distance, with the Nar to the right. The church and village of Castle Acre eventually come into view ahead.

7 Where the river comes close to the path, continue ahead on a track called Common Road, which ascends gently towards the village. Where the track meets a lane, turn right to the ruins of Castle Acre priory (EH). This was one of England's grandest religious houses, a Cluniac establishment on the pilgrims' route to Walsingham. The well-preserved prior's lodgings, adjoining the 12th-century west front of the church, include a beautiful oriel window.

Turn back to a lane on the right into the village and continue to the High Street and the pub car park.

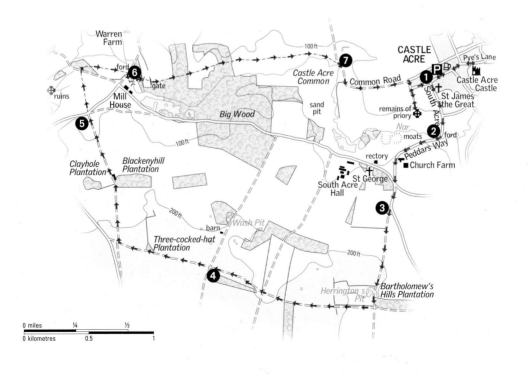

NORFOLK

2 Snettisham

Through woods and over a breezy sea causeway, spying summer wild flowers or wintering birds.

LENGTH 4 miles (2½ hours)

PARKING Beach car park at end of Beach Road

CONDITIONS Easy going; Beach Road may be busy with caravans and cars in summer

REFRESHMENTS Bars, shops and buffets serving caravan parks

1 With your back to the sea, turn left from the car park entrance along Beach Road. Pass a large caravan park on the right and rough ground on the left filled with seasonal wild flowers such as ragwort and fireweed. The road climbs over a long embankment – an old sea-defence line now superseded by a later one nearer the shore.

Follow Beach Road past further rows of caravans, then bungalows, to reach open country bounded by dark woods. Beyond Locke Farm, a wood with outlying gorse bushes begins to close in on the road. Continue to a modern stone house. Just past the house, turn left and go behind it to the small parish car park serving Snettisham Common. A notice gives information on the birds that have been seen on the common during the past year.

2 From the car park, take the bridleway that climbs up into the wood. The trees – mostly oaks, beeches and sweet chestnuts – are widespread at first but soon close in to form a high-ceilinged tunnel. Go through a gate and follow the bridleway near the edge of the wood with glimpses across meadows and broad fields of cereal crops to the distant sea. The path emerges from the trees by Lodge Hill Farm. The local red carstone of the farm's walls and chimneys contrasts strongly with the green background of trees.

3 Follow the path downhill as it swings to the left and sets off towards the sea, with convolvulus and ragwort woven into the wayside grasses. Make a brief dogleg to the right before turning left once again on a seaward course, crossing the track of a dismantled railway.

4 The path continues past a stunted, wind-tangled wood, to a stile with a footpath sign. Climb the stile and cross the field to a gap in the hedge on the far side. Go half-right across the next field, to reach a signpost that also marks a causeway over a stream. From this sign, go diagonally left across a third meadow.

5 At the end of the field, go through a kissing gate and continue over a grassy causeway. Turn left then after 100m turn right onto the redirected path, avoiding marshy ground, to the embankment of the present defences.

Follow the line of the path through rushes and sedge and clamber up to the top of the bank, with The Wash ahead. Away to the right is Hunstanton, with its broad sandy halo and in front, dimmed by distance, the tiny outlines of buildings in Lincolnshire.

6 Turn left and walk along the top of the embankment. Alternatively you can descend to the gravel beach. Beyond this, at low tide, are miles of mudflats and sandbanks which, together with the shingle and the marshes and pools on the inner side of the sea defences, make this one of the most important sites in Britain for waders and wildfowl.

More than 100,000 birds overwinter here, with many more passing through. There are also a large number of resident species, including oystercatchers and terns. In autumn and winter the combined multitudes advancing up the shore ahead of the incoming tide make an awesome spectacle. In summer, when the birds are fewer, there is great enjoyment in walking along the defences, where drifts of wild flowers, such as golden yellow horned-poppies, yellow weld and mauve sea rocket, grow out of the sand, shingle and thin soil.

Follow the embankment back to the car park. An entrance to Snettisham Coastal Park leads off the car park, with a board giving information on the area, including details of the 80 species of birds that may be seen in the appropriate seasons.

3 Burnham Overy Town

Two ancient seaports and views over saltmarsh, dunes and shore, each a separate wildlife habitat.

LENGTH 4 or 6 miles (2 or 3 hours)

PARKING In car park at rear of churchyard

CONDITIONS Mostly firm going over field and coastal paths

REFRESHMENTS Pub in Burnham Overy Staithe

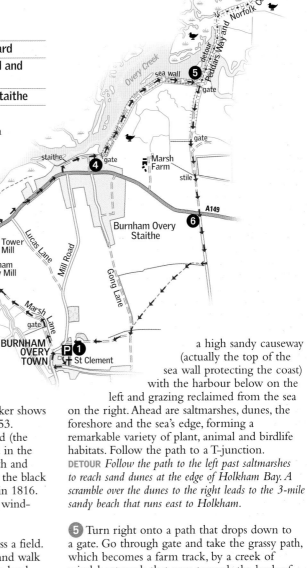

1 From the car park go ahead through a gate and then follow the path around St Clement's Church to the road. Turn right to the tiny village green backed by houses in the local flint, stone and brick, one of them decorated with massive stone heads. Turn right on a road signposted to Burnham Overy Staithe. After 100m, take the grassy, rutted track – Marsh Lane – on the left. Continue forward to the red-brick, late-18th-century buildings of Burnham Overy Mill, powered by the River Burn, running to the left of the track.

2 Take the lane that runs through the watermill. High on the front wall a marker shows where floods reached on January 30, 1953. Where the lane leads onto the coast road (the A149), continue ahead. At the first bend in the road, turn left over a stile onto a footpath and continue to another stile. To the right is the black and white Tower Mill, a windmill built in 1816. To the left saltmarshes stretch out, wild, wind-ruffled and lonely, to distant dunes.

3 Turn half-right onto a footpath across a field. Just before reaching the A149 turn left and walk along the edge of the field, then join the hard path along the road leading into Burnham Overy Staithe. After passing the former Maltings, now converted into houses, turn left down a lane to the quayside, or staithe, and to a forest of dinghy masts, both ashore and afloat, in the long, sheltered harbour. Just within living memory, coasting brigs and schooners used to call here; now it is a favourite haven of amateur sailors.

4 At the end of the staithe, take the well-trodden path above the harbour. Go through a gate and turn left to a nature reserve. Go along a high sandy causeway (actually the top of the sea wall protecting the coast) with the harbour below on the left and grazing reclaimed from the sea on the right. Ahead are saltmarshes, dunes, the foreshore and the sea's edge, forming a remarkable variety of plant, animal and birdlife habitats. Follow the path to a T-junction.

DETOUR *Follow the path to the left past saltmarshes to reach sand dunes at the edge of Holkham Bay. A scramble over the dunes to the right leads to the 3-mile sandy beach that runs east to Holkham.*

5 Turn right onto a path that drops down to a gate. Go through gate and take the grassy path, which becomes a farm track, by a creek of wind-bent reeds that runs towards the back of Burnham Overy Staithe. Continue ahead across fields through a gate then over a stile to the A149.

6 Cross the road and walk down the minor road ahead. After almost ¼ mile turn right onto a path, which at times is a narrow, sandy trail. At the end of a hedge follow the signposted path diagonally left across a field to a gap in the hedge in the mid distance. Go through the gap to a sandy track called Gong Lane. Cross the track and take the wide grassy path ahead, back to St Clement's churchyard.

CENTRAL ENGLAND

NORFOLK

4 Weybourne

An old railway station, wind-twisted woods,
stretches of gorse and heather, and bracing
coast along sand, farm track and shingle.

LENGTH 5 miles (3 hours)

PARKING Car park at Weybourne station

CONDITIONS Mostly easy going; heath paths may
be overgrown in summer

REFRESHMENTS Pubs at Weybourne, tearoom
at Kelling

1 From the station, a scallop-roofed gem of
1900 with old enamel advertisements and
porters' trolleys piled high with leather luggage,
go over the footbridge towards the waiting
room. At the bottom of the bridge turn right.
Cross over the road and enter Kelling Heath
Nature Trail, which runs beside the railway and
through a fairytale wood, mostly of oaks stunted
and twisted by salt winds off the sea. Pass a black,
still pool with water lilies, then take the right
fork that climbs up to the single platform of
Kelling Heath Park request halt.

2 The path continues behind the platform,
dropping down again into woods. At a grassy

drive through the trees, where the path divides,
fork right. The path becomes very steep and
sandy, bearing right to emerge on a broad,
pebbly track with the railway line running
through a cutting below.

3 Where the track reaches a cottage and level
crossing, cross the railway line with care and go
through a gate to take the access-restricted byway
on the other side. Here the terrain is heathland,
a mingling of golden gorse, purple heather and
browny green bracken, wrapped about by long,
dark arms of coniferous plantations running off
to arable fields and the sea.

4 Cross a minor road, then continue on a path
over Kelling Heath to the A149. At the road turn
left, then just before a war memorial and a book
and art shop, once the Kelling Reading Room,
turn right up a byway. Follow it round to the
right before the Quag.

5 Where the track reaches a hard-surfaced
parking area, follow it round to the right onto
the Peddars Way and Norfolk Coast Path. The
saltmarshes and wide sands to the west have
given way to a shingle desert.

6 Soon the path leads past the remains of
military installations from both world wars and
the radio masts and ever-spinning radar aerial of
today's RAF. Vigilance against invaders is an old
habit on this coast, where there is a deep-water
anchorage almost immediately offshore.
Continue along the top of the shingle ridge
to reach a reedy lake on the right. Drop
down to junction with Beach Lane and a
small car park shared with lobster pots and
inshore fishing boats. Early telegraph cables
from Germany came ashore at this point
in 1858. Beyond the lane, the shingle
beach gives way to eroded sandy cliffs.

7 Go right on Beach Lane to
Weybourne village. Its older houses
are composed of beach pebbles
framed with brick, and All Saints
Church is built into the substantial
remains of an Augustinian priory
founded in the 13th century. Turn
left on the A149 and, following
signs for the North Norfolk
Railway, turn right in front
of the church and then
left. Continue down
through the village and
on to Weybourne station.

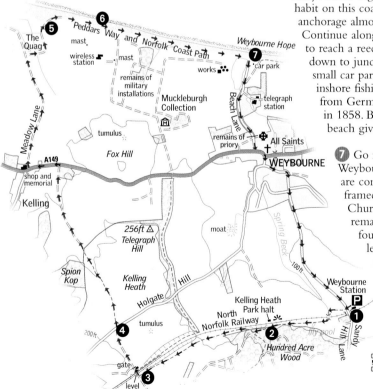

FIELDS AND THE SEA BY WEYBOURNE

NORFOLK

5 Ludham

A marshman's view of the Norfolk Broads, followed by a breezy stretch along the River Ant, busy with cabin cruisers.

LENGTH 5½ miles (3 hours)

PARKING In Stocks Hill beside churchyard gate

CONDITIONS Wear boots in wet weather

REFRESHMENTS Pub at Ludham; pub and tearoom at Ludham Bridge

1 With your back to the church, cross the road and walk past the King's Arms pub. Beyond the garage and Methodist church, turn left. The bridleway runs between wide, arable fields to meet a track called Goffins Lane. Cross the lane and take the marked footpath ahead.

2 At the hedgerow at end of the path, turn right and continue as far as a gap in the hedge on the left. Go through the gap and follow the path to a hedge at the other end of the field. Go through the gap in this hedge, and across a second field, then climb the bank to reach a grassy track.

3 Turn left and continue towards a modern house, Pinewood Lodge, on How Hill Road. Turn left and walk below tall trees to black, tarred Mill House, neatly converted from a tower mill. (Opposite is an entrance to How Hill House. The Broads Authority has a nature reserve in the grounds in which wetlands, fens and waterways are managed in the traditional Broadland way.) Continue on the road and turn right into the gateway and car park for Toad Hole Cottage.

4 Cross the car park and the meadow beyond, following signs for Toad Hole Cottage. On the left is the River Ant, busy with cabin cruisers and fringed by reed and sedge beds that are still cut for thatching. The little red-brick Toad Hole Cottage, built in 1728, was the home of generations of marshmen, who made a living out of reedcutting, wildfowling and catching eels. It now provides information on the life of the marshmen and is the starting point of a nature trail, which offers glimpses of terns, snipe, woodpeckers and marsh harriers, as well as lilies and other water-loving plants and the rare swallowtail butterfly.

5 From the cottage, take the path to the riverbank, cross the footbridge and turn left along the towpath. Follow the path as it runs between reedbeds and the river, with a view of How Hill House and its splendid garden on the left. The path veers out into marshy pasture on which cattle are fattened, as they have been for centuries, then bends left back to the River Ant.

6 Continue along the towpath for about a mile to Neave's Drainage Mill, on the right. Then continue along the towpath to Ludham Bridge, passing moored cruisers.

7 At Ludham Bridge, where there is a shop, a chandler's and a restaurant, turn left on the road. Pass the Dog Inn on the right and turn right onto a minor road signposted to Hall Common. On the left is red-brick Ludham Hall, whose arched-windowed wing – a former chapel – juts out from the rest of the building. The hall, now much remodelled, was in the 16th century the home of the abbots of St Benet's, whose scant ruins are visible across the marshes on the right.

8 Turn left at Ludham Hall and follow the bridleway sign through a farmyard and across open fields with Ludham church tower ahead.

9 At a T-junction turn left on a track which becomes a metalled road called Lovers' Lane. Continue to the A1062 and turn right to St Catherine's Church and the car park.

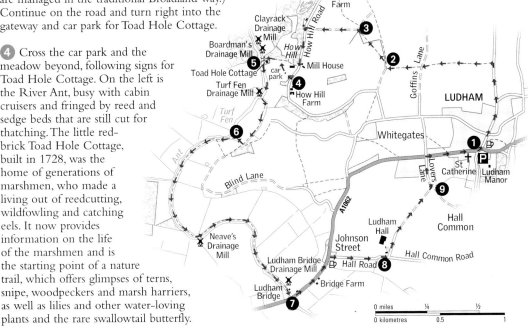

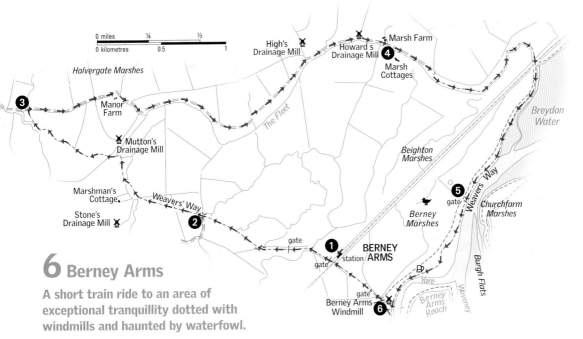

6 Berney Arms

A short train ride to an area of exceptional tranquillity dotted with windmills and haunted by waterfowl.

LENGTH	6½ miles (3½ hours)
CONDITIONS	Ground may be soft in places
REFRESHMENTS	Berney Arms pub

NOTE Check train times in advance for journey between Berney Arms and Reedham

1 This remote area of Norfolk is only accessible by train. The station is 2 miles from the nearest road. Descend from the train at Berney Arms station and turn left along the single platform. There are good views from the platform of the surrounding countryside – an enormous expanse of grass running to the horizon, seamed by broad, water-filled ditches and punctuated by windmills. At the end of the platform, walk beside the track for a few metres, then turn right through a gate, joining the Weavers' Way, a 56-mile route linking Cromer and Great Yarmouth. Follow the path through another gate to a footbridge. Cross this bridge and follow the path to a second footbridge.

2 Cross the bridge and continue diagonally across the open expanse of pasture ahead, heading roughly between the two windmills in the middle distance, to Mutton's Drainage Mill on the right. Beyond the mill, continue on the path for almost ½ mile to a point where a track joins from the right. The great plain may resemble a timeless wilderness, but it is, in fact, one of the most carefully managed areas of pastureland in Britain.

3 Turn right on the track, leaving the Weavers' Way. Continue to Manor Farm, alongside a wide drainage ditch where swans and mallards paddle.

Just beyond the farm, the track bends right, then wends its way across the marshes before following the course of the River Fleet past two more drainage mills to Marsh Farm.

4 Continue along the track for about ¾ mile to the railway. Cross the railway with care, climb the grassy embankment and turn right, rejoining the Weavers' Way on a raised causeway. The causeway runs above Breydon Water, which is mostly mud and sand when the tide is out, though there is always a marked navigable channel. The combined estuary of the Waveney and the Yare is a nature reserve and supports a large community of seabirds as well as birds of marsh and shoreline. Continue to a gate.

5 Go through the gate into Berney Marshes, owned by the RSPB. The water levels in the marshes are controlled by dams and sluices to induce shallow flooding in winter and spring, attracting huge numbers of birds. Among breeding species are swans and snipe, redshanks, teal and lapwings. Ahead, with cabin cruisers moored alongside, is the Berney Arms pub.

Beyond the pub, the Berney Arms Windmill (EH), built about 1870, is a landmark for miles around. Originally, it had two roles: lifting water out of the marsh with its scoop wheel and dumping it into the River Yare; and grinding cement cinder, which was then sailed down to the coast. On the far side of the estuary are the still substantial remains of Burgh Castle.

6 At the Berney Arms Windmill, turn right through a gate and follow a path running beside a wide ditch back to the station.

CENTRAL ENGLAND

NORTHAMPTONSHIRE

Several interesting long-distance trails cross Northamptonshire, including the Jurassic Way, the Brampton Valley Way and the Nene Way. The latter passes the village of Wadenhoe, focus of this hill and riverside walk.

1 Wadenhoe

From a meandering river and its extensive wetland along well-worn tracks to the haunting ruins of Lyveden New Bield.

LENGTH 7½ miles (3½ hours)

PARKING Car park by village hall

CONDITIONS Fairly easy walking, apart from muddy track approaching Lyveden

REFRESHMENTS Pub in Wadenhoe

1 From the car park, go through the gate and turn left to follow the Nene Way, with trees by the river to the left and St Michael and All Angels Church on the right. Continue on the waymarked footpath above the River Nene for 1 mile to the village of Aldwincle, crossing footbridges and stiles over several feeder streams.

In places the path may be overgrown with nettles, thistles and giant hogweed. The marshy land lining the river, with its diversity of plant life, is the most extensive area of riverside wetland in Northamptonshire. Just beyond a succession of back gardens on the right, turn right onto a footpath leading past a tall-spired church on the left and across a wide village green to Main Street.

Aldwincle's curious name, recorded in the Domesday Book as 'Eldewincle', meaning old corner or nook, is Anglo-Saxon. However, the discovery of a Bronze Age burial area and circular ditched enclosure suggests that there may have been a much earlier settlement here. The Romans built a timber bridge across the Nene east of the village.

2 Turn right and walk along Main Street, then after 200m turn left down Cross Lane, which soon becomes a broad track passing a

LYVEDEN NEW BIELD

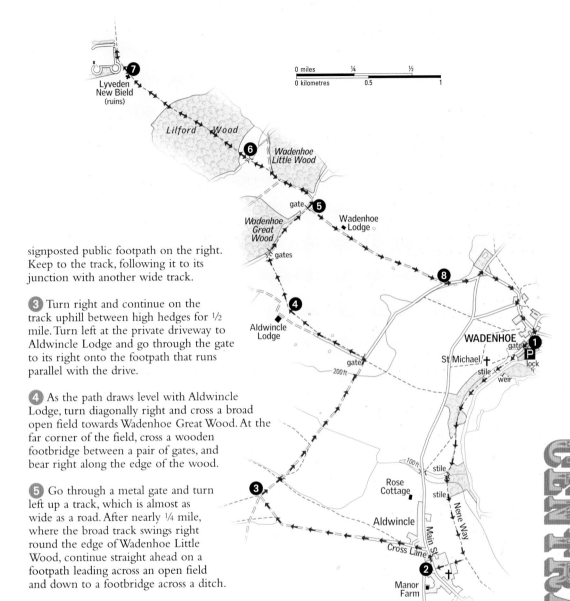

signposted public footpath on the right.
Keep to the track, following it to its
junction with another wide track.

3 Turn right and continue on the
track uphill between high hedges for ½
mile. Turn left at the private driveway to
Aldwincle Lodge and go through the gate
to its right onto the footpath that runs
parallel with the drive.

4 As the path draws level with Aldwincle
Lodge, turn diagonally right and cross a broad
open field towards Wadenhoe Great Wood. At the
far corner of the field, cross a wooden
footbridge between a pair of gates, and
bear right along the edge of the wood.

5 Go through a metal gate and turn
left up a track, which is almost as
wide as a road. After nearly ¼ mile,
where the broad track swings right
round the edge of Wadenhoe Little
Wood, continue straight ahead on a
footpath leading across an open field
and down to a footbridge across a ditch.

6 From the footbridge, follow the track up
into Lilford Wood between conifers, where it is
heavily cut by horses' hooves. The wood thins
out to give a dramatic view of Lyveden New
Bield, or New Building (NT), one of England's
strangest and most haunting ruins, which lies
ahead up the track.

Lyveden New Bield is a roofless stone-built
architectural shell, begun in 1594 by Sir Thomas
Tresham as a garden lodge to his new manor
house at Lyveden. Work proceeded slowly
because Sir Thomas had earlier converted to
Roman Catholicism and had been imprisoned
for years and heavily fined for his faith, depriving
him of the funds to complete it. Built in the
form of a cross, it is two storeys high above a
basement, with a surround of carved religious

symbols. Sir Thomas intended to lay out an
elaborate formal garden, of which a few faint
traces remain.

7 From Lyveden New Bield, retrace your
steps through Lilford Wood to the gate met
earlier at **5**. From the gate, bear left on the
track, which leads past Wadenhoe Lodge on
the left. Continue for ½ mile to a tarmac road.

8 Turn left onto the road. At the next fork turn
left then almost immediately right on the road
back to Wadenhoe, and past its thatch-and-stone
cottages to the car park.

CENTRAL ENGLAND

SHROPSHIRE

A particularly unspoiled county on the northern Welsh borders that offers wonderful walking on high, bare-ridged hills, across heathery plateaux and into richly cultivated valleys.

1 All Stretton

An energetic climb to craggy Caer Caradoc with its Iron Age hillfort and panoramic views of the Wrekin and the Marches.

LENGTH 4½ miles (3 hours)

PARKING National Trust car park just west of All Stretton

CONDITIONS Steep path to Caer Caradoc can be slippery in winter

REFRESHMENTS Pub and shop in All Stretton

1 Walk back on the lane to All Stretton, a village of assorted cottages dating from the 1500s. At the T-junction turn right onto the B5477 and take the first road on the left, called Farm Lane.

At the T-junction turn left, crossing a bridge over a stream, then continue ahead over a junction and a railway bridge to meet the A49.

2 Cross the A49 and go over a waymarked stile into a large field. With a fenced hedge on the left, cross the field and two more waymarked stiles. Head to the far corner of the next field and cross a waymarked stile on the left. To the left are the walk's first views of craggy Caer Caradoc, the site of an Iron Age hillfort.

Follow the track across fields past a series of dammed pools. Continue into a little wooded valley with a footbridge on the right.

3 Do not cross the footbridge, but take the higher of two tracks on the left, which leads onto scree and straight up the side of the hill towards the ridge of Caer Caradoc. Go over a stile, cross a path and continue up a steep slope for about ¼ mile. Follow the wide, well-worn path round to the left of the outcrop and along the ridge of the hill. At the top, there are exhilarating views of Church Stretton, Long Mynd, Lawley and the Wrekin. The path passes through the ramparts and up across the site of the hillfort.

Caer Caradoc is one of several hillforts in the Marches associated with the tribal chieftain Caradog – or Caractacus, as he was called by the Romans, whose advance he bravely resisted in AD 50. The remains suggest that some 600 people lived in square huts within the ramparts of the hilltop settlement. In times of peace they probably farmed the lower land.

4 Continue on the steep path downhill and where the slope becomes gentler, opposite a gate on the right and before a small valley, turn left and take the track downhill. Continue towards a hedge, and turn left at a waymark onto a path with a hedge on the right, which leads along the foot of the west face of Caer Caradoc.

5 At a fork, bear right downhill and continue over a stile. Walk downhill across a field, over a second stile and through a second large field. Go through the left-hand, metal gate and follow the track, bearing left through a copse.

Beyond the copse, the path turns right and goes over a stile. Cross the A49 and take the path ahead over a waymarked stile. Cross a field, then go over railway tracks and bear left across the corner of the next field. Cross a stile and turn right on an overgrown track. Where the track bends left, follow the path on the right across a small footbridge over a stream to a waymarked stile. Go over the stile and continue through a field with a hedge on the right. Cross a stile and turn left on a gravel track.

At the B5477 turn left through All Stretton. At the Yew Tree pub turn right down the road to return to the village hall and the car park.

ALL STRETTON

800 ft · 700 ft · stiles · stile · gate · stile · Hough Coppice · stile · stile · Caer Caradoc · 4 · 1400 ft · 1300 ft · 1200 ft · gate

1 · **2** stile · A49 · 600 ft · 700 ft · 800 ft · **5** · hedge

Three Fingers Rock

stiles · stile · stile · fence · gate

New House Farm · **3**

0 miles · ¼
0 kilometres · 0.5

2 Stiperstones

Over heathland and up to the Devil's Chair among the rocky outcrops of the Stiperstones.

LENGTH 4½ or 5 miles (2½ or 3 hours)

PARKING The Bog car park, on minor road off A488

CONDITIONS One moderate climb; rough underfoot on rocky track along ridge and sometimes slippery

REFRESHMENTS None on walk

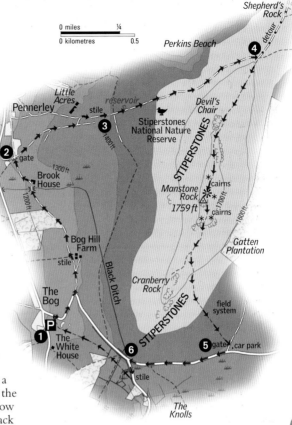

1 Turn right out of the car park, the site of a former lead mine in an area that, in the 19th century, produced ten per cent of Britain's lead ore. Follow the road uphill, leaving it at a sharp, right-hand hairpin bend to take the track ahead, which leads past Bog Hill Farm. At a gravel drive, take the track on the left, passing a stile on the left and several buildings. At the Natural England building take the right-hand track. Pass by Brook House to a gate at a junction of tracks.

2 Go through the gate and turn right along a gravel track that leads uphill past a cottage on the left and a metalled driveway on the right. Follow a small, handpainted footpath sign to a gravel track off to the left leading around the edge of a small farm. Turn right beside the farm onto another track and continue uphill, with the Stiperstones rocky outcrops in sight straight ahead.

3 Cross a stile beside a gate and go over a crossing of tracks onto the open moorland of the Stiperstones National Nature Reserve, which is characterised by steep slopes, deep valleys and heather moorland where meadow pipits, buzzards and kestrels can be seen.

Pass a small fenced service reservoir on the left and climb the track towards the first of the Stiperstones. About ½ mile beyond the gate is a series of ruined stone enclosures on the left from where the ground falls away into a deep-sided valley known as Perkins Beach. The craggy Devil's Chair, a natural rock feature, is clearly visible on the skyline to the right. Continue to a crossing of tracks

DETOUR *Turn left up the track and continue for ⅓ mile to Shepherd's Rock, a lone rocky outcrop offering exhilarating views.*

4 Turn right and continue up over the Devil's Chair and along the stony path, passing to the left of the main Stiperstones outcrop, a rock wall rising 15m (50ft). Continue to Manstone Rock,

standing 536m (1,759ft) above sea level, from where, on a clear day, views extend on the left to Cannock Chase, 40 miles to the east. To the west in Wales, Cadair Idris may be glimpsed. Ahead lie the Brecon Beacons and behind, to the north, is Beeston Castle in Cheshire.

Follow the path downhill, keeping to the left of the next outcrop, and continue down a grassy path to a gate at the edge of the Stiperstones car park.

5 Turn right out of the car park and the National Nature Reserve. Turn right on the road and continue ahead for about ½ mile.

6 At a road junction turn sharp left and, just past buildings on the right, cross a double stile on the right and head across the field towards the corner of a barn.

Go through a gate, then cross a series of stiles between fields of rough pasture where the call of the curlew can be heard. Continue over further stiles and across fields that descend towards The Bog. Go through a kissing gate under an electric overhead cable and follow the path past a small pond on the right and back to the car park.

SHROPSHIRE

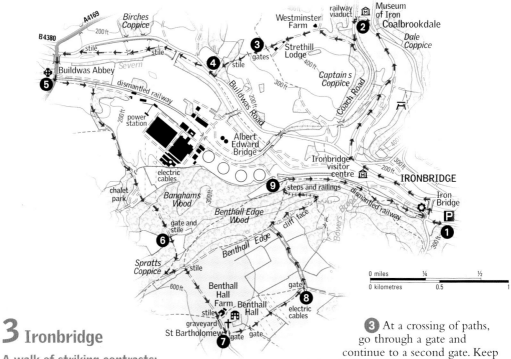

3 Ironbridge

A walk of striking contrasts:
from the ruins of a medieval abbey
to 16th-century Benthall Hall and
relics of the Industrial Revolution.

LENGTH 7 miles (3½ hours)

PARKING Long-stay car park beside Iron Bridge
on south side of River Severn

CONDITIONS Path beside the Severn can be
slippery in wet weather

REFRESHMENTS Full range in Ironbridge

1 Cross the Iron Bridge and turn left on the
road along the north bank of the Severn. The Iron
Bridge, built by Abraham Darby III in 1779, was
the world's first constructed from iron and spans
37m (120ft). After ½ mile, pass the Ironbridge
visitor centre and turn right up Dale Road,
signed to the Museum of Iron at Coalbrookdale.

2 The museum commemorates the first
smelting of iron ore with coke by Abraham
Darby I, the bridge-builder's grandfather. It also
includes the Rosehill and Dale Houses, the
restored homes of the first Quaker ironmasters.
Go through the grounds and under a railway
viaduct. Turn left along Coach Road and, just
before a second footpath on the right leading up
steps to Captain's Coppice, take the lane on the
right to Westminster Farm. Keep on the track to
Strethill Lodge on the left, then take the grassy
path straight ahead.

3 At a crossing of paths,
go through a gate and
continue to a second gate. Keep
right of a huge pylon and make for a
stile onto a path through a wood. Go over the
stile, cross the road and turn right along a narrow
pavement for 50m. Turn left on a footpath that
leads down to the river.

4 Turn right along the bank and go under
a bridge. Continue along the towpath, crossing a
stile into a long stretch of pasture, with views of
a power station's massive towers on the opposite
bank. Leave the field by another stile, and turn
left on the road. At a junction with the A4169,
turn left over the Severn. To the right are the
extensive remains of Buildwas Abbey (EH), a
Cistercian abbey built in 1135 and reached by
a road on the right, about 100m ahead.

5 Cross over an old railway line and turn left
along a minor road, which soon becomes a track
and bends right beside a fence on the right. The
massive towers of the power station then loom
up to the left and there are good views over
open countryside to the right.
　　Continue, passing through a park of holiday
chalets, which sits under two huge electric cables
carried by pylons. Follow the gravel track straight
ahead uphill and fork left under the electricity
cable onto another track, which climbs to a
waymarked gate and stile.

6 Cross the stile onto a path, which leads
uphill, bending right into a wood. At a junction
with another path, turn sharp left. Bear right over

the next waymarked stile and follow the track towards Benthall Hall (NT), a 16th-century stone house with mullioned windows and decorated plasterwork. Just past Benthall Hall Farm on the left, where the track begins to descend, ignore a signposted footpath to the right and continue straight ahead, past a small graveyard.

7 Just beyond the church, go through a narrow gate to the left. Follow the path across attractive parkland, past some fruit trees and through a waymarked gate. Continue along the edge of the farmland, crossing under power cables, to a waymarked swing-gate beside a larger gate.

8 Turn left on the track and continue, between hedges, across the farmland. The path becomes tree-lined, then passes through a barrier into Benthall Edge Wood. Turn right past a small limestone cliff, with rocks full of fossils, and go down a waymarked path. As the path swings to the right, turn left on a smaller path and walk down a series of wooden steps on the right. Keep on the path as it descends steeply into the Severn Gorge and bears right, down towards the River Severn.

9 At the river's edge, turn right and follow a narrow path beside it, walking along the edge of scrub woodland. The visitor centre is visible on the opposite bank.

After about 1 mile, the Iron Bridge and town beyond it comes into view. At the bridge, take the steps up back to the car park.

IRONBRIDGE

STAFFORDSHIRE

The county once famed for its potteries is otherwise gently rural, with unexpected features such as the spectacular sandstone ridge of Kinver Edge, and the old hunting ground of Cannock Chase.

1 Kinver

Over rocks and along a canal to explore a high ridge with ancient homes carved from sandstone.

LENGTH **7 miles (4 hours)**

PARKING **Signposted car park by Vale's Rock off Kingsford Lane, from west of Kinver**

CONDITIONS **Steep climbs at Kinver Edge**

REFRESHMENTS **Pubs in Kinver**

1 At the far end of the car park, take the path through a low gate into woods. Look up to see Vale's Rock, one of several cave houses dug out of the red sandstone around Kinver Edge centuries ago. Just before the rock turn right on a path. Where tracks and paths meet, fork left up a narrow path, which climbs steeply to a small reservoir. Fork left and then right on a track and continue to a T-junction.

2 Turn right on the road through Blakeshall. Where the road bends right out of the village, take the signposted footpath ahead. Continue along the bottom of the valley to two gates. Go through the left gate and climb the path between farm buildings. Pass a farmhouse on the right and turn right down a track, then cross a bridge over the River Stour and go past steelworks.

3 Cross a stile and turn left on the path along the Staffordshire and Worcestershire Canal. Continue on the towpath for 2 miles.

4 At Whittington Horse Bridge turn left on a track that crosses the River Stour. At Kinver's Anchor Hotel follow a road uphill then turn left at a T-junction with a residential road. At the T-junction by the Cross pub, cross the main road and go through a small swing gate opposite. Follow the path to a small road. Turn right and right again. At a T-junction with a major road turn left.

5 Just past the driveway to the House on the Hill, turn left at a footpath sign on a track towards Holy Austin Rock and the remains of an Iron Age hillfort, with magnificent views. Fork left on a wide track across the site of the fort towards its far edge, keeping to the right of the earthworks. Follow the broad stony track ahead along the ridge of Kinver Edge, a sandstone cliff rising out of wooded heathland. Continue on the main path to a crossing of paths by a map in a clearing. Fork right downhill and at the next junction of paths turn left back to the car park.

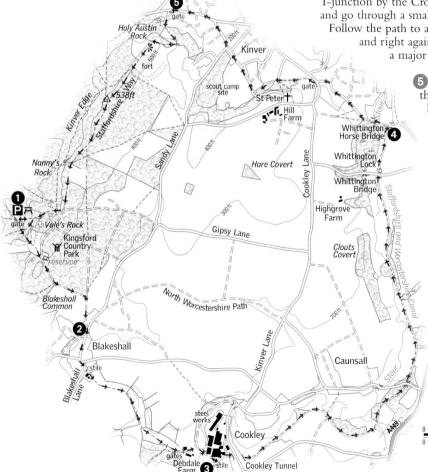

2 Milford Common

Heath, woodland and forest tracks, then beside a canal to a mansion and park full of classical wonders.

LENGTH 6 miles (3 hours)

PARKING Milford Common car park off A513 opposite Barley Mow pub

CONDITIONS Fair going, with some gentle climbs

REFRESHMENTS Pub at Milford village, restaurant and tearoom at Shugborough

1 From the car park, take the path marked Heart of England Way. Ignore a left fork and go ahead on a rising track between two tall pine trees with a fence on the left. Keep straight on to join a lane. Where the lane bends sharply right, keep ahead towards a house and turn left on another track, with the house on the right, past a wooden barrier onto a stony path through some trees. Go ahead at a multiple path junction to the next multiple path junction by Mere Pool.

2 Go straight ahead on a downhill stony track to the left of some wooden posts, signed to the Punch Bowl. At a path junction, turn right onto a wide track, following marker posts to the stepping stones across Sher Brook. Cross the stepping stones and go straight on to a track with a cycle track sign. Follow the track for 1 mile beside conifers and gnarled oaks. At the end of the track turn left to Seven Springs car park.

3 Walk left out of the car park to a junction with the A513. Cross the road and continue over the worn red cobblestones of Weetman's Bridge, built in 1887-8. Follow the lane under a railway bridge to a bridge over the Trent and Mersey Canal. The canal was designed by James Brindley and completed in 1777. Just before

the bridge go down steps on the right to the towpath, and turn left under the bridge to follow the canal. Ahead, Shugborough Hall (NT) comes into view; the 17th-century house was rebuilt in the classical style in the early 18th century. Pass under a bridge that ends abruptly at the banks of the Trent. At a bridge before a lock, turn left and go through a waymarked gap by a gate.

4 Continue ahead over the 14-arched Essex Bridge to reach Shugborough Hall lodge on the right. Go ahead on a tarmac track through rich pasture to the octagonal Tower of the Winds, built in the 1760s. Continue past red-brick Shugborough Park Farm on the right and soon pass a ha-ha – a walled ditch designed to keep out cattle without impairing the view from the house. Follow the road between the Shugborough Estate Ticket Office and car park, and continue to the A513.

5 Turn right and where the road straightens, opposite a red-brick house, turn right on a track leading to Cold Mans Slade picnic and parking area. Go ahead on a track through woodland, with a wire fence on the right. At a pair of reservoirs, follow the track as it bends left then right, then keep ahead on the narrow track just to the left of the reservoir gate. Head steeply downhill to meet the A513. Turn right and cross the road back to the car park.

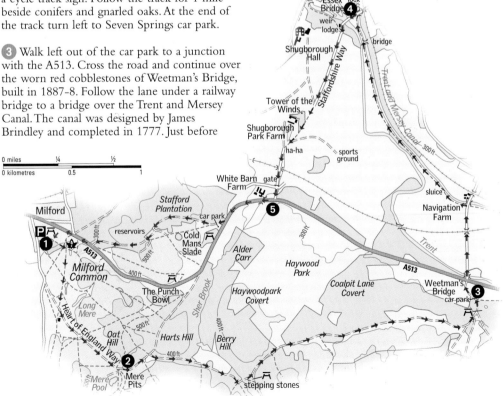

SUFFOLK

The rivers Orwell and Stour cut deeply into Suffolk's gentle agricultural landscape. Walking routes make the most of this water-rich countryside, leading from pretty villages that enjoy a special peace.

1 Cavendish

Through the Stour valley to Clare, an ancient market town with a country park around Norman ruins.

LENGTH 6 miles (3 hours)

PARKING In street behind village green between St Mary's Church and Five Bells pub

CONDITIONS A few gentle inclines

REFRESHMENTS Full range in Cavendish and Clare

CAVENDISH GREEN, THATCHED ALMSHOUSES AND CHURCH

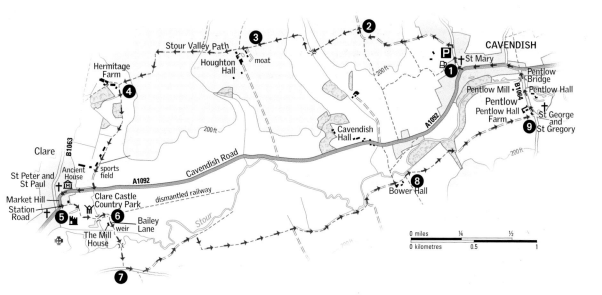

1 With St Mary's Church on the right, walk up the street and turn left just before a timber-framed house on the left. Follow the lane for about ¾ mile, ignoring two footpaths on the left, and head for a solitary house on the low ridge ahead.

2 Just beyond the house's garden hedge, turn left on the waymarked Stour Valley Path and continue along the ridge, with views over a broad valley of curved crop fields fringed by deep hedges and dotted with tall trees.

Follow a waymark sign across a plank bridge over a ditch, then cross a footbridge over a stream. On the far side, the path continues to the right and then left, gently ascending and crossing a culvert before reaching the brow of the hill.

3 Walk along the path past Houghton Hall farmyard on the left, ignoring a bridleway on the right. Continue ahead on a broad grassy track, then on a waymarked path that climbs alongside a dense hawthorn and blackthorn hedge.

Follow the path and hedge round to the left, then right towards Hermitage Farm. The little town of Clare can be seen in the valley below.

4 Where the path forks, just before the farm, turn left, continuing on the Stour Valley Path. It leads past an arable field, through the edge of a spinney, to a farmyard and then becomes a tarmac track around the edge of a sports field. When it reaches the A1092, turn right for Market Hill, at the heart of Clare, with the great Church of St Peter and St Paul towering above it. At a T-junction turn left into Market Hill, passing pastel-coloured houses and shops.

5 Turn left down Station Road and go through a gate to the old station buildings, which lost their railway lines in the 1960s. The buildings stand at the centre of a country park and on the site of a Norman castle, whose jagged remains crown the 305m (100ft), tree-clad motte. Its lords, the de Clares were for 300 years among the most powerful families in England.

From the station turn left and follow the line of the old railway over an iron bridge. Immediately turn left up a path with a handrail beside it, to the top of a green.

6 Turn right at the sign for Bailey Lane, towards the Georgian Mill House. Bear left, cross the weir and take the marked footpath half left across the meadow beyond. Cross the footbridge over the River Stour and continue to a road.

7 Turn left on the road. After about 200m turn left again onto a bridleway. Follow it almost to the river, then turn sharp right and, within a short distance, left on a path that leads through rich farmland, with low ridges on each side framing the valley. The path crosses a couple of tracks and reaches the riverside again before joining a driveway to Bower Hall.

8 Continue ahead, gaining a delightful view of the river at Bower Hall at a bend in the river, then along the edge of a field then through woods. From there join a bridleway to the B1064 at Pentlow.

9 Turn left into the riverside hamlet, which has an old red watermill, a timber-framed late-15th-century hall and the round-towered Norman Church of St George and St Gregory. Continue up the street, cross Pentlow Bridge and turn left to return to Cavendish.

SUFFOLK

2 Long Melford

From a village of glorious historical buildings,
beside a wood and across fertile fields to a
fine house where Tudor life is re-created.

LENGTH 5 miles (3 hours)

PARKING At upper end of village green

CONDITIONS Easy walking; gentle inclines

REFRESHMENTS Pubs in Long Melford and
Bridge Street

1 With the splendid Holy Trinity Church and
the red-brick almshouses on the left, walk across
the top end of the village green towards the
A1092, then turn left on the road. Before the
Hare Inn, cross the road and turn right past the
garden centre onto a concrete track called Hare
Drift. It leads through a belt of trees that soon
gives way to wide fields on both sides.

2 Cross the A134 and go through a gate onto a
grassy path, which leads through a landscape of
huge arable fields stretching towards dark distant
woods. After about ⅓ mile, follow the path as it
swings left along the edge of trees. Continue

with the woodland on the right – dense
blackthorn, hawthorn and a few taller oak trees
oddly interspersed with the occasional Second
World War concrete pillbox.

3 Just before the path reaches Chad Brook,
turn left on a path that runs parallel with the
water. Ragged robin, buttercups and dog roses
are among the wild flowers to be seen in season
along its banks as the path approaches the
Queech Plantation.

Continue beside the stream with the
plantation on the right, to a footbridge. Cross
the bridge and turn left on the other bank. Wide
arable fields can be seen on the right and the
wood soon dwindles to a tall double hedgerow
enclosing the path. Visible through the trees is
Ford Hall, an old Tudor-style timber-framed
building still partly surrounded by its moat.
Continue past it to a minor road.

4 Cross the bridge over Chad Brook and go
over the A134. Beyond the Rose and Crown
pub turn right and then left into the hamlet of
Bridge Street. Turn right up Aveley Lane for a
few metres, then turn left on a footpath and head
for open country. Overhead, larks ascend in
squadrons in spring and summer. At a post

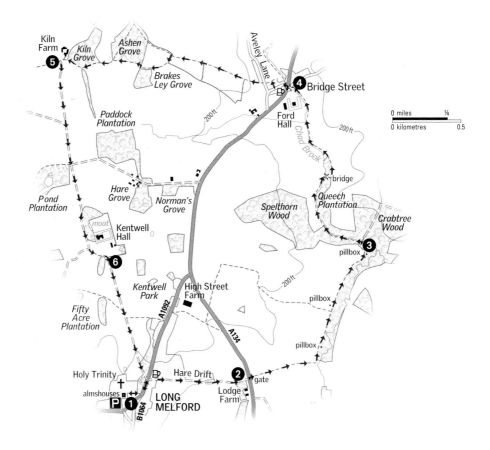

KENTWELL HALL

waymarked in three directions, turn left and follow the path. At the next waymark turn right towards woods. Continue along the edges of three small woods, Brakes Ley Grove on the left, and Ashen Grove and Kiln Grove on the right.

5 At a junction of paths near Kiln Farm buildings, turn left. Follow the long farm track, with broad acres on both sides extending to distant woodland. Continue straight ahead over several junctions. Ornamental trees can soon be seen in a copse on the left, and the pepperpot towers and terrace of Kentwell Hall appear. The path skirts the gardens of the Tudor red-brick mansion, built by the Clopton family, many of whom were buried in Holy Trinity Church. With its tall latticed windows, moat, large brick

dovecot and courtyard laid out in a brickwork maze, the hall has changed little over the centuries. Its attractions include the restored Elizabethan and Jacobean reception rooms, the timbered 15th-century Moat House, walled gardens and a rare breeds farm.

6 From the house, walk past the main gates and down the drive, a mile-long avenue of lime trees, many dating from the original 1678 planting. It passes a paddock where Suffolk Punch horses can be seen.

Closer to Long Melford, Holy Trinity Church and the almshouses appear across a meadow. At the end of the avenue, go through Kentwell Hall's park gates and turn right to return to Long Melford's village green.

SUFFOLK

3 Flatford Mill

The sinuous, willow-lined River Stour and lush Dedham Vale country – inspirations to the painter John Constable.

LENGTH 4 miles (2 hours)

PARKING Flatford Mill car park, south of East Bergholt

CONDITIONS Easy, flat going

REFRESHMENTS Pub and restaurants in Dedham, teashop at Flatford

1 Turn left from the car park and follow the road as it drops down. At the bottom, turn right on a waymarked path beside a stream. Turn left almost immediately on a rising path that runs beside a hedge, parallel with the road. Cross a minor road and rejoin the original road farther on through an opening on the left.

2 Cross a stile opposite into a field with wide views of open skies over the tree-lined River Stour and the luxuriant countryside of Dedham Vale. Follow the path half-right to another stile, and cross it to reach a junction. Turn right, ignoring a bridge on the left, then turn left over a stile at the next waymark. After 100m, cross a stile into a field. Follow the path through a series of fields and over two more stiles, keeping alongside a hedge to reach a stile at the corner of Fishpond Wood. Cross the stile into the wood, turn left over a footbridge and continue out of the wood. Turn sharp right, then after 25m turn left and follow a waymark to cross a stile and reach the junction with Donkey Lane.

3 Go straight ahead on the broad, tree-lined track through fields, with glimpses on the left

over the Stour of the Church of St Mary in Dedham, often painted by John Constable. Just past some cottages, turn left, following a waymark across a field to reach a road.

4 Turn left on the road. After 1/3 mile, cross the two bridges over the Stour. Boats can be hired from here. On the right is Dedham Mill, once owned by Constable's father and now converted into private flats. Constable painted the scene *Dedham Lock and Mill* in 1820. He spent his youth and early adult life in the Stour valley, and its languid water-meadow scenery inspired his most enduring work. 'I associate my careless boyhood with all that lies on the banks of the River Stour,' he wrote. 'Those scenes made me a painter and I am grateful.'

Opposite the mill, follow the waymark to a track and footbridges across a ford. Cross the bridges and follow a waymarked path on the right. Continue on the path past Dedham Rare Breeds Farm on the left, to a stile. Cross the stile into a field and continue beside a pond on the right and Dedham Hall on the left, to another stile. Cross the stile and turn right onto a gravel drive.

5 Where the drive meets a road, turn left into a field, on a path signposted to Flatford. Continue through a series of gates and stiles, signposted 'Flatford via River', to a wooden bridge over a stream and a stile. Turn right, crossing another bridge and stile beside the River Stour. Follow the path beside the meandering willow-lined river to a stile at Ram Lock.

6 Turn left and cross the bridge over the Stour to the thatched Bridge Cottage (NT), which houses a display on Constable and offers boats for hire. Turn right on a road to reach Flatford Mill and Willy Lott's House. These properties, and the nearby Valley Farm, were painted by Constable in the early 19th century and their charming riverside slumber has hardly been disturbed since. Constable's father owned Flatford Mill and the artist spent much of his childhood there. The group of buildings is owned by the National Trust but they are not open to the public.

Return to the bridge, following the road as it bears right. Take a path on the left, running beside the road, back to the car park.

4 Dunwich Heath

Sandy paths skirt a marshy nature reserve and lead to a town lost to the sea, by the crest of crumbling cliffs.

LENGTH 5½ miles (3 hours)

PARKING Car park by Coastguard Cottages (NT), about 5 miles south of Dunwich

CONDITIONS Easy; keep clear of the crumbling cliffs

REFRESHMENTS Café at Coastguard Cottages; pub in Dunwich; fish and chips on beach

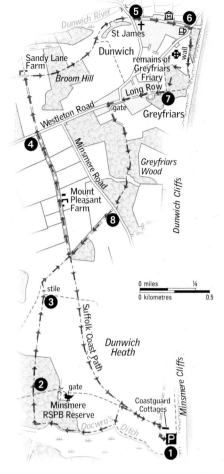

1 Walk through the car park gate and turn sharp left on a waymarked path. Ignoring the Suffolk Coast Path on the right, take the next left onto the NT footpath. The path drops down to Docwra's Ditch at the edge of Minsmere RSPB Reserve.

Turn right at the bottom of the ditch, beside a reedy lagoon. The marshes attract hundreds of birds, including avocets, bitterns and marsh harriers. Ignore two turnings to the right and continue on the path to a gate with Open Access and NT signs. Turn right and immediately left.

2 At a crossing of paths, turn right then left onto a sandy trail. Rising immediately to the right is Dunwich Heath – some of the last wild heathland in East Anglia, and home to nightjars, Dartford warblers, stonechats, red deer, common lizards and adders. On the left, behind an old parish boundary hedge, tank traps dug during the Second World War provide a sheltered haven for wildlife. Continue ahead to a gate and stile on the left.

3 Turn left over the stile and almost immediately turn right at a T-junction, to walk between hedgerows along old sheep walks. At a meeting of paths and farm tracks, turn left onto a farm track, passing between arable fields and to left of Mount Pleasant Farm. Continue to Westleton Road.

4 Cross the road to a track ahead, leading to Sandy Lane Farm. Turn right in front of the farm and follow a hedged bridleway to a crossroads by a church. Built in 1830, St James's is the last church left standing in Dunwich. The town's nine medieval churches succumbed to the sea over the centuries. The last of them, All Saints, disappeared in 1920, leaving behind a single buttress, which has been re-erected in St James's churchyard.

5 Walk ahead down St James Street, where a small museum exhibits a diorama of Dunwich demonstrating how relentless erosion by the sea has gradually destroyed this once prosperous medieval port and shipbuilding town. Continue to the Ship Inn at the end of the street.

6 Do not turn left on the road to the beach but turn right, and after a few metres turn left through trees onto the Suffolk Coast Path, which runs beside the walls of the ruined 13th-century Greyfriars Friary. On the other side of the path, brambles and bushes conceal the cliff edge and the last remaining headstones of what was once All Saints' churchyard. Follow the path right then left into a wood.

7 At the end of the wood turn right, passing the white wrought-iron gates of East Friars and a row of estate cottages on the left, to the junction with Westleton Road. Go forward on the road for about 30m, then turn left at a gate onto a private road, marked as a footpath. Continue through Greyfriars Wood to the junction with Minsmere Road.

8 Cross the road and follow a bridleway ahead, to a meeting of tracks and paths. Turn left on the waymarked path that leads back onto Dunwich Heath. The sandy path weaves through springy gorse and heather, offering a glorious panorama of sea and sky all the way back to the car park.

CENTRAL ENGLAND

SUFFOLK

5 Orford

Along the streets of a medieval port, across marshes, fields and woods inhabited by deer, and through parkland.

LENGTH 8 miles (4 hours)

PARKING Car park by quay

CONDITIONS Easy, but going can be heavy in the forest after rain

REFRESHMENTS Full range at Orford and Chillesford

1 Facing the Jolly Sailor pub, turn left out of the car park towards the quay. Turn left onto the quay path along the top of a grassy embankment, with marshes on the left, sailing dinghies on the right and Orfordness radio station in the distance ahead. Continue past the yacht clubhouse.

2 Turn left off the embankment down wooden steps. Climb a stile and follow the path across the first field to a T-junction with a grassy track. Turn left, along a drainage ditch, walking towards a colour-washed Georgian house in the distance, to a junction with a lane.

Turn left on the lane and follow it round to the right, skirting the wall of the Georgian house seen earlier. Turn right at the crossroads, with a thatched house on the left, and follow the lane to a T-junction. Turn left then, just before a group of new red-brick houses, turn right onto a signposted footpath. Follow the path leading across a field.

3 Turn right on the road and walk to the crossroads ahead. Turn left on a lane signposted 'Suffolk Coastal Route' (a cycling route) to meet the B1084. Turn right on the road and almost immediately right again on a marked bridleway overhung by branches. Continue ahead, crossing a farm road, and follow the field boundary on the right towards the tower of the isolated All Saints Church at the edge of forest. The church has a font dating from about 1200 and some fine 18th-century wood carving.

4 Cross the road beside the church, take the waymarked bridleway to the right of the Sudbourne Wood sign, and keep ahead between the trees. The track continues through gorse, bracken and mixed forest, where fallow and muntjac deer may be glimpsed. Ignore the rides and paths leading off to the left and right and

BOATS AT LOW TIDE, ORFORD

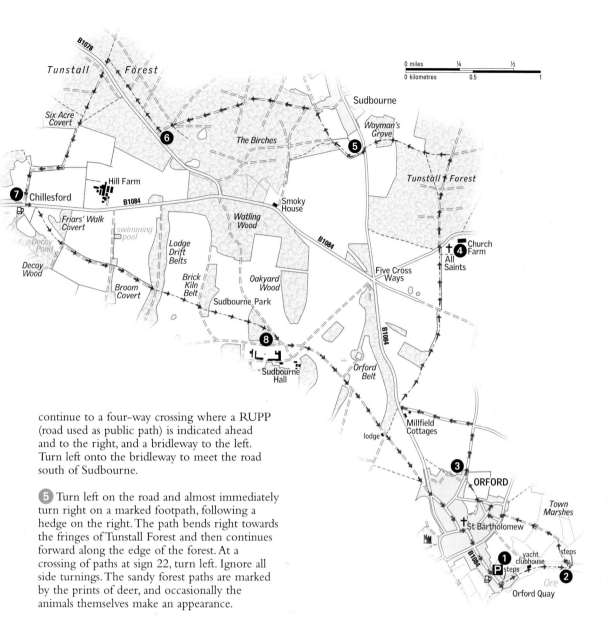

continue to a four-way crossing where a RUPP
(road used as public path) is indicated ahead
and to the right, and a bridleway to the left.
Turn left onto the bridleway to meet the road
south of Sudbourne.

5 Turn left on the road and almost immediately
turn right on a marked footpath, following a
hedge on the right. The path bends right towards
the fringes of Tunstall Forest and then continues
forward along the edge of the forest. At a
crossing of paths at sign 22, turn left. Ignore all
side turnings. The sandy forest paths are marked
by the prints of deer, and occasionally the
animals themselves make an appearance.

6 Just before the B1078 – traffic is audible and
visible through the trees – turn right on a path
running parallel with the road under power lines,
ignoring all side turnings. At the bend in the
power lines, when the path reaches a public
footpath, turn left to emerge onto the road.
    Cross the road to the bridleway opposite and
follow it through the wood, ignoring any side
turnings. Continue ahead across fields, bearing
right then left at a track to meet the B1084 at
Chillesford beside the Froize Inn, whose name
comes from a dialect word for 'friars'.

7 Turn left on the road, continue for a short
distance, then turn right onto a broad grassy
path, signposted to Orford. Walk through the
fields and coppices to enter Sudbourne Park. The
avenues of ancient chestnuts are reminders that

this was once one of the great estates of Suffolk.
Continue on the path to meet a drive joining
from the left.

8 Turn right on the drive, passing Sudbourne
Hall, fronted by lawns with urns on pedestals.
The original Sudbourne House was pulled down
after the Second World War, during which it
served as HQ for an army division. The present
building has been converted into flats.
    Follow the drive through parkland and
eventually out of the estate by a lodge building.
At the lodge, keep forward on a track, with
St Bartholomew's Church in view ahead. Where
the track meets the B1084 by an Orford village
sign, cross over to take the left fork into Orford
and return to the car park.

WARWICKSHIRE

This county's walks traverse a landscape that is typically English. Russet earth to the south meets green fields in a pleasing rural patchwork, while the gentle rise and fall of the land offers lovely views.

1 Fenny Compton

Through a country park, past the remains of a Saxon burial ground, to a grand medieval church that has long outlived its village.

LENGTH	4 miles (2½ hours)
PARKING	Memorial Road in village
CONDITIONS	A few steep climbs
REFRESHMENTS	Pubs in Fenny Compton

1 With Fenny Compton's village hall and fire station on the right, walk along Memorial Road to the T-junction. Turn left and after 20m, just past a thatched cottage called The Croft, turn right along a grassy waymarked path.

Continue over a stile onto a path with a fence on the left. Go ahead to cross another stile and then follow the waymarked path across two fields and over a cattle bridge.

2 Continue ahead, passing a barn on the right, as the path widens to a gate. Follow the waymark signs, across fields and pasture, towards Northend. Leaving the last pasture, turn left through a kissing gate, from where the path swings left past modern bungalows and cottages to join the road.

3 Turn left along the road. After about 130m, turn left along a lane at a waymarked no-through road. The lane climbs up past houses and then becomes a grassy path, as it approaches the 41ha (100 acre) Burton Dassett Hills Country Park. Follow the waymark arrows, passing over three stiles in quick succession, and bear right into a humpy hill pasture.

Pass between Bonfire Hill to the right and Pleasant Hill to the left. In 1908 quarrymen unearthed a Saxon burial place, containing 35 skeletons, at Pleasant Hill. They are thought to be the remains of Saxons killed in an unrecorded battle in the 6th or 7th century.

4 Cross a stile and, with Windmill Hill's beacon tower up on the right, follow an indistinct grassy path up a steep slope to join a road. There are magnificent views from the beacon, built by a local squire, Sir Edward Belknap, in the late 14th century, probably as a lookout tower.

Follow the road, passing some disused iron-ore quarries on the left. These were mined in the late 19th century and again, briefly, during the First World War.

At a T-junction, join the main road that bends round from the right and continue straight ahead, past Magpie Hill on the right. From the summit of the hill there are views to Edge Hill,

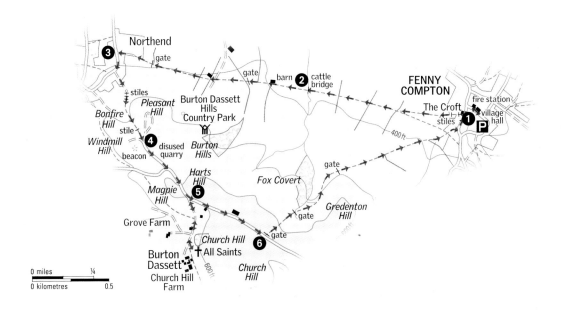

166

Stratford-upon-Avon and further to Bredon Hill, the Malvern Hills and, on a clear day, even the Clee Hills, rising up 52 miles away.

⑤ Fork right to Burton Dassett, then bear left to reach its imposing mellow brown ironstone church, All Saints, which is built into the hillside. Inside, the floor slopes 4.6m (15ft) between its two ends. The church has massive Norman doorways and is crammed with many other fine decorative features, including wall paintings, lancet windows and delightful carved figures on the capitals of its pillars, which date from the 13th and 14th centuries, when All Saints stood at the centre of a thriving market town.

The population of Burton Dassett was severely depleted by the Black Death (1348-9) and, in Tudor times, the eviction of large numbers of tenants by Sir Edward Belknap, who enclosed

243ha (600 acres) to raise sheep for their profitable wool. The town's sizeable church now serves only a tiny community. Retrace your steps to the fork in the road and turn sharp right towards Fenny Compton, passing a group of farm buildings on the left.

⑥ After about ¼ mile, turn left through a field gate. The indistinct path bears right and goes downhill, across pasture to another gate. Follow the waymarked path past Fox Covert, the copse on the left, and round Gredenton Hill on the right, and then bear right to a gate. Follow the path towards Fenny Compton, beside a hedge with fine views beyond it to the left and fields to the right, for ½ mile. Cross a small field, going straight over a crossing of paths, and bear right to join the road. Turn left past the stone cottages and houses, then right into Memorial Road.

THE BEACON ON WINDMILL HILL

WORCESTERSHIRE

Some of the county's most attractive paths ascend from mellow towns into the Cotswold Hills, following high ridges into broadleaved woods and farmland. Fine views extend to the Malvern Hills and the Vale of Evesham.

1 Broadway

A stiff climb to a folly tower on top of a Cotswold escarpment and downhill through beech woods.

LENGTH 4 miles (2½ hours)

PARKING Car park in Leamington Road (B4632)

CONDITIONS A demanding walk with one steep climb of about 210m (690ft)

REFRESHMENTS Range in Broadway

1 Turn left out of the car park and left again, passing the fine medieval stone Priory Manse on the corner, onto the broad main street lined by a wide green and chestnut trees.

2 After 200m, turn right into an alleyway, following an acorn sign for the Cotswold Way and Broadway Tower. After a gate, then a kissing gate, the path crosses a small stream and passes an orchard. Continue uphill to another kissing gate, then cross a field to its opposite corner, passing a waymark post in the middle.

3 Where the path forks, continue along the Cotswold Way across the next field, beside hawthorn bushes. The serious climb up the Cotswold escarpment then begins.

Follow marker posts to a stile in the upper right-hand corner of the field and carry on

upwards beside a stone wall. The last part of the climb is eased by steps and a handrail. From seats near the top of the hill, there are extensive views over the Vale of Evesham. The climb now becomes easier and the top of Broadway Tower can soon be glimpsed jutting above the brow of the hill.

4 As the path crests the escarpment the tower, with its three canted walls sandwiched between crenellated towers, is fully revealed.

The folly was built around 1800 by the 6th Earl of Coventry to please his new wife, who believed that it would be visible from her family home near Worcester. She proved her theory was correct before building began by ordering a beacon to be lit on the site.

From the tower, go through the gate and continue on the Cotswold Way, which bends sharp left on top of the escarpment. The path winds for about ½ mile along the edge of the escarpment through thorn bushes.

5 Where a broad farm track sweeps across the path, turn left and then right at a Cotswold Way marker post. Head down a little hollow into woods dominated by magnificent beech trees, and follow the waymark posts to the A44.

6 Cross the road and go down steps into a wood, leaving the Cotswold Way. Where a path joins from the left, keep straight ahead on the higher level and continue through the beech wood. As the path descends, look for a marker post and turn right up the steps. Head uphill and follow the path to the left along the edge of the wood. The path wriggles through trees for about ½ mile – ignore any side tracks. Turn left at a marker post and follow the steps down to a stile and a road.

7 Cross the road and a driveway, and climb a stile to a path, signposted to Broadway. As the path descends a magnificent panorama of the escarpment stretches away to the horizon.

Continue downhill past marker posts and waymarks, eventually going under the A44 and into Broadway.

8 At the junction with Broadway's main street, turn right into the town past traditional Cotswold buildings, and turn right again to return to the car park.

2 Overbury

A stimulating walk to the summit of Bredon Hill, at the northwest frontier of the Cotswolds.

LENGTH 6½ miles (3½ hours)

PARKING On road near St Faith's Church

CONDITIONS Good paths; one moderate climb

REFRESHMENTS None on walk

1 With the Church of St Faith and Overbury Court on your left, follow the road round a right bend past Church Row cottages. At a T-junction, turn left and follow the road that climbs steadily through Overbury, a village of mellow Cotswold stone and half-timbered houses.

2 At a road junction, continue straight on uphill on a lane signed 'No Through Road'. Fork right on a footpath that climbs steadily along the walled side of a predominantly beech wood, edged with ash trees.

3 At the end of the wood, bend right then left to continue alongside a bramble-covered drystone wall on the left, to a farm track. The path bears slightly right across the track and heads upwards towards another wood. Follow the path up the left side of the wood to reach a crossing with a broad track. Turn right; soon there are extensive views to the south. Where the track reaches a stone wall at a path junction, turn left and continue uphill towards another wood.

4 At a gate turn left and follow the well-trodden path along the edge of the wood. Go through a gate into a field and follow the path, with a fence on the left. Continue along the ridge, with views of the Vale of Evesham and the Malvern Hills, through a gate and alongside a drystone wall. The path and wall bend left towards 18th-century Parson's Folly, which marks the 293m (961ft) summit of Bredon Hill, the site of an Iron Age hillfort. On a clear day the Welsh mountains can be seen in the far distance.

5 With the tower on the left and a drystone wall on the right, continue ahead to go through a gate, along a field edge and through another gate into a narrow wood. Ignoring a downward-branching path on the right, follow the main track to a waymarked stile on the left. Turn left over the stile, walk along the edge of the field, and continue ahead to pass to the right of a barn

with a sundial on its side, Sundial Farm. Go through a gate and continue to a T-junction.

6 Turn left through a waymarked gate and continue uphill, with a wall on the right. Where a broad track known as the Belt joins from the right, turn right through a waymarked gate. At a junction with a metalled lane, turn right and descend steadily on the lane through trees. Ignore a right fork and continue past The Lodge on the right and across a stream.

7 At the entrance to Overbury Park, cross a cattle grid and turn right on the road back to Overbury village. Turn right towards the Church of St Faith. The church dates from the early 11th century; gargoyles adorn the corners of its 14th-century tower. St Faith, who was martyred by the Romans in AD 268, is depicted in a window in the north aisle. A bishop holding two croziers is carved into stone panels on the remarkable Norman font. From the church return to the parking place.

CENTRAL ENGLAND

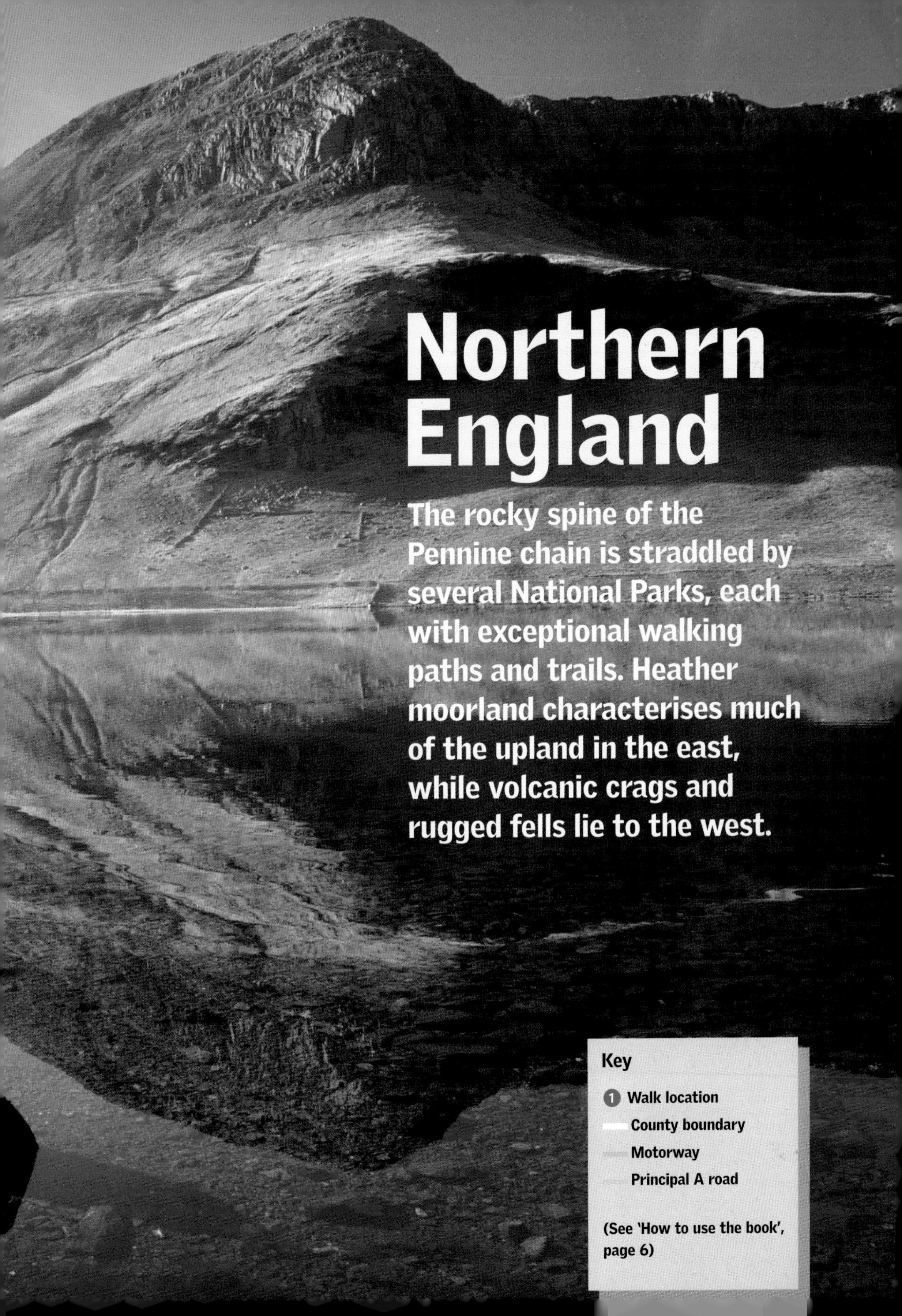

Northern England

The rocky spine of the Pennine chain is straddled by several National Parks, each with exceptional walking paths and trails. Heather moorland characterises much of the upland in the east, while volcanic crags and rugged fells lie to the west.

Key

1 Walk location

County boundary

Motorway

Principal A road

(See 'How to use the book', page 6)

CUMBRIA

The Lake District in Cumbria is one of Britain's most distinctive and beautiful landscapes – dramatic fells and peaks mirrored in long, deep 'waters' or lakes. The region's walks are bracing and the views matchless.

1 Dent

From a Dales village by riverside meadows and a stony beck, and along the foothills of rugged high fells.

LENGTH 5 miles (3 hours)

PARKING In car park opposite village school

CONDITIONS Mostly clear riverside and valley tracks, but some quite steep ascents

REFRESHMENTS Pubs and tearooms in Dent

1 From the car park, face the village school and turn right on the main street, then just before the tearoom turn right on the footpath towards the River Dee. Cross the field and go through the stile. Turn right beside the wall and go through the narrow gate, then turn left immediately along the fence. Go through another stile and continue to the river. Ahead are the farm buildings of High Hall and Low Hall, among pastures and meadows, and steeper fells, rising to Aye Gill Pike.

Turn right on the Dales Way, an 81-mile trail linking the National Parks of the Yorkshire Dales and the Lake District. Ash and wych elm, oak and sycamore trees shade the path, and in summer the banks of the Dee are hidden in a dense carpet of marsh flowers. Cross over a dry stream, then a footbridge and climb up the steps to the road.

2 Cross the road to the squeeze stile and go down the steps by a path signposted to Mill Bridge, passing Dent village green on the right. Go through the wicket gate, cross the field, then turn left through a wicket gate by a large metal gate, to go over connected bridges. Rejoin the riverside path for about ½ mile.

3 After crossing a footbridge, the path bears right as it leaves the River Dee to continue beside Deepdale Beck, a stony side stream. Like many other becks in the limestone uplands, it has dry stretches where the water vanishes into chambers and channels under the ground. Continue along the beck through a series of stiles and gates to the junction with the road.

Turn left along the road then, just before the bridge, cross the road and go through a wicket gate to join the path signposted to Deepdale Lane. Soon, where the path divides, fork right up a track and continue uphill onto an open field. Turn left and walk along the edge of the trees with the field rising to the right. Continue to a wall, then turn right and go steeply uphill along the wall. After about 50m, where a path joins from the right, turn left through a stile and go straight along the contour and above the line of trees, with the hill on the right.

Before the end of the field, bear left below the remains of an old limekiln to reach a wall stile. Cross the stile and take the path leading towards the right-hand corner of a derelict building. Ahead and left is the austere whaleback slope of Whernside. At 736m (2,415ft), its summit is the highest of the Three Peaks, which include the nearby Ingleborough (724m/2,375ft) and Pen-y-ghent (693m/2,273ft).

4 Go through the stile, climb the bank and turn right on the track, keeping to the left of the field, which climbs past farm buildings and through several gates to a road. Cross the road and take the broad concrete track opposite, signposted to Nun House Outrake. Where the track bears right to High Nun House, continue ahead on a stony track, climbing steeply out of woodland. Follow the track along the walled

ALONG THE FOOTHILLS OF THE HIGH FELLS
DENTDALE

outrake, a lane used to drive flocks of sheep to and from the valley farms. On each side is rough pasture, pockmarked by 'shake holes' where underground limestone beds have dissolved and the surface has collapsed. Continue to a gate and a walled track on the right, signposted to Keldishaw.

5 Turn right and cross a small stream. The track follows the contour of the fellside, crossing springs and gills and scars of old mine workings, with the valley spread out to the right. Ahead in the far distance are the Howgill Fells. Continue for about 1¼ miles, to cross a bridge across Flinter Gill, a cleft in the limestone flanked by a stand of rowans, to a side track on the right signposted to Dent.

6 Turn right, go through a gate and continue downhill. To the right, the cleft of Flinter Gill becomes a wooded gorge. The track becomes a steep sunken lane, edged by hazel, elm and hawthorn. Where the lane meets the road, walk ahead to the main village road and the car park.

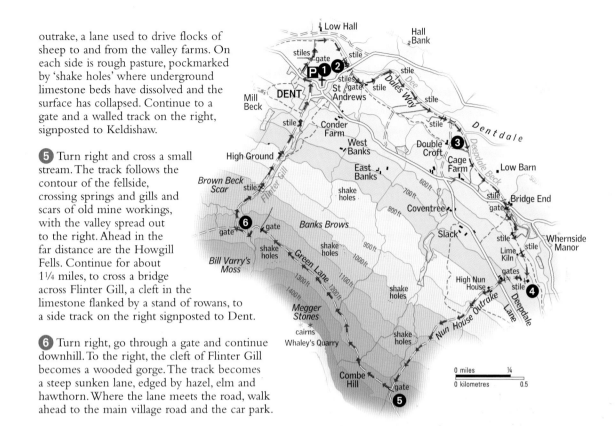

CUMBRIA

2 High Wray

Through woodland, by England's largest lake, climbing gently to a moorland summit with superb views of southern Lakeland.

LENGTH 4½ miles (2½ hours)

PARKING On road marked Windermere via Ferry, in car park at end of surfaced road

CONDITIONS Two steady ascents, but neither is steep; clear paths, tracks and minor roads

REFRESHMENTS Pubs and teashops in Hawkshead

1 Cross the gate at the end of the surfaced road onto the lakeside track marked 'Vehicular Access' to Belle Grange, a lone house amid luxuriant rhododendrons. Just after Belle Grange turn right onto a flagstone path signposted to Hawkshead, part of the old carriage road to Hawkshead. The woodlands are a haunt of red and roe deer. Continue to a division in the path.

2 Fork right, on the path marked Hawkshead via Guide Posts. Keep to the main path, past a Claife Estate National Trust sign and alongside the forestry fence to a path junction.

3 Go across the junction, then immediately fork right and go over another junction towards Hawkshead, now following part of a waymarked route from the Windermere

ferry to Latterbarrow. Numbered posts line the path, as well as white-topped wooden posts. Follow the path to post 11.

4 Turn right and follow the clear winding track through partly cleared woodland, then cross a stile and climb to the summit cairn. The moorland hill, despite its modest 244m (803ft) height, affords a superb view over Windermere, backed by Wansfell Pike, The Old Man of Coniston, Bow Fell, Fairfield, Langdale Pikes and Dollywaggon Pike. From the cairn take the well-trodden path that drops sharply to the left, in line with distant Hawkshead village. Continue down to a path running along the edge of the trees, above the stream and a wall; turn right along it, descending steadily to emerge at a road.

5 Turn right onto the road and where the road divides, fork left towards Hole House. At the next fork, bear right. Where the road bends right, continue ahead on a signposted track to Wray Castle, past a house and through fields, with views to the left of Blelham Tarn. Leave a second field by a stile, ignoring a gate to the left, then follow yellow waymarkers through three more fields to a gate by the road.

6 Turn left, then after about 300m turn right onto a driveway between entrance pillars at the gatehouse of Wray Castle. The mock-medieval castle, now a telecommunications training college, was built in 1845 by Dr James Dawson, a retired surgeon. In 1882, at the age of 16, Beatrix Potter was brought here by her parents on her first holiday in the Lake District. There she met Canon Rawnsley, a founder of the National Trust, who later suggested Frederick Warne as a publisher for her first book, *The Tale of Peter Rabbit*.

7 Follow the drive to the left of the castle and go down the steps on the left, then follow an enclosed path, with a field fence on the left. At the end of the field turn left onto a path along the edge of woodland to the right, and continue to a junction of paths at Windermere's Low Wray Bay.

Turn right on the lakeside path, along wooded shores dotted with villas, many built in the 19th century by wealthy magnates. On leaving the woodland through a gate and emerging into a field, keep near the lake shore.

At High Wray Bay, with its two stone boathouses, go through the gate ahead and turn left onto the lakeside track, then continue about ¾ mile back to the car park.

3 Coniston

An energetic walk combining mining relics and views across Coniston Water, ending on a lakeside path.

LENGTH 5½ or 5¾ miles (3½ or 3¾ hours)

PARKING At National Park information centre

CONDITIONS Fairly demanding

REFRESHMENTS Full range in Coniston; small shop at Coniston Hall

1 From the car park, turn left on the road and walk past the Crown Hotel and St Andrew's Church, where the 19th-century critic and author John Ruskin is buried. At the junction with the A593, turn left, cross the bridge then immediately turn right. Just past the Sun Inn, turn right on the road. At the end of the road turn left through a waymarked gate and continue on the track ahead. After a field and a footbridge, the track ascends alongside Church Beck for about ¼ mile to a waterfall by Miners Bridge.
DETOUR *The track ahead leads to Coppermines Valley, the scene of intense mining activity from 1599 until the 1890s. Scattered about are the remains of engine houses, inclines and wheel shafts, and miners' cottages.*

2 Do not cross the bridge, but turn sharp left on a rising path, which gives views of Coniston Water. After crossing a footbridge over Scrow Beck, follow the left side of two fields to a stile in a bend in a narrow road. Walk ahead to the bend to the right, take the track ahead and go through a gate. Follow the grass track to Heathwaite Farm, ignoring the enclosed path to the left.
   Just before the farm turn left down the field edge to a farm road. Turn right into the farmyard then left opposite the farmhouse, signed Torver. Cross a small yard and follow the side of the field; in the next field keep near the top edge and go through the gate ahead. Turn left onto the path then fork right on a path between walls, ignoring a gate on the left. Join the end of a road by a house and descend to the A593.

3 Cross the road and turn right. Where the road bears right, go through a signposted gate on the left. Continue along the course of an old railway line, through a gate into woods, then on the road serving a caravan park.
   Where the road bears right to meet the A593 continue ahead. After about 100m turn left through a gate onto a grassy track, passing under power lines. Continue along the length of the field, go over a footbridge and into woodland then back into a field. Here, follow the waymark left to Hoathwaite Farm.

Turn right in the farmyard, following yellow waymarks into a field, then turn left through a gate into woods. At the next field, cross half right and follow the track past Brackenbarrow Farm on the right to a T-junction with another path.

4 Turn left on the path, through a gate, the first of several into Torver Common Wood. Follow the main track through woodland (ignoring a fork to the right and then left), through a gap in an old wall to a clearing and on to the lakeside path.
   Turn left on the path, from where Brantwood, John Ruskin's former house, can be seen across the water. Keep to the lakeside until the route enters a campsite; at the T-junction with the campsite road turn right. Continue past Coniston Hall on the right, distinguished by its massive chimneys.

5 Beyond the hall, where the road bears left, take a broad path ahead then left away from the lake. At the end of the field bear right through a gate. Turn left at the road junction, into Coniston.

175

CUMBRIA

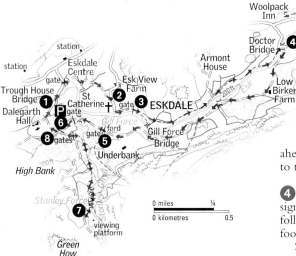

3 Go through the gate to a division of paths. Look for a grassy path bearing slightly to the left, which might not easily be seen when the bracken is high, ignoring the main path that swings to the right to Gill Force Bridge.

The path soon loses sight of the river and rises through rough grazing land. Walk on, with views towards Hardknott Pass and neighbouring fells ahead and slightly to the right, before descending to the river by Doctor Bridge.

4 Cross the bridge and fork right on a track signposted to Dalegarth. Past Low Birker Farm follow the track as it bears right, crossing a footbridge over a stream.

Soon after the footbridge, the track passes a small conifer wood on the left. Visible through the trees is a secluded tarn, the haunt of herons. Continue for about ½ mile, past Gill Force Bridge on the right, to the corner of a wall and a waymarked bridleway on the right.

5 Continue ahead on the main track, crossing a ford and going through a gate into woodland. Soon after crossing a footbridge over Stanley Ghyll, the track leaves woodland through another gate into a field. At the end of the field go through a gate to a signpost.

6 Turn left on the path signposted to Stanley Ghyll and Birker Fell. After about 100m go through a gate into woodland on the left, then follow the main path up the wooded ravine, crossing and recrossing Stanley Ghyll by footbridges to the Stanley Force waterfall.

7 Just before the third footbridge, leading to the waterfall's main pool, a steep path on the right leads to a viewing platform for a dizzying sight of falls and sheer 45m (150ft) drops.

Return downstream to the signpost and the junction with the track walked earlier.

8 Turn left on the track and then immediately right on the path, passing Dalegarth Hall on the left, with its tall chimney stacks. Part of the hall dates from the 13th century, but it has been extended over the centuries. The local breed of Herdwick sheep, one of the hardiest in the country, can often be seen grazing by the hall.

At a junction of paths, bear right to return to the car park.

4 Eskdale

Alongside the fast-flowing River Esk, with charming vistas of fell and pasture, and a climb to a hidden waterfall.

LENGTH 3½ miles (2 hours)

PARKING Trough House Bridge car park, on narrow road just west of Dalegarth station, west of Boot

CONDITIONS Clear, mostly level riverside tracks and paths; one climb to Stanley Force waterfall

REFRESHMENTS None on walk; café at Dalegarth station; pub in Boot

1 From the car park turn right towards the main Eskdale road. Cross the bridge over the Esk and continue for about 100m, then turn right through a gate on a path signposted to St Catherine's Church.

The path soon emerges from trees, and then continues, enclosed by drystone walls, to a junction of paths near the church.

2 Turn right to the church, which was largely rebuilt in 1881. The first church on this site is thought to have been built in the 12th century. Some features of a 14th-century structure remain in the present church – the east window and the font, which spent 60 years in a nearby farmyard before being returned here in 1876. By the door, a board records the 18th-century 'poor stock' donations that were given to the church so that it could help the needy.

Just past the church turn left on the riverside path signposted to Doctor Bridge, and then continue to a gate.

5 Grange

Around the head of Derwent Water and up steep woods to a tumbling beck and a magical tarn, over two packhorse bridges.

LENGTH 6½ miles (4½ hours)

PARKING Near Methodist church

CONDITIONS Steep and stony leaving Borrowdale

REFRESHMENTS Full range at Grange and Rosthwaite; tearooms at Watendlath

1 Walk away from the bridge and through the farming village of Grange, past Holy Trinity Church, and along a winding lane past houses and farm buildings. Just beyond a stream, turn right through a gate onto a path signposted to Lodore.

Cross a stream and fork right through two gates to a boardwalk across a marshy area. The path skirts Great Bay, at the south end of Derwent Water, a refuge for wildfowl. Follow the path and boardwalk to a footbridge over the Derwent. There are good views to the left of Derwent Water and over Keswick to Skiddaw. Beyond the bridge turn right; cross a fence stile and bear left away from the river, across another stile to a road.

2 Turn left on the road. Past the Borrowdale Hotel, cross the road and go through a farm gate. The track bears left behind a farmhouse, then zigzags steeply up through birch woodland. Continue on the main path and at the crest of the hill, go over a fallen wall and downhill towards Watendlath Beck. Go through a gate at the end of a wall, with an attractive waterfall on the left, and follow the path through oak woodland to a junction. Turn right on a broad stony track, go through a gate in a wall and turn left towards a footbridge.

Turn right just before the footbridge to follow the beck, a haunt of dippers, grey wagtails and common sandpipers. Where the beck forks, follow a path through a gate in a wall and along to stone steps and through another gate. Continue with Watendlath visible ahead, going through two more gates. Follow the wall leading left to the beck, then bear right on a rocky path to a gate. A packhorse bridge crosses the beck to Watendlath, a hamlet built on the site of a Viking settlement.

3 Continue ahead with the beck on the left and go through a gate. Fork right on the path signed to Rosthwaite, gaining superb views. Past the brow of the hill, the path descends steeply. Shortly after crossing a stream, ignore a path to the right and continue down to go through a gate in a wall. Follow the path downhill through two more gates to a crossing with a metalled track.

Turn right and go over a packhorse bridge to a road. Turn left on the road, then turn right through the farming village of Rosthwaite. The walled lane becomes a track. At the river, do not cross it, but follow the path to the right and continue to a packhorse bridge on the left.

4 Cross the bridge, go through a gate, then bear right along the river. Go through a gate and into woodland, bearing left away from the river. Ignore paths to the right. Follow the path through gaps in two walls as it rises, then falls to meet the river. Follow to the left through a gate, then right across two streams. Follow the walled track to a junction with a metalled lane, and turn right into Grange.

177

CUMBRIA

6 Langdale

A walk punctuated by waterfalls and rivers coursing over stones and rocks, and passing a working slate quarry.

LENGTH 5½ miles (3 hours)

PARKING Silverthwaite car park off B5343 between Skelwith Bridge and Elterwater

CONDITIONS Moderately demanding, involving some short but steep slopes and rough terrain

REFRESHMENTS Café and pub at Skelwith Bridge; pub at Elterwater

1 From the entrance to the car park, cross the road and take the path signposted to Langdale and Elterwater. Follow the path through a belt of woodland to a gate with a field beyond.

At the far side of the field, turn left on a riverbank path beside the Brathay. Continue through a gate into the woods, past a footbridge to Skelwith Force, a wide, surging waterfall – not high, but carrying a large volume of water.

A short distance farther on is the main road in the village of Skelwith Bridge. Do not continue ahead to the main road, but return to the footbridge and cross it. Keep following the clear path, passing houses, until joined by another path on the left at a waymarked post.

2 Continue uphill through a gate on the far boundary of the wood, into fields. The path merges with a track; carry straight on, passing to the left of a house, and continuing through two kissing gates to Park Farm. On the far side of the farmyard turn right on a waymarked path between outbuildings, and go through a gate leading into fields. Continue over stiles and into a wood and finally to a stile leading onto a minor road.

3 Turn right and follow the road for a short distance, then cross a stile on the left signposted to High Park. The footpath immediately divides; take the right-hand fork. The path follows the wooded riverbank upstream, past the spectacular waterfall of Colwith Force, to a gate on the woodland boundary.

4 Go through the gate and follow the path across fields and straight through the farmyard at High Park, to a minor road. Turn right and follow the road to the neighbouring farmhouse of Stang End. Immediately beyond the buildings turn right, through a gate, onto a wall-lined path, and continue across a footbridge to a gate on the edge of a minor road.

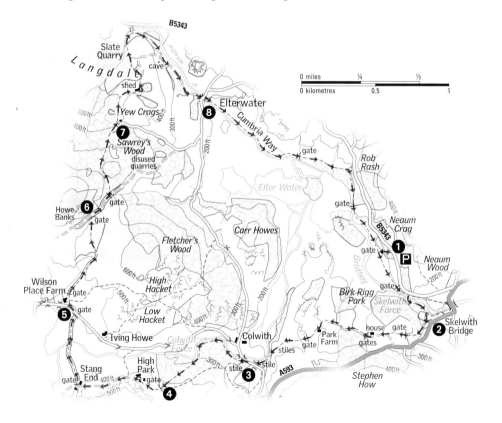

5 Turn left on the road for about 75m, then follow a track on the right, past Wilson Place Farm, to a gate. The waymarked path beyond the gate climbs across two fields before reaching a kissing gate that leads onto a bridleway.

6 Go through the gate and turn right on the bridleway. Go through another gate 200m along the track, then turn left on a path through Sawrey's Wood. Continue to a crossing of paths and turn right to emerge onto a minor road, then turn left. Almost immediately, the road reaches the end of a bridleway on the right, leading past a house.

7 Turn right along the bridleway, which winds clearly through a working slate quarry. Just after passing the last shed, turn left on a road. Continue for a short distance, then take a path on the left identified by green signs. The path leads down to Great Langdale Beck, then follows its right bank downstream. Ignore a footbridge that leads to a road into Chapel Stile village; stay on the right bank. The path rejoins the quarry road. Keep left, parallel to the river, as far as a minor road on the edge of Elterwater village.

8 Turn left towards the village centre and cross a bridge over Brathay, then immediately turn right and walk through a NT car park to join the riverside path. This is part of the Cumbria Way, some 70 miles of path linking Carlisle to the north and Ulverston to the south. The gnarled slopes of Huntingstile Crag and Scartufts climb to the left; later, to the right, Langdale Pikes can be seen looking back over Elter Water.

Continue through the gates bounding the woodland around the lake until you arrive at the path on the left, used at the start of the walk. Turn left and retrace your steps to the car park.

WATER ROARS AND CHATTERS THROUGH THE WOODLAND
RIVER BRATHAY, UPSTREAM OF COLWITH FORCE

CUMBRIA

7 Buttermere

A circuit popular since Victorian times – around a quiet lake mirroring elegant crags and fells.

LENGTH 4 miles (2½ hours)

PARKING National Trust car park in village

CONDITIONS Level paths, but some sections are narrow and uneven

REFRESHMENTS Full range in Buttermere village

1 Walk into the village and turn right on the road beside the Bridge Hotel, and continue to the Fish Hotel. Facing the hotel, take the track on the left of the building, which bears left through a gate. Continue ahead through another gate, ignoring a gate and path on the right. There are views ahead of Red Pike and Sourmilk Gill cascade.

2 Go through another gate and turn right to cross a footbridge over Buttermere Dubs. (Dubs are deep pools in a stream, a haunt of large trout.) Go through a wicket gate into Burtness Wood and take the broad lakeside path signposted 'Lake Shore Permitted Path'. At a shingle beach, take the left fork along the shore for good views of Hassness with the slopes of Robinson towering 738m (2,420ft) above.

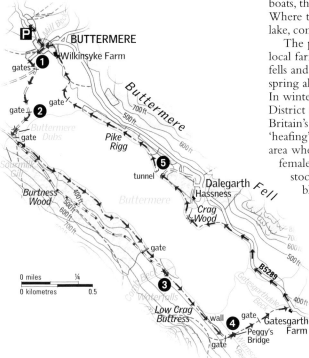

At the end of the wood, go through a gate in a wall and continue over a footbridge across Comb Beck. There are impressive views of the hanging valley on the shoulders of High Stile and High Crag.

3 Continue ahead to a wall on the left. Follow the path along the wall, then at a junction with a waymarked bridleway, turn left through a gate and cross a footbridge over Warnscale Beck. The views to the right are magnificent. On one side of the tumbling brook is a ridge rising sharply to Fleetwith Pike; on the other is the hummocky summit of Haystacks.

4 Follow the broad track through a gate and continue ahead, passing to the left of Gatesgarth Farm, to reach a road. Turn left on the road; it is not usually very busy, but walk on the right-hand side to face the traffic. After about 200m cross to the left side of the road to take a short footpath, avoiding a difficult corner.

Where the road bends left along the edge of the lake, turn left on a path, which for several hundred metres is rough, stony and often quite muddy. It goes through several gates and over a footbridge, along a terrace in the rocky slope and through a tunnel. This was built in the 19th century by a local landowner to keep his workers gainfully employed during winter.

5 The path comes out of the tunnel and passes a small landing stage for fishermen's rowing boats, then continues through several more gates. Where the shore bends left at the head of the lake, continue ahead.

The pasture on the left is important to the local farmers, most of whose grazing is on the fells and commons where the grass is poor; in spring all these fields are full of ewes and lambs. In winter and summer, the high fells of the Lake District are populated by Herdwick sheep, Britain's hardiest breed. They are noted for their 'heafing' instinct – never straying far from the area where they were raised. Both male and female are long-haired, short-legged and stocky; ewes are hornless. Lambs are born black, and become paler as they age. 'Herdwycks' were recorded in the Middle Ages, when they were kept by the Cistercian monks at Furness Abbey.

Go through a gate and over a slab bridge, then bear right to climb around a rocky knoll and turn left towards Buttermere village. Follow the path through Wilkinsyke Farm to meet the road. Turn left and follow the road back to the car park.

8 Derwent Water

Beautiful lakeside, steep wooded slopes, high windswept fells and views of rugged mountains.

LENGTH 4 or 6 miles (2½ or 4 hours)

PARKING Lakeside car park outside Keswick

CONDITIONS Generally level paths; steep, rocky climb to the top of Walla Crag

REFRESHMENTS Keswick lakeside tearoom

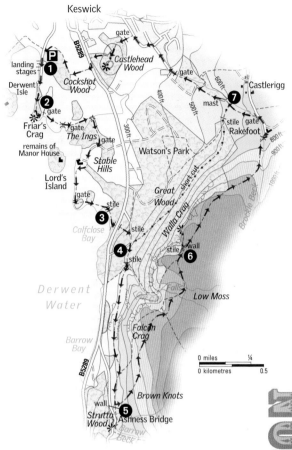

1 Keeping the shore to the right, follow the road past the landing stages. Ahead and to the right is Derwent Isle; in the 18th century it was owned by a millionaire who built a Gothic mansion, a fort and a stone circle there.

The road beside the lake soon becomes a broad track, signposted to a superb viewpoint called Friar's Crag. The track bears left before reaching the rocky outcrop, but a path leads directly to the viewpoint. Along this path is a memorial stone to Canon Rawnsley (1851-1920), one of the founders of the National Trust.

2 Cross the gate on the landward side of the crag and follow the main lakeside path to the right. Lord's Island, ancestral home of the Radcliffe family, is to the right.

Go over several bridges and through a gate into a marshy woodland called The Ings, bearing right after a footbridge. At the edge of the wood, go through a gate and turn right, past buildings at Stable Hills and along the shore on a permissive path. Beyond another gate, the path bears left to a footbridge over a stream.

3 Continue along the shore to the National Trust collecting cairn, then turn left on a path to a squeeze stile in a wall. Cross the road and go through another squeeze stile, and continue into Great Wood, crossing a car park exit road. Go across an open wooded area, bearing right to a path junction. The forest was once used by charcoal burners whose 'pitsteads' or platforms survive as clearings.

SHORT CUT Turn left at the junction and continue up a woodland path, ignoring paths to the left. At the end of the forest, go through a stile. Follow the track to a wall and stile. Continue from **7**.

4 Continue ahead at the junction. On the edge of the forest, cross a footbridge, go downhill alongside a wall and bear left. The path rises gently through scrubby hillside at the foot of Falcon Crag cliff. Follow the path signed to Ashness Bridge to a wall and gate. For a view of the Derwent Fells, go through the gate to a packhorse bridge.

5 Just before the gate, turn left and climb the hill. Follow the path for 1 mile, making for a distant tree-studded hilltop. Eventually the path meets a wall; for views over Derwent Water and the fells, cross a stile in the wall to reach Walla Crag.

6 Follow the path to the right as it descends into a valley, then bear left to a gate in a wall. Go through the gate and follow the track over a bridge to Rakefoot farm, then turn left on a narrow road. After 200m, turn sharp left through a gate at the bottom of a road bank and cross a bridge. Follow the path to the right along a stream.

7 At a fork keep ahead, past a radio mast on the left. The path swings right, reaches a junction facing a stream and bends left towards a gate and a road. Continue on the road; after the second field turn left on a hedge-lined path to Castlehead Wood. Go through a gate, fork right and bear left uphill, to a fenced corner on the right and a view of Keswick and Bassenthwaite Lake. A path on the left climbs Castlehead for views of Derwent Water and Borrowdale. Follow the main path to the road. Cross and turn left onto a pavement, then right down steps and onto a hedge-lined path to Cockshot Wood. Turn right for the car park.

NORTHERN ENGLAND

CUMBRIA

9 Rydal Water

Past Wordsworth's front door and into the heart of the poet's beloved landscape, then along slopes that were mined for slate.

LENGTH 4 miles (2 hours)

PARKING White Moss Common car park, off A591 between Rydal and Grasmere

CONDITIONS Undemanding, on well-marked paths

REFRESHMENTS Café at Rydal Hall

1 With your back to the entrance of the car park, take the path on the right-hand side, running parallel to the main road. Where the path emerges onto the roadside by a postbox, turn left onto a signposted footpath and past a waterfall to the left. The path becomes enclosed between stone walls and leads through a gate to a crossing path, with a pair of cottages immediately beyond.

2 Turn right and carry straight on along a frequently gated path, with the side of 609m (2,000ft) high Heron Pike rising to the left and Rydal Water stretching out below. The route is known locally as the old coffin road because it was used in the past by pallbearers walking between Ambleside and consecrated ground at Grasmere.

About ½ mile beyond the cottages, there is a large stone block beside a wall on the left, where the bearers rested their loads. Continue through more gates to emerge onto a minor road at Rydal.

3 Turn right and follow the road down past Rydal Mount, the house to which Wordsworth moved from Dove Cottage in 1813, and where he lived until his death in 1850. The property was purchased by the Wordsworth Trust in 1970 and is open to the public.

Continue past the entrance to Rydal Hall to meet the A591, at the bottom of the hill.

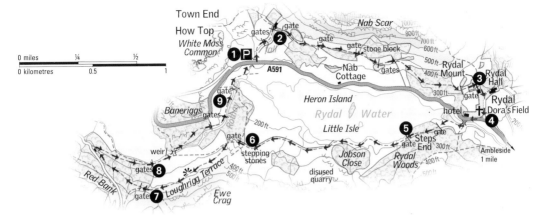

Town End
How Top
White Moss Common
Nab Scar
800ft
700ft
600ft
500ft
Rydal Mount
400ft
Rydal Hall
Rydal
Dora's Field
A591
Nab Cottage
Heron Island
Rydal Water
Little Isle
stone block
gates
300ft
hotel
Baneriggs
gates
gate
200ft
gate
stepping stones
Jobson Close
Steps End
300ft
gate
Rydal Woods
400ft
Ambleside 1 mile
weir
disused quarry
500ft
Red Bank
gates
Loughrigg Terrace
400ft
500ft
Ewe Crag
gate

0 miles ¼ ½
0 kilometres 0.5 1

4 Turn right and follow the road for 100m to a path on the left leading through a gap in the wall opposite a hotel. Continue over a footbridge crossing the River Rothay, then almost immediately turn right and continue, keeping close to the riverbank, to a gate.

Go through the gate into Rydal Woods. Woodlands around Rydal and in some other parts of Cumbria are among the last strongholds in England of the red squirrel. Just beyond a gate on the far boundary of the woodland, the path divides.

5 Fork right, walking close to the lake shore for a short distance before the path veers away from it, following the side of a wall below Loughrigg Fell. Continue along the base of the mountain to a fork in the path by a corner of the wall.

6 Bear right, crossing some easily negotiated stepping stones. After 100m, ignore a gate on the right leading into woodland, and instead carry straight on to a seat positioned by a fork in the path. Keep left, following a path along Loughrigg Terrace, looking across Grasmere to Helm Crag. The slopes on the left were mined for slate and contain Rydal Cave, a broad, lofty gallery cut into the hillside. Immediately beyond a gate leading into woodland, the path divides.

7 Take the right-hand fork, going through a gate on a path signposted to Grasmere. The path descends through mixed woodland containing oaks, copper beeches, holly and ecologically unwelcome rhododendron bushes.

Turn sharp right in front of a gate leading onto a minor road, following the signpost to Grasmere Lake. The path joins another one following the side of Grasmere. Turn right and continue along the lake shore to two gates on the boundary of woodland.

8 Go through the gate on the left and continue across a footbridge over the Rothay, just downstream of the river's outlet from Grasmere. Turn right on the far side of the bridge and follow the path through woodland beside the river to a gate leading to fields. Continue through two more gates to a junction by a footbridge on the right.

9 Keep left, following a gravel path. After a short distance, the path divides again. Fork left and continue on the path, which emerges on the roadside, opposite the entrance to the car park.

RYDAL WATER

NORTHERN ENGLAND

183

CUMBRIA

10 Glenridding

Stunning lakeland views from the open fells, and the dramatic scars of old mine workings at the end of a steady climb.

LENGTH 5½ miles (3 hours)

PARKING National Park information centre

CONDITIONS Demanding, involving a climb to 457m (1,500ft); do not attempt in mist

REFRESHMENTS Full range in Glenridding

1 Leave the car park by the telephone boxes, turn left and follow the road to the A592. Turn left on the pavement on the far side of the main road and continue beside a wall. Where the wall ends, fork right on a path close to the side of Ullswater; there is a fine view across the lake of the 657m (2,155ft) high summit of Place Fell. The path soon rejoins the roadside.

2 Turn right. Immediately beyond the bridge over Mossdale Beck, turn right on another lakeside path that leads past delightful little wood-backed shores before winding back to the road. Continue on the path parallel to the road for a short distance until you see a track on the far side signposted to Seldom Seen and Glencoyne.

3 Turn onto this track, which then divides in three. Take the centre track and walk steadily uphill, over a cattle grid. Glencoyne farmhouse, which dates from 1629, lies in the valley to the right, with the slopes of Gowbarrow Park forming a backcloth. There are fine views over Ullswater towards Pooley Bridge at the end of the lake. Continue along the track for ½ mile to Seldom Seen, the cottages of a tiny former mining and quarrying community, on the right.

4 The path continues uphill to the left of the cottages to a stile and onto the open fell with a wall on the right. Follow the path to the end of the wall, where there is a gate.

5 Go through the gate and follow the path to the left of a tall standing boulder and then to the top of the pass at Nick Head. The valley on the right is a fine example of a 'hanging valley' formed during the Ice Age.

6 Fork right over the ridge and down the hill (over ground that can be very boggy when wet) towards the spoil heaps from the Greenside lead and silver mine workings. Head for a timber bridge over a stream.

7 Cross the bridge and follow the path to the left, marked by stone cairns, and down a series of zig-zags towards the valley of Glenridding Beck. The ridge on the other side ends in Striding Edge, a narrow ridge leading to the top of Helvellyn – at 950m (3,116ft) the third highest mountain in England. But it is the remains of the old Greenside mine, now stabilised and landscaped, that dominate the immediate scene. Worked for lead and silver since the 17th century, the mine, driven deep under the mountains, was in operation until 1962.

At the bottom of the zig-zags turn left onto the track that comes down the valley.

8 The track passes through an old mine building restored as a camping barn on the left and an outdoor pursuits centre on the right, then past the Helvellyn Youth Hostel. Sheffield Pike rears up to the left and Birkhouse Moor to the right. Continue along the track, past some former miners' cottages and onto a surfaced road to Glenridding and the car park.

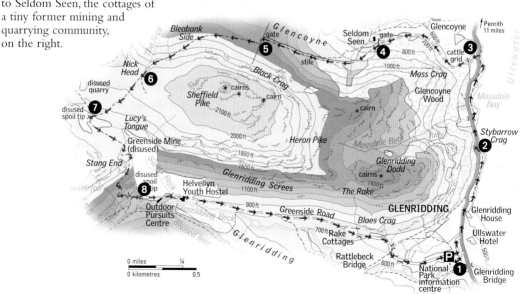

11 Glassonby

An idyllic pastoral landscape of fields, hedgerows and small copses stretching along the River Eden.

LENGTH 6 miles (3½ hours)

PARKING Layby on left of the Kirkoswald road out of Glassonby

CONDITIONS Boggy patches in fields

REFRESHMENTS Tearoom at Little Salkeld Watermill (limited opening)

1 From the layby, follow the footpath sign into the wood and uphill. Cross a stile out of the wood and head diagonally across a field to follow the escarpment above the river. The route dips down to the River Eden, crosses a plank footbridge and follows a length of plank walkway, into a pine

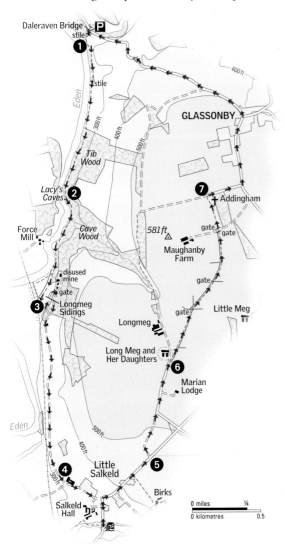

plantation. Follow the walkway through the wood, then continue along a sandy path climbing to a sandstone bluff above the river.

2 As the path drops steeply from the bluff, fork right along a narrow ledge to Lacy's Caves. The grottoes were created by Colonel Samuel Lacy, an 18th-century local landowner. From the caves, return to the main path and continue up the river, past another bluff above a weir with views of an old mill on the far bank. The path skirts the abandoned sidings of a gypsum mine and follows the route of an old railway towards a viaduct on the main line to Carlisle.

3 The path zigzags round an electricity substation to join a concrete track signposted to Little Salkeld. Follow the track to the village, passing a flat sculpture constructed by local children depicting the course of the Eden.

4 At the end of the track bear left and at the road junction turn right to visit 18th-century Little Salkeld Watermill. Colonel Lacy lived at nearby Salkeld Hall. Retrace your steps and head up the road signposted to Glassonby and Druid Circle. At the top of the hill there are distant views to right of Cross Fell, the highest peak in the Pennines.

5 Immediately after the village sign for Little Salkeld turn left onto a stony lane, and follow it as it bends right and becomes a grassy track between hawthorn hedgerows. The track joins a tarmac road leading to the arrangement of standing stones known as Long Meg and Her Daughters. Long Meg is a monolith inscribed with a faint spiral pattern. The 'daughters' form a ring nearby. The stone circle probably dates from about 2500 to 1500 BC. When viewed from its centre, 3.5m (12ft) high Long Meg indicates the position of the midwinter sunset.

6 Follow the path along the field edge to the right of the stone circle, and continue ahead, crossing several gates and passing a pine plantation on right. Cross the lane to Maughanby Farm, then continue across another field to Addingham church. The original village was washed away by floods in 1160, but the church was rebuilt on this safer site. Fragments of ancient stone crosses and tomb lids dredged from the river are displayed in the porch.

7 Follow the path round the church to the churchyard gate and walk up the lane to the road. Turn left into Glassonby, then bear left at the village green along the road signposted to Kirkoswald. Continue along this lane for ¾ mile to return to the parking place.

DURHAM & TEESSIDE

There are some real gems for the walker in this northeastern county. They include the impressive river valley of Teesdale, the Durham Heritage Coast and the Durham Dales, crossed by 40 miles of the Pennine Way.

1 Bowlees

Majestic waterfalls, white-water rapids and rare wild flowers amid the awe-inspiring scenery of Upper Teesdale.

LENGTH 4 or 5 miles (2½ or 3 hours)

PARKING Bowlees visitor centre car park, off B6277 about 3 miles southwest of Forest-in-Teesdale

CONDITIONS Generally firm paths, but slippery rocks at High Force

REFRESHMENTS Hotel on B6277 near High Force

1 From the car park, cross a bridge over the stream to the visitor centre, which contains natural history and geology displays. From the centre, take the path that joins a lane down to the road. Cross the lane and go through a gate into a field, following the footpath through a second gate to a wynch bridge. An earlier wynch bridge here, built in 1704, collapsed in 1802, plunging 11 lead-miners into the River Tees – only one was drowned.

2 Bear left through a gate beside the life-belt stand, then turn right at a footpath sign up a grassy bank, crossing a tumbled drystone wall. Cross the field to a stile by a stream, keep the stream on the left and follow it to a wall. Cross a stone slab bridge over the stream and continue alongside the wall to a gate. Go through the gate and follow the track to a tarmac lane.

3 Turn right and continue ahead to an isolated hill farm, one of many scattered on the valley's upper slopes. Grazing by sheep encourages the growth of wild flowers that would otherwise be smothered under grass. Go through the farmyard and continue through a pasture beside a stone wall.

4 Just beyond a gate, swing down to join a path along the riverbank beneath isolated Holwick Head House. Do not cross the footbridge, but continue on this path upstream, immediately climbing back to higher ground. Cross a stile and follow the path through dense growths of juniper. The area is noted for its unique community of plants, 'the Teesdale assemblage'. Rare yellow mountain saxifrages, spring gentians, mountain pansies and wild orchids have thrived on the high limestone slopes since the Ice Age.

Soon, a mighty roar of water can be heard as the path nears High Force, where the river plunges into a chasm 21m (70ft) below.

5 Retrace your steps to the footbridge under Holwick Head House, but do not cross the river. Follow the path downstream. The river churns in white-water rapids, diverting around rocky islets to form pools of still, dark water. The force of the river is unpredictable, but the valley surrounding it has been tamed by man. Neat stone walls line the fields that climb towards a rocky escarpment on the valley's upper slopes. From this point, there is little sense of the lonely wilderness that lies beyond the skyline: 15 roadless miles of windswept Pennine moor, rising well above 610m (2,000ft).

6 Cross a stile and continue ahead on the banks of the river beside Low Force, where gushing rapids form a series of waterfalls. Bright yellow globeflowers and pink bird's-eye primroses thrive in the limestone soils of the banks. The falls are best viewed from the wynch bridge. Cross the bridge and return to Bowlees car park.
DETOUR *Continue through the car park, following a footpath through the wooded gorge to Gibson's Cave, where ferns and primroses grow from the rockface to create a natural hanging garden. In this mysterious, romantic setting, a waterfall splashes down from overhanging rocks, curtaining a shallow cave behind.*

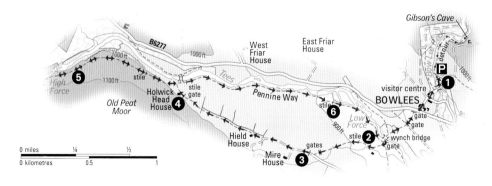

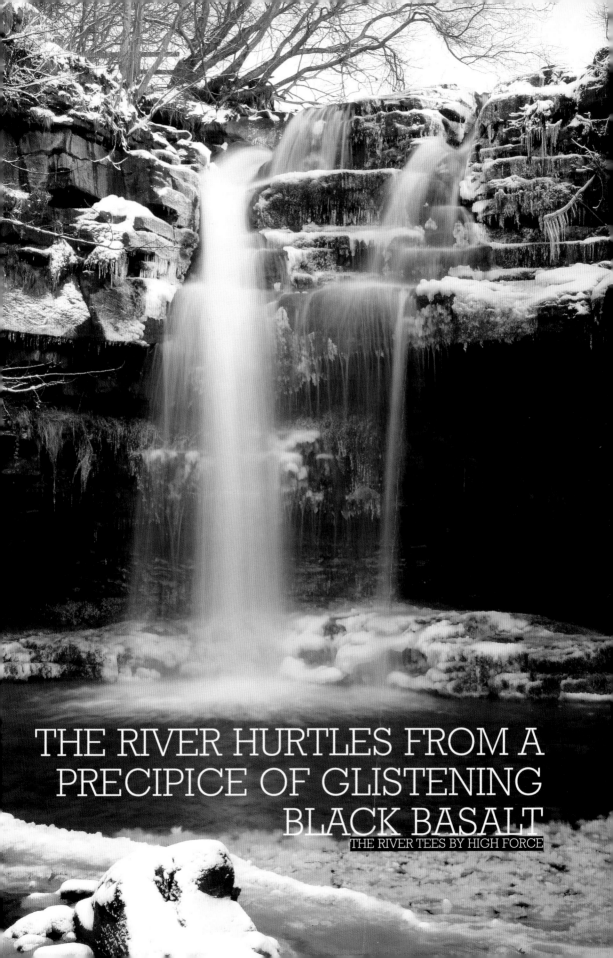

THE RIVER HURTLES FROM A
PRECIPICE OF GLISTENING
BLACK BASALT
THE RIVER TEES BY HIGH FORCE

NORTHUMBERLAND

England's most northerly county is lonely and unspoilt – a wilderness of outstanding natural beauty. Walkers can experience a tremendous sense of space and distance on the upland tracks of this remote landscape.

HADRIAN'S WALL, BY VINDOLANDA

1 Vindolanda

An exploration of the Roman Empire's northern frontier, taking in a fine stretch of Hadrian's Wall.

LENGTH 5 miles (2½ hours)

PARKING Eastern car park, off A69 east of Henshaw

CONDITIONS Paths firm and dry; some short but moderately steep climbs

REFRESHMENTS Café at Vindolanda

1 Turn right out of the car park. At the footpath sign just before a Roman milestone, turn right over a stile beside a stream, then bear left across a field. When High Shield Farm is visible, head to its right. Cross a stile, bear right across the field and cross a stile in the far corner onto the road.

2 Turn right along the Military Road (the B6318), built by General Wade in 1751 after the Jacobite Rebellion. Walk along the grass verge for nearly ¼ mile, then turn left through a gate at a footpath sign. Continue across the vallum, a broad ditch that defined the zone of Roman military control, and then the Roman Military Way, a supply road that ran the length of the frontier with links to every turret, milecastle and fort. The wall and its defensive structures were constructed by the Emperor Hadrian between AD 122 and 126.

3 Turn right over a stile before a gate. Follow the wall to another stile, ignoring a path on the left to Hotbank Farm. The climb is steep, but is rewarded with a view of the wall along a sheer escarpment, with moors and forests stretching towards the Cheviots to the left.

4 At a junction with the Pennine Way continue along the wall up Cuddy's Crags, bearing left on a steep climb. To avoid the climb, turn right across a stile and follow the Military Way along the lower slopes, returning to the wall at Milecastle 37. This fort, a gateway through the wall, is well preserved, with massive walls and a two-room barracks for its 16-man garrison. Just beyond the fort, climb steps to walk along the top of the wall above the precipice of Housesteads Crags.

5 Enter Housesteads by the West Gate. Built in AD 124, before the wall was finished, the fort was garrisoned by a regiment of 800 auxiliaries from Belgium. The barracks, granaries, hospital and latrines can be seen, as well as the spacious house of the commanding officer. A path from the South Gate leads to the museum, containing military equipment and other artefacts.

6 From the museum, turn sharp right on a tarmac lane below the buildings and follow this down to Military Road. Cross the road and go over a stile, then continue ahead on the bridleway to a ridge. Follow it down a dip, keeping to the right of the rock face, and on to East Crindledikes. Follow the path through the farmyard onto a tarmac lane.

7 After about ¼ mile, turn right along the road. Continue for ½ mile and bear left at a junction signposted to Bardon Mill. After ½ mile, turn right to Vindolanda. A fort was built here after the Roman campaign in northern Britain in AD 75, and was later reconstructed as a base for troops working on the wall. The museum's collection includes clothing, shoes and writing tablets from the garrison's official files – among the most revealing documents about the Roman occupation ever found. From the museum return to the car park.

NORTHERN ENGLAND

NORTHUMBERLAND

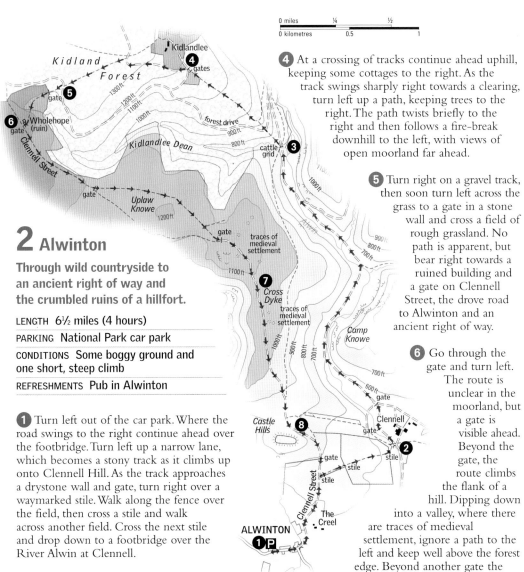

Kidlandlee

Kidland Forest

4 gates

5 gate

6 gate, Wholehope (ruin)

Clennell Street

1300 ft
1200 ft
1100 ft
1000 ft
900 ft
800 ft

forest drive

Kidlandlee Dean

cattle grid **3**

gate

Uplaw Knowe

1200 ft

2 Alwinton

Through wild countryside to an ancient right of way and the crumbled ruins of a hillfort.

gate

traces of medieval settlement

900 ft
800 ft
700 ft

7

Cross Dyke

traces of medieval settlement

Camp Knowe

1100 ft

LENGTH 6½ miles (4 hours)

PARKING National Park car park

CONDITIONS Some boggy ground and one short, steep climb

REFRESHMENTS Pub in Alwinton

700 ft

600 ft

gate

Clennell

gate

2

stile

1 Turn left out of the car park. Where the road swings to the right continue ahead over the footbridge. Turn left up a narrow lane, which becomes a stony track as it climbs up onto Clennell Hill. As the track approaches a drystone wall and gate, turn right over a waymarked stile. Walk along the fence over the field, then cross a stile and walk across another field. Cross the next stile and drop down to a footbridge over the River Alwin at Clennell.

Castle Hills

8

gate

gate

stile

stile

Clennell Street

stile

ALWINTON

1 P

The Creel

2 Cross the footbridge and turn left up a forest road, following the river upstream. The level road leads up for 1½ miles through a valley of bare, scree-covered slopes where sheep and cattle graze beside the shallow stream. There are pine woods far ahead in the upper reaches of the valley, but no other signs of cultivation. The only sound is the gentle gurgling of water.

3 Cross a cattle grid into a pine forest and turn left up the path signposted to Kidlandlee. The path is steep for ¼ mile, cutting through the pine trees. Cross a forest drive, continue climbing, then bear left along a broad grass track towards the hilltop. Approaching the summit, go through two gates to a junction of forest roads. To the right is the isolated Kidlandlee farm, perched over alpine fields.

4 At a crossing of tracks continue ahead uphill, keeping some cottages to the right. As the track swings sharply right towards a clearing, turn left up a path, keeping trees to the right. The path twists briefly to the right and then follows a fire-break downhill to the left, with views of open moorland far ahead.

5 Turn right on a gravel track, then soon turn left across the grass to a gate in a stone wall and cross a field of rough grassland. No path is apparent, but bear right towards a ruined building and a gate on Clennell Street, the drove road to Alwinton and an ancient right of way.

6 Go through the gate and turn left. The route is unclear in the moorland, but a gate is visible ahead. Beyond the gate, the route climbs the flank of a hill. Dipping down into a valley, where there are traces of medieval settlement, ignore a path to the left and keep well above the forest edge. Beyond another gate the route is clear, following a ridge with deep valleys to the left and right.

7 Continue on the track through the prehistoric Cross Dyke. The bank and ditch across the ridge were probably dug in the late Bronze Age, 3,000 years ago. At Castle Hills, ½ mile farther on, are the crumbled ramparts of a ruined hillfort commanding a magnificent site above Coquetdale.

8 From Castle Hills continue ahead on the drove road, which leads back to Alwinton. Awe-inspiring views stretch on all sides of the road to encompass wild moorland scenery, interspersed with forests and rivers and studded with farms. Beyond a gate the route rejoins the first leg of the walk, and returns to Alwinton.

3 Craster

From medieval Dunstanburgh Castle along the rocky coastline to the beach at Craster, where kippers are still smoked.

LENGTH	3 miles (1½ hours)
PARKING	Quarry car park
CONDITIONS	Easy
REFRESHMENTS	Pub and kiosk in Craster

1 Cross the road from the entrance to the car park in Craster's old quarry – now a small nature reserve where such birds as red-breasted flycatchers, reed warblers and wrynecks can be seen. Go through a gate opposite. Follow the path ahead through a copse, before emerging into a small field filled with bracken. At the far end of the field go through a gate. Follow the well-defined path ahead, with gorse-covered slopes on the right and open fields on the left.

2 Where another path joins from the right, continue ahead. The path leads between gorse bushes swathed in a heady coconut scent in spring and summer, then widens to a broad grassy track that can be muddy at times.

Steep, gorse-covered whinstone crags, known as Dunstanburgh Heughs, rise steeply to the right. Hard-wearing and dark, whinstone was quarried here until the 1930s. The stone was unsuitable for building, but was used extensively in the metalling of roads. Follow the path along the foot of the crags, bearing gently to the right to a kissing gate.

3 Go through the gate and turn right onto a gently rising stony track. As the slope levels out, the sea comes into view ahead, and to the left are the awe-inspiring ruins of Dunstanburgh Castle (EH/NT), set on a low grassy headland. Continue ahead towards a wide gate.

4 Ignore the gate ahead and instead go through the gate on the right, following a path that runs close to a barbed-wire fence on the left. Go through the first gate on the left and follow the path downhill beside another wire fence towards a junction with the coast path.

5 Turn left and go through a gate, then continue ahead on the coast path towards the castle. Where a path joins from the left, continue ahead, following the shore line, and make your way to the castle ruins.

The castle has been a ruin since Tudor times. Building began in 1313 under the direction of Thomas, Earl of Lancaster, Henry III's grandson. Under Henry IV, son of the Duke of Lancaster, John of Gaunt, the castle became a Lancastrian stronghold in the early 15th century. Approaching the castle from the south, its large curtain wall with two towers forms what was the most well-defended part of the castle. A grassy plateau to the north of the main ruins provides spectacular views over Embleton Bay. The low whinstone cliff on which the castle stands is known as Gull Crag, and is noisy with the cries of many seabirds, including kittiwakes, fulmars and cormorants.

6 Retrace your steps to the gate, go through it and continue along the coast path towards Craster. At low tide the beach is lined with rock pools. As Craster comes into view, smoke can be seen rising from the roof of a building in the centre of the village. Craster kippers are smoked here over fires of oak sawdust, although not in the quantities they were in the early 19th century when Craster had a large herring fleet. A few Craster boats still fish for crab and lobster, but the herring for the smokehouse is brought in from larger ports. The smokehouse is open to visitors.

7 Where the coast path reaches the village, go through two gates to join a tarmac road leading past the tiny, sheltered harbour. When the Craster quarry was active, whinstone was carried to the harbour by overhead cableway and then transported down the coast as far south as London. A concrete structure used to support the loading bin can be seen on the south pier. At the T-junction turn right to return to the car park.

NORTHUMBERLAND

4 Kirknewton

Through the foothills of the Cheviots, past waterfalls, forested mountain slopes and prehistoric settlements.

LENGTH 5½ or 6½ miles (2½ or 3 hours)

PARKING In lane beside St Gregory's Church

CONDITIONS After heavy rainfall the ford at start of Step 2 may be challenging, but the water is usually only a few inches deep. Fairly gentle climbs

REFRESHMENTS Full range in Wooler

1 From the church, walk up the village street and turn left onto the B6351. Follow the road about ¼ mile to a gate on the left just before a bridge over the river. Go through the gate and follow the track above the riverbank to a ford. Cross the ford and turn left. (If the riverwater looks high, ignore the gate, cross over the road bridge and immediately turn left onto a path, and walk alongside the river to the ford.)

2 Ahead lies an enticing wilderness of empty hills and wooded valleys. Follow the path slightly right as the river and path diverge, heading across the grass and through an opening in a fence. Climb up to a metal gate, then over a ladder stile in a wall. Continue ahead through fields to follow the steep valley edge above the river. The valley is cloaked in ash and oak woods, while beside the path mountain goats sometimes clamber through the tumbled stonework of a prehistoric settlement. Continue to a stile in the fence to the left of the path.

3 Cross the stile and follow a narrow path downhill to meet a fence. Walk alongside the fence to another stile. Cross it and follow the path above the river – the grassy bank is a good vantage point from which to watch for salmon in the College Burn. The river tumbles through a rocky gorge where ferns and honeysuckle overhang clear pools below the Hethpool Linn. The valley was once used as a route by Scots and English 'reivers' during border raids.

4 Do not cross the footbridge, but continue along the same bank of the river as it swirls through the rocks. Unexpectedly, the valley opens out to form an almost alpine pasture around Hethpool's manor house and cottages. Keeping the house to the right, follow the path through field gates and over stiles to meet a track.
DETOUR *Turn right on the track, which joins a lane that serves the valley. Turn left on the lane to open pasture where a circle of boulders – a Neolithic shrine – forms an enigmatic pattern in the turf.*

5 Turn left across a bridge over the stream, then turn left at a footpath sign. The path climbs steadily through gorse and scrub to a pine plantation. Continue over a stile and through the plantation, which is so dense that voices echo off the trees.

6 As you emerge from the conifers by a stile, continue over the bare hillside to another stile ahead. Cross the stile and bear right at a path junction, dipping through a wooded glen, then climbing a stile back onto open hillside. Pass to the right of a ruined sheepfold and over rough

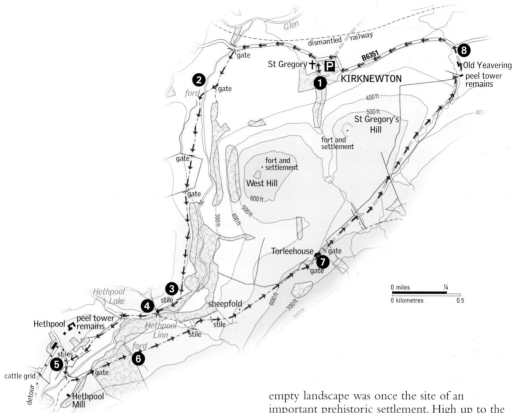

fields into another pine plantation. From here the path gives way to a stone track to Torleehouse, an isolated hill farm.

7 Past Torleehouse, the track becomes a gravel drive, descending from the Cheviots down into the valley of the River Glen. This wild and empty landscape was once the site of an important prehistoric settlement. High up to the right of the track is the windswept summit of Yeavering Bell.

8 The track meets the road just beyond Old Yeavering farm, where the base of a 16th-century peel tower has been converted into a barn. The field opposite was the site of Ad Gefrin, a 7th-century Anglo-Saxon township. Turn left onto the road to return to Kirknewton.

NORTHUMBERLAND

5 Holy Island

Across golden sand dunes in a birdwatcher's paradise, an historic island-seat of worship and a once-mighty fortress.

LENGTH 4½ miles (2½ hours)

PARKING In car park to left of road shortly after causeway

CONDITIONS All level paths and sand, apart from short climb to priory ruins

REFRESHMENTS Full range in village

NOTE Details of safe crossing times to the island are available from tourist information centres and local pubs, or from www.northumberlandlife.org/holy-island

1 From the car park, follow the road towards the causeway, and at a footpath sign turn right through a gate. The path runs beside a field, with views to the left across the vast expanse of muddy sand that separates the island from the mainland. Where the path heads toward the dunes bear right and follow a fence as it swings round beneath the waste of sand that mark the island's northern shore. Continue to a drystone wall and a wide raised bank, marking a clear division between fields.

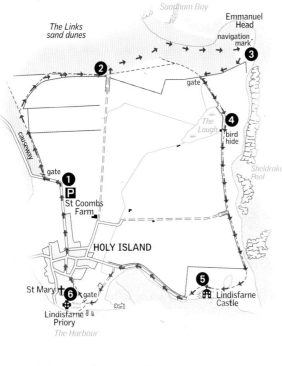

2 Follow the footpath sign to the left for a very short distance, then bear left again towards the dunes. There is not, at first, much sign of any path, but soon a stretch of track winds upward between the dunes. Follow this and, after crossing a high point in the dunes, within sight of the sea, descend into a dip and turn right, then left, around the edge of the dunes; aim for the tall pyramid of the navigation mark on Emmanuel Head.

3 From the navigation mark, bear right towards Lindisfarne Castle, visible ahead on Beblowe Crag, the highest point of the island. Turn right onto a grassy track beside a wall, then turn left through a wooden gate. The high causeway was originally a route for wagons hauling lime and ironstone from quarries on the northern shore. To the right is the Lough, a reed-fringed freshwater lake where whooper swans, grebes, tufted duck, shovelers and teal are but a small selection of the birdlife regularly seen by observers from a hide.

4 The track follows the shore, above low cliffs and rocky beaches, to the castle. At its foot stand a set of massive kilns built in the 1860s when trade in lime and coal linked Holy Island with Dundee. Lindisfarne Castle (NT) was built during the reign of Henry VIII as a defence against the Scots. The last action that it saw came unexpectedly in 1715, when its two-man garrison was temporarily overwhelmed by a pair of Jacobites. In the early 20th century the ruins were transformed into a country house by the architect Sir Edwin Lutyens.

5 From the castle follow the lane towards the village. At a footpath sign bear left along the harbourside, passing several of the ancient upturned boats that islanders use as fishing huts.

The path winds uphill towards a former coastguard station. Before the top bear right through iron gates to the priory ruins. This is not the austere Lindisfarne monastery founded by the Irish missionary Aidan in 635, and of which the more venerated Cuthbert was prior later that century. That early seat of learning was sacked by Viking raiders in 793. The existing ruins are of a grander priory founded in the 12th century, when Lindisfarne was renamed Holy Island.

Following the Dissolution of the Monasteries in 1537, the island became in turn a fortress, a fishing station and an outpost of the mining industry, before its isolation was appreciated by romantic-minded visitors.

6 Follow the fingerpost directing visitors towards the castle through the village, passing the island's small winery. In the 1850s Holy Island had a population of 1,000 and ten pubs, but today the village is quiet out of season. To return to the car park, follow the main road to the causeway.

LINDISFARNE CASTLE, HOLY ISLAND

Blood, sweat and tears in the high Pennines

Walkers in the Pennines should reflect on the amazing ingenuity and effort that went into building the Settle to Carlisle railway.

The Ribblehead Viaduct is one of the architectural marvels of the North Pennines. Its 24 arches carry the Settle to Carlisle section of the Midland Railway across the Ribble Valley, some 14 miles south of Horton-in-Ribblesdale. It is visible from the three famous, long-distance trails: the Three Peaks Walk, the Pennine Way and the Dales Way.

All three of these routes make for demanding hikes, capable of leaving even the fittest walker gasping. But as ramblers on these routes pause to ponder the engineering genius that made the Ribblehead Viaduct possible, they might also reflect on the amazing amount of human effort that went into building both it and the railway that runs along it.

The privations of the army of at least 2,000 Victorian labourers who, between 1869 to 1876,

lived and dug and drank and toiled – and died, some of them – on the bleak Pennine moors make the modern, long-distance walker's fatigue seem inconsequential.

Astonishing achievement

The Midland Railway, from London to Scotland, came into being as competition for its rivals: the Great Northern Railway along the east coast and the London & North Western Railway along the west. The 72 miles between Settle and Carlisle were some of the most difficult to construct.

Far from civilisation, the area was a wilderness of bleak hills and rain-soaked, stream-sodden bogs, under which lay clay so sloppy in wet conditions that it resembled thick glue and could drown a man or a horse. When dry, the clay would harden enough to blunt the pickaxes

RIBBLEHEAD VIADUCT, SETTLE TO CARLISLE RAILWAY

aimed at it and jar the bones of the navvies wielding them, and could only be shifted by gunpowder blasts.

A succession of seemingly endless tunnels, viaducts, cuttings and embankments, with their associated culverts, portals, masonry, abutments and foundations – extending down 7.5m (25ft) – pushed the line through this tricky country. Such mighty works were built by hand, with pick and shovel, hauling spoil and materials by horse and cart – or horse and sled across the worst bits of bog, where a wheeled vehicle would sink and never be recovered. The Settle to Carlisle railway was the last hurrah of the old-style labourer, tough and energetic, a law unto himself, a man who could shovel 20 tonnes of earth and rock, earn ten shillings and eat more than 1kg (3lb) of beef a day.

Legacy in the landscape

The most poignant and striking site along the Midland Railway's moorland route is at Batty Green, in the shadow of the Ribblehead Viaduct. Here a maze of grassy hummocks marks the sites of the rows of crude huts where up to 2,000 men, women and children lived rough and ready. Here are the outlines of the shops where they bought goods at contractors' prices, the mission house, the library and post office, the hospital and the school – the navvies' families followed them to their site of work and shared their hardships.

The men fought bare-knuckle matches on Sundays, cooked beef they slaughtered themselves, and – many of them – drank themselves stupid. Over one weekend, one of them was reported to have 'drunk all his wages, a Whitney pea-jacket with mother-o'-pearl buttons, six flannel shirts, two white linen ditto, sundry pairs of stockings, a pair of boots, and a silver watch with a gilt chain'.

The most fitting memorial to the railway navvies is not carved in stone. It remains to be read in the mountainous spoil heaps and the outlines of jerry-built huts and shops that litter the moors. And it lies also in the parallel lines of the railway track, as it curves across a viaduct or emerges from a tunnel mouth, carrying another rattling train of goods or passengers through the rainy Pennine hills.

YORKSHIRE

The Yorkshire Dales National Park spans the central Pennines and provides superb walking amid rugged scenery. To the east, routes cross pretty dells, high moorland and skirt rocky shores.

1 Market Weighton

A gentle walk along a former railway trackline and a Roman road to the secluded landscaped grounds of a country estate.

LENGTH 6½ miles (3½ hours)

PARKING By the Londesborough Arms pub

CONDITIONS Clear tracks and paths in gently undulating country

REFRESHMENTS Full range in Market Weighton; pub in Goodmanham

1 With the church on the right, walk along Londesborough Road to the end of the churchyard. Turn right, then left into Station Road. Just after passing between bollards, ignore the first path on the right and continue to another path on the right. Follow this to a junction of three paths. Take the broad path ahead, the Hudson Way, which follows the route of a former railway line.

2 Follow the Hudson Way, soon passing under a brick bridge and entering a small nature reserve. Continue for 1 mile to a junction with a road.

3 Turn left. At a junction turn left into Goodmanham, then turn right on the narrow road by the churchyard, following the sign for the Wolds Way.

4 Continue ahead, passing under a former railway bridge. Follow the signposted bridleway to the right, and continue ahead past a waymarked side path on the right. After a sharp right bend, the Wolds Way goes along a short section of a Roman road that once ran from Malton, north of Market Weighton, to Brough on the Humber. The cooling towers of Drax power station are visible in the distance. Continue ahead to a junction with the A163.

5 Cross the road and take the track ahead. Continue ahead at the junction with a farm road then turn left on a waymarked grassy track, descending through parkland with views ahead of the early 19th-century Londesborough Hall. The red-brick mansion was home to railway magnate George Hudson, after whom the Hudson Way is named. The route passes between two small lakes, created as part of the landscape scheme for the grounds; a telescope installed here enables walkers to observe waterfowl. Continue to a junction with a track, then turn left to another waymarked junction of tracks below prominent arches.

6 Turn left on the track signposted Wolds Way, and go through the Londesborough Park estate to the gatehouse. Turn left on the road, then turn right shortly after on a waymarked path. Continue along the left side of two fields, then cross a stile into another field, where hummocks mark the site of Towthorpe in the Thistles. This village, recorded in the 11th century, was abandoned in 1612; many other villages throughout the Wolds met the same fate when large-scale sheep farming brought an end to the labour-intensive open-field farming system. Follow the tarmac track ahead through a gate and past farm buildings to the A163.

7 Cross the road and follow the path ahead along the left edge of fields. At a road junction turn left along the pavement and return to Market Weighton town centre.

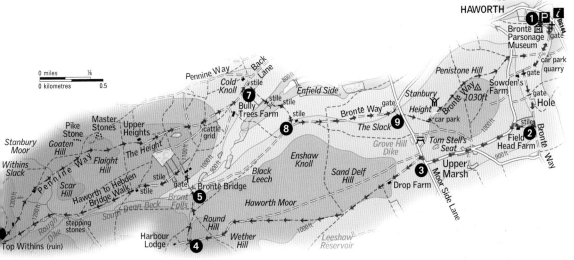

2 Haworth

Brontë country – the writers' family home, the moors and the house that inspired _Wuthering Heights_.

LENGTH 7 miles (4 hours)

PARKING Car park at Brontë Parsonage Museum opposite West Lane Baptist Church

CONDITIONS Good paths; some hard climbing

REFRESHMENTS Full range at Haworth

1 Turn left past the entrance to the Brontë Parsonage Museum, the former home of the literary sisters, to the Church of St Michael and All Angels. Following signs to Penistone Hill and Oxenhope, turn right through the graveyard and out through a kissing gate. Pass a smallholding and car park on the left, and continue on the Brontë Way, round Sowden's Farm towards Hole and Oxenhope. Go through a gate and continue to the left through fields and another gate to pass just above the hamlet of Hole. Go through a gap in the wall and across a large field.

2 Just before the stile on the far side of the field, turn right onto a walled track to Field Head Farm, to meet a road. Turn left, go through Upper Marsh and on to a T-junction.

3 Turn right, then left up a track over a cattle grid signposted to Brontë Falls and Top Withins. To the left, beyond Drop Farm on the moorland, the glistening water of Leeshaw Reservoir can be seen. At a crossing of paths, bear half right towards Brontë Falls. At a marker post at the top of the ridge turn left on a track to Harbour Lodge.

4 Just before Harbour Lodge turn right, go down to a footbridge and follow the path beside the stream and then steeply downhill as the water is transformed into the spectacular Brontë Falls.

5 At South Dean Beck cross Brontë Bridge and continue up the opposite bank through a kissing gate, following signs to Top Withins.

At a crossing of paths, turn left past ruined buildings, across several fields. Where a path joins from the right, cross a ladder stile and continue along a sandy track overlooking the beck and the slopes beyond. Cross stepping stones over Rough Dike and continue on the steep sandy path beyond.

6 At a signpost turn left and continue to Top Withins, which inspired Emily Brontë's _Wuthering Heights_. Return to the signpost and take the Pennine Way towards Stanbury and Haworth over moorland, past several farms and cottages, with Ponden Reservoir on the left. Lower Laithe Reservoir appears ahead.

Continue on the Pennine Way, over a cattle grid at a crossing of paths, past Bully Trees Farm on the right and onto Back Lane.

7 At Cold Knoll, the first farm on the left, turn right over a stile and take the well-trodden path downhill. Cross a stile, then a footbridge over South Dean Beck, turning right and then left around a group of trees up a steep path to a ladder stile. Go left around the edge of the field. Then follow the path steeply uphill over a ladder stile beside a ruined farmhouse on the left and over a short rise beyond it.

8 Turn left in front of the farmhouse onto the wide Brontë Way. At a cattle grid, go through a gate, following the signpost right across a patch of moorland to the roadside higher up the hill.

9 Cross the road onto the path ahead and, at a crossing of paths, go left on the Brontë Way, bearing left across a car park and around Penistone Hill. Bear left to a road, cross it and follow signs for Haworth down a walled track.

At the bottom turn left back to the church and museum.

YORKSHIRE

3 Hardcastle Crags

A climb to the moors, a stark mill below the crags along Hebden Water, and a village with dramatic church ruins.

LENGTH 4½ or 5½ miles (3 or 4 hours)

PARKING NT car park, New Bridge, off A6033 just north of Hebden Bridge

CONDITIONS Hard climbs; some muddy tracks

REFRESHMENTS Pubs in Heptonstall; tearoom at Gibson Mill

1 Walk back along the road for 25m and turn left on a bridleway between stone walls. After a short, steep ascent, turn right up a wide track and climb for nearly a mile in the shade of tall trees above Crimsworth Dean Beck on the right.

Just beyond Abel Cote Wood, look up a track on the left to Abel Cote Farm, for a glimpse of Abel Cross, a medieval double cross that may once have marked the old packhorse route. A

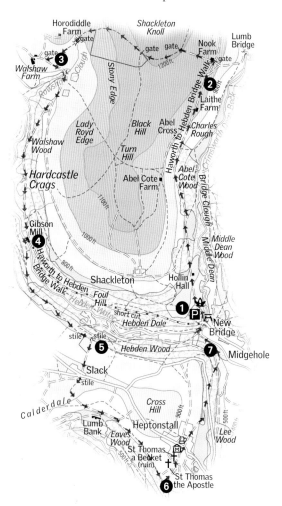

farmer who planned to use it as gateposts split its base in two. Pass Laithe Farm on the right and continue to the next signpost, which indicates Grain Water Bridge ahead.

(From the signpost, a steep path down to the right offers a short detour to Lumb Bridge, which spans Crimsworth Dean Beck at a point where protruding bands of gritstone have made a spectacular little waterfall.)

2 From the signpost continue ahead to a gate just before Nook Farm. Turn left in front of the gate up a slope and onto a steep path between walls. Go through a gate and turn left beside a wall with heather and bilberry-covered moorland to the right. Go through another gate on the left, then turn right along the top of the field with a wall on the right. As the path descends, Horodiddle Farm is seen ahead across the moor. Go through a gate, then cross a bridge over Rowshaw Clough and continue along the track to Walshaw Farm.

3 Go through a gate and turn sharp left on a tree-shaded gravel track waymarked to Hardcastle Crags. At a fork, follow the yellow waymark. Continue between Scots pine, ash and oak and pass towering crags on the right to Gibson Mill (NT), a starkly imposing structure built in 1800 and now a visitor centre.

Although cotton manufacturing at the mill ceased in the late 1890s in the face of competition from larger local mills, the building took on a new role as a place of entertainment – first as a 'dining saloon', and later as a roller-skating rink, dance hall and boating pond. This palace of leisure finally closed at the start of the Second World War.

SHORT CUT *Pass the mill and continue along the main track for just over a mile, back to the car park. The track remains in Hebden Dale, making its way through woodland, with Hebden Water on the right.*

4 Just beyond the mill, branch right into the mill yard, bear left over a stone bridge across Hebden Water and left again onto a path. Where the path divides just ahead, take the right fork uphill through woodland. Ignore a track bending sharp right, pass a set of steps and continue climbing on the rocky winding path high above Hebden Water, out of the trees and along the top of the wood beside a fence to a squeeze stile. Go through the stile and turn left beside a wall across a short field.

5 Go through another squeeze stile and turn right on a track between walls up to Slack, where garden flowers overflow onto the path. Cross the road and follow the footpath ahead through a squeeze stile to the right of a garden gate. The path leads beside a stone wall on the left and a garden fence. As the wall swings left, continue ahead over rough ground along the edge of back gardens, and turn left downhill on a gravel track. At a junction turn left onto the Calderdale Way between neat stone walls.

Where the path divides, take the left uphill path with a wall on the left. At the end of the short track, turn left on a road then turn right through a waymarked gap in a wall into woodland on a rock-strewn path. At a waymarked post, turn left uphill. Continue along the top of woods among crags dropping steeply to the Calder valley on the right.

6 At the path's end turn left through a gap in the wall onto a walled waymarked path through the outskirts of Heptonstall. Cross two roads and continue to the Church of St Thomas the Apostle and the ruins of St Thomas a Becket Church beside it. With the churches on the left, go down stone-paved West Laithe.

Turn left up Heptonstall's stone-paved main street. Just before the Cross Inn, turn right into Northgate towards an octagonal 18th-century Methodist chapel. Where the road divides, fork right by a metal waymark, down a steep track with fine views over Hebden Bridge on the right. Cross a road, follow the waymarked bridleway ahead down through woods, cross a road and descend under trees to Hebden Water.

7 Turn left beside the river. Pass a working men's club and, after a short distance, turn right over the stone bridge. At a postbox, turn left on the road to the car park.

GIBSON MILL ON HEBDEN WATER

YORKSHIRE

4 Malham Cove

Across a dramatic limestone landscape
shaped by ice, and through a peaceful glade,
with a detour to a spectacular gorge.

LENGTH 3½ or 4 miles (2 or 2½ hours)

PARKING Yorkshire Dales National Park visitor
centre at Malham

CONDITIONS Grass and stony paths; some steps
to climb at cove; care needed on uneven
limestone pavement

REFRESHMENTS Full range in Malham

1 Turn left on the main road to join the
Pennine Way, which runs for 256 miles from
Edale in the Peak District to Kirk Yetholm over
the border in Scotland. The road begins to climb
through a patchwork of stone-walled fields.
Turn right along the gravel track towards the
spectacular amphitheatre of Malham Cove,
½ mile away, following the course of Malham
Beck, the brook that winds below.

2 At a waymarked junction, turn right to the
cove, thought to have been formed by a rare
combination of ice and water erosion. The cove's
62m (240ft) high limestone cliff is popular with
rock climbers. Retrace your steps, bearing right
on the Pennine Way to steep stone steps that
snake to the top of cove. At the top, the dramatic
scenery of Malham is surrounded by views of the
dales, stretching as far as Pendle Hill in Lancashire.
    The limestone pavement on top of the cove
was formed in the Ice Age, and consists of
blocks or clints divided by deep fissures called
grykes. Follow the Pennine Way around the top
of the cove with care – it is easy to twist an
ankle here.

3 Turn right over a ladder stile towards Gordale
Bridge. To the right the path and brook can be
seen winding along the valley floor. The path
meets a stone wall for a short section, then
continues across a grassy hilltop to a road.

4 Cross the road and join a path to Gordale,
¾ mile away, which leads between a stone wall
and a rocky outcrop. At a gate turn right and
take the steps down to a ladder stile in a stone
wall. Follow the path ahead through a gently
sloping meadow. At the bottom, continue to a
road, where the narrow Gordale Bridge stands.
The limestone bridge was built to allow
packhorses to cross the stream.
DETOUR *To go to the Gordale Scar gorge, turn left,
following the road as it bears right, then turn left
again. The track soon becomes a stony path as it meets*

LIMESTONE PAVEMENT ABOVE
MALHAM COVE

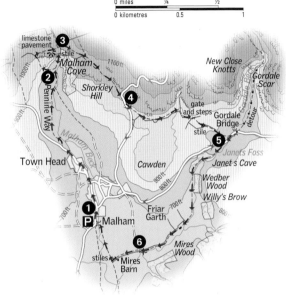

Gordale Beck and passes through the narrowing valley of Gordale Scar. The spectacular, twisting gorge with 91m (300ft) high limestone walls was scoured out by meltwater from Ice Age glaciers, and conceals two waterfalls. Return to Gordale Bridge.

5 With Gordale Bridge on the left, turn right on the road. Continue ahead for a short distance, then take the path on the left to Janet's Foss, through dense woodland of ash and sycamore, ignoring a small path to the left.

A cave in this peaceful glade, swathed in ramsons and dog's mercury, was said to be the home of Janet, or Jennet, a fairy queen. In the 18th century it was used by smelters from nearby copper mines. The foss, a Norse word meaning 'waterfall', makes a short drop over a 3.5m (12ft) wall of limestone into a pool once used for sheep dipping. The distinctive drumming of woodpeckers can sometimes be heard in the wood in spring.

6 At a meeting of paths by a footbridge, go straight on, following a waymark, with a stone wall on the left. The field barns dotted around were built to store hay and provide shelter for cattle in winter. They fell into disuse in the 20th century when farming methods became more intensive and cattle were overwintered in large numbers in sheds.

Cross a ladder stile on the left and continue ahead to a junction. Turn right to rejoin the Pennine Way, which follows Malham Beck into Malham village. Cross the footbridge behind the Old Smithy and walk along the road to return to the car park.

NORTHERN ENGLAND

YORKSHIRE

5 Clapham

Through limestone dales and gorges, past a vast hidden cavern, towards one of Yorkshire's highest peaks.

LENGTH 6½ or 8½ miles (4 or 5 hours)

PARKING National Park Centre car park

CONDITIONS Steady ascent, except steep climb from Gaping Gill to Little Ingleborough; easy scramble at Trow Gill; take a compass

REFRESHMENTS Full range in Clapham

1 From the car park turn right on Gildersbank, past a packhorse bridge across the beck on the left and the entrance to Ingleborough Hall on the right. Just before St James's Church bear left and cross the bridge. Turn right and follow the road as it bears sharp left, then turn right on the walled track signposted to Ingleborough. Woodland soon gives way to open views of pastures and meadows to the left. Across the valley to the right are Thwaite Scars, a typical limestone scar of bare grey stone, shattered and weathered into columns, shelves and tors resembling ruined battlements. The drystone wall along the track is a virtual rock garden, hung with clumps of dog's mercury, bluebell, herb-robert and crosswort.

Continue with Clapdale Wood on the right and go over a stile by a gate. The track climbs away from the valley woodland, soon reaching Clapdale Farm.

2 Continue through the farmyard. Cross a ladder stile beside a gate ahead and turn right on the path signposted to Ingleborough Cave, dropping steeply down the valley with views of Thwaite Scars. The path reaches the bottom of the hill at a broad track by Clapham Beck. Turn left to Ingleborough Cave.

The cleft from which Clapham Beck emerges, visible on the left by the ticket office, gives no clue to the secret world hidden beyond it. Over

BRIDGE AT CLAPHAM

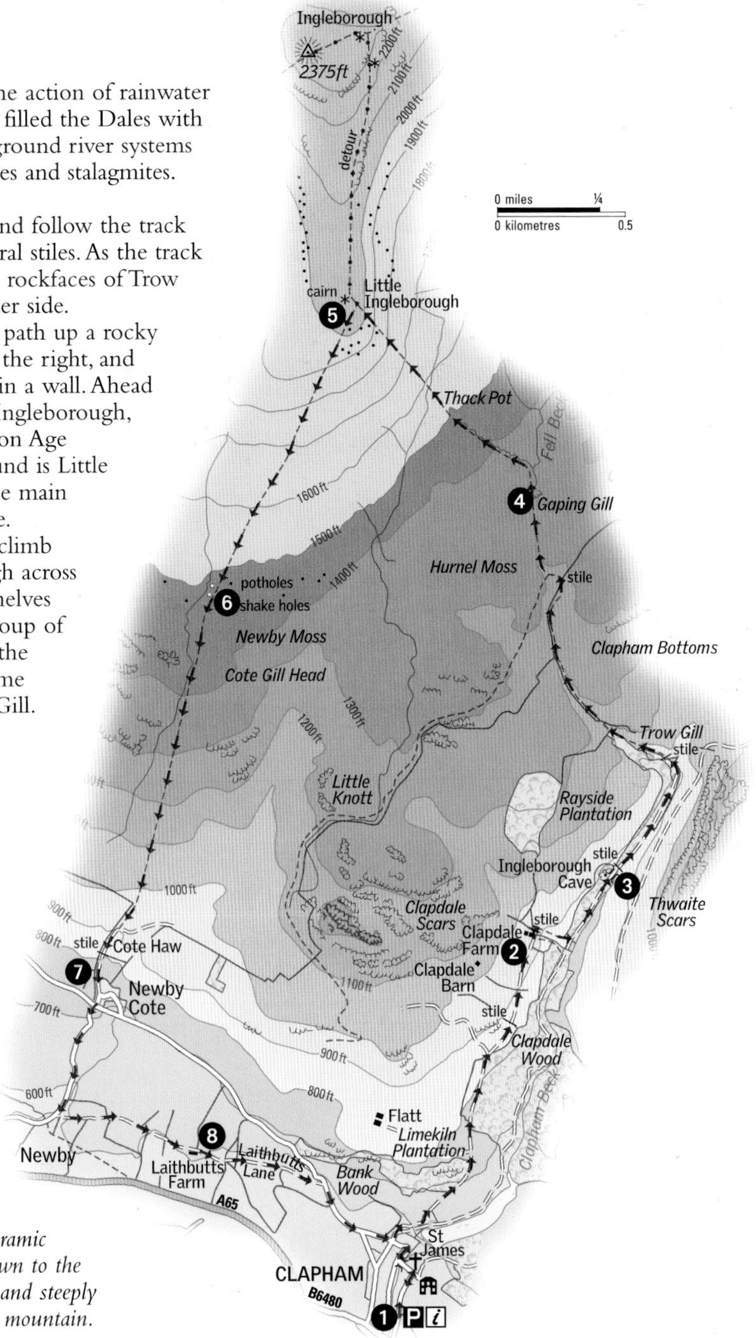

many thousands of years the action of rainwater on the local limestone has filled the Dales with caves and potholes, underground river systems and caverns full of stalactites and stalagmites.

3 Cross the footbridge and follow the track up the valley, crossing several stiles. As the track bears left, the tree-covered rockfaces of Trow Gill gorge close in on either side.

The track narrows to a path up a rocky cleft, passing a pothole on the right, and climbs gradually to a stile in a wall. Ahead is the table-top profile of Ingleborough, the site of an important Iron Age settlement. In the foreground is Little Ingleborough, linked to the main summit by a narrow saddle.

The path continues to climb towards Little Ingleborough across open sheepwalk, passing shelves of bare limestone and a group of fern-lined shake holes on the left, then bears right to some more potholes at Gaping Gill.

4 Gaping Gill is perhaps the most famous pothole in Britain. Here Fell Beck plunges more than 105m (350ft) into the main chamber, Britain's biggest known cave chamber. From the fence at the main entrance to the cave, turn left along the beck. The path soon bears left to Little Ingleborough, crossing Thack Pot then climbing steeply to the cairn on the 631m (2,070ft) summit.

DETOUR *To reach the summit of Ingleborough, and its panoramic views, follow a stony path down to the saddle joining the two peaks and steeply up the right-hand side of the mountain.*

5 Stand on the west side of the cairn at Little Ingleborough and continue on a bearing of 210 degrees, through an area of stone shelters and hollows. The path is not always clear; make for the left side of a blunt ridge in the near distance. Some small piles of stones eventually act as waymarks. The path levels out slightly and continues past some small ponds.

6 Beyond the ponds the path clears, and soon the village of Newby comes into view in the valley. Eventually the path widens into

a track. Cross a ladder stile by a gate and continue to a junction of roads.

7 Continue ahead on a road signposted to Newby. After about ¼ mile, at the end of a wall on left, turn sharp left on a waymarked bridleway to Laithbutts Farm.

8 Follow the clear track ahead. At the road turn right then turn left on a side road into Clapham. Return to the car park.

205

YORKSHIRE

6 Buckden

Along the Dales Way to the River Wharfe past an ancient 'parliament', climbing to exhilarating views and visiting three hamlets.

LENGTH 6½ miles (3½ hours)

PARKING Car park at northern edge of Buckden

CONDITIONS Gentle climbing, some rocky paths; take care at stepping stones when water is high

REFRESHMENTS Pub and shop in Buckden; pubs in Hubberholme and Cray

① From the entrance to the car park, cross the B6160 and take a short gravel path ahead. Turn right on a lane. Beyond a humpback bridge, turn right over a stile on the Dales Way towards Hubberholme to the River Wharfe, which winds along the wide valley floor.

② Continue along the pebbled banks of the river, swinging left after ½ mile alongside a stone wall. Follow the wall and then turn right on the road to Hubberholme. The village stands beside the river and the narrowing valley of Upper Wharfedale. The George Inn is the site of the 1,000-year-old 'Hubberholme Parliament', held on the first Monday in January, when the grazing rights to a nearby field are auctioned to raise money for the sick and poor people of the area.

③ Turn right over the bridge beside the George Inn and go through a gate to the right of the 13th-century Church of St Michael and All Angels. The ashes of the writer J.B. Priestley lie here, and are marked by a plaque. Behind the church, take the left fork to Yockenthwaite, following the

Dales Way along the river, which is lined with sycamore, beech and elder. In places, the path passes through meadows carpeted with wild flowers in summer. Continue for 1½ miles to Yockenthwaite, crossing a footbridge on the way.

④ On reaching a farm building, turn right at a fingerpost, then immediately left through a gate. Beyond the farmhouse, turn right up a gravel track. Near the top go through another gate and bear right to the top of the hill; the path becomes steep and rocky. After ½ mile, cross a stile and footbridge over a small ravine then continue through a sycamore and beech plantation.

⑤ Go through a gate behind Scar House, following a yellow waymark, and fork left towards the hamlet of Cray; soon there is a good view of Buckden and the valley below. Follow the path as it winds gently along the terraced hillside, past a cairn on the slope's summit. Then follow a stone wall to a footbridge across a small waterfall, and continue ahead through meadows.

⑥ At a meeting of paths, take a stony fingerposted track to the left through farm buildings, and cross the road at Cray. Use the stepping stones over the stream with care, especially when the water is high. Follow the path towards Buckden, zigzagging steeply for a short stretch.

⑦ Turn right at a path junction and look back for a bird's eye view of Cray. Continue along the ridge, which links the forts at Bainbridge and Ilkley and was once tramped by the Romans. As the route bears left just before the wood of birch, hazel and hawthorn, Buckden comes clearly into view. The rocky path drops steeply through sparse woodland before leading back to the car park.

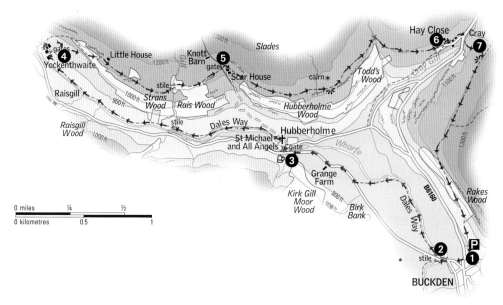

7 Lofthouse

A fertile valley in the middle of the moors and a hilltop village with timeless views.

LENGTH 3 or 3½ miles (2 or 2½ hours)

PARKING Car park in village centre

CONDITIONS Two steep ascents; rest easy going

REFRESHMENTS Pub in Lofthouse; café on detour at How Stean Gorge

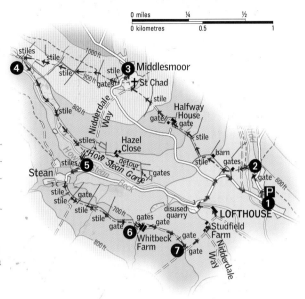

1 From the car park, turn right on the road to a stone cross above a water trough, then turn left along an alleyway between stone walls. Go through a gate and along a track to a footbridge over the River Nidd, flowing over shelves of limestone bowered by sycamore, ash and wych elms.

2 Cross the bridge, go through a gate and continue to a minor road. Cross the road and go through a wicket gate, then continue ahead to the left of a barn to two gates. Go through the gate on the right and walk up the field to a stile, with a barn on the right. Follow the path uphill across another stile, through meadows and pastures.

St Chad's Church appears between the trees ahead. To the right are views across Nidderdale to Thrope Edge and Lofthouse Moor. Go through a gate into the farmyard of Halfway House. Keep to the right on the concrete drive, with stone buildings to the left and barns and byres to the right. At end of the drive go through a gate on the left and continue up the path and some steps, then over a stile to St Chad's, which contains a remarkable stone cross dating from Saxon times.

3 Follow the cobbled lane into Middlesmoor. Turn left at the road. Opposite the former Wesleyan chapel, turn right through a stile in the wall, with a house on the right. Continue past farm buildings, through two gates and along a broad track, with How Stean valley to the left.

Go through a gateway in a wall and bear half left to a stile by a gate in the far left of the field. Cross the stile and follow the fence over a beck. Then cross another stile in a wall under a tree, and continue across a field to reach a waymarked gap in the fence on the left. Bear slightly left, heading down through the bracken to cross a stile in a wooden fence. Turn left to another stile.

4 Cross the stile, follow the path through woodland to How Stean Beck and walk along the bank. Cross a stile in a fence just before the woodland ends and continue past a limekiln and across a ladder stile in a wall. Continue to cross another stile before a T-junction.

DETOUR *To go to How Stean Gorge turn left, signed Nidderdale Way, and cross a stile. Then, ignoring a Nidderdale Way sign to the left, cross the field towards gates. Go through the gate on the right and across the next field, then go through a gate by a barn and turn right through another gate leading to the car park and café. The gorge was created by glacial meltwater; its cascades, rock terraces, tunnels and caves can be explored by hiring a torch from the neighbouring shop.*

5 Turn right through a gate over the beck, then climb the steps and continue to a road. Turn right. Where the road bends right opposite Beckside Cottage, turn left on a narrow path, cross a footbridge and continue ahead on the grassy path with a wall to the left. Cross a stile and continue across the field to cross another stile.

Walk between a house and a byre to a wicket gate at the corner of wall. Continue ahead, with a wall on the left, through a stile and across a footbridge. Fine views of Middlesmoor and the church on the hill can be seen to the left. Continue through a stile and down the bank, then go through a wicket gate and across the footbridge to reach Whitbeck Farm.

6 Go through a gate into the farmyard, through another gate on the left, then turn right to follow the wall round the side of the house. At the end of the garden, go through a wicket gate and turn left along a track. Follow the track to buildings, where it meets a walled lane.

7 Turn left along the lane. By a caravan park, where a track joins from the right, turn left, following the signposted Nidderdale Way, and walk through the farmyard. Follow the track along the river to reach the road. Turn right and cross the bridge, then continue to a junction. Turn right to return to Lofthouse and the car park.

YORKSHIRE

8 Rievaulx

From Rye Dale's pastoral idyll to woodland dells and a quiet valley, and the glory of 12th-century monastic ruins.

LENGTH 5 miles (2½ hours)

PARKING Abbey car park

CONDITIONS Undemanding, but woodland paths can be muddy and overgrown

REFRESHMENTS Café at Rievaulx Abbey

1 From the car park, turn right and walk back up the lane to some stables and a gate on the left. Go through the gate into the Duncombe Park grounds, which stretch up Rye Dale from the stately house near Helmsley. The path runs beside the empty channel of an old canal, cut to supply water to the religious community in the abbey, and along the edge of Air Bank Wood. Continue down a flight of stone steps and through a footgate onto an unmetalled lane. Head downhill to Bow Bridge.

RIEVAULX ABBEY, VIEWED FROM RIEVAULX TERRACE

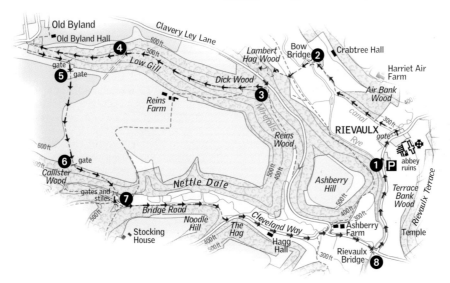

2 Cross the bridge, an elegant stone-built structure dating from 1713, and walk straight ahead. The upper reaches of Rye Dale come into view as you climb farther up the slope. Continue into Lambert Hag Wood to reach a metalled drive. Turn left. After a short climb, the drive merges with Clavery Ley Lane; turn left again and follow this to a bridleway on the right.

3 Turn off the lane and follow the bridleway downhill through Dick Wood, into a shaded, secluded valley. The numerous hazel trees in the woodland have been coppiced, originally by the monks from Rievaulx, who used the cut branches to make sheep hurdles.

A concreted section of the track leads steeply down to the bottom of the valley to cross a beck. Immediately after the beck, turn right onto a track leading up Low Gill. The enclosed valley has a timeless atmosphere – its silence broken only by birdsong and the chatter of the stream.

Follow the path, ignoring any turning off to the left, to an old stone wall covered in moss.

4 Go straight ahead through a gap in the wall. Continue to a junction near the head of the valley. Turn left on a path that doubles back and climbs to the boundary of the wood.

5 Go through the gate on the right at the top of the wood and follow the path to a second gate, crossing a track on the way. There is a good view across the valley to the village of Old Byland.

Like Rievaulx, Old Byland was the location of a 12th-century abbey. However, it proved a less attractive retreat than its neighbour and was abandoned after only four years. Go through the second gate. The path descends across fields towards Nettle Dale, with views ahead of the

stone-walled fields of Scawton Moor and the forestry plantations of the Hambleton Hills. Continue to a gate on the edge of woodland.

6 Go through the gate and turn left onto a path that drops to a footbridge in Nettle Dale. Cross the bridge and head for a stile on the other side of the field. Go over the stile and ahead through a gate. The path leads to stepping stones across a beck.

7 Cross the stepping stones and immediately turn left onto Bridge Road, passing a string of ponds on the left that are a perfect habitat for waterfowl. At the junction with a tarred lane turn left, along the Cleveland Way.

The mock Tuscan temple on Rievaulx Terrace can be glimpsed above the wooded slopes ahead. Carry straight on past a left turn across a stream to Ashberry Farm. Rievaulx Bridge, built to replace an earlier 13th-century crossing that was swept away in a flood in 1754, lies a short distance farther on.

8 Cross the bridge and turn left immediately, following a lane beside the River Rye towards the ruins of Rievaulx Abbey (EH), founded in 1132 and, before its dissolution by Henry VIII in 1538, one of England's wealthiest monasteries. More than eight centuries ago, when St Aelred was abbot, the abbey was said to have 'swarmed like a hive of bees'. Nowadays, on a summer's evening, when the last rays of the setting sun are glinting on the wooded slopes and the ruined cloisters, Rievaulx's arcadian setting leaves a lasting impression. Continue along the lane to the car park.

NORTHERN ENGLAND

YORKSHIRE

9 Lockton

A fairly arduous walk rewarded by magnificent views over forest to the high moor, with a stretch on an old drove road.

LENGTH 5½ or 6½ miles (3 or 4 hours)

PARKING In cul-de-sac off crossroads in village

CONDITIONS Some steep climbs

REFRESHMENTS Pub in Levisham

1 Cross the stile at the end of the cul-de-sac and walk along a footpath between gardens to a wooden bench, where the path divides. Fork left along the top of the escarpment, above slopes that are cloaked with bracken and mixed

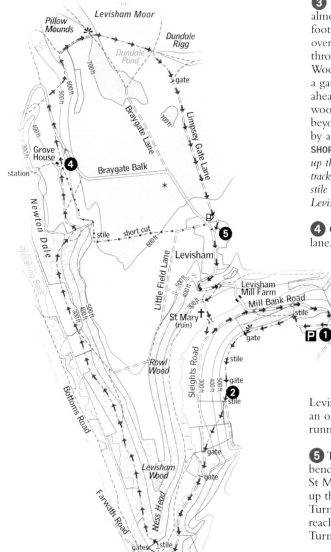

woodland. The little ruined church of St Mary can be seen far down in the valley. Continue over fields, through several gates and stiles, to a stretch of open hillside above dense thickets of gorse.

2 At a waymark next to a broken line of hawthorns turn right and head diagonally downhill on a clear path through the gorse. At a second waymark, follow the fenceline steeply down to a stile. Cross the stile, turn right and go down the hillside through hawthorn trees. Continue ahead straight across the field to a track.

Turn left on the track and continue along the valley bottom, through gates and across fields, into the thick woodland beside the stream. The track emerges from the wood near Farwath, a farm by the North Yorkshire Moors Railway. Continue to a gate on the right, close to the farmhouse.

3 Go through the gate, onto a farm track, then almost immediately turn right again, over a footbridge. Cross a stile into a field and bear left over to an opening in the fence opposite. Go through and walk up to the edge of Levisham Wood, then bear left and follow the path through a gate that leads to a well-defined track. Walk ahead for about 1½ miles, through belts of woodland and across rough fields. Continue beyond a forestry plantation to an open slope cut by a broad grassy track.

SHORT CUT *Turn sharp right and continue diagonally up the slope. Beyond the head of the little valley, the track arrives at a stile set in a stone wall. Cross the stile and turn left onto a field track to the village of Levisham, to rejoin the walk at* **5***.*

4 Continue ahead, then turn left on a tarred lane. Just before reaching a hairpin bend, turn right on a footpath and follow it steeply uphill. At the top is a magnificent view over Langdale and Cropton forests to the high moors. Bear right, directly away from the slope just climbed, and follow the path beside a drystone wall across Levisham Moor. Continue ahead to a junction of paths on the far side of Dundale Pond. Take the signposted track to the right to Levisham, soon joining Limpsey Gate Lane, an old drove road. Continue to a minor road running through Levisham village centre.

5 Turn left through the village. After a hairpin bend turn right down a track past the ruin of St Mary's Church. Cross a footbridge and walk up the slope to meet Sleights Road, a broad track. Turn left and follow the track along the valley to reach Mill Bank Road on the edge of Lockton. Turn right back to the centre of the village.

10 Cloughton

Through fertile fields and a wooded valley to a hidden gorge and waterfall, and back past a rocky smugglers' shore.

LENGTH 4½ miles (2 hours)

PARKING In Newlands Lane

CONDITIONS Easy, over level ground

REFRESHMENTS Hotel in Hayburn Wyke

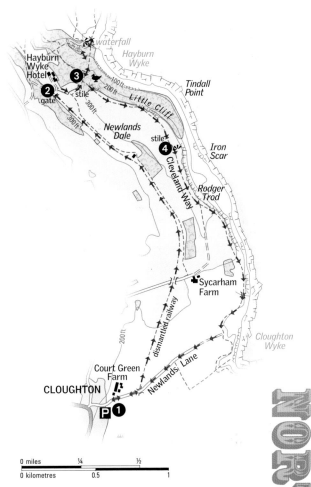

1 Walk along Newlands Lane, away from Cloughton, a village that developed during the 19th century as a result of quarrying for building stone and limestone. Although the sea is only ½ mile ahead, there is little sense of being near the coast in this fertile strip of farmland wedged between moors and clifftops. Continue on the lane to a bridge over a dismantled railway. Turn left on a path that follows the course of the old railway, which once carried stone and minerals south and brought trainloads of summer visitors and day-trippers north, to the small resort of Whitby. With the rails and sleepers long gone, the old line provides a quiet walkway.

Cross a farm drive and continue through the secluded woods and fields of Newlands Dale, and past a pretty whitewashed cottage, to reach a gate by a lane.

2 Go through the gate and turn right on the lane, which leads to a hotel. Before reaching the hotel, turn right on a path that leads over a stile into a field. Follow the downhill path to another stile on the edge of woodland fringing a nature reserve.

3 Cross the stile. Immediately beyond it the path divides beside an information board. Fork left down into a densely wooded valley. The path emerges from wind-sculpted trees above the little beach of Hayburn Wyke. Ahead lies a footbridge where Hayburn stream pours through a rocky gorge on its way to a waterfall over the cliff edge. Badgers, foxes and roe deer frequent the area.

Retrace your steps to the information board and fork left, uphill, joining the Cleveland Way. Continue along the path, through a pine wood partly replanted with broad-leaved trees, to reach a stile.

4 Cross the stile to enter open headlands above Rodger Trod, where there are fine views along the coast. Looking back, the scene is of a procession of ever-higher cliffs that plunge 90m (300ft) into the sea; looking ahead, the ruined battlements of Scarborough Castle (EH) can be glimpsed in the distance, rising beyond ranks of

rocky ledges and platforms. Descend steps cut in the path to a footbridge. Beyond the bridge the path winds around gull-tenanted cliffs and steep banks backing the small rocky bay of Cloughton Wyke. Once, it is thought, smugglers beached their boats on the shore below.

Carry on to a car park, then turn right, away from the coast, along a narrow road – the end of Newlands Lane. Follow the road back over the dismantled railway to return to the parking place on the edge of Cloughton.

YORKSHIRE

11 Swainby

Past the walls of an ancient fortress to a tree-mantled hill and windswept moorland edges.

LENGTH 7 miles (3½ hours)

PARKING In street opposite village church

CONDITIONS Moderately challenging, involving a climb to open moorland

REFRESHMENTS Full range in Swainby

1 Cross the bridge over Scugdale Beck in the middle of Swainby and follow the road, which leads out of the village, over a dismantled railway line, to the ruins of Whorlton Castle.

The impressive gatehouse, with guardrooms and fireplaces open to the sky, dates from the 14th century, although the vaults behind are Norman. The castle was later home to the Earl of Lennox whose son, Lord Darnley, married Mary, Queen of Scots. During the Civil War the fortress defences were dismantled.

Farther along the road, the picturesque ruins of 12th-century Whorlton Old Church lie abandoned, behind an avenue of ancient yew trees. Continue to the second of two gates on the outside of a sharp right-hand bend.

2 Turn left through the gate and follow the path straight ahead, across fields. Ahead, the steep escarpment of the moors climbs to the summit of cone-shaped, 320m (1,050ft) high Roseberry Topping, with the towns of the Cleveland Plain discernible on the hazy horizon stretching away to the left. Follow the path up steps and over a stile to a broad grassy path leading over open hillside to a gate at Whorl Hill Farm.

THE CLEVELAND HILLS BY SWAINBY

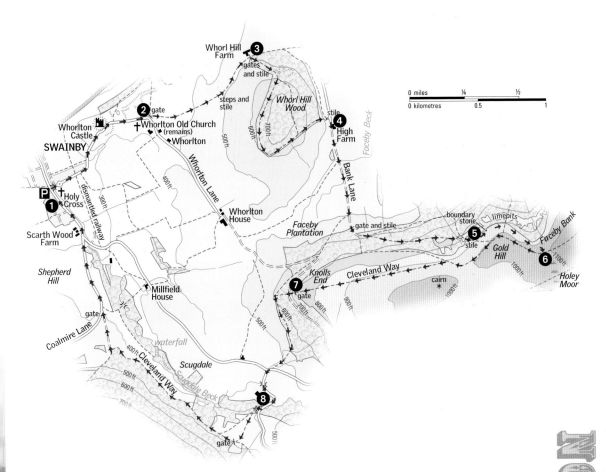

3 Go past this gate, then through a second gate to cross a farm track to a stile; climb over another stile on the right. An uphill track leads into Whorl Hill Wood. The smooth, grey trunks of beech trees march away on both sides; in spring the woodland floor is carpeted with bluebells.

As the path begins to level off, fork right to follow the edge of the wood around the shoulder of Whorl Hill; there are glimpses through the trees of Swainby down in the valley, and Shepherd Hill on the far slope. Continue just inside the perimeter of the wood. The path eventually narrows through bracken and gorse. At a fork, go right. The path goes downhill, parallel to a fence, widening again to a forest ride.

Soon, when the path begins to move away from the fence, a faint path forks off to the right. Head downhill on this path between straight ranks of beech trunks, again in line with the perimeter fence. Cross a stile into a paddock and emerge by a house on Bank Lane.

4 Turn right and follow Bank Lane, past High Farm and over Faceby Beck, to a gate immediately below the forested slopes of the moor. Go over the stile to the left of the gate, into a forestry plantation, and follow a track that bears left to climb diagonally up the slope. Ignore the left

fork at the start of the climb and continue until the path levels out, then take a right fork going steeply uphill to a stile in the wall ahead.

5 Cross the stile, turn left and follow the wall along the top of the plantation. The crags of Gold Hill can be seen on the right. Continue along the uphill grassy path that leads from the corner of the plantation, to the Cleveland Way.

6 Turn right along the Cleveland Way. Continue ahead along a stretch of the high moorland escarpment, devoid of trees and signs of human habitation. Continue downhill, to arrive at a footgate on the lower boundary of the moor.

7 Go through the gate and stay on the Cleveland Way. The path drops steeply and bends round to the left before emerging onto a lane. Walk ahead down the lane opposite, past a farm and over a small bridge to a track on the right.

8 Turn along the track, which leads over a footbridge and across a field to a gate into forestry. Turn right beyond the gate. At a fork with a track signposted to Swainby turn right. At the end of the track, go right through a gate onto the road and continue ahead into Swainby.

YORKSHIRE

12 Great Ayton Moor

A bracing walk over forested slopes to a hill dedicated to a Viking god of war and a monument to a mighty mariner.

LENGTH 4½ miles (2½ hours)

PARKING Car park off Dikes Lane, 1½ miles east of Great Ayton station, by cattle grid

CONDITIONS Generally level paths, but steep climbs to Roseberry Topping and Captain Cook's Monument

REFRESHMENTS None on walk; full range in Great Ayton

1 Facing uphill, turn left off the road onto the signposted Cleveland Way. The path climbs a flight of steps cut into the slope, then continues alongside a fence and a drystone wall marking the upper boundary of a forestry plantation.

To the right, an expanse of rolling heather moorland stretches seemingly to infinity, while clearings in the trees on the left reveal glimpses of the distant, smoky landscape of the factories and power stations of Teesside.

Follow the Cleveland Way as it bends left around Slacks Wood, to reach a gate in a drystone wall.

2 Go through the gate and continue ahead on a path towards Roseberry Topping, a distinctive cone-shaped hill visible for miles around. Perhaps on account of its uncompromising symmetry, Roseberry Topping was regarded by the Vikings as a sacred place; they dedicated it to Odin, the supreme creator and god of war.

Halfway up the hill, just past a Cleveland Way waymark stone, branch right and go up the short path to the 320m (1,050ft) summit. There are sensational views over precipitous rockfaces, caused by centuries of quarrying for sandstone, iron, coal and jet.

Descend from the summit back to the Cleveland Way, and turn right to come to a gate.

3 Go through the gate and follow the path along the left-hand side of a field. To the right, above a steep escarpment, is a folly – a grand shelter for 18th-century shooting parties. Continue downhill along the edge of two fields.

4 Turn left on a path immediately beyond the second field, past a cottage and across fields towards Airy Holme Farm.

In 1736 the young James Cook moved to the farm with his father, the newly appointed bailiff. In those days the moorland slopes of Roseberry Topping, now cloaked with the dark shapes of conifer plantations, would have provided extensive rough grazing for livestock.

The path bends right and joins a downhill lane. Continue past a disused quarry, where roe deer may be glimpsed through the undergrowth, to Dikes Lane, an old drove road used by farmers taking livestock from the moors to market.

5 Cross Dikes Lane and continue ahead on a minor road past a group of whitewashed cottages. Beyond the cottages the lane deteriorates into a muddy track that sidles along the flank of Round Hill towards the forested slopes of Easby Moor.

The path leaves the open hillside and enters a plantation of larches. Take the right-hand path along the edge of the trees, with a fence on the right. Go through a gate at the far boundary of the plantation, back to open hillside. Kestrels can

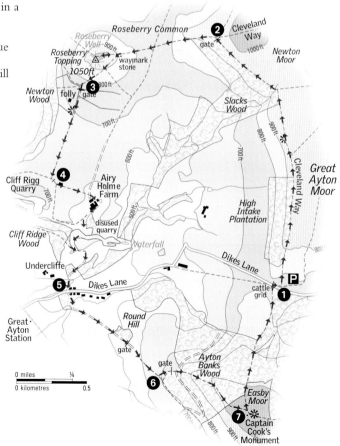

often be seen hovering above as they scan the ground for small prey emerging from the cover of the gorse that grows on the slope. Keep left along the edge of a field, then follow the path up through bracken and gorse, with a drystone wall on the left. At the corner of the wall, turn sharp left uphill to reach a gate leading into a plantation.

6 Go through the gate and immediately fork right onto a steep sandy path running through Ayton Banks Wood. Continue straight ahead over a crossing forest track. The path emerges from the trees onto

open moorland and leads between a pair of old stone gateposts to Captain Cook's Monument. Erected in 1827, the 15m (50ft) column commemorates the explorer and sailor, born in the nearby village of Marton, whose great voyages of discovery helped to open Australia and New Zealand to colonisation.

7 With your back to the ascent path, turn left and follow the waymarked Cleveland Way downhill over heather and back into forestry. The path follows a fire-break back to the car park.

A HILL DEDICATED TO A GOD OF WAR
ROSEBERRY TOPPING

YORKSHIRE

13 Hinderwell

A hinterland of fields and woods behind mineral-encrusted cliffs, once-busy harbours and mining works.

LENGTH 4½ miles (2 hours)

PARKING Roadside on village road off A174 (from Staithes turn right; from Ellerby turn left)

CONDITIONS Good, level paths and lanes; steep section in Staithes

REFRESHMENTS Full range in Staithes, pub at Dalehouse and between Port Mulgrave and Hinderwell

1 Follow the lane away from the main road, past houses to a footpath signposted off a sharp left-hand corner. Follow the path across a stile by a gate, and continue across fields into the wooded valley of Borrowby Dale. To the right the smoking chimneys of Boulby potash mine can be seen. The 1,143m (3,750ft) shaft makes this the deepest mine in Britain and the workings extend out under the sea for 2 miles.

Follow the path over a stile, down through woodland and across a footbridge over Dales Beck. Continue uphill across a field to a stile on the edge of a wood.

2 Cross the stile and turn right, following the path along the side of a steep valley. The path continues along a slope that has been planted with oak and ash trees, to reach a stile by a gate.

3 Climb over the stile and cross a footbridge over the beck immediately beyond, then follow a metalled track signposted to Dalehouse, a hamlet of mine-workers' cottages. At the junction in the hamlet turn right and pass the Fox and Hounds pub, whose inn sign shows a grinning fox hiding from the hunt under the old stone bridge behind the pub. Continue to a junction with the A174.

4 Turn right for a short distance then turn left on a minor road to Staithes. Continue all the way down the road to the harbour.

The old town, with its sheltered anchorage, was once the busiest fishing harbour on this stretch of the coast, and the local, colourfully painted fishing boats, known as cobles, may still be seen moored along the narrow creek above the harbour. A youthful James Cook worked as a grocer's boy in Staithes before signing to a Whitby shipwright. The village has changed little since his time, with its maze of narrow alleyways, flights of winding steps and tiers of gaily painted cottages – all clinging to the steep slopes climbing away from Staithes Beck.

5 Turn right at the waterfront and follow Church Street steeply uphill. The street peters out into a track then, high above Staithes, a spectacular clifftop path with dizzying views 90m (300ft) down to crashing waves. Behind, Boulby Cliffs soar to 203m (666ft), making them the highest on England's east coast. This part of the walk follows the Cleveland Way, which starts in Helmsley, on the edge of the North York Moors National Park, and ends 110 miles later at Crook Ness, on the coast near Filey. Continue along the tops of cliffs, where bands of pale sandstone alternate with a hard black lignite – the source of the polished and carved jet jewellery so popular in the 19th century. The path reaches a tarmac lane.

6 Turn right and follow the lane through Port Mulgrave; the abandoned harbour is now a nature reserve, but ironstone mined from deep below the headlands was shipped from here until the early 1900s.

Continue up the lane into Hinderwell. At the junction by St Hilda's Church turn left. In the churchyard is a well dedicated to the saint, who founded the abbey at Whitby. The small shrine of weathered stone shelters a little pool. Return to the roadside parking place, which lies on the far side of the main road.

Map

Staithes Harbour

Cowbar **5**

Old Nab

car park

Cleveland Way

Staithes

A174

Cliff Farm

4

Dalehouse

Seaton Hall

Thorndale Shaft

200ft

stile

3

Beacon Hill △377ft **6**

Port Mulgrave

Dales Beck

Cliffs

Plum Tree House

Borrowby Dale

Oakrigg Wood

St Hilda †

P HINDERWELL

stile **1**

gate

A174

stile stile

2

0 miles ¼ ½

0 kilometres 0.5 1

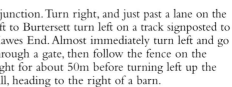

14 Bainbridge

Along a meandering river to a secluded lake, through fellside pastures and on to a Roman road.

LENGTH 5 miles (3 hours)

PARKING By village green

CONDITIONS Two steep ascents, otherwise easy going

REFRESHMENTS Pub and tearoom in Bainbridge

1 Cross the green past the stocks and the post office, then turn right on the A684. Cross the bridge over the River Bain. The grassy mound on the left is Brough Hill, the site of a Roman fort called Virosidum. As the road curls up and to the left, turn right through a squeeze stile in a wall onto a path signposted to Semer Water. To the right is the River Bain, 2½ miles long, reputed to be the shortest river in Britain. Continue past a barn to a fingerpost.

2 From the fingerpost continue to another fingerpost on the brow of the hill ahead, then continue on the same line, heading for the next rise. Continue to a wall.

3 Go through the right-hand of two stiles and follow the path over the top of Bracken Hill. The path is indistinct as it heads along the ridge but becomes clear again as it runs along a wall ahead to a stile. There are excellent views of Semer Water and the surrounding hills and moors.

Cross a stile ahead and continue through two fields, crossing stiles. In the third field, head to a ladder stile between a barn on the left and the river bend on the right. Cross another stile and follow the path ahead alongside the river.

4 Where a path joins from the left, cross a stile to continue straight ahead on the path signposted to Semer Water. The route crosses more stiles to reach a triple-arched bridge. Semer Water, reached along a road on the left from the bridge, is a natural lake – a rarity in the Dales. Turn right to cross the bridge and walk up the steep road to

a junction. Turn right, and just past a lane on the left to Burtersett turn left on a track signposted to Hawes End. Almost immediately turn left and go through a gate, then follow the fence on the right for about 50m before turning left up the hill, heading to the right of a barn.

5 Go through a gate to the right of the barn, then cross a stream and climb uphill, bearing left of a barn on the hillside ahead. Close to the barn the path meets a wall; continue alongside it to a squeeze stile on the left. Go through the stile and bear slightly right uphill on an indistinct path, making for a dip in the hill crest with a wall on the left. At the dip, go through a squeeze stile in the wall ahead and continue with the wall on the left. The local sheep are adept at climbing – hence the barbed wire along the top of the walls.

6 At the top of ridge, go through a gate and turn right along the road, passing hills and hollows made by old mine workings. Soon, turn right through a squeeze stile and follow a path signposted to Horton Gill Bridge, over tussocky grasslands to a walled track.

7 Turn right on the track. This is Cam High Road, a Roman road built to link Virosidum with a fort at Ridchester in Lancashire. Follow the track for just over a mile, until it meets a road. Bear left downhill to return to Bainbridge.

217

YORKSHIRE

15 Gunnerside

Forgotten pathways through the fellside past old lead mines and smelting mills at the head of a tumbling beck.

LENGTH 5½ miles (3½ hours)

PARKING Village car park or beside B6270

CONDITIONS Fairly demanding

REFRESHMENTS Shop and pub in Gunnerside

1 From the car park or roadside, cross the bridge in the direction of the King's Head, and turn left on a track signposted to Gunnerside Gill. Follow the beck upstream to a white gate with stone steps to the right. Climb the steps and continue along the walled path, through a wicket gate and round a large house. Continue ahead with the beck to the left, through an old wall and across fields.

2 Where a side valley cuts in from the right, continue ahead past ruins of disused mines on the right. Go through a gate into woodland, across a little brook and alongside the boulder-strewn riverbed. Pass through another gate and up steps. Continue ahead through Birbeck Wood, climbing above the beck on the edge of the woods. The path then descends to the beck.

3 Cross a tiny stream and go through a squeeze stile in a wall. Soon, where a fence meets the wall, turn right through a squeeze stile in the wall, ignoring another one in the fence. Continue ahead with the wall on the left and a barn to the right. Cross a marshy field with bracken-covered mounds and continue ahead across two more fields with extensive ruins.

4 The path skirts remains of a 19th-century mine, including a wheel-pit where the galena (lead ore) was crushed – and the bouse teams, a row of bays into which ore was piled. Keep left of the ruins. Cross another stile, then follow the path, seeing more ruins on the other side of the beck, up to a stile leading onto open fellside. Follow the wide path past field enclosures and a small, ruined barn, then along a wall.

5 Follow the path as it leaves the wall, and the Botcher Gill Nook gorge comes into view across the valley to the left. Soon, to the right, Swina Bank Scar forms an amphitheatre of scree and weathered sediment. The ground is always marshy here. Farther along, across the valley, a chute of rubble marks the remains of the Dolly Leadmine. Continue past other disused mines. There is an air of melancholy about the abandoned workings, where so many men once toiled.

6 After two stone cairns, at the junction of paths, fork left down to the beck. The path eventually leads to the right of another ruined building, which once stored peat from the surrounding fells for use as fuel in the smelt furnace. Just past the peat store is the Blakethwaite smelt mill, where galena would have been smelted.

7 Cross the footbridge over the beck and follow a wide, clear track to the left up the slope, climbing to the shoulder of the valley. The path cuts across banks of heather and crosses a stone bridge embankment, then rises and falls, eventually meeting a broader track at the head of Botcher Gill Nook.

8 At the path junction turn left on the broad track across the gill to a stile beside a gate. Cross the stile and continue for a mile, descending towards the ridge end.

9 As the track bends to the right with a small cairn to the left, turn left onto a grassy path heading towards houses at the foot of the valley. The path passes a group of shake holes on the right – circular depressions caused by underground erosion. Follow the path as it bends to the right, and on to cross a stile to the left of a house to return to Gunnerside.

Map labels:

ruins of Blakethwaite smelt mill
Lownathwaite Mea
Gorton Hush
North Hush
disused mines
disused mines
Bunton Hush
Gunnerside Gill
Lownathwaite
Swina Bank Scar
disused mines
Dolly Lead Level
Botcher Gill Nook
1600ft
Botcher Gill Gate
stile
Silver Hill
Gunnerside Beck
shake holes
1600ft
stile
stile
disused lead mine
gate
Jingle Pot Edge
stile
barn stile
Birbeck Wood
1200ft
gate
1100ft
shake holes
900ft
gate
shake holes
stile gate
GUNNERSIDE
B6270

0 miles   ¼   ½
0 kilometres   0.5   1

218

HAY BARNS AT GUNNERSIDE

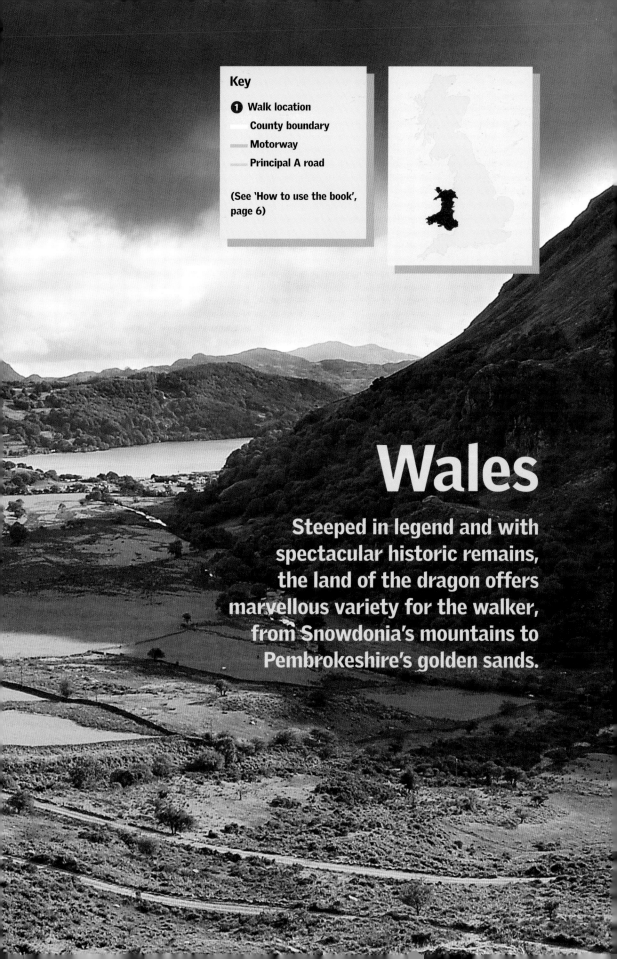

Key

1 Walk location
County boundary
Motorway
Principal A road

(See 'How to use the book', page 6)

Wales

Steeped in legend and with spectacular historic remains, the land of the dragon offers marvellous variety for the walker, from Snowdonia's mountains to Pembrokeshire's golden sands.

SOUTH WALES

The dramatic southern and southwestern coasts of Wales, including the beautiful Gower Peninsula, offer some of the region's best walking, rivalled only by the lonely Preseli Hills and the winding lower Wye Valley.

1 Tintern Parva

From a former railway station along the Offa's Dyke Path to a view of a ruined medieval abbey by the River Wye.

LENGTH 4 or 5 miles (3 or 3½ hours)

PARKING At Tintern Old Station

CONDITIONS A steep climb and rocky descent

REFRESHMENTS Café at Old Station; pub at Brockweir; pub and café at Tintern Parva

1 Facing the river, turn left and go along the the old railway bed; the line closed in 1964, but the station is preserved. Where the track ends, climb the steps, cross the bridge into Brockweir and turn right on the lane. The tiny village was once a busy port and boat-building centre. The unruliness of its inhabitants was curbed by the opening, in 1833, of a Moravian church, built by a Protestant sect tied to no particular doctrines. The church still functions, and is reached by a footpath beside the Brockweir Inn.

2 Continue past Gregory Farm and turn left on a wide track, signposted to 177-mile Offa's Dyke Path. Go through a metal gate, with a hedge on the right and a wooded valley on the

left. Just before a stone barn, turn right on a narrow waymarked path, between tall hedges, and continue to a stile.

3 Cross the stile and turn right beside a fence. After 40m, follow the waymarks slightly to the left and uphill, then continue as the path winds up between trees to the top of the rise. Follow the path as it bears right along the edge of an escarpment, to an information board at the start of a spectacular section of Offa's Dyke. This huge bank-and-ditch earthwork was built by King Offa of Mercia in the 8th century AD, as a border separating his kingdom from what is now Wales.

Continue up the stony path, which narrows to a shady tunnel, passing through trees. Continue to a crossing track, with a signpost to Tintern.

4 Continue ahead to the Devil's Pulpit, an isolated limestone pinnacle commanding a superb view of Tintern Abbey, which is set within a loop of the River Wye. Legend has it that the Devil used to harangue the monks in the abbey from this spot, pelting them with rocks.

Return to the Tintern signpost. Turn left on the steep downhill path through towering beeches and continue to a junction with a broad forestry track, where the trees thin out. Turn right on the track. Opposite a TV/radio mast, turn left onto a narrow path with a yellow waymark. This becomes a steep, natural rock staircase.

5 At foot of the hill, turn right towards a bridge parapet, where the Wye comes into view. Bear left on a broad track that narrows as it passes to the left of a metal gate. Beyond some steel posts, the track meets the course of the old Wye Valley Railway. Turn right to emerge opposite Tintern Abbey, then follow the track round to an iron-girder bridge, dating from 1872, which once carried a branch line of the railway. Cross the bridge and continue past Abbey Mill and its wharf – all that remains of a once busy industrial complex – to a junction with the A466.

DETOUR *Turn left to visit the well-preserved ruins of medieval Tintern Abbey (Cadw).*

6 Turn right and continue for about ½ mile. Just before the Wye Valley Hotel, turn right onto the signposted Wye Valley Walk. Go through the churchyard of St Michael's Church then follow the riverbank, crossing several footbridges over little streams. At the brick abutment of the old railway, climb the steps on the left and then turn left to reach Tintern Old Station and the car park.

2 Oxwich

An energetic walk on a wooded headland with sea views, a secluded Norman church and an impressive Tudor mansion.

LENGTH 3½ miles (2 hours)

PARKING Car park at Oxwich Bay

CONDITIONS Muddy in parts after rain, with some steep and rough paths

REFRESHMENTS Café and hotel in Oxwich

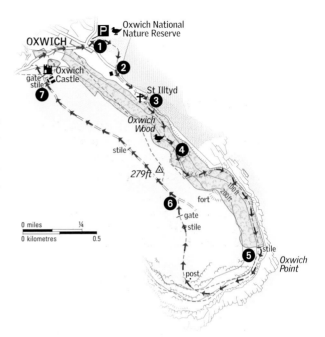

1 Head towards the sea; to the left is an area of sand dunes, part of the Oxwich National Nature Reserve. The dunes support plants such as sea holly, prickly saltwort, orchids and evening primrose. Turn right along the top of the sandy beach, heading towards a hotel. Continue to the end of the beach and go right through a gap in the wall to join a road.

2 Turn left; the road soon becomes a rough track, then a narrow path at the edge of a steep wooded hill to the right. Continue along the path past the Norman Church of St Illtyd, with its sturdy battlemented tower and tiny chancel, approaching a wooded area, also part of Oxwich National Nature Reserve. Trees reach down to the rocks on the shoreline below, many of them stunted by strong winds.

3 Just beyond the church, bear right uphill, following the path through a broad-leaved woodland of oak and ash. The long, steep climb is eased by flights of steps. In spring and summer the surrounding air is heavy with the scent of wild garlic.

4 Towards the top of the hill, where the path divides, turn left along a path through the trees. Follow the path around the flank of the hill, with tree roots weaving underfoot, eventually emerging at the edge of the wood with a narrow area of grassland to the right. Continue ahead, bearing left back into woodland.

The path then descends, sometimes steeply on steps, sometimes gently, passing dark crevices in the rock. Continue downhill back to the shoreline. Ivy carpets the ground on either side of the path and climbs the trunks of gnarled oak trees. The path eventually passes a small clearing on the cliff, with views along the south Gower coast towards Threecliff Bay, High Tor and Pwlldu Head to the left and the rocky shoreline of Oxwich Point to the right.

Continue along the edge of the wood, with the shoreline and waves lapping against rocks on the left, to a stile.

5 Cross the stile, leaving the nature reserve. Follow the yellow-waymarked path ahead. The cliff curves down to Oxwich Point, and the path opens out, surrounded by mouse-ear hawkweed and devil's bit scabious. Continuing ahead, the path is lined with rich yellow gorse and purple bell heather in summer. Continue ahead until a small, grassy outcrop extending over rocks to the left comes into view. Take any of the indistinct paths up the cliff to the right, before or at the outcrop. Halfway up the cliffside, bear left on a path running parallel with the shoreline, which eventually swings round below rocky outcrops to the clifftop.

At the top, carry straight on across grass past a yellow-waymarked post. Follow the path through a patch of gorse and head for a stile by a gate opposite. Cross the stile and follow the yellow waymark to reach a stony farm track.

6 Turn left on the track. Where it divides, go straight on, following the sign to Oxwich Green. Views to the left extend over Port-Eynon Bay. At the end of the track, cross a stile.

7 Continue ahead to a road, passing the remains of Oxwich Castle, once a magnificent 16th-century fortified mansion. It was built by the Mansels, a powerful Gower family, and their family crest is carved into the wall. The castle's gateway and curtain wall were designed to impress rather than to defend.

Turn right at the road, passing an old limekiln. At the crossroads continue ahead to return to the car park.

WALES

223

SOUTH WALES

3 Manorbier

From the shadows of a Norman castle, along the Pembrokeshire Coast Path to cliffs above surf-scoured rocks.

LENGTH 6 miles (3½ hours)

PARKING Beach car park

CONDITIONS Strenuous clifftop walk; wear good walking shoes or boots

REFRESHMENTS None on walk; full range in Manorbier

1 Walk along the path leading from the car park to Manorbier beach, then turn left and follow the signposted Pembrokeshire Coast Path over shingle. Go up some steps at the end of the beach and follow a narrow path along the edge of the bay.

After a short distance the path reaches King's Quoit, a 5,000-year-old burial chamber consisting of a huge horizontal slab of rock supported on smaller uprights.

2 Carry straight on along the path from King's Quoit to the end of the headland, where the cliffs leading eastwards to Old Castle Head come into view. The path bends left, rounding the headland, to run along the base of a steep slope.

Rock ledges run out to sea, separated by long, seaweed-filled gullies where the sea surges and gurgles. The path skirts an inlet with a tall stack – an isolated pillar of rock – guarding its mouth, then climbs to the clifftops before descending into a steep, narrow coomb. The headland beyond the coomb flanks a sandy bay, with Old Castle Head at its far end.

Follow the winding, undulating path, past deep fissures and sudden drops, to a stile on the high ground above the bay.

3 Cross the stile and walk along the edge of a field to reach the perimeter fence of Manorbier Camp – a military base. Turn right and follow the waymarked route of the Pembrokeshire Coast Path, across three more stiles, to the entrance to the base.

4 Turn right on the road through the base then immediately left on the side road beside the fence. After a short distance the road divides; fork right to a picnic area, where the road divides again. Turn left. The tarmac soon gives way to a grassy track that leads to a stile.

5 Cross the stile onto a footpath that rounds Skrinkle Haven before reaching the edge of the land at Church Doors – tiny twin coves.

Continue along the cliff path, with Lydstep Point immediately ahead. The small rocky isthmus of St Margaret's Island, joined to Caldey Island by a natural rock causeway, can be seen out to sea, before the path goes steeply downhill into a coomb with a flight of wooden steps leading out of it.

6 Climb the steps and turn left at the top on a track leading to a stile. Beyond the stile the path divides. Fork right, through a gate, and follow the wide path to Lydstep Point, where high cliffs tower over the sandy crescent of Lydstep Haven. The path bends to the right beyond the point, following the edge of the land past Whitesheet Rock and back to the steps leading into the coomb.

Retrace your steps to the main road through the camp and turn right towards an estate of houses. Continue to a track on the left just before the houses.

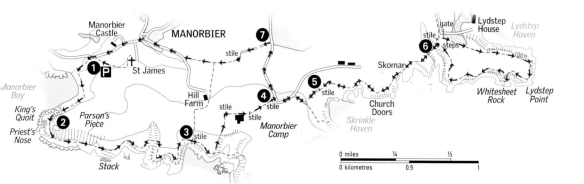

7 Turn left along the track, which leads across a field. Turn left again at the far side of the field and follow the boundary down a small dip to arrive at a stile. Cross the stile and turn right on a wide path enclosed between old stone walls. The path, signposted to Manorbier, merges into a surfaced farm lane, which leads to a T-junction in the village. Turn left and follow the beach road, passing Manorbier Castle, where the medieval scholar Gerald of Wales was born in 1146. Gerald's father, the Norman knight William de Barri, ruled the estate on which the castle stands and linked his family with the Welsh royal line through marriage. Continue along the road to the car park.

MANORBIER BAY BEACH

SOUTH WALES

4 Stackpole Quay

Wild clifftops and wheeling seabirds, giving way to a serene lake with waterfowl among the reeds.

LENGTH 6½ miles (3 hours)

PARKING Stackpole Quay car park, off road from Stackpole to Freshwater East

CONDITIONS Up-and-down clifftop path leads to level walking beside an ornamental lake

REFRESHMENTS Café at Stackpole Quay, pub at Stackpole

1 Take the path that leads from the bottom left-hand corner of the car park, signposted to Barafundle. Continue to a flight of steps on the right, above the little harbour of Stackpole Quay. Climb the steps to join a grassy path over the clifftops and continue over a small rise, where the sandy sweep of Barafundle Bay comes into view. The path descends to an arch in a stone wall.

2 Go through the arch and down a long flight of steps to reach the beach. The path runs just above the line of high tide to a flight of steps leading from the far side of the bay into a small wood. Continue to a stile. Cross the stile and stay on the clifftop path, past natural arch formations, to the end of the headland. The scene along the coast constantly changes, with new headlands, coves and islets continuously coming into view – all crowded with colonies of bickering guillemots and fulmars. Continue to a stile at the head of a narrow cliff-lined cleft called Raming Hole.

3 Climb over the stile and follow the path, which rounds the next headland then skirts the back of a small cliff-locked bay and continues to the headland of Saddle Point. Here cross a stile and descend towards Broad Haven – a sweep of sand backed by dunes. Follow the path away from the coast, skirting a stretch of brackish water. Continue to the side of a deeply indented ornamental lake created as part of the 18th-century landscaping of the Stackpole Estate.

4 Bear right, keeping the lake to the left. Its extent is soon apparent: three long fingers of water stretching between wooded ridges – a home for waterfowl, which bob and weave between beds of water lilies and other water plants. The dunes give way to dune grassland and open woodland. Continue along the path to a stone footbridge.

Cross the bridge and immediately fork right. Carry straight on, with the water now on the right. After about ¾ mile continue past a graceful stone bridge with eight arches, then past a boathouse that has been converted into a hide for birdwatchers. The path bends away from the shore before climbing to a small archway.

5 Turn right through the archway then turn left and climb a flight of broad, formal steps to a terrace where Stackpole Court once stood; now only the stable block that adjoined the house remains. Follow the right-hand edge of the terrace, which curves around to join a drive. Turn right on the drive then immediately take the signposted footpath on the right to a walkway over a weir. On the far side turn left and continue to a minor road.

Turn right and follow the road uphill through firs and broad-leaved woodland to Stackpole. Beyond the village, where the road divides, fork right. At the next junction turn right to return to the car park.

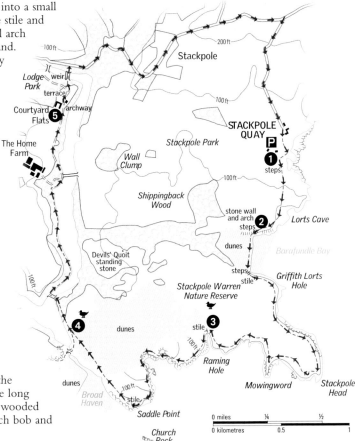

5 Porth Clais

Along the far-western rim of Wales, across quiet countryside then along a clifftop path with foam-flecked waves below.

LENGTH 5½ miles (3½ hours)

PARKING St David's, Bishop's Palace car park

CONDITIONS Undemanding walk along clifftop paths and quiet lanes

REFRESHMENTS Full range in St David's

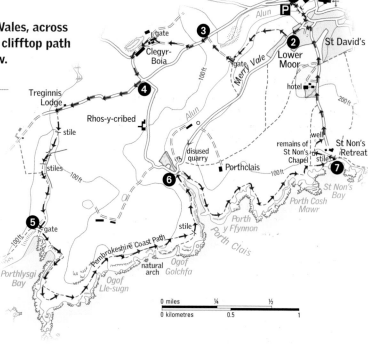

1 Turn right out of the car park and cross a bridge over the River Alun. Immediately beyond a left turning leading towards the cathedral, turn right to a T-junction, then turn right again and follow the road for 200m to a signposted footpath on the right.

2 Follow the footpath – a wide grassy track between stone walls, with rough pasture beyond. The path bends left, alongside the River Alun, to a gate beside a house. Go through the gate and turn right, across a footbridge over the river, then continue ahead to emerge onto a minor road.

3 Turn left on the road for 100m, then take a broad track on the right towards a rocky outcrop. The track divides just before reaching a cottage; fork right and walk past barns to a gate. Go through the gate and turn left on a track leading to a lane, at Clegyr-Boia, then turn left again. Continue along the lane for a short distance to a crossroads. There are views to the left of the tower of St David's Cathedral and to the right of the rocky, ragged end of the Pembroke peninsula.

4 Turn right at the crossroads, signposted 'No Through Road', to a house called Treginnis Lodge. Turn left opposite the house, along a signposted footpath that leads across a field to a stile. Cross the stile and follow the path along the edge of a field to a small footbridge. Go over the bridge and two stiles immediately beyond it. The path now follows a narrow valley to a gate just behind Porthlysgi Bay, a rocky cove.

5 Go through the gate and turn left on the Pembrokeshire Coast Path, which leads down to the stony beach then crosses a stream and climbs onto a low headland. Out to sea, colonies of seabirds wheel over islets, and as the path rounds the headland there is a long view eastwards of a spiny, cliff-fringed coast.

Continue along the clifftop path to a stile. Cross the stile and follow the path alongside Porth Clais to a lane at the head of the inlet.

6 Turn right on the lane then immediately right again towards some old, round limekilns. Before reaching the kilns turn left along the coast path – a rocky track that follows the other side of the inlet back to the open clifftops. Continue around the small bay of Porth y Ffynnon into the wider bight of St Non's Bay, where the ruin of St Non's Chapel lies beyond a stone stile on the left.

7 Cross the stone stile and follow a footpath away from the coast, past the ruined chapel – dedicated to St David's mother – to a kissing gate. Go through the gate; beyond it there is a holy well with a shrine on which it is recorded that the spring that feeds it appeared on the day the saint was born.

After a short climb the path meets a lane. Turn left. The tower of St David's Cathedral comes into view ahead. Walk straight on along the lane, past a hotel, to a road junction. Turn left then immediately right to re-enter the city on Goat Street. Turn left down Deanery Hill to return to the car park.

wales

227

SOUTH WALES

6 Wolf's Castle

Up steeply banked lanes and over rough pasture to a mountain crowned with strangely shaped, eroded rocky outcrops.

LENGTH 5½ miles (3 hours)

PARKING Parking space opposite chapel in village

CONDITIONS Varied and demanding, along hilly lanes and over field and mountain tracks

REFRESHMENTS Pub in Wolf's Castle

1 Turn left in front of the chapel opposite the parking area, and follow the lane to the A40. Turn right on the main road and follow it across a bridge over a railway, then turn right again, onto a minor road signposted to Hayscastle. Continue uphill, between high, grassy banks. At the top of the hill, there is a view to the left, across rolling countryside, to the craggy outcrops of Great Treffgarne Mountain. Beyond Bank Farm the road goes into a dip, before climbing again and reaching the end of the driveway that leads to Cold Comfort farm.

2 Turn left onto the farm driveway and continue past the farmhouse and through two gates in close succession. At a pair of gates, hung side by side, go through the right-hand one into a field. Walk straight ahead along the field edge and go through a gate into the next field. Just before the far boundary of the field, the path reaches a stone stile on the right.

3 Go over the stile and then follow the edge of a field to reach a second stone stile. Go over this stile onto a minor road, with a wooden stile on the opposite side. Cross the road and go over the wooden stile into an area of rough pasture that is covered with thickets of blackthorn and gorse. Continue following the path to where it meets a broad track.

THE POLL CARN OUTCROP, GREAT TREFFGARNE MOUNTAIN

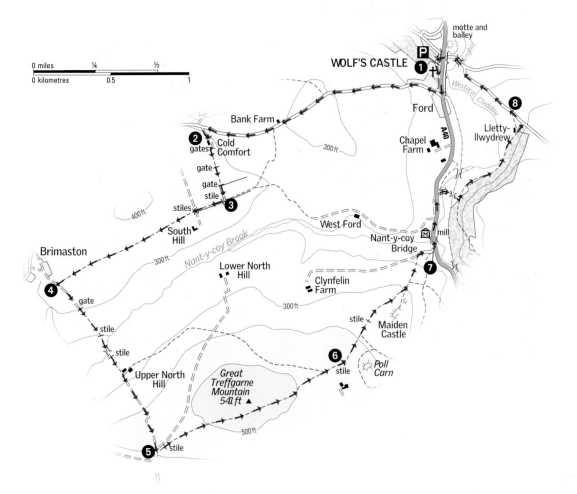

WOLF'S CASTLE

motte and bailey

P **1**

Ford

8

Bank Farm

2 Cold
gates Comfort

gate

gate
stile

stiles **3**

South
Hill

Brimaston

4

gate

stile

stile

Upper North
Hill

Great
Treffgarne
Mountain
541 ft ▲

500 ft

5 stile

Lower North
Hill

Clynfelin
Farm

300 ft

West Ford

Nant-y-coy
Bridge

mill

7

stile

Maiden
Castle

6

stile

Poll
Carn

Chapel
Farm

Lletty-
llwydrew

Nant-y-coy Brook

Western Cleddau

A40

300 ft

400 ft

4 Turn left on the track, which peters out a short distance beyond a gate. Keep straight ahead over springy turf, across two stiles with a small stone footbridge between them, to emerge onto the driveway of Upper North Hill. Cross straight over, following a waymarked path, which soon merges into a surfaced, uphill track. At the top of the rise, there are views behind of Strumble Head and of Milford Haven ahead. Continue over the brow of the hill to a meeting of tracks.

5 Go sharp left on a broad waymarked track to reach a stile on the right, built of concrete blocks. Immediately beyond this, there is a 'private road' sign across the track. Cross over the stile and walk straight ahead up a slope to the summit of Great Treffgarne Mountain. Stay on the path, which continues straight on from the summit, to reach a stile, below the strangely shaped outcrops of Poll Carn.

6 Cross the stile and follow the path, which bends left to another stile, above the even more surreal-looking rocks of Maiden Castle. Go over this stile and continue on the path beyond it,

which soon becomes indistinct. Walk down the ever-steeper slope, over yet another stile, to join a path at the foot of the hill. Turn left on the path, then continue ahead to reach the A40.

7 Turn left on the road and follow it downhill to Nant-y-coy Bridge, where a former mill houses a museum and craft centre. After a short distance turn right down a signposted path, opposite the drive to West Ford Farm, to a footbridge over the Western Cleddau river. Cross the bridge and continue under a railway bridge, beyond which the path divides. Fork left, along the edge of a forestry plantation, with the river to the left. The path joins the drive to a house called Lletty-llwydrew. Go up the drive to reach a minor road.

8 Turn left and continue downhill to a junction. Turn left again and cross a bridge over the River Anghof. The mound-and-ditch construction of an old motte and bailey – the original Wolf's Castle – lies just past the bridge, commanding the confluence of the Anghof and Western Cleddau rivers. Follow the road under the bridge to return to the parking place.

WALES

SOUTH WALES

7 Crymych

To the tops of the Preseli Hills, where the remnants of a lost Celtic civilisation haunt a landscape redolent of ancient Britain.

LENGTH 4 miles (3 hours)

PARKING On roadside verge below Foeldrygarn, 1½ miles southwest of Crymych on road to Maenclochog

CONDITIONS Exposed hilltops; wet underfoot

REFRESHMENTS None on walk; full range in Crymych

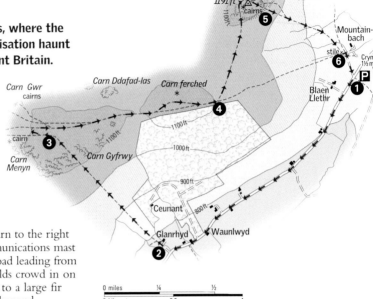

1 With the summit of Foeldrygarn to the right and a hill crowned by a tall communications mast to the left, walk along the quiet road leading from Crymych. Small, stone-walled fields crowd in on both sides, climbing on the right to a large fir plantation, with the Preseli Hills beyond.

After about ¾ mile, the fields to the right are broken by a block of fir trees. Continue on the road for a short distance to reach a junction with a broad farm track joining from the right.

2 Turn right on the track and continue past some buildings to a stile. Cross the stile onto open moorland and walk straight ahead, aiming for the middle of three rocky outcrops at the top of the slope. There is no clearly defined path up the hillside and there are likely to be frequent boggy patches. Higher up the slope, the ground tends to become drier.

Head towards the saddle between Carn Gyfrwy and Carn Menyn, which lie just below the top of the hill. These rocky outcrops were sources of the huge pieces of stone taken from the Preseli Hills for the building of Stonehenge.

From the top of the hill, a spectacular panorama of moorland and sky opens up ahead. The wide, rolling landscape stretches towards the distant Pembrokeshire coast, with patches of tussocky grass and pockets of reedy ground marking frequent springs. Cairns and outcrops of natural rock punctuate the bleak terrain, although the area is rich in Bronze Age and Iron Age remains – an indication that it once enjoyed a milder climate.

3 From the top of the hill, walk straight ahead, descending a short distance to where the route is crossed by a well-defined path. Turn right on the path, heading towards the top edge of the large plantation of firs that was seen from the road at the start of the walk. Continue over the tops of the Preseli Hills, heading for the far corner of

the fir plantation, to reach a junction with a broad, well-defined track, leading away towards higher ground.

4 Turn left on the track, heading over gently rising ground towards the top of Foeldrygarn, the highest of the nearby summits. Near the top of the climb, the path bends to the left to skirt the ramparts of an Iron Age hillfort and a ragged line of craggy outcrops. The three great piles of stones on the summit of Foeldrygarn are said to mark the burial place of Bronze Age chieftains. These look across stretches of bleak peat moorland to similar sentinel-like cairns, standing guard on the neighbouring hilltops.

5 Turn around for a view of the rolling hills of Carmarthenshire, stretching away to the east. Walk down the slope towards these eastern hills, crossing the encircling ramparts of the fort to join a wide green track. Continue downhill on the track, through an area of rough pasture, studded with large boulders and crisscrossed by numerous small streams.

Keeping on the track as it descends, head in the direction of a small windbreak of trees to the right of a farmhouse – called Mountain-bach – to reach a stile on the lower boundary of the open hillside.

6 Cross the stile and follow a signposted path that joins a farm track. Follow the track downhill, past some small fields, to reach the roadside. Turn right on the road to return to the parking place.

8 Poppit Sands

From the sea shore to the soaring heights of the clifftops, accompanied by the mewing of gulls and the muffled boom of the surf.

LENGTH 5½ miles (3½ hours)

PARKING Poppit Sands car park, on B4546 north of St Godmaels

CONDITIONS Fairly demanding

REFRESHMENTS Shop and café at car park

1 Turn left out of the main entrance of the car park. Follow the road around the perimeter of the car park and uphill, with an ever-widening view across the Teifi estuary to Cardigan Island. Beyond the brow of a hill, the tiny harbour of Cei-bâch can be seen down the slope to the right. Past a youth hostel, at a fork in the road, continue ahead as the road starts to go uphill again, to a cattle grid.

2 Cross the cattle grid and immediately fork right on a partially surfaced track. Continue past a small pond and a house to the edge of a farmyard. Climb over the stiles on both sides of the yard and carry on to another stile. Cross this and turn right on a broad grassy track. Just before a gateway across the track, climb a stile on the right and turn left, so that you are walking parallel to the track, now on the far side of the fence. A long grassy bank sloping down to Cemaes Head can be seen

ahead. Continue walking along the track until you reach a stile on the left, where the way ahead is barred by a fence.

3 Cross the stile and continue on the coast path along the tops of high cliffs, with spectacular views. The path eventually makes a steep descent behind the bay of Traeth y Rhedyn. At the bottom of the steep, narrow valley at the far end of the bay, the path divides.

4 Fork left. Cross a footbridge over a small waterfall and climb a flight of wooden steps on the far bank. At the top, turn right on a grassy path beside a fence. Continue along a deep wooded cleft, cut by the stream, to a stile near the head of the valley. Cross the stile and turn left to follow the edge of a field to another stile, leading onto a track. Turn right and follow the track through the farmyard at Granant-isaf, where it merges into the surfaced driveway to the house. Continue along the drive to emerge onto a minor road.

5 Turn left on the road, which bends sharp right to reveal a chequerboard of small fields rising to hills rolling away as far as the eye can see. Further on, the Teifi estuary comes into view, in a fold in the landscape. Beyond the small Victorian chapel at Cippyn, the lane sweeps ever more steeply down the side of a valley, with woodland below on the right and rough gorse-and-bracken-clad fields above. Continue down the hill to reach the side of the dune-backed estuary and the car park.

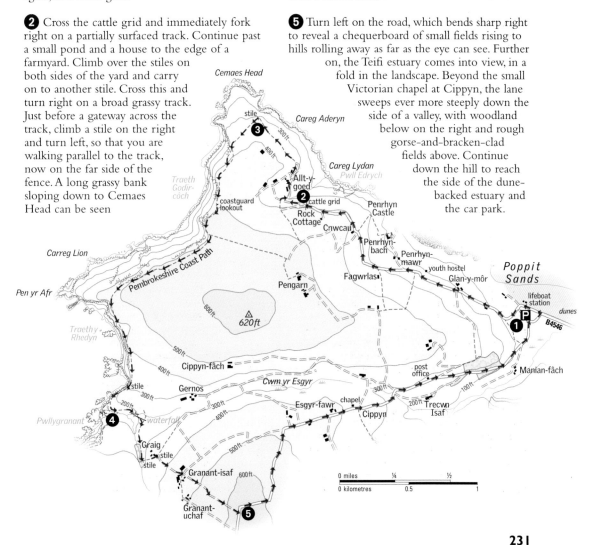

NORTH & MID WALES

There's a lifetime of upland walking in this magnificent region, including the Brecon Beacons and the hills of mid Wales. Monuments and curiosities pepper the trails, but never detract from the sublime beauty of nature.

1 Penderyn

From a path behind the cascading curtain of the Sgwd yr Eira waterfall to panoramic views from the summit of Moel Penderyn.

LENGTH 6½ miles (4 hrs)

PARKING Roadside in Penderyn

CONDITIONS Boggy and slippery in areas; wear good walking shoes

REFRESHMENTS Pub in Penderyn

1 Facing the road junction, take the track waymarked to the Sgwd yr Eira waterfall. After about 300m, go through a small kissing gate, next to a larger gate, then continue across open countryside with fine views of the Brecon Beacons to the right.

2 At a meeting of paths, fork right, following the signs 'Advisable path to waterfall'. In wet conditions, this stretch will be very muddy. Take care on the approach to the waterfall; a sign warns that the rocks around the gorge are dangerous. By the waterfall, follow the well-used path to a signpost at a fork in the path.

3 Continue straight ahead to the waterfall, following the stepped path that descends very steeply and is sometimes slippery. A public footpath runs along a recess behind the curtain of the fall; a 19th-century engraving shows a shepherd driving his sheep this way. Weak shale between two layers of resistant sandstone has been eroded by water to create this passage. Take extreme care on the wet rocks. From the falls, retrace your steps to the signpost and turn right, following the signs to Pontneddfechan and Craig y Ddinas – Dinas Rock. From this path, there are good views of the heavily wooded gorge of the river. Follow it through the forest to a T-junction in a clearing.

4 Ignore a turning to the left and continue on the path ahead, which almost immediately bends to the right. Continue for about ½ mile through a conifer and hardwood plantation, until it emerges into an area of bracken. The wooded river gorge appears below to the southwest. The path descends gently through a sparse, broadleaved wood to more open countryside, which is dotted with rocky outcrops.

5 At a signpost to the Gunpowder Works, turn right on a narrow, stepped path leading to the river. Cross the footbridge and turn left onto a track, passing to the left of the old gunpowder factory, established in 1857 by the Vale of Neath Powder Company. Gunpowder was produced here until 1931 and stored here until 1940. Follow the track through the wooded gorge, with the river on the left.

6 At a fork in the track just beyond a house, bear left. Where this track joins a lane at a T-junction, turn left along the lane and cross the stone bridge over the river. Turn immediately left on the other side of the bridge, then follow the signpost indicating Rhaeadr Waterfall, with the cliff face at Craig y Ddinas on the right.

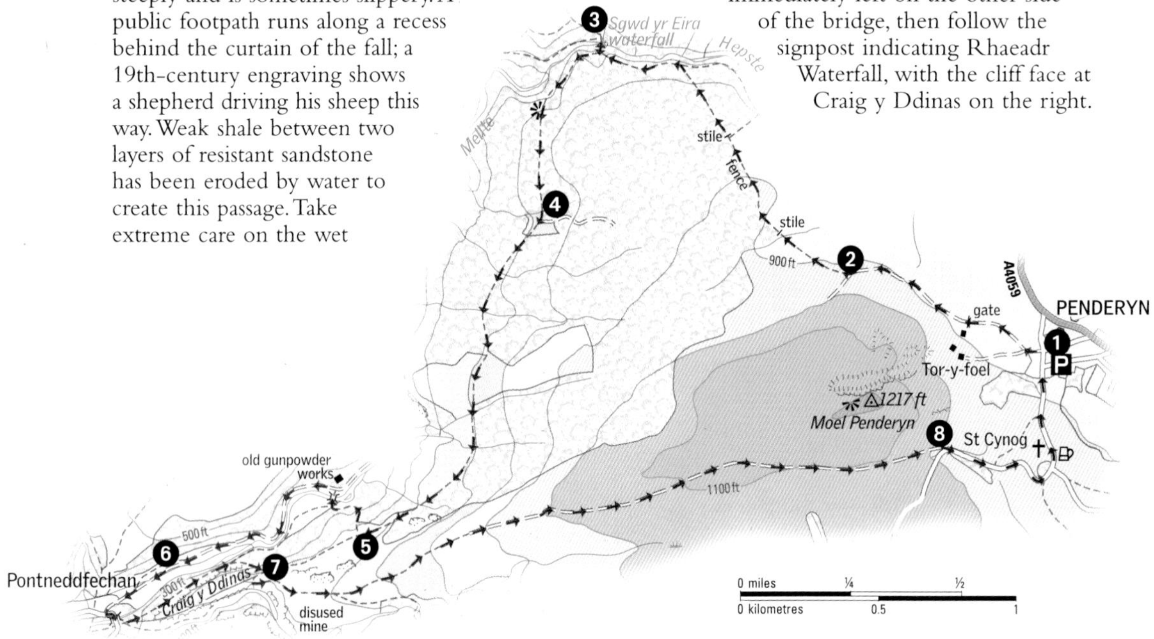

3 Sgwd yr Eira waterfall
Mellte
Hepste
stile
fence
stile
900 ft
4
2
gate
PENDERYN
A4059
1 P
Tor-y-foel
1217 ft
Moel Penderyn
8 St Cynog
1100 ft
old gunpowder works
5
500 ft
6
7
Pontneddfechan
Craig y Ddinas
disused mine

0 miles   ¼   ½
0 kilometres   0.5   1

SGWD YR EIRA WATERFALL

7 At the next junction, which is about 100m farther on, continue ahead to climb up a steep rocky path that soon levels out and passes through open hillside. The ruins of a disused mine can be seen to the right of this path.

At a signpost, keep straight ahead towards Penderyn, ignoring a path that goes off to the right. Continue climbing uphill as the path becomes a track that heads up towards the summit of Moel Penderyn. Panoramic views of the surrounding countryside soon begin to open up, with the Brecon Beacons becoming visible in the distance to the left. Stay on the path as it leads on past the summit, continuing towards Penderyn.

8 Where the path reaches a T-junction with a lane, turn left along the lane and continue on past the Church of St Cynog and its graveyard and the Tafarn Llew Goch pub. The lane drops steeply down into the village and leads back to the start of the walk.

wales

233

NORTH & MID WALES

2 Mynydd Illtud Common

Past wetland nature reserves in the Brecon Beacons to the summit of Twyn y Gaer and remains of an Iron Age hillfort.

LENGTH 6 miles (3 hours)

PARKING Brecon Beacons Mountain Centre, off A470 at Libanus

CONDITIONS Grassy common land, muddy in wet weather

REFRESHMENTS Tearoom in visitor centre

1 Leave the car park through the gate beside the cattle grid and turn left at the road past the visitor centre. The centre provides information about the Brecon Beacons National Park.

2 Go straight across a T-junction, then join a track along the left edge of the common. The Brecon Beacons rise to the left, and the upland mass in the distance ahead is Craig Cerrig-gleisiad a Fan Frynach, a National Nature Reserve. When the enclosed farmland in view to the right comes to an end, continue ahead past a gate in the fence on the left for about 250m.

3 Turn right opposite a stile in the fence – signposted to Pont Llech in the opposite direction – onto an indistinct grassy track that bends right then left in the distance. Keep to the widest and best-defined track. The boggy area marked by small trees on the right is the wetland nature reserve of Traeth Mawr. The sheep and ponies on the common belong to local farmers, who have commoners' rights to graze their animals here. Near to the road ahead, a pool harbours damselflies and dragonflies.

4 At the road turn right along a track parallel to the road. At the next road junction turn right.

DETOUR *Continue across a cattle grid then go through a gate on the right to the site of St Illtyd's Church, demolished in 1995 because of lack of maintenance funds. The enclosure is believed to be a pre-Christian site, possibly dating from the Bronze Age.*

5 Just before the cattle grid, turn left on a path. Cross the road and take the path ahead, with a fence on the left. Cross a farm track. By the road to the right is a Bronze Age standing stone that aligns with the site of St Illtyd's Church and with a standing stone on the west of the common. Continue ahead along the fence.

6 Where the fence bends in an arc to the left, leave it and follow the track ahead, rejoining the fence at the other side of the arc. Continue along the fence until reaching a road to the left.

7 Leave the fence and cross the road, then walk up to the summit of Twyn y Gaer. Around the triangulation pillar are traces of an Iron Age hillfort. Views extend to the Sugar Loaf in the southeast, and to Black Mountain, the major summit in the west of the National Park (not to be confused with the Black Mountains to the east).

8 Turn sharp right and take the broad grassy path back to the road. Turn left on the road, then turn right at the next road junction. Turn left on either of two tracks following a fence, and continue ahead for 1 mile to return to the car park.

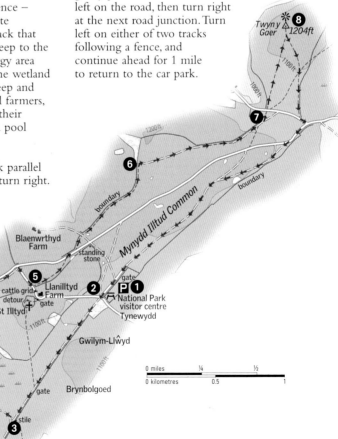

3 Skirrid Fawr

Up through woodland to an isolated hill overlooking breezy Welsh moors to the English border.

LENGTH 3½ miles (2 hours)

PARKING Layby on left of B4521, 1½ miles east of junction with A465 by Abergavenny

CONDITIONS One steep climb and a rocky path; very muddy in places after rain

REFRESHMENTS None on walk

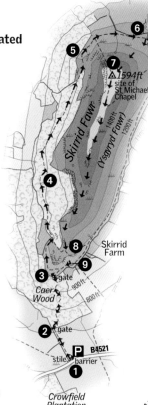

1 Leave the layby at its barrier end and follow the broad track as it bends right, avoiding the stile ahead. The track leads up to Caer Wood.

2 Go through a gate into the wood, entering the Skirrid Estate (NT). Among the many birds that may be spotted are chiffchaffs, blue tits, coal tits, long-tailed tits, blackcaps and buzzards. At the first fork keep right and follow Beacons Way waymarkers to the top of the wood, ignoring any other paths and tracks that cross the way.

3 Go through a gate and immediately turn left, following a drystone wall for about ¼ mile. Continue along the thinly wooded slopes of 486m (1,596ft) high Skirrid Fawr, or Ysgyryd Fawr in Welsh. This, and the 596m (1,955ft) high Sugar Loaf to the west, are outlying peaks of the Black Mountains.

4 As the wall eventually drops away, glorious views appear on the left of the Sugar Loaf, with its unmistakable pointed summit, and the Black Mountains beyond.

The undulating path becomes rocky and uneven as it continues below the steep slopes of the Skirrid mountain on the right.

5 Continue through a rocky cleft – the result of a glacial landslip that gives the mountain its remarkable profile, and gave rise to various superstitions. Legend tells that it is the heel mark of Jack o'Kent, a wizard who delighted in making a fool of the devil, who jumped off Sugar Loaf onto Skirrid. For many centuries people also believed that Skirrid was a holy mountain. Some thought its russet soil was so holy that no snail or worm could live in it, and

local farmers scattered its earth on their lands to ensure a good harvest. Beyond the valley are fine views to Titterstone Clee Hill in Shropshire, the Malvern Hills and Golden Valley in Herefordshire, and to Radnor Forest in Powys. The path bends right and is then joined by a fence on the left.

6 Just before the fence bends right uphill, and where there is a waymarker arrow on a small gate in the fence on the left, climb the slope on the right. A well-used path begins about a quarter of the way up Skirrid Fawr, making a short but steep climb to the triangulation pillar on the summit.

Two stones by the triangulation pillar are all that remains of a medieval pilgrimage chapel to St Michael. Drawn by such legends that Noah's Ark had once landed on the hill when the waters of the Flood receded, and that Skirrid was formed by an earthquake at the time of the Crucifixion, pilgrims climbed the mountain on St Michael's Eve to hold mass at the chapel. In 1680, at a time of Roman Catholic persecution, some 100 adherents are said to have clambered up the mountain to say mass.

7 From the triangulation pillar, continue straight on along the ridge, where views extend southwards across Gloucestershire and the Severn estuary, with Steep Holm island prominent in clear weather, to the Mendip Hills in Somerset.

8 At the far end of the ridge, descend into a cleft with hawthorn trees. Turn left on a steep downhill path.

9 At a junction in front of a fence and tumbledown wall, bear right. Some 100m farther on, turn left through a gate and descend through Caer Wood on the path taken early in the walk, then follow the track downhill back to the layby.

wales

NORTH & MID WALES

4 Llanthony

Past 12th-century abbey ruins deep in sheep country, then along the secluded, bracken-clad Vale of Ewyas.

LENGTH 5 miles (3 hours)

PARKING Car park by priory

CONDITIONS Some short, steep climbs; route partly obscured by bracken in summer

REFRESHMENTS Abbey Hotel in priory ruins

1 From the car park, follow the road to a T-junction. Cross the road to a track opposite and slightly to the left, and walk past a house with a postbox in its wall. Cross a footbridge and turn right through a small gate. After a second gate cross a stony track and go over a field, following a sign for Cwm bwchel. Cross a stile into woods.

2 Beyond the next footbridge, climb a stile, turn left over another stile and continue up the left edge of a field. Passing farm buildings on the left, climb to a waymarked stile ahead. Ignore a path to the right and continue straight on up beside a sunken path.

3 Climb a stile and turn right at a signpost to follow the path through bracken, with good views of the Vale of Ewyas. Follow the fence on the right, until the path crosses a small wooded ravine with two streams.

4 Climb a stile at a gate and follow a line of trees ahead. Continue past Nant-y-carnau, a typical Welsh longhouse.

5 Just beyond the longhouse, turn right on a track that descends to a road. Turn left on the road, and just past a stone farmhouse go through a gate on the right and follow the right edge of a field. Cross a stream by a footbridge and turn right through a gate. After 100m, the path rises up a bank, leaving the stream below. At a fence bear left to cross it at a waymarked stile. Go along the top edge of the field and cross the next stile on the left.

6 Cross a track and stile at a road junction and walk up the steep right side of a field to climb another stile. Turn right and walk along the left side of a fence.

After the next stile, the path leads through sparse woodland past stone ruins. Follow the line of trees and then, without descending, continue ahead across a pasture hillside.

7 Cross a stile in the fence on the left at the far end of the pasture, before a house. Turn right along the fence. After 200m go through a gate. Descend to a waymarker post, turn left past conifer plantation on the left, then cross a field to ruins of a stable block in trees ahead.

8 The ruins are all that remains of Siarpal, or the Sharples, a grand mansion that poet Walter Savage Landor began in the early 19th century.

At a meeting of tracks go straight on, avoiding the steep path to the left. Pass to the left of Wiral Farm, go through a gate and continue to a signpost by a stone wall.

9 Turn right, signposted to Llanthony, go through a gate and follow a fence on the left to a gate into Wiral Wood, a haunt of redstarts, goldcrests, nuthatches, wood warblers, and green and great spotted woodpeckers.

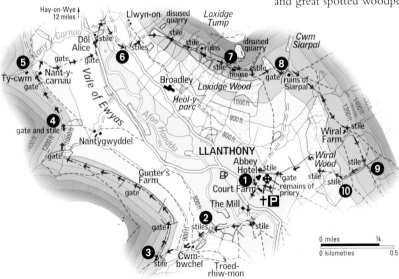

ANCIENT ABBEY RUINS
LLANTHONY PRIORY

10 Turn right on the track through the wood, then head across a field to the ruins of Llanthony Priory (Cadw), founded by Augustinian monks in 1108. The priory church is 61m (200ft) long and the square tower in the centre was originally 30m (100ft) tall. By the priory is a small church dedicated to St David, built on the site where the saint is said to have lived as a hermit. After the Dissolution of the Monasteries in 1536 the priory was left to decay until bought by Walter Savage Landor in 1807. Landor set about improving the estate by planting specimen trees and a beech avenue, improving roads and importing sheep. But after becoming bankrupt he was forced to sell the estate in 1814, leaving his great plans unfinished. Turn right along the priory boundary wall and continue round to a gate on the left that gives access to the grounds and car park.

wales

5 Glascwm

Along an old drovers' track up to a lonely pass and a trek across tranquil moorland bearing signs of ancient man.

LENGTH 4 miles (2 hours)

PARKING On verge by church

CONDITIONS Easy

REFRESHMENTS None on walk; pub at Hundred House on A481

1 With the church on your left, follow the road to where a side road joins from the left by a telephone box, opposite the former school and youth hostel.

Turn left on the side road. After about 50m, at the edge of the village, the road bears left. Do not follow it, but carry straight on on a lane ahead, immediately crossing a stream, then follow the lane uphill to a four-way junction.

Until the 19th century Glascwm was an important stop on a drovers' route, along which livestock was driven to fairs in Herefordshire.

DROVERS' TRACK BY GLASCWM

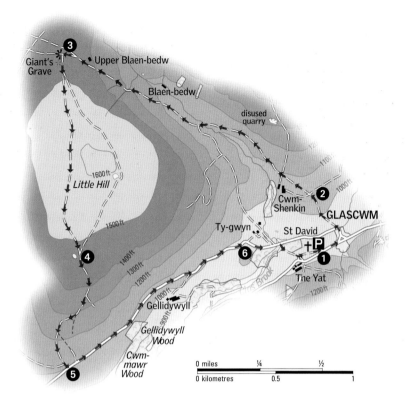

They came from the Wye valley, over Aberedw Hill, past a shoeing forge at Cregrina, through Glascwm and on to Colva and Newchurch. In its heyday Glascwm was busy enough to support four inns and a racecourse.

2 At the junction, go straight ahead along a level farm track, and continue, ignoring a path to a farm on the left. The track begins to rise steadily, eventually climbing to the shoulder of a hill to the left of a conifer plantation visible on the distant skyline. In some places along the track there are lines of stone slabs that in medieval times were often used as field boundaries in this part of mid Wales.

3 At the top of the climb, the view opens out ahead towards the sparsely populated uplands of the Eppynt and the Cambrian Mountains. In the foreground is the craggy hill known as Carneddau, which has evidence of Bronze Age settlers as well as an Iron Age hillfort.

Turn left, passing a track to a Bronze Age burial mound known as the Giant's Grave. Where the path divides after about 100m, fork right on a track over the open moor of Little Hill, a haunt of skylarks and grouse. Continue ahead, with impressive views on the right to the peaks of the Brecon Beacons National Park, to a dewpond.

4 Just beyond the pond the track begins to descend more steeply and Glascwm comes into view on the left. Follow the track as it bends right and then left to join a narrow unfenced road.

5 Turn left and continue for just over a mile, ignoring a sharp right turn to Gellidywyll, to where the road forks.

6 The left fork leads to a farm. Take the right fork across a confluence of streams. Just beyond the stream confluence, turn right up a track and follow it as it bends left to Glascwm's Church of St David. The church stands on a round mound – possibly a prehistoric barrow – flanked by yew trees, and owes its dedication to a visit by St David, the patron saint of Wales, in the 6th century. He left behind a handbell with supposedly magic powers, which has long since disappeared.

A later visitor was the Victorian vicar and diarist Francis Kilvert in 1871, who recorded in his diary that the church belfry doubled as the village school; it was 'fitted up with desks, forms and master's desk and fireplace'.

Walk through the circular churchyard – like many others in the area, it was deliberately designed without corners 'by which the devil may enter' – back to the parking place.

wales

NORTH & MID WALES

6 Vale of Rheidol

An energetic walk, mostly through woodland, to the idyllic River Rheidol and its fish ladder, built for salmon and trout.

LENGTH 4 miles (3½ hours)

PARKING At end of lane leading past Rheidol Power Station, off A44 east of Aberystwyth

CONDITIONS Fairly hard going in places, with some steep climbs

REFRESHMENTS None on walk; café at power station visitor centre

1 Walk back along the lane, passing a footpath on the left, and after a few metres turn right over a stile and follow the path up a steep hill. Turn left at a T-junction and continue uphill for ⅓ mile, passing an area of cleared forest, to a stone house.

2 Turn left through a waymarked gate into the yard and through a gate on the other side. Keeping close to the hedge on the right, walk down the field, from where there are views over the Rheidol. Go through a gate near the bottom of the hedge and follow the fenced track ahead. At a junction with a gravel track, turn right and walk uphill to a gap in the fence on left.

3 Turn left through the gap and follow the rough track downhill, then turn right through a kissing gate and cross a stream. At a junction of paths, turn sharp right to climb steeply through oak forest, with the stream below to the right. Go through a kissing gate, entering Coed Simdde-lwyd nature reserve – 34ha (85 acres) of oak, beech and elm woodlands.

4 Turn left. With the fence on the left, follow the path along the hillside for about ½ mile to a crossing of forest paths. Turn right, uphill, on a waymarked path, and continue climbing for ¼ mile, ignoring easier paths to the left, to reach a stile at the top of the wood.

5 Cross the stile into a field, from where there are superb views across the Vale of Rheidol. Here a short detour up the fence line leads to a dramatic view of the Bwa-drain waterfall at the head of a steep-sided gully. Return to the stile.

Walk half right uphill from the stile, to a group of trees beside the remains of a building. Cross a stile and stream and continue up to the top of the field, then go through a gate to reach a minor road. Turn left to reach a gate into a farmyard.

6 Go through the gate and, still on the minor road, cross a small bridge over a stream. Turn left off the road, with the stream to the left. Ignore a footbridge on the left but look for a small footbridge to the right and in a few metres go through a field gate. Follow the hedge on the left, then turn right in front of the next gate to reach a ruined farmhouse. Continue ahead to pass through another gate. Turn right along the fence line to reach the ruins of Castell Bwa-drain, an Iron Age fort, from where there are panoramic views of the Vale of Rheidol. Return to the gate.

7 Follow the path, keeping ahead at the end of the fence, and soon descend towards woodland. Just below the left-hand corner of a field take a well-marked path entering woodland, descending steeply. Go through a kissing gate then, ignoring a second kissing gate just off the path on the left, continue through another kissing gate to a gate with a house just ahead. Continue along the drive and through a field gate to reach a minor road.

8 Turn right and after passing a house turn left on a footpath signposted 'Bysgod Fish Ladder'. Cross a footbridge past a waterfall and the fish ladder, built to help sea trout and salmon make their way upstream. Follow the river upstream with waterfalls on the left, then swing right up a field to reach ruined mine buildings.

9 Just beyond the old mine buildings, cross a stile into woodland and follow the path, passing old mine shafts on right. Continue on this path for just over 1 mile, with the Vale of Rheidol railway to right, ignoring a footpath on right.

10 At a junction of paths, take the centre path with a fence on the left, then bend left steeply downhill to reach a wider path. Cross a stile, continue across a footbridge and turn right at the lane to the parking place.

Map labels: Bwa-drain; gates; Castell Bwa-drain; gate; 6; 7; gate; 900 ft; waterfall; stile; gates; 800 ft; 600 ft; Vale; 5; stile; 8; gates; Rheidol Falls; 0 miles ¼; 0 kilometres 0.5; Glyn-Rheidol; 800 ft; Coed Simdde-lwyd; 2; stile; 500 ft; 400 ft; gate; 4; gate; 700 ft; 500 ft; 3; 1; P; disused mines; 9; stile; 300 ft; Rheidol; gate; Troedrhiwsebon; 200 ft; stile; Vale of Rheidol Railway; gate; 10

7 Ynyslas

Golden sands, an immense expanse of dunes, a nature reserve and extensive views across Borth bog and the Dyfi estuary.

LENGTH 4 miles (2 hours)

PARKING Beach car park by Ynyslas Nature Reserve visitor centre

CONDITIONS Easy walking, on the flat

REFRESHMENTS None on walk

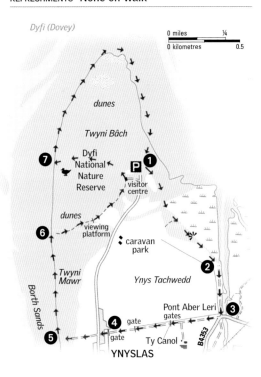

1 Facing Aberdyfi across the estuary, turn right out of the car park and head along the empty expanse of Ynyslas sands. The Welsh name means 'blue island', from a time when the sands were cut off at high tide. Continue walking along the obvious high-tide mark.

When the sands give way to estuary marsh, follow a sandy track, with low dunes on the right and marsh on the left, ignoring a path that joins from the right. There are views back across the estuary to Aberdyfi and the hills behind.

2 Continue along the sandy track between the edge of the lower dunes on the right and the marshland on the left, to a boulder-lined car park. Turn right on a stony track by the edge of a creek, which channels the River Leri into the Dyfi estuary. After a short distance pass a boatyard on the left.

3 Where the track meets a road, turn right and immediately right again, crossing a cattle grid, onto a tarmac track. The track leads towards the sea across the flats. Dotted with farmhouses perched on low rocky outcrops, the flats were drained for pasture. As the track sweeps left towards a farm, go straight ahead on a grassy path through a small gate into a field. Go straight ahead through more gates to reach houses and a track leading to the road.

4 Cross the road to a stony track opposite. Walk straight across the links and the shingle to Borth Sands. The long expanse of flat sands is inviting, but red flags and signs warn visitors against swimming on account of the treacherous currents at the mouth of the River Dyfi.

5 Turn right and walk for ½ mile along the beach, with the wide expanse of Cardigan Bay on the left and ranks of dunes, sprouting their uneven growth of coarse grass, to the right. This area is known as the Ynyslas Nature Reserve, part of the Dyfi National Nature Reserve.

6 Turn right by a 'Danger' notice, crossing pebbles, to follow a sandy path to a raised viewing platform. The fenced areas protect a number of ground-nesting birds, such as ringed plover, and also help the marram grass to become established.

The reserve provides habitats for a wide variety of plant and animal species. Between the dunes, damp hollows in the calcium-rich sand make an ideal environment for orchids. Rabbits attract predators, including polecats. Butterflies are common in summer, and dunlin, sanderling and oystercatcher can be seen on the beach, probing and sifting for tasty morsels.

From the viewing platform there are spectacular views across the dunes to Cors Fochno, or Borth bog, and the estuary. The mudflats are a haven for waders and wildfowl, such as cormorant, curlew and common sandpiper.

During spring and autumn migrations, the wader population increases dramatically; in winter the wildfowl population includes Greenland white-fronted geese and large numbers of wigeon. Continue ahead, first on a boardwalk, then on a marked path, to reach the visitor centre. Continue along a boardwalk then turn left onto a sandy path back to the sea shore.

7 Turn right at the beach and follow the shoreline for about ½ mile towards the mouth of the River Dyfi. There are fine views across the estuary to the line of pretty waterfront houses in Aberdyfi. Stay with the high-tide mark as it bends round to the right and eventually leads back to the car park.

wales

A world away

Ancient monasteries – once rich outposts of civilisation – reward the walker in Wales's remoter countryside and river valleys.

Remains of monasteries abound in rural Wales. The country as it was in the early Middle Ages – wild and remote – offered the safe refuge from the world, the flesh and the Devil that monks were seeking. The monks retained, however, their aesthetic sensitivities, and these are still very much in evidence in many of the monasteries' buildings. Their intricate stone carvings, sumptuous stained glass and decorative tilework often seem at odds with the austere rules of the religious orders that created them.

But walkers that pass such masterpieces of craftsmanship can only be thankful. A rambler journeying along the lengthy Cistercian Way, which weaves a 650-mile circular route through the heartlands of Wales, may take in no fewer than 17 monastic sites of considerable architectural worth and interest.

Those who break their journey at Strata Florida (Abbey of the Flowery Way), 15 miles southeast of Aberystwyth at the edge of the Cambrian Mountains, will be well rewarded, as

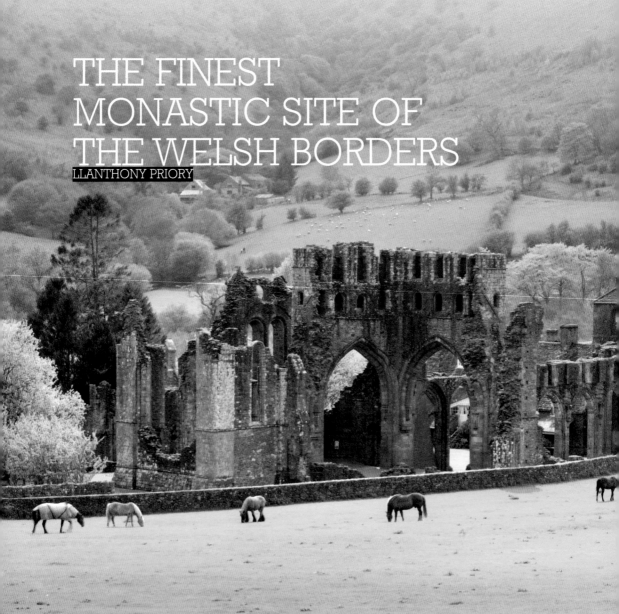

THE FINEST MONASTIC SITE OF THE WELSH BORDERS
LLANTHONY PRIORY

they feast their eyes on the beautifully figured medieval tiles. The abbey was founded in 1164 and was a pilgrimage site and rallying point for Welsh nationalists for centuries. Several Welsh princes lie buried here, as does the great 14th-century poet Dafydd ap Gwilym. Among the headstones in the modest burial plot is also one bearing the incised outline of a leg and the curious inscription: 'The left leg and thigh of Henry Hughes Cooper was cut off and interred here, June 18th 1756.'

The monks of the Cistercian Order, scouring the Welsh Borders early in the 12th century for sites on which to build their establishments, were especially keen on remote, unspoilt landscapes.

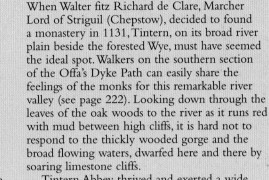

When Walter fitz Richard de Clare, Marcher Lord of Striguil (Chepstow), decided to found a monastery in 1131, Tintern, on its broad river plain beside the forested Wye, must have seemed the ideal spot. Walkers on the southern section of the Offa's Dyke Path can easily share the feelings of the monks for this remarkable river valley (see page 222). Looking down through the leaves of the oak woods to the river as it runs red with mud between high cliffs, it is hard not to respond to the thickly wooded gorge and the broad flowing waters, dwarfed here and there by soaring limestone cliffs.

Tintern Abbey thrived and exerted a wide influence for nearly four centuries, then – like so many similar establishments – it declined and decayed, until the Dissolution of the Monasteries finally swept it away in 1536. The monks and so many of their treasures all disappeared, but the abbey's Gothic church, light and exquisite, still stands. An empty stone shell on the riverside, it sits in what many consider the most perfect monastic setting in Britain. Tintern's atmospheric ruins and romantic setting have inspired many artists, including J.M.W. Turner.

Austere lives

The Black Mountains of the Welsh Borders hold several monastic sites in their steep, winding valleys, too. The finest is undoubtedly Llanthony Priory, deep in the Vale of Ewyas, directly below Hatterall Ridge and the Offa's Dyke Path (see page 236 for the walk starting at Llanthony). Legend claims that the patron saint of Wales, St David himself, build a chapel here in the 6th century, where he lived a life of prayer, existing on a diet of wild leeks. Other stories say that a Norman knight, William de Lacey, stumbled on the ruins while out hunting and vowed to spend the remainder of his days here as a hermit. But it was Augustinian monks who built the site's beautiful priory church, of which the graceful arches still stand.

Three miles up the valley, the visionary Reverend Joseph Lyne – better known as Father Ignatius – tried to re-establish the monastic way of life in the 1870s at the site he named Llanthony Tertia. Unfortunately, his version of Benedictine rule proved too harsh and his monks not tough enough. The Llanthony Tertia community lasted a mere 30 years, although its tottering church ruins continue to cast their shadow over the hillside at Capel-y-ffin.

Most poignant of all the Black Mountains monastic ruins are those of Craswall Priory. Built by the monks of the severe Grandmont Order in 1225, it now lies, almost lost and forgotten, under grassy hummocks and yew trees in a side cleft of the Monnow Valley. These days, its rough walls, chapels and altar are visited mainly by sheep.

wales

NORTH & MID WALES

8 Penmaenpool

Woodland tracks to a mountain road used by goldminers, and braided tidal flats.

LENGTH **5 miles (3½ hours)**

PARKING **Car park by toll bridge**

CONDITIONS **Demanding, over a variety of terrain**

REFRESHMENTS **Hotel bar near car park**

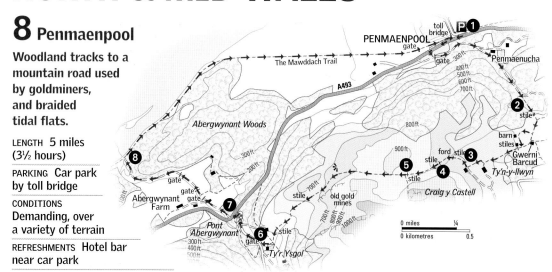

❶ From the car park turn right on the main road, then take the signposted footpath on the left, just behind the hotel. Follow the path to a small iron gate leading to a metalled drive. Turn left on drive and continue uphill.

Just before the gate to Penmaenucha house, fork right on a surfaced track and continue to a small reservoir. Turn right on a steep woodland path leading away from the reservoir to a ladder stile at the top of a wood.

❷ Cross the stile and walk ahead to a field track. Turn right on the track, which divides in front of Gwerni Barcud cottage. Take the right fork – a *tir cymen* (permissive path). The track winds past copses of small oaks, while looming ahead is Cadair Idris – the mountain chair of the giant Idris. Pass to the left of a stone barn and continue over two ladder stiles to the yard at Ty'n-y-llwyn.

❸ Turn right in the farmyard and go through a gate between a stone barn and a Dutch barn, into a field. Then turn left and follow the field boundary uphill to reach a track. Turn right. Follow the track over the brow of the slope to a ladder stile. Cross the stile and a small ford immediately beyond, then turn left through a gap in a field wall. Walk straight ahead to a ladder stile over the wall at the top of the field.

❹ Cross the ladder stile and continue ahead, skirting flat marshy pasture where springs seep through cotton grass and lady's smock to join a weed-filled channel.

Beyond, on the left, are the boulder-strewn slopes of Craig y Castell (Castle Rock), a haunt of cuckoos in spring and early summer. Cross another ladder stile at the top of the field to emerge onto an old mountain road – the highest point on the walk.

❺ Turn right, soon rounding the side of a slope for widening views down the Mawddach estuary to the sea. Continue past old gold mines, marked by tell-tale fans of spoil spilling from their entrances, towards the wooded Abergwynant valley. The steep slopes of Cadair Idris come into view on left, like a rampart across the head of the valley. Continue over two ladder stiles to a gate beside a towering lime tree, to meet a valley lane.

❻ Turn right on the lane and follow it downhill. Below you in the trees is the fast-flowing Afon Gwynant. As you wind down the lane, through the limes, sycamores, beeches, oaks and alder, you may see an old weir, complete with salmon steps. Walk down to the A493.

❼ Turn left and walk a few metres towards a stone bridge over the river, then turn right, onto the drive to Abergwynant Farm. Follow the driveway until just before it bends left over a bridge to reach the farm. Walk straight ahead through a gate, keeping the river on the left.

A short distance farther on, fork left through another metal gate and continue to a third gate on the edge of woodland – this one is distinguished by the remains of a carving of an owl on the right-hand gatepost. Follow the track to the shingly shore of the Mawddach estuary.

❽ Turn right on the surfaced Mawddach Trail. One long stretch lies along a low causeway, where cream-coloured bladder campion spills down the embankment in early summer. High ribbons of reed – home to buntings that can often be seen on the swaying stems – mark channels through the estuary flats.

Continue along the trail to a gate at the end of a cutting, then walk along a tidal channel in front of the hotel to return to the car park.

9 Llanystumdwy

To the sea and back, by the winding River Dwyfor, through the childhood village of David Lloyd George.

LENGTH	5½ miles (3 hours)
PARKING	Village car park near pub
CONDITIONS	Easy going on good paths
REFRESHMENTS	Café and pub in Llanystumdwy

1 Turn right on the main village street, passing Highgate cottage on right. This was the home of the British prime minister and statesman David Lloyd George until 1880, when he was 17, and also his uncle's shoemaking workshop. Also on right is the Lloyd George Museum.

Just before reaching the bridge over the River Dwyfor, turn right. At the end of a terrace of houses, turn left on a footpath. This runs past the grave of Lloyd George and down to the river.

2 Cross a footbridge, go through an iron gate and follow the path through woods beside the river, which leaps down a series of rapids. Cross a stone clapper bridge over a stream, beyond which the river dashes down a narrow rocky gully. Ignore a bridge over the river and keep to the same bank. The opposite bank now rises steeply to rock faces dripping with fern. Dippers and kingfishers may be spotted. Follow the path as it climbs briefly away from the river, then go through a gate and descend again to the water's edge. Approaching a farm (seen through the trees), turn right at a broken-down stone wall, through an archway, onto a stony path emerging onto a farm road.

3 Turn right on the farm road, and walk along the edge of woods to the right, with fields divided by drystone walls to the left.

4 At a farm entrance, go through the gate and turn left on a concrete road skirting barns. Go through two more gates and along a field edge with a wall to the right, then enter another field. At the end of a small wood beside a house, go through a small gate in the corner and walk between the cottages and down the drive.

5 Turn right on a minor road. After a house on the right, turn left on the driveway to Cae-llo-Brith. Go through a gateway by the farm and follow the track to a metal gate. Cross a field, with stone wall to the left, go through a gate and turn right on a broad track between stone walls. Beyond a patch of wood beside houses turn left to meet the A497.

6 Turn left on the pavement. Just beyond a line of fir trees on the opposite side of the road, turn right by a footpath sign. Continue straight on over a stone stile on a footpath that crosses the railway and heads down to the sea.

7 At the shore, turn right on a path above a sandy beach. To left is a distant headland crowned by Criccieth Castle. Follow the path close to the sea's edge, passing to the left of an area of reedy marsh. At the mouth of the River Dwyfor, turn inland along the riverbank, beside marshland.

8 Go through a kissing gate and cross to a stone wall at the edge of the marsh. Keep to the path beside the riverbank, through first one then a second kissing gate.

9 Turn right along the field edge. Follow the field edge to join a track and cross the railway. Follow the track, over stiles, to a farm, then follow a broad concrete road past the farmyard, with the wooded Dwyfor valley to the left, to reach the A497. Cross the road to a wooden gate opposite and take the path between houses to the bridge. Turn right to return to the car park.

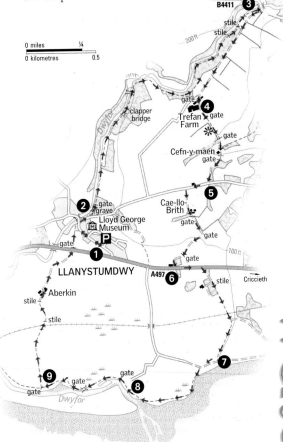

wales

245

NORTH & MID WALES

10 Llithfaen

Dramatic sea views over granite-quarried hillsides and a summit crowned by a remarkable hillfort.

LENGTH 5½ miles (4 hours)

PARKING In car park on left of road ½ mile north of Llithfaen

CONDITIONS Some strenuous rough mountain paths. In poor weather, summit may be covered in cloud, so check weather forecast

REFRESHMENTS None on walk

1 Turn right out of the car park onto the road. After 100m, turn sharp left on a broad track heading up the flank of the hill, towards a radio mast. The track rises steadily through heather moorland and rocky outcrops. Immediately below and to the left are the levels and inclines of old granite quarries, overlooking the village of Porth y Nant, built in 1863 for the quarry workers. The wider view ahead and behind looks up and down the length of the Lleyn Peninsula.

Where the broad track dips down, take a narrow level path on the right through heather. This eventually rejoins the broad track, which passes below the radio mast and rises. At the top of the rise, a view emerges of Trefor village, the bay beyond and the surrounding hills.

2 At a quarry gate, turn right on an indistinct path beside a fence and continue downhill past a waymark post. Where the fence turns sharply left, ignore a clear path heading straight ahead on a line above the top of the crags, and bear left downhill between the fence and a line of telegraph poles to meet a wall at an angle. Turn sharp right, following the waymark and keeping a wall to the left. Where the wall begins to swing away to the left, carry on downhill to the bottom of the field. Go through a fallen wall, then past a ruined building on the left to a small gate in another wall beneath the crags. Beyond the gate, the path becomes a more obvious green track, beneath the dramatic, rocky hillside. Follow the track, with a short, sharp climb, to a kissing gate.

3 Go through the gate and follow the level path towards the left edge of a patch of conifers. Going through a series of gates, continue along an avenue of trees beside a wall, and emerge on a road. Turn right.

4 Beyond farm buildings on the left, where the road begins to bend left, go through a kissing gate on the right, following an arrow, to head slightly uphill to the top of a rise. The path is indistinct here, but continue straight on to a derelict ladder stile in the fence ahead. Cross the stile and carry straight on, passing a farm on the left. Cross a second derelict stile, walk across the field and go through a gate to reach the B4417.

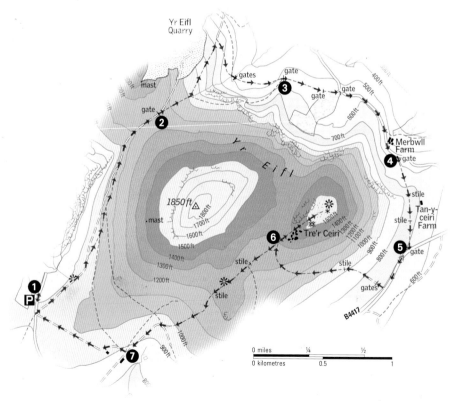

5 Turn right on the road. After 300m, turn right by a footpath sign and take the steps to a kissing gate. Go through the gate and follow the path beside a wall leading steeply uphill. Go through another gate into an area of sheep pens. The path swings left below the crags to a ladder stile. Cross the stile and follow the path, which becomes a narrow, stony track through heather.

6 Where the path divides at the top of the ridge, turn right towards the rocky summit of one of three peaks, known as Yr Eifl (the Rivals). A path leads up beside a jumble of rocks to the entrance to Tre'r Ceiri – Town of the Giants – the Iron Age fort that tops the hill. It is hugely impressive, with a high defensive wall, and a walkway beneath the parapet. The views from the summit are superb, right down towards the peninsula tip, with the sea in view on either side, and inland to Snowdonia.

Return to the path junction and carry straight on along a narrow path through heather to a stile near a gate in the wall opposite. Take the clear path ahead to climb over a ridge, where another fine view of the coast opens up. Follow the path down, over a stile and past a waymark post, and head towards Llithfaen.

7 Where the track divides just before houses, turn right towards the right-hand end of a line of conifers. At a house, turn right on a path beside a wall. Continue uphill on a broad green track, which tops the rise, then head downhill back to the car park.

TRE'R CEIRI, THE 'TOWN OF THE GIANTS'

NORTH & MID WALES

11 Newborough Forest

Sand dunes on Anglesey's southwest coast, and avenues of pines that lead to the holy island of the 'St Valentine' of Wales.

LENGTH 4 miles (2½ hours)

PARKING In Newborough Forest, at beach southwest of Newborough

CONDITIONS Easy

REFRESHMENTS None on walk; café and pubs in Newborough

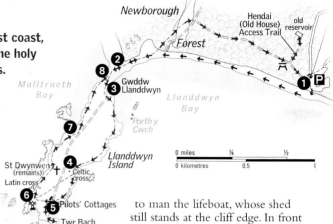

1 From the seaward end of the car park, go through the gap in the dunes and turn right along the sandy beach towards the long, low hump of Llanddwyn Island. On the right are high dunes and behind them the Corsican pines of Newborough Forest, created in the 1950s on 700 acres of the dunes. The 'New Borough' of the Middle Ages comprised the homes and farms of villagers moved by Edward I from the neighbourhood of his castle at Beaumaris, but the clearance of the scrub for farming exposed the land to the westerly winds, and storms in 1331 buried homes and farmland in sand. The beach gets more shingly towards Llanddwyn, with a variety of sea shells.

2 At the end of the beach, go through a natural gateway formed by enormous, pillow-shaped mounds of lava rock forced up from undersea volcanoes, and head for an information board. At exceptionally high tides you may have to wait a short while for the tide to recede before attempting to reach the 'island'. The board tells the legend of Dwynwen, Wales's patron saint of lovers, who lived as a hermit on this island after falling in love with Prince Maelon but then had to repel his advances when he tried to seduce her.

3 Behind the information board, follow yellow arrows up steps to the left. The path runs above the shore, passing secluded bays where tufts of thrift spring from the lichen-covered rocks. (Some bays are closed to the public during the bird-nesting season.) The grassy banks on the right are bright with herb-robert, bird's-foot trefoil and speedwell in season. The sandy path emerges over a brow to reveal the lighthouses, crosses and tumbled buildings that dot the tip of the island.

4 At the Celtic cross, turn left towards a neat, whitewashed terrace of pilots' cottages. Two cottages have been restored to appear as they were around 1900, when pilots based here guided ships into the Menai Strait and helped

to man the lifeboat, whose shed still stands at the cliff edge. In front of the cottages is the cannon that once summoned extra lifeboatmen from Newborough.

5 Beyond the cottages, yellow markers guide you up a path surfaced with compacted sea shells, then across a wall at the head of a sandy bay to Twr Bach, an old beacon tower topped by a modern flashing light, on a pretty headland dotted with sea campion and thrift. Return across the headland towards the disused lighthouse, built in 1845 to replace the beacon. The cliffs and offshore rocks are the nesting places of the countless seabirds that wheel around Llandwyn, including cormorants, shags, and the red-billed oystercatcher.

6 From the lighthouse, climb the shell path up to the Latin cross on its outcrop. This cross commemorates the death of St Dwynwen in AD 465. On the right are the ruins of a 16th-century church, built on the site of Dwynwen's own chapel, and an enclosure grazed by the unusual Soay sheep, with their curling horns.

7 Where the grassy path reaches the main track, fork left up steps for a last switchback course along the western side of the island. A sandy cove at the foot of the cliffs is reached where the coast path drops to a little valley, with a view across Malltraeth Bay and its long sandy shore.

8 Return along the Llanddwyn Bay beach; at a break in the dunes, turn left into the forest and bear right along a broad track through pines. At a picnic site 50m before the metalled road begins, turn left at a red marker post to a clearing. Ahead, outlined in the sand, are the remains of one of the buildings of the sand-drowned Newborough village, and beside it the rectangular basin of an old reservoir. Retrace your steps to the main track, and turn left to the car park.

12 Conwy Mountain

To a summit hillfort with spectacular views over Conwy's estuary and sandy beaches, a 13th-century castle and town walls.

LENGTH 6½ miles (4 hours)

PARKING Long-stay car park by Bodlondeb council offices, Conwy

CONDITIONS Some strenuous hill-walking

REFRESHMENTS Full range in Conwy

1 Walk to the right of the council offices and join a metalled path leading downhill. Fork left, and just beyond Butterfly Jungle on the left, fork right through woodland. As you continue, grand views open up on the right over Conwy estuary and the castle. The path soon bends left and climbs steeply to meet another path. Turn right. Continue ahead close to the edge of the wood. On leaving the wood, turn left on a lane and walk to a T-junction with a residential road.

Turn left past a school. Cross the A547, then go over a footbridge over the railway. Turn left on a lane and continue past the gates of Beechwood Court, where the lane becomes metalled.

2 At a junction, turn right on a lane uphill, gradually rising above Conwy. Shortly after going through a gate alongside a fence, Conwy Mountain comes into view. Fork right up the hill, gaining more fine views of Conwy Castle and the estuary. As the path levels out, ignore all paths up Conwy Mountain on the right and keep straight on towards Allt Wen hill ahead. Pass a small pool on the left and join a track coming in from the right. Continue to a farm track.

3 Turn left and follow the track, winding downhill. About 50m before joining a road, turn right down a grassy path that heads steeply down

Sychnant Pass, with Allt Wen on the right. On joining a metalled lane at a hairpin bend, turn right downhill to the small village of Dwygyfylchi. About 100m after entering the village, turn right over a footbridge crossing a small stream and turn immediately right.

4 The path leads round houses and up the hill. Continue on up concrete steps and into a small patch of pine forest. At a cluster of beech trees before a fence, fork right on a waymarked path uphill. As the path levels off at the edge of trees, there is a wide view of Anglesey and the rough scree slopes of Penmaen-bach. Leave the woods over a stile beside a gate and bear right.

5 Where the path divides by a sycamore tree, fork right up a very steep, grassy incline. At a crossways, ignore a path on the right leading to the top of Allt Wen and go straight on over the saddle between two small hills. Soon after passing a pool on the right, turn right on a farm track.

6 Turn left at the footpath sign met at **3**. At the small pool fork right, then turn left up a path towards the summit of Conwy Mountain. Stay on the path to the top of the hill, ignoring all paths that cross. At the top, once the site of an Iron Age hillfort, there are remains of several circular stone huts and panoramic views of Anglesey, Great Orme, Little Orme and Conwy Bay.

Follow the most worn path along the ridge towards Conwy. Nearing the town, the path drops down to a stile near some cottages.

7 Cross the stile, then turn left at a T-junction on a lane. Continue past a turning on the left and follow the lane to a T-junction. Turn left and follow the road over a railway bridge to a junction with the A547. Turn left, and after 80m turn right into the car park.

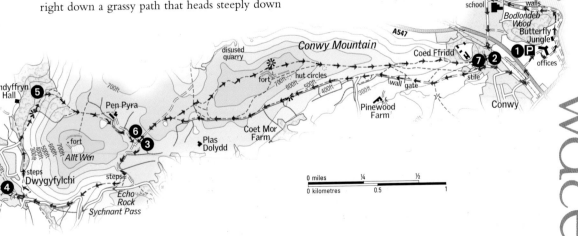

NORTH & MID WALES

13 Llanberis

Through woods on a mountainside, once busy with men quarrying for 'grey gold', and a climb to a medieval hilltop castle.

LENGTH 4 miles (2½ hours)

PARKING Off A4086 next to 'Electric Mountain' centre

CONDITIONS Mostly easy, but some rocky ascents; boots or stout shoes needed

REFRESHMENTS Cafés and pubs in Llanberis; cafés at Slate Museum and Quarry Hospital

❶ From the far end of the car park, walk to the lakeside and turn right over the footbridge, then beyond the swing gate bear left alongside the lake to the grey gash of the slate quarries cut into the hillside. Soon the whistle can be heard of one of Llanberis's two steam railways. Cross a footbridge and soon turn left into the Welsh Slate Museum, where old workshops tell the story of the Dinorwig Quarries, which once employed 3,000 men but closed in 1964. Close by at Gilfach Ddu station is a memorial to Thomas Jefferson, the US President whose ancestors came from this area.

❷ To the right of a waymark sign and a diving school go through a short tunnel for a dramatic view of the steep face of Vivian Quarry, reflected in a still pool at its base. Return through the tunnel and turn left up steps beside a steep incline, left at the waymark post and left again at a footprint marker.

❸ Ignore waymarked steps on the right and go past banks of slate softened by the hazel, birch, oak and sycamore that are colonising the slopes. The path rises to the Quarry Hospital, restored to appear as it was in 1876. The hospital was well equipped and staffed for its time, and even had hot and cold running water. From the terrace in front of the hospital there is a view of Llyn Padarn and, behind it, the soaring backdrop of the Snowdon massif.

❹ Leaving the hospital, turn right past the mortuary and follow the yellow waymark between the slate gateposts. The path winds through oak woods, the lake glimmering beyond the trees. At a seat and viewpoint, ignore a green marker to the right and continue ahead. The path soon drops steeply, then swings to the right; ignore steps that lead down to a mill on the left.

DOLBADARN CASTLE

5 At the stream, pass through a swing gate and cross a slab footbridge. After 25m turn right through a swing gate, following yellow waymarks. The rocky path climbs through a gorse-clad clearing, but soon re-enters woodland and recrosses the stream amid a series of waterfalls. Bear left to the top of the hill, reaching a fence made of upright slabs of slate.

6 Ignore a stile on the left, but continue ahead up a clear stony track between lichen-covered oaks and birches, where bluebells carpet the glades in spring. Ignoring a yellow waymark heading right, continue to the top of the hill where a stile leads onto a bracken-covered hillside. Follow the grassy path and go over another stile. Continue uphill, with a fence on the right then a slate wall on the left, and join a track to a gate, where the path descends sharply to the right. Cross a stile and continue ahead, ignoring a blue waymark for the Vivian Trail to the right. From here, the view

opens out onto Vivian Quarry below, where climbers challenge the cliffs over which quarrymen once dangled on ropes for their livelihood.

7 Follow the path round the top of the quarry and continue steeply downhill, following yellow and blue waymarks. At the foot of some steps, turn left through a cutting in the rock into tiny Anglesey Barracks. The two tiny rooms of each of these houses were, until 1939, the weekday homes of up to four quarrymen who came from Anglesey by boat and train.

8 Return through the cutting and continue downhill. Fork right over a footbridge, past the winding machinery of the old tramway. The path zigzags downhill between high slate walls.

Just before a broad seat set into the wall on the right, turn left through a break in the wall. Do not continue past this seat; the walled path is permanently blocked lower down. Follow the rocky path downhill to a road and turn right towards the Welsh Slate Museum entrance.

9 Just before the museum buildings, turn left across the footbridge crossed early in the walk, then turn left to pass under the Llanberis Lake Railway. Follow the path through a car park and across the road to 13th-century Dolbadarn Castle. Its position on a rocky outcrop gives the single round tower a commanding presence out of proportion to its size. Stairs spiral up within the thick walls, with openings looking across Llyn Peris and Llyn Padarn.

Retrace your steps to the footbridge. Follow waymarks left towards the shore of the lake to return to the car park at the start of the walk.

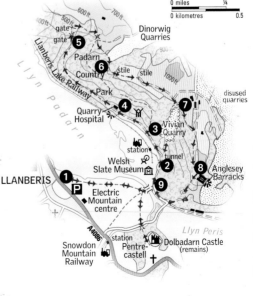

wales

NORTH & MID WALES

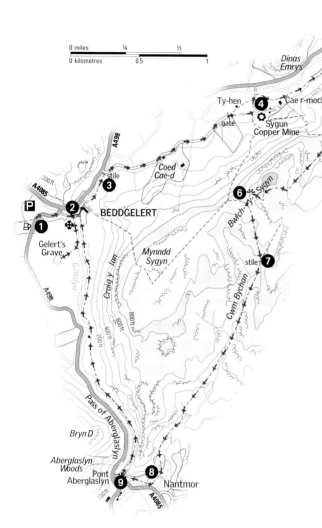

the grave commemorates the hound that is said to have saved the life of 13th-century Prince Llywelyn's infant son, only to be slain by the prince, who wrongly thought it had killed his heir.

2 Retrace your steps and cross the footbridge over the Glaslyn – here a gentle stream, but met in more turbulent mood later in the walk. Pass to the left of colour-washed cottages and follow the river, crossing a lane. The path soon descends through tall rhododendron bushes.

3 Cross a ladder stile and turn right on a lane. Where the lane ends, go through a gate and bear right towards a water wheel at the entrance to Sygun Copper Mine, where underground tours of the former workings give a vivid picture of the way copper was wrested from the rocks just over a century ago.

4 From the mine, follow footpath arrows above the river, through gates and alongside a drystone wall backed by rowan trees. The tree-covered rock outcrop across the river is Dinas Emrys – linked in legend with Merlin, King Arthur's

14 Beddgelert

A Snowdonia 'classic', to the heights above a hill-girt lake and down to the Glaslyn's tumbling cataracts.

LENGTH 6½ miles (4 hours)

PARKING Near Royal Goat Hotel

CONDITIONS One 244m (800ft) ascent, many rocky paths; boots or stout shoes needed

REFRESHMENTS Cafés and pubs in Beddgelert

1 Walk along the A498 to the road bridge. Just before the bridge, turn right down a lane by the river towards Gelert's Grave – Beddgelert in Welsh. Do not cross the footbridge over the Glaslyn, but instead continue along the river. Soon a path on the right leads to the 18th-century grave of a dog famed in Welsh legend;

magician, and the scene of titanic struggles between red and white dragons from which the Red Dragon emerged as the symbol of Wales.

5 Soon Llyn Dinas opens out beside the path. At the beginning of the lake, go through a kissing gate then bear right up a zigzag path. The steep ascent through heather and bracken is rewarded by views back across the lake in its attractive setting of wooded and bracken-covered slopes, with a drystone wall snaking up one crag like a miniature Hadrian's Wall. Continue along the slate-strewn track, marked with yellow arrows, rising gradually to Bwlch-y-Sygyn pass.

6 At a signpost at the head of the pass, among rocky outcrops, turn left to Aberglaslyn. (A shorter route back to Beddgelert continues straight ahead.) A brief clamber up through rocks and heather to the top of the mound on the right gives a satisfying view of the path you have just walked.

7 At a wire fence, turn right over a ladder stile, down Cwm Bychan, with a view to the sea. As the valley broadens, the stilt-like supports of an old miners' cableway are seen ahead. Sheep find precarious footholds on the flanking boulders, and suck at lichen on the rocks.

A cavern marks the entry to old mine workings, and there are tumbled remains of old buildings. The path crosses a stream, and beyond a gate there is a small waterfall before the path descends by rocky steps through woods of oak, birch and chestnut.

8 Beyond the woods, in a clearing, follow a sign pointing left to Pont Aberglaslyn. The path crosses under the track of the Welsh Highland Railway. Follow a slate marker pointing uphill to Pont Aberglaslyn, passing behind the toilets in the car park at Aberglaslyn. Go through a swing gate and pass above an old cottage before descending through woods to the bridge.

9 Do not cross the bridge, but turn right to follow the Glaslyn upstream, as it bounds over a boulder-strewn bed, widening here and there into calm pools. The Fisherman's Path follows a terrace above the river, in places emerging dramatically onto the riverside boulders. There are chains and boardwalks attached to the rockface to help your advance through the pass. (After prolonged, heavy rain this path may be impassable. At such times it is necessary to return to the bridge, cross it and turn right along the A498 back to Beddgelert.)

As the pass widens, the path becomes more secure and crosses the relaid track of the Welsh Highland Railway. Continue ahead along the riverside path back to Beddgelert.

THE HILLSIDES BY CWM BYCHAN

NORTH & MID WALES

15 Llyn Geirionydd

Two mountain lakes set among dramatic hills, patched with conifer forests and deciduous woodland.

LENGTH 5½ miles (3½ hours)

PARKING Car park at south end of Llyn Geirionydd, off A5 west of Betws-y-Coed

CONDITIONS Some rocky paths; wear good walking shoes

REFRESHMENTS None on walk; pubs and cafés in Trefriw and Llanrwst

1 Walk back to the entrance of the car park, then turn right by a gate onto a waymarked gravel track, with a Forestry Commission sign. Cross the end of the lake and turn left on the other side. Follow the track for about ¼ mile as it rises steeply through woodland and round a sharp S-bend.

2 Turn right 30m after the S-bend on a broad stony track that climbs steeply for about 200m. Rejoin the gravel track uphill for about 50m, and when it bends right keep forward on the steep waymarked path ahead. Continue through mixed woodland and conifers. The path rises steeply for a short while and then enters much denser coniferous forest through a gap in a wall and levels out. Go through a gap in a fence and descend through woodland, crossing a stream. As you near the edge of the wood, views of the hills of Snowdonia open up.

3 At the edge of the wood turn left on a path, just before a stile. Glimpsing Llyn Crafnant Reservoir through the trees, follow the path over stepping stones across a small stream. Leave the woodland by a stile, turn left on the lane ahead and Llyn Crafnant Reservoir, surrounded by hills, comes fully into view. Follow the lane for ½ mile past Maes Mawr farm to a gate.

4 Go through the gate and turn right on a waymarked gravel track. Cross a bridge and go through a gate. Just before reaching a house, turn right over a footbridge and turn left. Go uphill and over another stile, then continue to a T-junction.

5 Turn right on a track and continue for about ¼ mile to reach the southern end of the reservoir. Walk along the shore and enter the edge of the forest, which soon gives way to open bracken-covered hills rising steeply on the left. This is an excellent spot for birdwatching. Continue to the end of the lake.

6 Go through a gate, cross a bridge over a stream and turn left at a T-junction onto a lane, leaving the lake and following a stream. Opposite a car park by a picnic spot, fork right up a steep gravel track. At a right hairpin bend, go straight on and climb a stile to a steep path, shortly passing the tunnel of an old slate mine. The path bends right and left past ruins of mine buildings.

7 Follow the obvious path, ignoring smaller side paths, and enjoy a fine view down the Crafnant Valley. The well-worn path descends through a gap in a wall, crosses a ladder stile and leads up to the top of a hill. Llyn Geirionydd comes into view. Walk towards it, passing a monument to the 6th-century Welsh poet Taliesin, who is believed to have been born near here. Beyond the monument head towards the lake.

8 Turn right at the lake's edge to go through a small gap in a wall, then over a stile on a path along the wooded edge of the lake. Climb a stile out of the woodland, then another to the gravel track at the end of the lake and turn left. At the metalled lane, turn left to return to the car park.

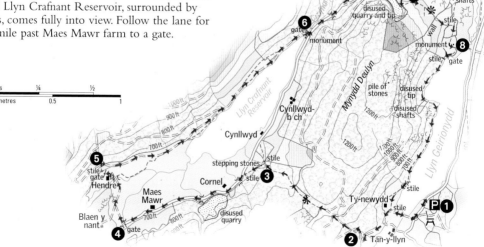

level clearing covered with heather and bilberry. Go straight across a broad gravel track beyond the clearing and walk downhill, across another junction, to a crossing track with red and blue waymark posts.

16 Loggerheads

Through forest and up heather slopes to a hilltop ruin, then beside a river at the foot of wooded bluffs.

LENGTH 6 miles (4 hours)

PARKING Loggerheads Country Park car park, off A494 north of Tafarn-y-Gelyn

CONDITIONS Demanding, hilly walk

REFRESHMENTS Café at car park

❶ Turn right on the minor road at the entrance to the car park and follow it uphill, with the top of Moel Famau, the highest hill in the Clwydian range, soon coming into view. At a T-junction turn right, then left onto a track signposted as a footpath. Continue beside a stream and through a gate, ignoring a stile on the left. Go through a second gate, immediately beyond which the track bends sharp left to a stile on the right, beside a signpost for Moel Famau. Cross the stile and walk across the corner of the field to reach a prominent stile on the edge of forestry.

❷ Cross the stile and turn right to arrive at a ladder stile. Climb this and after 20m cross another stile on the left, by a waymark signposted Coed Clwyd. Head uphill into the plantation and at the first waymark turn left and continue to a wide gravel track. Turn left and follow the track, past a turning on the left leading to a cottage, to the second of two tracks on the right. This leads straight ahead from a left-hand bend into forestry. Continue up a gentle slope into a fairly

❸ Turn right and follow the track uphill to a fork where the red and blue routes separate. Keep right, on the red-waymarked track, and continue uphill to emerge onto a steep slope leading to the ruined Jubilee Tower on the summit of Moel Famau. Built in 1810 to mark King George III's 50 years on the throne, the tower was badly damaged by a storm in 1862. Even so, its walls offer magnificent views.

❹ Continue in the same direction to meet a fence on the right bounding forestry. Continue downhill, ignoring a stile over the fence, to meet a crossing track at the corner of the plantation. Turn right and walk downhill, with forestry to the right and open hillside to the left, into rough, gorse-covered pasture. Keep a wall and fence to the right. Go through two gates to a fork in the track.

❺ Turn right and continue through two more gates before emerging on a minor road. Turn left downhill. At a T-junction take the path ahead to cross a footbridge over the River Alun. Go through a gap in the wall beyond, then turn right up a steep stony path. Soon the path meets the dry course of an old leat, or manmade water channel. Turn right to a minor road. Go through a gate on the far side of the road and continue past boarding kennels to a gate in a stone wall.

❻ Go through the gate and fork right on the winding path running parallel to the river, below increasingly higher limestone bluffs. Cross a two-arched stone bridge where the path emerges from the wood to return to the car park.

wales

NORTH & MID WALES

17 Horseshoe Falls

Past the ruins of a Cistercian abbey to the natural ramparts of a high escarpment and castle battlements.

LENGTH 6½ miles (4 hours)

PARKING Horseshoe Falls car park, off B5103 northwest of Llangollen

CONDITIONS Demanding, involving steep climb to castle ruins

REFRESHMENTS Full range in Llangollen

1 From the entrance to the car park turn right, then almost immediately take the footpath on the left, signposted to Valle Crucis Abbey. Continue up the steps leading into a birch wood and follow the path until you reach a stile.

2 Cross the stile onto a bracken-covered hillside studded with boulders. The path winds gently upwards above the Dee valley floor, and bends around the flank of a hill. After a short distance the dramatic craggy ruins of Castell Dinas Bran, on the far side of the valley, come into view. Follow the path beside a fence to a fork. Take the right-hand path, signposted to the abbey, and continue downhill over a stile to the A542.

3 Turn left on the road and after 100m turn right through a wooden gate, signposted to the abbey. Continue on a path across fields to 13th-century Valle Crucis Abbey, where the tracery of a rose window and an elaborately vaulted chapter house survive. Leave the abbey grounds by the main entrance, and fork right on a track through a caravan park. Where the track bends left, walk straight ahead on a waymarked path to a footbridge over the Eglwyseg river.

4 Cross the footbridge and climb a flight of wooden steps on the far bank to emerge on an open slope above the river's wooded margin. Turn left on a path, signposted to Tan-y-fron, and continue along the foot of the slope to a ladder stile by Abbey Cottage. Cross the stile and turn right on a track for a few yards before crossing a second ladder stile. Turn left on the far side of the stile and continue to a junction.

5 Turn sharp right, doubling back along a broad grassy track signposted to Bryn-hyfryd. Continue along a hillside covered with gorse and bracken, crossing a stile by a gate. Follow the path over a second stile by cottages, then fork right and follow the track downhill to reach a minor road. Turn left on the road and walk uphill to a farm driveway on the right leading to Dinbren Isaf.

6 Turn right and follow the drive to the farmyard, then into a field beyond. Keep left across the field to a stile and gate in the corner. Cross the stile and follow the path downhill, with a fence on the left, to a gate. Go through

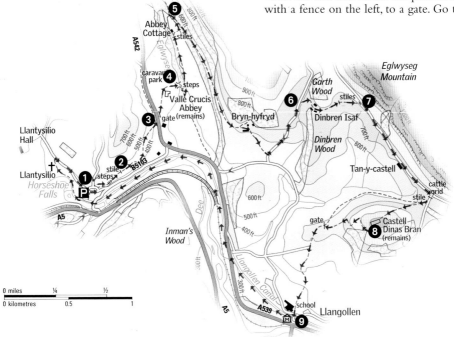

the gate and walk across the field, passing to the left of an old limekiln before reaching a stile beside a gate leading onto a minor road beyond.

7 Turn right on the road and continue in the shadow of the limestone scarp, passing a house on the right called Tan-y-castell. Turn right over a cattle grid and down a surfaced lane to a stile on the right signposted to Castell Dinas Bran. Follow the path beyond the stile to the remains of the 13th-century castle, where views stretch down the Vale of Llangollen towards England in one direction, and into the hills and valleys of the Welsh heartland in the other.

8 Keeping the castle ruins to the left, follow a stony path that zigzags downhill to a gate. Go through the gate and continue straight ahead over a crossing track to a kissing gate beside a house. Go through the gate and descend steps to another gate, beyond which the path leads to a bridge over Llangollen Canal.

9 Cross the bridge and turn right on the canal towpath. Continue for about 1½ miles to Horseshoe Falls: an elegant curved weir built across the Dee by the engineer William Jessop to siphon water into the canal system. Go through an iron gate beside the weir and through two more gates on the path past St Tysilio's Church, to the road. Turn right to the car park.

VIEW FROM CASTELL DINAS BRAN

Scotland

Gentle, fertile lowlands contrast
with the remote splendour of the
Highlands in this wild, romantic
land of fresh and sea-water
lochs, glens and offshore islands.

Key

1 Walk location

County boundary

Motorway

Principal A road

(See 'How to use the book',
page 6)

NORTH HIGHLANDS
& ISLANDS
300-311

Durness

Thurso

Wick

A99

A9

Lairg
A837

Ullapool

5

4
A835

6

A9

A9

2

1

Elgin

A96

13

Fraserburgh

A952

Peterhead

Skye

Portree

7

8

Nairn

Inverness

Loch
Ness

11

12

A95

10

8

Cairngorms
National
Park

7

9

Braemar

A90

Aberdeen

A93

A96

Kyle of Lochalsh

A87

A887

A87

Mallaig

A830

Newtonmore

A82

A86

Grampian Mountains

CENTRAL
274-297

A9

6

Pitlochry

4

A93

Forfar

A92

A90

Fort
William

14

15

16

A828

A82

3

2

Dundee

St Andrews

Mull

17

18

Oban

A85

A819

A85

A82

Crianlarich

5

Perth

6

Loch Lomond &
The Trossachs
National Park
Loch
Lomond

3

A84

A9

A91

M90

Stirling

A811

Kirkcaldy

5

Edinburgh

A1

1

Lochgilphead

Dumbarton

A78

A737

Glasgow

M8

A70

A702

SOUTHEAST
266-273

2

Peebles

3

Coldstream

4

A83

East
Kilbride

Irvine

Kilmarnock

A70

M74

M73

Hawick

A7

Jedburgh

A68

4

Ayr

2

A76

Moffat

A701

SOUTHWEST
260-265

A77

Dumfries

A75

1

Stranraer

A75

SOUTHWEST SCOTLAND

The walks of Scotland's southwest take in wooded hills, river valleys, sandy beaches and shingle banks. At Callander Crags, moorland paths lead to hilltop cairns with magnificent views.

1 Carsethorn

Along the Solway estuary shoreline, then inland past the birthplace of an American hero and the glorious gardens of Arbigland.

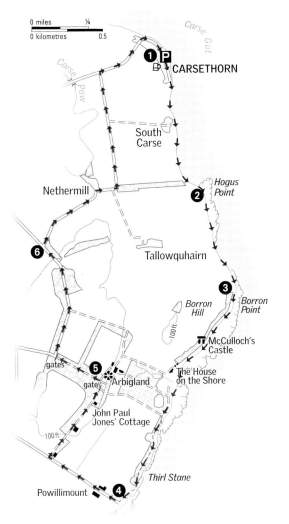

LENGTH 5 miles (3 hours)

PARKING Car park opposite Steamboat Inn in Carsethorn

CONDITIONS Check tide times – sand at low tide, pebbles or rough turf at full tide

REFRESHMENTS Pub in Carsethorn

1 From the car park turn left down a lane with houses on either side. Beyond the last house on the left, turn left at the groyne – the sand-covered wall of posts and planks designed to slow down beach erosion. Turn right along the high-tide mark. The shore descends in tiers, as massive granite boulders give way to pebbles and then sand and mud at sea level. Walk along the tideline, usually marked by cockleshells, tellins, periwinkles and mussels, passing South Carse, the buildings on the right.

The sand and mudflats are covered for an hour or two at high tide but more often the sea is distant, about a mile away to the east. The Solway estuary is an important site for wading birds. Even in summer, when many species are nesting in the Arctic, flocks of sanderlings, oystercatchers, ringed plovers and dunlin can be seen.

2 Continue past Hogus Point. The rock spurs of the point are a favourite roost for gulls; at high tide they feed in the rich waters of the Gulf Stream or scavenge fields. To the right, only a few

metres above the spring tideline, is a bank topped by hawthorn and sycamore trees, swept into bouffant styles by the prevailing westerly winds.

From Hogus Point, keep to the tideline on shellsand, above the rock bands. The salt-tolerant plants growing among the shingle include white campion, orache and silverweed. Grass tufts are topped by sea plantain and thrift.

3 Continue around Borron Point and along a broad bay with a high tree-covered slope to the right. Bracken, undersown with bluebells in spring, covers any open ground. Halfway around the bay, and hard to spot when trees are in leaf, is the hummock of McCulloch's Castle, an Iron Age hillfort. Excavations have revealed that a fortified tower house was later built within the moated earthwork and was in use as late as 1500.

Continue past buildings including the House on the Shore on the right and a round garden shelter. The huge granite boulder to the right, perched on a reef of ancient sandstone, is known as the Devil Stone. According to legend, when the Earth was still hot, the Devil bit the boulder out of Criffel, the local mountain, and spat it into its present position.

Continue down the coast – either along the shore or, at high tide when the shore is not accessible, along a narrow, winding, grassy path that follows a wall above the beach for about

2/3 mile, passing through trees before descending to Thirl Stane, an impressive natural stone arch, and the grassy parking area beyond.

4 Turn right onto a lane and walk through the farmyard of Powillimount and past a pair of farm cottages. At Arbigland's west lodge, turn right into a private avenue that passes, on the right, the birthplace of John Paul Jones, who has been acclaimed as the founder of the American naval tradition for his actions in the American Revolutionary War. Continue to the entrance gates on the right of Arbigland, an 18th-century mansion set in exotic gardens, where roses, azaleas, rhododendrons and camellias flourish in a climate similar to that of Torquay. John Paul Jones's father was head gardener here in the 18th century.

5 Turn left onto the broad driveway leading away from the entrance, with trees on both sides. Go through some white gates and turn right along the road. Pass a driveway to the House on the Shore on the right and continue ahead with the slopes of Criffel ahead.

6 At a junction at the end of the woods turn right. Follow the road past Nethermill on the left. The road then veers left, and after about 1/2 mile reaches a junction. Turn right to return to Carsethorn and the car park.

SCOTLAND

SOUTHWEST SCOTLAND

2 Straiton

Across wooded hillsides and a river valley, ending with a steep climb to a panoramic moorland viewpoint.

LENGTH 5 miles (2½ hours)

PARKING Car park at western edge of village

CONDITIONS Easy gradients through fields and woodland; track may be muddy in places and grass may be slippery on the steep climb up to the monument

REFRESHMENTS Pub in Straiton

1 From the car park, where a noticeboard describes 20 miles of paths around Straiton, turn right and cross the footbridge over Lambdoughty Burn. Turn right on a track, following the burn south through sheep pasture, and cross a wooden bridge over the peaty brown Water of Girvan. A smaller bridge follows, then a stile leading to a lane. Turn left on the lane past Bennan Farm and follow a farm track downhill to the right.

2 Ignoring a track on the left, keep straight on through a gate into a field. Continue up the field, passing clumps of boulders on the right; these gave a dry base for stacking corn before the days of combine harvesters. At the top of the field, the track bends left before a drystone dyke, leading down to Bennan Wood.

3 Climb over the stile into the wood and follow the track through a spruce plantation, fringed by the occasional silver birch. Roe deer may sometimes be spotted in the shadows. In spring, the grass verges are covered in bluebells. After about ½ mile, at a hairpin bend, leave the track, cross a boardwalk ahead over a ditch and go through a gate.

4 Beyond the gate, spruce gives way to broad-leaved trees, mainly oak. Shortly, a delightful view opens up: the pasture sweeps down to the Water of Girvan and rises up from the opposite bank to the exposed slopes of Craig Hill and Craigengower, on whose summit stands a tall stone obelisk. The track then wends downhill, sometimes over muddy stretches, through a gate towards Craigfad Farm.

5 At Craigfad, swing left past the front gate of the whitewashed farmhouse. Turn left on the metalled road and cross the river. At a T-junction, turn left and walk for about 1½ miles along the valley floor. On the right, the valley side rises steeply with rocky outcrops. The road is quiet, but watch out for traffic on the bends.

6 Turn right over a metal stile into a field before Straiton primary school and follow the clear track uphill to the wooded lower slopes of Craigengower.

At the top of the field, climb the stile and follow a track through trees for a short distance. At a waymarked T-junction turn right and walk to a second waymarker, also at a T-junction. Continue straight ahead over a boardwalk across a ditch and follow the path through the plantation to a stile over a stone wall. Climb the stile to reach the upper slopes of Highgate Hill. The final stretch to the summit is steep.

7 At the summit stands a memorial to Lt Col James Hunter Blair, killed at the Battle of Inkerman in 1854. The panorama stretches from Straiton to the Christmas-pudding form of Ailsa Craig, protruding out of the sea in the Firth of Clyde.

Return to the road, turn right and walk through Straiton, where whitewashed terraced cottages face each other across the main street. The village's tranquil setting belies a turbulent history. In the late 17th century, during the 'Killing Time', government troops garrisoned near the village hunted down Covenanters who were opposed to Presbyterian bishops. The tomb of one 'martyr' can be found in the village churchyard, on the left, on the way back to the car park.

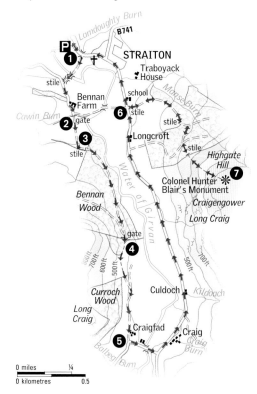

3 Callander Crags

Beautiful woods, a waterfall plunging through a river gorge and an ascent to the summit of the Crags.

LENGTH **4 or 5 miles (2 or 3 hours)**

PARKING **In Station Road car park**

CONDITIONS **Good paths and tracks with short sections of minor road and steep climb to the summit of Crags; steps near Bracklinn Falls may be slippery in wet weather**

REFRESHMENTS **Range in Callander**

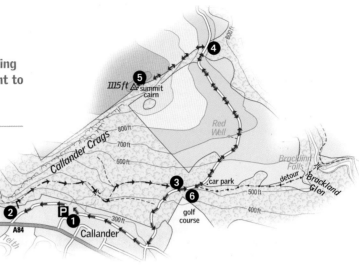

1 With your back to the car park entrance, turn left through a subsidiary parking area. Bear right up a grass bank onto a housing estate road. Turn left and, just past the flats, turn right on a lane signposted 'To the Crags' and 'Wood Walks'. Follow the lane, which becomes a rough track, to a sign and information board that includes details of the Callander Crags and the woodland.

2 Turn right on a path that ascends through woodland, its floor lined with bluebells in spring, below the Callander Crags. The older chestnuts, beeches and firs were planted here in the 18th century, when the land belonged to the Earls of Ancaster.

Follow the path for 1/3 mile, bending right over a footbridge. At a crossing of paths, turn left uphill and continue until the path meets a forest track. Turn right and follow the track through the woods below the Crags. Descend on the track to emerge on a tarmac road. Turn left on the road and follow it, as it climbs upward, to reach Bracklinn Falls car park.

DETOUR *Turn right on a level path towards the Bracklinn Falls, passing an information board giving general details of the Trossachs area and of the Falls. Alongside the path, you may see wild plants with medicinal properties, such as eyebright, self-heal and tormentil. Roe deer may be spotted here in the morning or the evening. At the end of the path, go down some steps to the Bracklinn Falls, popular with sightseers since Victorian times. A local legend says that Sir Walter Scott rode over the waterfall, which cascades over giant sandstone blocks, on a shaky old bridge as part of a wager. He used the Bracklinn Falls, 'so black and steep', in his poem* The Lady of the Lake.

3 Continue ahead and follow the road as it climbs steeply, opening out into meadows, with the Callander Crags away to the left. Just off the road to the left, a path leads to a semicircular

stone wall with a plaque in the centre. This marks the Red Well, a mineral spring from which water that is coloured bright iron-red flows; it is supposed to have restorative powers. After about another 2/3 mile, where the road bends to the right on entering the woods, you reach a worn, green sign that points left to Callander Crags.

4 Turn left and follow a narrow path climbing through birch woodland and out onto the open moor. Continue up to the summit cairn, the highest point of the Callander Crags at 340m (1,115ft). Magnificent views of the surrounding hills and countryside stretch for miles in all directions. A marble plaque on the cairn bears the inscription 'Queen Victoria's Diamond Jubilee Cairn 1897'.

5 Turn back and descend on the same path, with stunning, unobstructed views opening out all around. Directly ahead, above a dense pine plantation, is the prominent 665m (2,181ft) summit of Uamh Bheag. Follow the path down to the road and turn right, back downhill towards the Bracklinn Falls car park.

6 Continue ahead on the road for around 2/3 mile, passing a golf course behind some trees on the left, to reach the rear of Arden House. This was used in the popular 1960s television series *Dr Finlay's Casebook* as the residence of Dr Finlay, Dr Cameron and Janet, their housekeeper.

Take the footpath that runs downhill to the left of a garden wall. Continue on past Arden House and then past another house to finally emerge on Ancaster Road. Turn right and follow the road back to the car park.

SCOTLAND

263

SOUTHWEST SCOTLAND

4 Whiting Bay

On the Isle of Arran, past ancient tombs and a torrent-scoured gorge to a commanding view of the Firth of Clyde.

LENGTH 5 miles (2½ hours)

PARKING Seafront layby near bridge over Glenashdale Burn

CONDITIONS Fairly demanding hilly walk on forest tracks and paths

REFRESHMENTS Full range in Whiting Bay

1 With your back to the sea, walk through a gap between the youth hostel and Glenashdale Burn to a track signposted to the Giants' Graves. Continue along the track, which follows the riverside, into broad-leaved woodland. After a short distance the track divides.

2 Fork left, signposted to the Giants' Graves, and walk uphill past a ruined building into a forest plantation of mature trees. Climb a long flight of steps leading up a steep bank.

At the top of the steps turn left on the forest track then continue up a more gentle gradient, past a grove of mature trees that have been labelled with their names. A view opens out over Whiting Bay and Holy Island; past the far end of the Bay looms the mountain of Mullach Mor. Beyond the opening the track is enclosed between tall dark trees for a short distance before it bends to the right into a clearing around the Giants' Graves – a tumbled group of chambered neolithic burial cairns, once covered by earth, which date back at least 4,000 years.

3 Turn around and retrace your steps to the side of Glenashdale Burn, then turn left and follow the path signposted to the waterfall. Continue beside the river, which enters a broad-leaved woodland containing stands of birch, ash and alder.

Ahead, an ever-louder roar advertises Glenashdale Falls. Carry straight on to reach a path branching to the right.

4 Turn right and make the short steep descent to a viewing platform over the falls, which plunge more than 30m (100ft) through a narrow rocky gorge, colonised by wild flowers and draped with curtains of dripping moss.

Return to the main path and turn right, emerging onto a patch of open ground beyond the top of the falls, beside a footbridge leading to the far bank.

5 Cross the bridge, over placid pools that give no hint of the torrent that occurs such a short distance downstream, and walk straight ahead

away from the river. Soon the path goes through a gap in a stone wall then immediately divides; fork right, on a path signposted to Whiting Bay via an Iron Age fort. The ramparts of the fort command a wide view over the south of Arran and the surrounding sea.

Continue on the uphill path from the hillfort to meet a forest road.

6 Turn left and carry on climbing until you reach a T-junction with another forest road; turn right, signposted to Lamlash. Follow the road for about a mile – it runs more or less parallel to the coast – to reach a large clearing. Walk to the far side of the clearing, where there is a panoramic view over Lamlash Bay and Holy Island, then retrace your steps to the start of the clearing.

7 Turn left on the forest track, following the signposted route to Whiting Bay via Hawthorne, and continue downhill through a forest glade to emerge on a minor road. Turn right.

The road soon deteriorates into an unsurfaced rutted lane, flanked by grassy banks and hedges, above which there are occasional glimpses of the roofs of Whiting Bay and its long beach of sand, rock and shingle. After a left-hand bend the lane meets the A841 on the edge of Whiting Bay. Turn right and follow the road along the seafront, past shops and hotels, to the bridge over the Glendale Burn and the parking place.

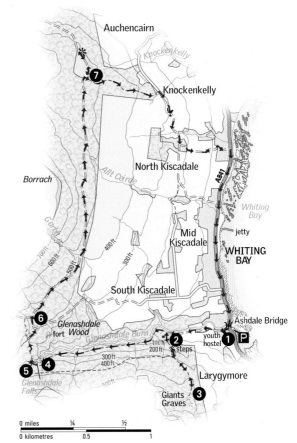

HOLY ISLAND, VIEWED FROM WHITING BAY

SOUTHEAST SCOTLAND

Edinburgh's waterfront – the Firth of Forth – is a fascinating coastline for walkers. South of the city there are three easy ranges of hills, and south again is the border country, with good tracks on the old drovers' roads.

1 St Abbs

Through a nature reserve teeming with birdlife to an ancient priory on a clifftop overlooking the sea.

LENGTH 5½ or 6 miles (2½ or 3 hours)

PARKING Northfield visitor centre car park

CONDITIONS Clear, firm paths through the conservation area; some walking on sand and rocky shore

REFRESHMENTS Tearoom at visitor centre and kiosk at Coldingham Bay (summer only)

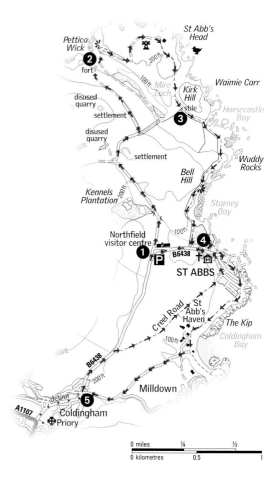

1 Turn right out of the car park and follow the road to St Abb's Head for 1½ miles to the inlet of Pettico Wick. Cliffs stretch into the distance on the left. Inland is the man-made Mire Loch, where seabirds feed and preen. Continue along the road to a small car park near the lighthouse.

2 Go left across the grass to the cliffs and offshore rocks. From April to June, a teeming mass of birds cram onto every tiny ledge and outcrop. St Abb's Head is a National Nature Reserve, managed jointly by the NTS and the SWT. It is one of the most important nesting and breeding areas for seabirds in Britain. In spring and early summer, more than 60,000 birds gather here, including cormorants, fulmars, guillemots and shags.

To the left, the view from the cliffs stretches to Fife Ness on the east coast. The promontory is above a geological fault and this area of coast has provided important information about the formation of rock strata. Return to the road and cross over to continue around the lighthouse, walking to the right of the former lighthouse-keeper's cottage, ahead to the cliff path. Follow the cliff path inland, a little behind Kirk Hill.

3 Cross a stile and continue along the path back to the coast, climbing over Bell Hill where the view south encompasses St Abbs village and the cliffs along the coast to Eyemouth and beyond. Follow the path to a road and turn left into the village, passing a small museum of local history in the old school.

4 Fork left to the harbour, usually busy with fishing boats and divers. Boat trips around the Head can be taken from here. Take the path climbing out of the harbour and turn left at the top. Walk between the houses to a tarmac path at the end of the road, turning right towards the golden sands of Coldingham Bay. From the bay, turn left onto the access road and continue ahead, using the path to the right of the road for ½ mile to reach Coldingham village.

DETOUR *Turn left into Coldingham and left again to visit Coldingham Priory. Established 900 years ago by Edgar, King of the Scots, on the site of a nunnery founded by St Ebba, the priory was largely rebuilt in the 17th century, and still serves as the parish church.*

5 Turn right towards St Abbs. After about ½ mile, turn right on the ancient Creel Road, now partly a tunnel of trees that provide a sheltered walk. Turn left into St Abbs on reaching the first houses in the village, then left again along the road back to the car park.

2 Abbey St Bathans

Riverside scenery and the remains of a highland broch, leading to part of the Southern Upland Way.

LENGTH **5 miles (3 hours)**

PARKING **Riverside car park**

CONDITIONS **Firm paths and roads**

REFRESHMENTS **Restaurant in Abbey St Bathans**

1 Turn left out of the car park and follow the road out of the village, walking by the river at first, then climbing away to the right. In just under a mile, at a sharp bend with a sign warning drivers to 'Toot', leave the road, going to the left and following the steps down to a footbridge over the Eller Burn.

2 Cross a stile and follow the path ahead, which soon climbs away from the burn. Continue across open ground, climbing to a gate at a field border. Go through the gate and turn left, downhill, towards another gate. A circular shooting lodge dating from the late 18th century, Retreat House, is visible on the other side of the river, through the trees to the left.

3 Go through the second gate and bear right, uphill. The path is indistinct in places but Edin's Hall Broch soon appears ahead, set on a natural platform on this side of Cockburn Law.

This impressive defensive structure would originally have been higher, but the layout of the double walls, with chambers between, is clear. Relatively little is known about these mysterious brochs. They are believed to date from around the 2nd century AD and are found mainly in the Highlands. Continue ahead on a clear path, downhill to a narrow metal gate.

4 Go through the gate and continue ahead, with a fence and trees on the left. Cross the steps over a wall, which can be slippery after rain. Ignore any signs pointing to the broch, which lead from another parking area. Follow the path along the bank above the Whiteadder. The woods across the river contain,

for this area, a high proportion of oak trees. Cross some more steps over a wall. Follow the riverbank to a meeting of paths.

5 Fork left along the lower path. Go through a gate and cross the footbridge over the river by the cottages at Elba. Turn left, cross a bridge over Otter Burn and swing right with the main track. Walk uphill through the woods for about ¼ mile to a minor road.

6 Turn left along the road, climbing steadily for about 1½ miles. Ignore the next road to the left, continuing ahead to the houses at Moorhouse, where another road joins from the right. There are excellent views from this stretch of the walk.

7 At the road junction, turn left off the road. Cross a stile at a field boundary and follow a path through Edgar's Cleugh (a cleugh is a narrow valley). The route then gradually curves to the right and passes underneath some power lines to Whare Burn.

Turn left at the burn, joining the Southern Upland Way for about a mile. The long-distance path runs for 212 miles from Portpatrick on the west coast to Cockburnspath in the east. Follow the track, then the lane, back to the Whiteadder. Cross the river to return to the car park.

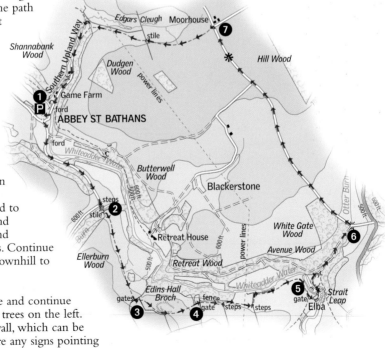

SOUTHEAST SCOTLAND

3 Traquair

Following the Southern Upland Way past an ancient well, on the way to the top of Minch Moor and breathtaking views.

LENGTH 8 miles (4 hours)

PARKING At Traquair village hall

CONDITIONS Mostly good paths and tracks but boggy and thick heather in places, with moderate climb on first part of route

REFRESHMENTS None on walk

1 From the car park, turn left and go up the track, following signs for Southern Upland Way (SUW, a 212 mile long-distance path that crosses southern Scotland, from Portpatrick in the west to Cockburnspath in the east). The steadily climbing track is at first enclosed on both sides by fine examples of drystane dyking, the Scottish equivalent of drystone walling. Where the track bends left, look back for exhilarating views up the Tweed valley and over the village of Innerleithen to Lee Pen hill.

2 Continue uphill on the track to enter the forest. A good deal of conifer felling takes place

FIELD GATE NEAR TRAQUAIR

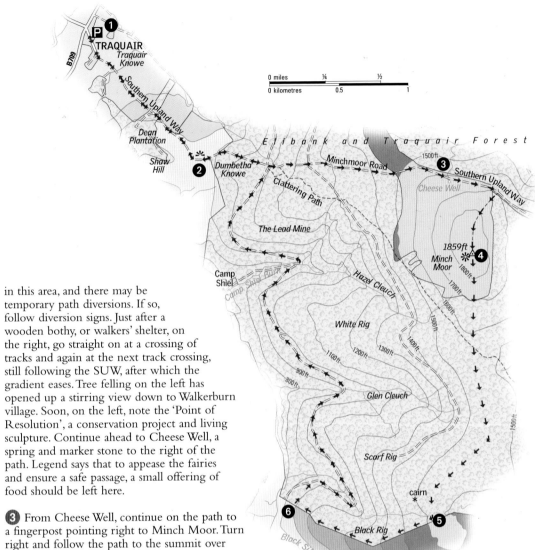

in this area, and there may be temporary path diversions. If so, follow diversion signs. Just after a wooden bothy, or walkers' shelter, on the right, go straight on at a crossing of tracks and again at the next track crossing, still following the SUW, after which the gradient eases. Tree felling on the left has opened up a stirring view down to Walkerburn village. Soon, on the left, note the 'Point of Resolution', a conservation project and living sculpture. Continue ahead to Cheese Well, a spring and marker stone to the right of the path. Legend says that to appease the fairies and ensure a safe passage, a small offering of food should be left here.

3 From Cheese Well, continue on the path to a fingerpost pointing right to Minch Moor. Turn right and follow the path to the summit over open, heathery ground.

At the 556.5m (1,859ft) summit is a cairn, a tall landmark mound of stones. The views and purity of air here are intoxicating. To the east the three Eildon peaks below Melrose are prominent, and to the west the higher Tweedsmuir Hills crowd the horizon.

4 From the summit, head south on a narrow path down a heathery ridge. Ahead is a wavy pattern of sinuous slopes and rounded summits hazing into the distance. Re-enter forest and continue ahead, following the line of an old stone wall; the heather is thick in places. On reaching more mature trees, cross a gap in the wall to the left then curve right with the wall into a tree tunnel and swing left. The path in the tree tunnel can be boggy in parts, although this may be avoided by crossing to the other side of the wall as necessary.

5 Just before reaching the boundary wall, turn right to follow a steadily descending path that is quite rough in places. Just discernible on a low ridge ahead is a memorial to Learmont Drysdale, who was a leading Scottish composer of the 1890s and 1900s.

6 Before reaching the corner of the forest turn right onto the waymarked Tweed Trail. Continue to follow the waymark arrows until you meet a more substantial path, and an expansive view. Turn right and continue on the track as it bends right and drops again to cross Camp Shiel Burn, then left before climbing around a small hill to rejoin the outward route. Turn left and walk downhill back to Traquair and the car park.

SOUTHEAST SCOTLAND

4 Melrose

From stately abbey ruins to the Eildon Hills, with memorable views and signs of ancient Iron Age and Roman civilisations.

LENGTH 4 miles (2½ hours)

PARKING Car park opposite entrance to Melrose Abbey

CONDITIONS Good paths; some stretches may be muddy; strenuous climb up North Eildon

REFRESHMENTS Full range in Melrose

1 From the car park turn left then right up the road away from Melrose Abbey (HS), with the Eildon Hills in the distance ahead. On the left is Priorwood Gardens (NTS), which grows flowers that are used in dried flower arrangements, and has many old and unusual types of apple tree. Continue to Market Square with its cross of 1645.

2 From Market Square go straight on to the B6359, Dingleton Road, and under the bypass. Soon turn left down steps between houses, following the Eildon Hills Walk 'triple peak' signs. For a time you also follow St Cuthbert's Way, a footpath from Melrose to Lindisfarne in Northumberland. Cross a footbridge over a burn to reach a flight of steps.

3 Climb the steps and cross a stile. Take the path ahead between fences and then along the side of a field, through gates, to reach an open

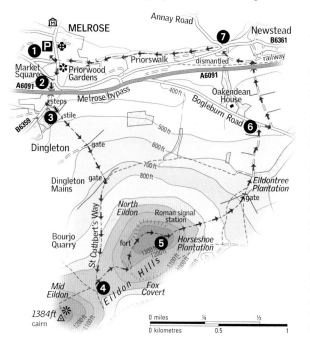

hill. Looking back, there are fine views of Melrose, with the abbey prominent and the River Tweed beyond.

Follow a rising path to the right through gorse to the saddle between Mid Eildon and North Eildon. To the right are the remains of Bourjo Quarry, which provided stone for the rebuilding of Melrose Abbey in the 15th century. Wide views open out, especially to the west along the Tweed valley to Galashiels and beyond.

The predominantly heather and grass-covered Eildon Hills are masses of ancient hard rock, partly volcanic, exposed by millions of years of weathering and glacial action. Birdlife on the hills includes the linnet, willow warbler and the red grouse.

4 From the saddle between the hills, turn left and follow the track rising steadily to the top of North Eildon, passing through the Iron Age ramparts of a fort of the Selgovae tribe. The Romans demolished the fort and set up a signal station, and it is easy to see why: the view encompasses half the Borders. To the south, the line of Dere Street is apparent, parallel to the A68, and the Waterloo Monument on Peniel Heugh stands out. Farther west, the cone of Rubers Law rises above the Teviot valley. To the northeast are the village of Newstead and Leaderfoot viaduct, with the site of the Roman fort of Trimontium between them.

5 From the summit and facing towards Melrose, turn right on a steeply descending path – care is needed with footing. Lower down, the gradient eases and the path runs between gorse to a gate. Go through the gate and follow the – sometimes muddy – track between fences to emerge on Bogleburn Road.

6 Turn right on the road, then turn left down a lane with Newstead ahead. Follow the lane as it bends left and right under the A6091 bypass and then under an old railway line. At a T-junction of paths, turn left and follow the path to reach a road at the west end of Newstead.

7 Turn left and cross the road diagonally towards some stables. Follow the Eildon Walk signs through a gate and onto a path between stables and a row of houses. Follow the path along a hillside ledge with a stream on the right. The view extends across the Tweed to woods and farmland beyond, and ahead to Melrose.

Where the path reaches houses, continue straight ahead. Near the end of the houses, before the road veers left uphill and beyond an electricity sub-station, keep to the right to walk through a small park, then go across a footbridge over a burn to Melrose Abbey and the car park.

5 South Queensferry

Under Britain's most famous rail bridge to long strands by the Firth of Forth and views of Edinburgh.

LENGTH 8 miles (4½ hours)

PARKING Car park near Hawes Pier, on the shore road

CONDITIONS Long, flat walking on tracks and beaches beside the Firth of Forth

REFRESHMENTS Full range in South Queensferry

1 Walk towards the Forth Rail Bridge, passing Hawes Pier, the departure point for the car ferry to Fife before the road bridge opened in 1964. In summer, boats still transport holidaymakers from the pier to Inchcolm Island far out in the seaward approaches to the firth. Hawes Inn was the traditional gathering place for ferry passengers; it features in Sir Walter Scott's novel *The Antiquary* (1816) and Robert Louis Stevenson's *Kidnapped* (1886).

The cantilever rail bridge, opened in 1890, dwarfs everything nearby. The huge tubes and girders – the design was massively overspecified as a response to the Tay Bridge disaster a few years earlier – casts a latticework of shadows over the road.

Turn left along the broad track immediately beyond the bridge and follow the edge of woodland by the firth's rocky shore to a gate.

2 Go through the gate and continue along the shore past Long Craig Pier and Whitehouse Bay. The tanker berth off Hound Point can be glimpsed ahead as the track winds through woodland, always remaining close to the shore. Pass a grassy track on the right leading between two hillocks, then turn left a short distance farther on and follow the path down to the sheltered waters of Peatdraught Bay. Walk along the edge of the water to Hound Point, where the path rejoins the track.

3 Continue on the track beyond the headland, through a wood and past a side track on the left to Fishery Cottage. The broad tidal expanse of Drum Sands stretches towards a horizon rimmed with the rooftops of Edinburgh. The track emerges from the wood onto the top of the beach, then bends away from it again to reach a fork.

4 Fork left to walk past Barnbougle Castle, a private house built by the 5th Earl of Rosebery, Britain's prime minister from 1894 to 1895. It was modelled on a stronghold that stood on the site until 1820. After a short distance, the track emerges from the wood into parkland between Dalmeny House (open three days a week in high summer) and the firth. Follow the track to a signposted shore walk on the left.

5 Follow the shore walk, which crosses a golf course then bends right along the shore, before descending into the little valley of the Cockle Burn. Cross the footbridge over the burn. The path leads into Long Green Wood. Continue ahead to join a wider, tree-lined track, then turn left to a row of cottages, where the track ends.

6 Continue on the path from the end of the track to Snab Point, where there is a fine view behind to Hound Point. Continue over a footbridge across Linklin Burn to Eagle Rock, named after its worn carvings – supposedly made by members of the Roman garrison in the fort at Cramond. A short distance farther on the path ends at Cobble Cottage on the River Almond, where a ferry (daily except Fridays) serves Cramond.

From Eagle Rock, return to the car park at South Queensferry by the same route.

SCOTLAND

SOUTHEAST SCOTLAND

6 Craigmead

Bracing moorland air and magnificent views on the way to the highest point in the Lomond Hills.

LENGTH 5½ miles (3 hours)

PARKING Craigmead car park, west of Falkland on Lomond Hills road signposted to Leslie

CONDITIONS Fairly demanding; over exposed moorland

REFRESHMENTS None on walk

1 Go through a gate at the back of the car park and walk straight ahead to a stile. Cross the stile and follow a grassy track, which soon merges with a wider track joining from the right. Continue over open moorland with views over the surrounding countryside.

The smooth grassy ramparts of Maiden Castle, an Iron Age hillfort more than 2,000 years old, can be seen a short distance to the right. Buzzards wheel overhead in wide circles, scanning the ground for prey and carrion, while skylarks ascend towards the clouds. Continue along the track to where it divides, with a narrower path branching to the right.

HARPERLEAS RESERVOIR AND WEST LOMOND HILL

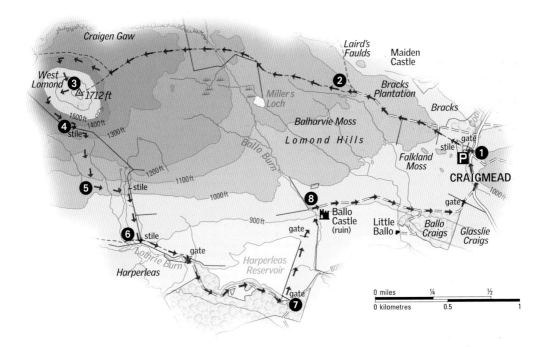

Fork left, staying on the wider path, which after some distance starts to bend towards the dominant high point of West Lomond – at 522m (1,712ft), the highest hill in Fife. The view behind shows the sister hill of East Lomond rising beyond the road from Falkland to the car park. Red grouse may catapult themselves from the heather underfoot, taking off on whirring wings and making a clucking call that sounds like an exhortation to 'go back, go back'.

Continue on the path, which follows a ridge to the top of West Lomond, climbing in two or three steepish spurts broken by flatter stretches. The views from the summit reveal the entire route of the walk and much of Fife, including the nearby watery expanse of Loch Leven to the southwest.

With your back to the ascent path, turn right and follow a grassy path down the crest of a broad ridge. The path merges with a narrower one. Turn left and wind around the side of the hill, slightly above a drystone wall on the right. Pass a sign by the wall, indicating that there is a way over it ahead, and continue to a stile.

Cross the stile and immediately turn left, with the wall now on your left. At the first opportunity turn right and start to descend the rough hillside – there is no clearly marked path to follow. Skirt a wet patch where springs rise on the hillside, and continue down a more abrupt slope to meet a path running across the face of the hillside.

Turn left on the path and continue to a stile over a stone wall. Do not cross the stile but turn right and follow a grassy path downhill to a corner between stone walls, where there is another stile, on the left.

Cross the stile and follow the path beside Lothrie Burn towards Harperleas Reservoir. Go through a gate where the path joins a track, and continue over a footbridge across the reservoir inlet. Enter a forest plantation on a firm, metalled track, and follow it as it winds around the margin of the reservoir before arriving at a gate.

Go through the gate and follow the path alongside the low dam impounding the reservoir, to a second gate. Beyond the gate the path climbs towards Ballo Castle, a ruined manor, where it meets a track.

Turn right onto the track. Pass the drive to Little Ballo farmhouse on the right then, beyond a shelter belt of trees, follow the track as it bends left and continues through a gate flanked by stone posts before emerging onto a minor road. Turn left and follow the road for a short distance to return to the car park.

CENTRAL SCOTLAND

Much of Scotland's most dramatic and best-loved scenery lies within this region, from majestic Loch Lomond and the peaks of the Central Highlands to the spectacular granite domes of the Cairngorms.

1 Edzell

A beautiful riverside path, a rocky gorge and an intriguing link with the Napoleonic Wars.

LENGTH 5 miles (2½ hours)

PARKING In the main village street

CONDITIONS Easy going on riverside paths, with some road walking

REFRESHMENTS Café and pubs in Edzell

1 Go down the lane to the left of the garage, signposted to the Shakkin' Brig. Pass a picnic area and continue to the broad River North Esk. Turn left on the riverside path. Ignore Shakkin' Brig on the right and continue ahead along the riverbank past many fine trees, including handsome old beeches. Below to the right, the river rushes by, tumbling over small rock falls. There are views north up Glen Esk to the high hills beyond. After about a mile, go round a small inlet and pass above a waterfall, by a footbridge, to reach a road bridge. This is the graceful, single-arched Gannochy Bridge, which spans 16m (52ft) and rises 20m (65ft) above the fast-flowing waters of the North Esk.

2 Cross the bridge and turn left through a gate. Follow the riverside path for ½ mile through beautiful scenery. At one point, huge slabs of rock extend into the river, narrowing its flow. The path passes to the left of the Burn, a study centre in a mansion built between 1791 and 1796 by Lord Adam Gordon, who was commander-in-chief of the army in Scotland.

When Lord Gordon bought the estate in 1780, the land was used only for sheep-grazing. He cleared the heathland for farming, planted gardens and woodlands, and laid out 6 miles of walks. It is said that he had the riverside path made by French prisoners from the Napoleonic Wars. Some beech, horse chestnut and walnut trees survive from Lord Gordon's original planting.

3 From a footbridge over an inlet, retrace your steps to Gannochy Bridge and turn left on the road, passing the driveway to the Burn on the left. Continue past the Glen Esk road on the left and take the next road right, signposted to Northwaterbridge. Follow the road, with woods on each side, for 1 mile to the first junction, at which there is a house on the left.

4 Turn right on a track signposted to Arnhall Quarry. There are splendid views to the right of the hills at the head of Glen Esk. Beyond the entrance of Arnhall Quarry, the track narrows and passes a house on the right. A plaque on its front wall states that this is the Barracks, built in the early years of the 19th century, during the Napoleonic Wars, for the soldiers guarding the French prisoners of war who were being used as unpaid farm labour. Continue to the end of the track, past a notice stating 'Edzell by foot only' and through a group of mill houses.

5 Pass to the right of the last house and continue on a footpath to the river. The path follows the riverbank for a short distance, then reaches the Shakkin' Brig.

6 Cross the suspension bridge, which, as its name suggests, shakes a little as you walk over it. Turn left beside the river and then right to return to Edzell.

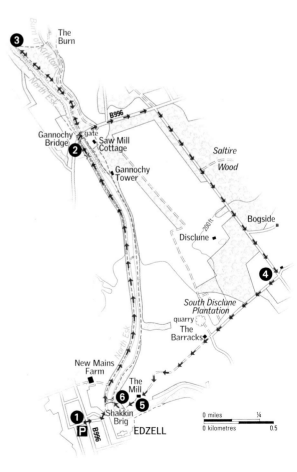

2 Arbroath

Superb clifftop scenery with spectacular rock formations and abundant birdlife along the way.

LENGTH 5 or 5½ miles (2½ or 3 hours)

PARKING At far end of the promenade from the harbour

CONDITIONS Easy going, with one climb up to cliffs

REFRESHMENTS Full range in Arbroath

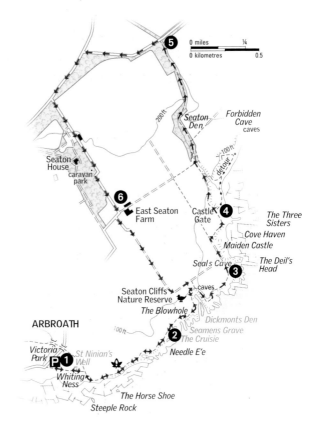

1 Take the tarmac path that leads up to the cliffs, passing on the left St Ninian's Well, named after the saint who brought Christianity to this part of Scotland 1,400 years ago. If you look back along the path, Arbroath and its long promenade are visible. The large grassy area behind the promenade is known as Victoria Park, opened in 1897 to mark the Diamond Jubilee of Queen Victoria. Continue along the clifftop path, passing numbered posts. At post 3, look down to the right to see the Needle E'e, a remarkable natural rock arch, cut through by the incessant pounding of the sea. It is unusual in being parallel to the coast – such arches more often lie at right-angles to the coast. The red sandstone along this stretch is about 350 million years old.

Pass a sign indicating that this is a SWT reserve to reach a small inlet known as the Cruisie, from its supposed resemblance in shape to the old lamps known as 'cruisies'.

2 Continue on the cliff path, passing on the right a collapsed cave called the Blowhole, through which, at high tide, the sea spray can sometimes spurt upwards, like a whale expelling a plume of air and water. Follow the path as it skirts round a large inlet known as Dickmont's Den, that is said to have been much used by smugglers in the days before a customs sloop was stationed in Arbroath in 1740. The steep cliffs of the Den are usually alive with the cries of birds; in spring, the abundant flora includes banks of thrift, gorse, primroses and wood violets.

3 Where the tarmac ends, the path then becomes a little rougher and continues past The Deil's Head, a dramatic isolated rock stack, formed by the gradual erosion by the sea of the surrounding cliffs. You can walk down to the foot of the stack, unless the sea is high. Birds to be spotted here include oystercatchers, sandpipers and curlews. Continue beyond post 12 to a division of paths, passing the scant remains of the Iron Age hillfort of Maiden Castle on the right, which dates back about 2,000 years.

DETOUR *Take the right fork, leading down to the broad Carlingheugh Bay. There is a fine view of the headland rocks known as the Three Sisters, or the Camel's Back because of their hump-like outline. Continue to the grassy area at the foot of the cliff and the multicoloured pebbles of the beach.*

4 Take the left fork and follow the path through a wooded ravine called Seaton Den. Cross a burn by a single plank, turn left and follow the path up the Den, a lovely shaded walk among old beech trees. Cross the burn again and follow the path to a minor road.

5 Turn left on the road and left again at the next junction. After ¼ mile, turn left by the high wall of the Seaton Estate. Follow the road to a caravan-park entrance. Do not go into the park, but keep straight ahead on a clear track, still by the wall, to the junction at East Seaton Farm.

6 Turn right for 50m, then left on a broad track, through a gate, and back towards the cliffs. Straight ahead, 11 miles out to sea, is the Bell Rock lighthouse. Follow the path to the left, then right, to meet the cliff path at Dickmont's Den. Turn right and return along the cliff path, back down to the promenade at Arbroath.

SCOTLAND

275

CENTRAL SCOTLAND

3 Glamis

Pictish stones, a prehistoric hillfort, sweeping views of the Angus hills, and the 'devilish' gates of a royal castle.

LENGTH 6 or 8½ miles (3 or 4½ hours)

PARKING Car park off Main Street

CONDITIONS Easy going, mostly on quiet roads

REFRESHMENTS Pubs in Glamis and Charleston; restaurant at Glamis Castle

1 Walk to Main Street and turn left, then turn right at the junction. On the right are the entrance gates to Glamis Castle. The gateway, known as the De'il Gates and decorated with heraldic beasts, was built in 1680. The wrought-iron gates were a golden wedding gift in 1931 to the 14th Earl and Countess of Strathmore from their son-in-law and daughter, the Duke and Duchess of York, later George VI and Queen Elizabeth.

2 Turn left on the road opposite the De'il Gates to the junction with the A94. Turn right then soon turn left on a straight road signed to Newtyle, to a road on the left signposted to Slaughs.

3 Turn left and follow the tree-lined road as it rises steadily towards woodland. After a sharp right bend there is a wide view to the left of the Angus hills. The road then continues between fields grazed by cattle and passes between forest edges to Holemill. There is a small waterfall hidden in the woods behind the former mill, which can be heard but is almost impossible to reach.

DETOUR *Continue straight on and follow the road past disused quarries. After about a mile turn left on a track to climb the hill of Denoon Law. On the summit is a prehistoric fort offering grand views.*

4 Turn left and follow the road past Wester Rochelhill farm and then carry on past Mains of Rochelhill farm to reach a junction with the A928.

5 Turn left. After ½ mile turn left on a minor road leading downhill into Charleston, a village established in 1833, principally for weavers. At the north end of the village is a wonderful view of Glamis below, with the Vale of Strathmore beyond. Continue downhill to meet the A94.

6 Cross the A94 and take the path opposite into a lane. Just before the first house turn right on a path and follow it to a road. Turn left then first right to meet Dundee Road. Turn right and then turn left on The Mill, passing the former mill buildings. Glamis once supported a linen industry, and a flax-spinning mill was built on the Glamis Burn in 1806.

At the next road, Forfar Road, turn right, crossing the Glamis Burn.

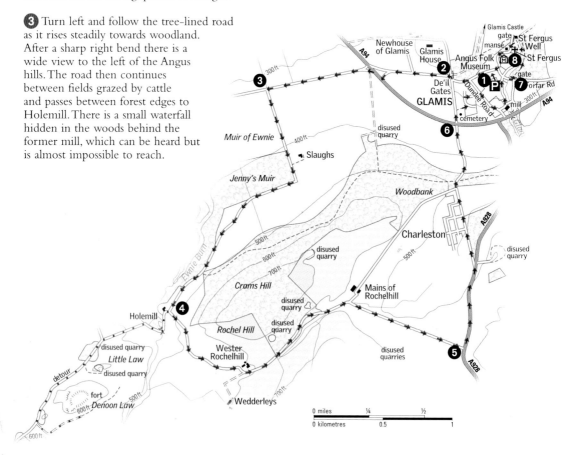

7 Over the stream, turn left through a gateway on a riverside path. Turn left over a footbridge and continue behind the kirkyard of St Fergus to St Fergus's Well, named after an 8th-century Irish missionary who founded a church at Glamis.

Walk back a short way and turn right up steps. Go through a gate and turn left on a road, the Kirkwynd, to St Fergus's Kirk. The building dates from 1790. Over the road in the manse garden is a carved Pictish stone, dating from the early 8th century and showing a Celtic cross and other symbols.

8 Follow the Kirkwynd past the Angus Folk Museum (NTS). Bear right into Main Street and turn left into the car park.

GLAMIS CASTLE

CENTRAL SCOTLAND

4 The Hermitage

Under the soaring trunks of Douglas firs to a forest-shrouded folly and a cascade-lined gorge.

LENGTH 5½ miles (3 hours)

PARKING The Hermitage car park, off A9 just north of Dunkeld

CONDITIONS Moderately demanding walk along riverside paths, lanes and forest tracks

REFRESHMENTS Full range in Dunkeld

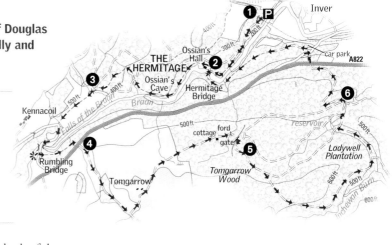

1 Take the footpath from the back of the car park, signposted to the Hermitage. Continue through mixed woodland of ash, beech, oak, larch and Douglas fir, inhabited by red squirrels. At first, the River Braan can only be heard, but after a while the roaring torrent can be glimpsed between the trees.

Further on, the path joins the riverbank. Continue walking along it, upstream, to reach Hermitage Bridge, where the path divides.

2 Do not cross the bridge, but stay on the same side of the river to reach Ossian's Hall. This 18th-century folly is named after a legendary Celtic bard, whose supposed collected poems – translated and published in the 1760s to wide acclaim – turned out to be a literary fraud.

Continue along the signposted Braan Walk to reach Ossian's Cave – a round stone hut – then follow an uphill path away from the river, over a crossing path, to join a track along the edge of a felled area.

3 Turn left and continue on the track to cross a footbridge over Craigvinean Burn. This section of the walk follows the line of the old military road between Coupar Angus and Amulree. Continue ahead until you emerge onto a minor road. Turn left on the road and walk downhill to Rumbling Bridge, which stands at the head of dramatic waterfalls. Immediately beyond the bridge, there is access, on the right, to the rocks above the Falls of Braan, a long, wild stretch of foaming rapids that are contained in the chute of a narrow, rocky gorge.

Continue up the minor road for a short distance, then turn left on a woodland path that leads to a clearing with more dramatic views of the bridge and the gorge. The path winds up a slope, crossing two small footbridges before reaching the A822.

4 Cross the road and continue on the track ahead, signposted to Glen Garr. After about ⅓ mile, turn left, following a signpost, and go past Tomgarrow Farmhouse into Tomgarrow Wood, a predominantly birch woodland. Walk past a cottage in the wood and cross a small burn, a short distance ahead, to arrive at a gate in a deer fence.

5 Go through the gate and continue along a forest track to a junction. Turn right onto the track signposted Inchewan Walk and follow it as it bends left above Inchewan Burn. Walk straight on at the next junction, following the signs for Inver, to arrive at yet another junction of tracks.

Keep right, following a track that offers views beyond the tops of the forest trees to the heather-covered hills. Continue until you reach a junction of broad tracks.

6 Turn left onto the track signposted Braan Walk. Continue downhill as the track bends left then right before reaching a gate leading onto the A822. Cross the road and follow the track ahead to a minor road lower down the slope, and then turn right into Inver car park. Cross to the far left-hand corner of the car park and follow a broad path that leads towards Hermitage Bridge.

On the way to the river, there are good views of a 65m (212ft) high Douglas fir growing on the far bank; it is said to be the tallest tree in Britain. Cross Hermitage Bridge and turn right immediately to retrace your steps beside the river to the Hermitage car park.

5 Comrie

Waterfalls and bubbling pools, an imposing monument, and woods that are home to red squirrels, roe deer, sparrowhawks and jays.

LENGTH 4½ miles (3½ hours)

PARKING Car park in School Road

CONDITIONS Good path and tracks. Steep climb to the Melville Monument

REFRESHMENTS Full range in Comrie

1 From the car park exit, turn right along the main street. Pass St Serf's, Comrie and Strowan's parish church on the left. Where the main road turns sharply left, signposted to Crianlarich, continue straight on past the Deil's Cauldron restaurant to reach a sign for the Glen Lednock Circular Walk.

2 Following the arrow, turn right on a track into deciduous woodland, where roe deer can sometimes be seen. Continue uphill along the winding track.

3 At a sign to Wee Caldron, make a short diversion to view the rapids on the River Lednock. Walk on to rejoin the main path, turning right. Continue uphill above the river and gorge.

4 Where the path levels out, at the side of a minor road, go right beside a wall parallel to the road. Soon a flight of wooden steps leads down to a platform overlooking the Deil's Caldron (Devil's Cauldron) – a bubbling pool of water fed by a waterfall. Legend has it that the hollow was the haunt of a water elf, called in Gaelic *Uris-chidh*, who enticed victims into the pool.
  Continue along the road to a gate on the left.

5 Turn left through the gate and climb the steep path up to the Melville Monument. Built in 1812, it commemorates Henry Dundas, 1st Viscount Melville, Lord Advocate for Scotland and a government minister under Pitt the Younger; he was known as 'King Harry the Ninth', such was his influence. On a clear day, the views are stunning. When the obelisk was struck by lightning in 1894, the steeplejack who repaired it claimed he could see Castle Rock in distant Edinburgh. Return to the road, turn left and continue to where it bends to the left.

6 Leave the road and follow the sign straight ahead on a rough track that leads around to Laggan Wood. Go down a short slope and across the river on the Shaky Bridge, so called because one end is balanced in a large sycamore tree. On the other side, turn right. A little farther on, cross a stile over a fence and then ascend some steps. At the top, turn right and continue along a farm track, which may be muddy.

7 The Melville Monument comes into view at the summit of Dun More. Moorland birds and birds of prey can be seen, as well as herons on the river. Bear left on the path away from the river and continue to a wall that runs along the edge of a forestry plantation.

8 Go through a gate into the woodland. Sparrowhawks, noisy jays, red squirrels and roe deer find shelter among the trees. Follow the track as it climbs and then descends through the trees. At a sign saying Circular Walk, continue ahead.

9 At a junction of tracks and another waymark sign, turn right. The path soon begins to descend steeply towards Comrie. The woodland becomes more open and there are fine views over the town and the surrounding countryside. Descend some steep steps and continue down a slope into the glen. Go right at a path junction with a wooden waymark sign. The path then bears slightly to the left, beside the river again on a more level stretch.

10 Pass a weir and follow the river path as it winds pleasantly through the glen. Go through a gap in a wall and turn right, following a sign to the village centre. Cross the river by a wooden bridge and follow the surfaced path to a junction and another sign to the village centre, pointing left. On reaching the main village street, turn right to return to the car park.

Map labels: Shaky Bridge, stile, 500ft, 600ft, gate, Glen, Dun More, gate, steps, Deil's Caldron (waterfall), Melville Monument, Lednock, 600ft, 500ft, Laggan Wood, Wee Caldron, 300ft, 100ft, weir, 200ft, COMRIE, St Serf, P, Dalginross

0 miles ¼ ½
0 kilometres 0.5 1

SCOTLAND

279

CENTRAL SCOTLAND

6 Killiecrankie

South from the battlefield where Bonnie
Dundee's Highlanders routed the forces of
William III, beside rivers and a loch.

LENGTH 8½ miles (4 hours)

PARKING Visitor centre car park outside village

CONDITIONS Undemanding

REFRESHMENTS Kiosk at visitor centre

1 A path leads from the car park to the visitor centre, whose information about the area includes the story of the 1689 Battle of Killiecrankie, when rebel Highlanders led by Viscount 'Bonnie' Dundee defeated a much larger government force.

Take the path leading from the rear of the visitor centre, signposted to the Pass, Soldier's Leap and Linn of Tummel. It goes down a flight of steps to the River Garry, where a short path to the right leads to Soldier's Leap, named after a fleeing English soldier who saved his life by

AUTUMN COLOURS, LOCH FASKALLY

jumping the 5.5m (18ft) chasm. Turn left and follow the path downstream, beneath Joseph Mitchell's impressive railway viaduct, 16.5m (54ft) high and over 152m (500ft) long, which was opened in 1863.

Continue through woodland, following the river for a mile to reach an old milestone and a footbridge over the Garry.

2 Turn right and cross the bridge. Turn left by the river and walk downstream to pass below Garry Bridge. Continue along the waymarked path, which veers away from the riverbank to some steps. Climb the steps and continue across a narrow, wooded neck of land lying between the confluence of the Garry and Tummel rivers.

A small stone beside the Linn of Tummel waterfall commemorates a visit by Queen Victoria in 1844. From the stone, walk upstream for about ¾ mile to Coronation Bridge, a small suspension footbridge financed by public subscription to commemorate the accession of George V to the throne.

3 Turn left and cross the bridge, then follow the path as it bends left and climbs up a slope before emerging onto a minor road. Turn left and continue along the road, following the right bank of the Tummel. There are fine views across Loch Faskally to 841m (2,760ft) Ben Vrackie and, beyond the head of the loch, to the Pass of Killiecrankie.

Continue past Clunie power station, where the hydroelectric energy from Loch Tummel is harnessed. Clunie Arch, a memorial beside the power station, is dedicated to the workers who lost their lives during the five years that it took to complete the project. The arch incorporates a section of tunnel that conveys the water from Loch Tummel under the mountain. The road bends round beside Loch Faskally, a narrow finger-like stretch of water, before reaching Clunie Footbridge.

4 Cross the bridge, which runs below the busy A9 road bridge, and turn left immediately on the far bank. Follow the waymarked shore path along the side of a small bay.

Beyond a second footbridge the path climbs away from the water's edge up the side of Dunmore Hill, meeting a broader path through the woodland. Turn left and continue towards Loch Dunmore, a small lake reached along a footpath branching to the right. Continue around the side of the lake to emerge onto a minor road.

5 Turn left and continue along the road to the signposted entrance to a freshwater fish research laboratory. Turn left along a footpath leading to the side of Loch Faskally, then continue on the shore path to the head of the loch and the confluence of the Garry and Tummel rivers.

The path follows the Garry upstream to rejoin the outward route of the walk at the footbridge over the river. Retrace your steps to the car park.

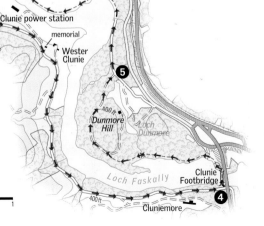

CENTRAL SCOTLAND

7 Braemar Castle

From a turreted castle where Highland Games are played to pathways with wide views of mountain peaks.

LENGTH 3½ or 4½ miles (2 or 3 hours)

PARKING Car park by Braemar Castle, on the A93, ½ mile north of Braemar

CONDITIONS Mainly moderate climbs; very steep detour up Creag Choinnich

REFRESHMENTS Full range at Braemar

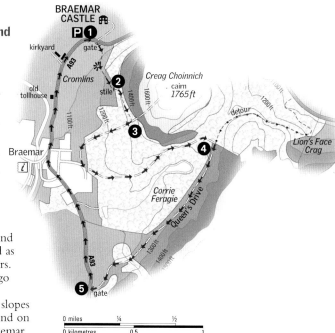

❶ From the car park, turn left on the A93 and walk up to the entrance to Braemar Castle. The castle, orginally constructed by the Earl of Mar in 1628 and rebuilt for the Farquharsons of Invercauld as a fortress-home in 1748, is open to visitors. Cross the road in front of the castle and go through a wooden gate.

Follow the stepped path up the lower slopes of Creag Choinnich, with fenced woodland on the left and glimpses of the turrets of Braemar Castle behind you. At a viewpoint with a striking panorama of the River Dee and the distant hills, an indicator board gives details of Deeside's wildlife and identifies 13 mountain peaks. The nearest, just left of Braemar, is the 860m (2,818ft) Morrone (from the Gaelic *Mòr Shròn*, meaning 'big hill'). The fields sloping down on the right are known as the Cromlins, from the Gaelic for 'crooked fields'. Continue on the stepped path as it levels out to reach a gate and a stile.

❷ Go over the stile into the wood and follow the markers to the right, along the occasionally narrow and indistinct path. Continue on this path to a waymarked T-junction with a wide track. To the left is a hard, steep ½-hour climb up to the 538m (1,765ft) summit of Creag Choinnich (Kenneth's Hill), capped by a cairn built by an English soldier in 1829.

❸ Take the right turning at the T-junction and follow the track as it goes downhill through larch woodland. Near the bottom of the hill, a path goes off to the right towards a fence, gate and some houses. Ignore this and continue on the track as it bends sharply to the left and goes uphill again through the forest. Continue ahead, ignoring a side track on the right, until reaching a sharp bend to the right and another T-junction. DETOUR *Turn left and follow the path up a gentle hill to the Lion's Face Crag. Any resemblance there may once have been to a lion's face has been eroded, but there are views across the Dee to the 17th-century Invercauld House and its vast estate.*

❹ Turn right onto a wide track, known as Queen's Drive after Queen Victoria, who often rode this way in her carriage from Balmoral Castle. Seats along the route provide many opportunities for appreciating the stunning view. Ahead is the heavy bulk of Morrone. Continue to a gate and a junction with the A93.

❺ Turn right on the road to Braemar, taking care to avoid the fast-flowing traffic. At the entrance to the village, on the right-hand side, a plaque on a house records an extended visit by the Scottish novelist and poet Robert Louis Stevenson in 1881. Stevenson wrote part of *Treasure Island* here.

Braemar is also home to the most prestigious of the Highland Games – the famous Braemar Gathering, held every year on the first Saturday in September. It includes athletic events, such as pole vaulting and tossing the caber – a 15m (49ft) long pole that weighs about 40kg (88lb), as well as piping competitions.

Follow the road through the village, past the old tollhouse and the ruins of a kirk, or church. Among the graves in the kirkyard is that of Peter Grant, the last of the Jacobite rebels and known as 'Dubrach' after the name of his farm. He died in 1824, aged 110. Continue on to the car park.

8 Glen More

Classic upland walking on a high and lonely trail, once used by bands of Highland rustlers.

LENGTH **5 miles (3 hours)**

PARKING **Glenmore Lodge National Mountaineering Centre, east of Coylumbridge**

CONDITIONS **Demanding hill walk on forest tracks and mountain paths; wear walking boots and carry waterproofs and a compass**

REFRESHMENTS **Shop at the visitor centre**

1 Turn right at the car park entrance and follow the broad forestry track away from Glenmore Lodge. Continue ahead for ¼ mile, ignoring tracks branching off to the left, to reach a bridge over the Allt na Feithe Duibhe – a small upland burn that flows into Loch Morlich.

2 Cross the bridge, which lies on the boundary to the SWT reserve of Ryvoan. The track skirts a strip of low-lying, boggy ground, flanking the burn and bounded on the far bank by a wall of Scots pines. The forest extends well up the slopes of Meall a' Bhuachaille, affording a glimpse of how the Highlands were before the Clearances, when the trees were torched to make way for sheep pasture. Follow the track, squeezed

against the side of the burn by the steep slopes of Creag nan Gall on the right, to An Lochan Uaine – a small lake cupped between the hills.

3 Follow the path between the loch and the burn. Ryvoan Pass, the narrow notch in the landscape beyond the far end of the loch, lies on the old Rathad nam Meirlach – a road down which caterans, marauding clansmen, from the glens around Lochaber, swept silently and swiftly on cattle-rustling raids. Continue along the track, which recrosses the Allt na Feithe Duibhe, before reaching a fork at the head of the glen.

4 Fork left towards Ryvoan Bothy, a shepherd's hut converted into a mountain shelter, its gable sharp against the skyline. The track now becomes stonier and more uneven, as it climbs steeply to arrive at a path junction beside the bothy.

5 Turn left on a winding uphill path over the open slopes of Meall a' Bhuachaille. Behind, the caterans' road snakes across a wide upland plateau on its way to the lowlands of Forres and Elgin. Continue upwards to the summit cairn. At 810m (2,657ft), Meall a' Bhuachaille is perfectly positioned for a good view over the surrounding countryside. Below, Glen More stretches from Loch Morlich into the ancient kingdom of Badenoch and the wild massif of the Monadhliath Mountains. Ahead and to the right, broad, ochre-coloured moorland surges around the dark green of Abernethy Forest. To the left, Bynack More, 1,089m (3,574ft) and Cairn Gorm, 1,245m (4,084ft), dominate a long ridge.

6 Walk straight on from the cairn, on a well-worn path towards Creagan Gorm, the next summit. The path descends into a broad saddle between the two high points, where it divides.

7 Go left and follow the downhill path over open ground to reach the upper boundary of the Queen's Forest. The path plunges below the tree line and broadens into a track along the banks of Allt Coire Chondlaith. Continue beside the stream, ignoring any side tracks. The track emerges by the visitor centre car park; walk past it to emerge on a minor road.

8 Turn left and follow the road through the forest, passing the Reindeer House, to reach Glenmore Lodge and its car park.

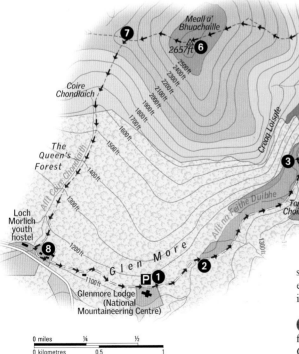

Meall a' Bhuachaille
2657ft
Ryvoan Bothy
Coire Chondlaich
Creag Loisgte
The Queen's Forest
Ryvoan Pass
An Lochan Uaine
Creag nan Gall
Tom Da Choimhead
Loch Morlich youth hostel
Allt Coire Chondlaith
Allt na Feithe Duibhe
G l e n   M o r e
Glenmore Lodge (National Mountaineering Centre)

0 miles ¼ ½
0 kilometres 0.5 1

CENTRAL SCOTLAND

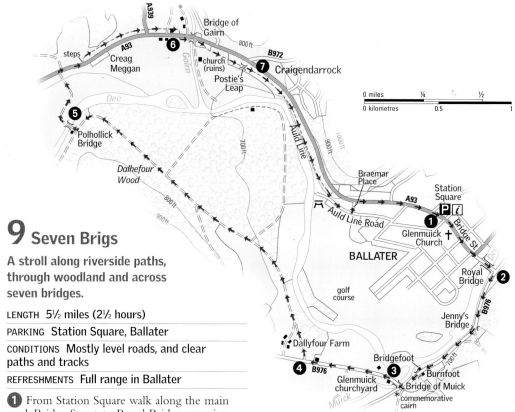

9 Seven Brigs

A stroll along riverside paths, through woodland and across seven bridges.

LENGTH 5½ miles (2½ hours)

PARKING Station Square, Ballater

CONDITIONS Mostly level roads, and clear paths and tracks

REFRESHMENTS Full range in Ballater

1 From Station Square walk along the main road, Bridge Street, to Royal Bridge spanning the River Dee. The bridge is the fourth to be built on or near this spot. The first and second were swept away by floods in 1799 and 1839 respectively; the third lasted until 1885, when the present bridge was opened by Queen Victoria.

2 Cross the bridge and turn right on a road wedged between the river and a steep wooded hill. Just before a bend to the right, at a spot known as Spinnin' Jenny's after an ancient witch, is the second bridge of the walk, Jenny's Bridge. Some steps lead from the low, moss-covered parapet on the left-hand side to a seat above.
    Continue past two facing cottages, called Bridgefoot and Burnfoot, and cross a third, small bridge over a stream, to a junction. A commemorative cairn marks the site of one of Queen Victoria's last public acts, when she took the salute at a march past of the Gordon Highlanders in 1899, before the regiment left for the Boer War.

3 Turn right over the Bridge of Muick, built in 1878. In Glenmuick churchyard, to the left, old tombstones include that of John Mitchell, who was apparently aged 126 when he died in 1722. To the right, the rounded summit of Craigendarroch towers above the village and its

golf course. Continue to a building and copse on the right, just before Dallyfour Farm (once home of the long-lived John Mitchell), and turn right on a wide gravel track.

4 Follow the track through the thick conifer woodland at Dalhefour Wood for just over 1 mile. After a sharp bend left at the river, turn right over the elegant Polhollick Bridge. The suspension bridge, 58m (190ft) long and 1.2m (4ft) wide, was built in 1892 to replace a ferry service. The deep, clear pool under the bridge is a popular angling spot.

5 Follow the track to the right along the river then left to the A93. Turn right on the road, being careful of the traffic, and cross where a sign points left to a disused quarry. Steps climb to a path above the road, clear of traffic. Turn right on the path, dropping down to cross another road, then continue to meet the A93 again.

6 Cross the road and turn left over the Bridge of Gairn, where the River Gairn, the River Dee's longest tributary, ends its 20 mile journey. To the right are the ruins of the old parish church of Glengairn. At a farm road on the

right, marked 'Bridge of Gairn Farm', turn right and then immediately left on a path that drops down to the Auld Line. In the 19th century this was the planned route of the Ballater to Braemar railway, but the railway line was never constructed and the path has now become a popular riverside trail. The walk's seventh bridge spans a ravine at Postie's Leap.

⑦ Follow the path along the river, with views across it of a wooden chalet built for the late Queen Mother. When you reach a picnic area, follow the path to Auld Line Road. Take the first road on the left, known as Braemar Place, then turn right on the A93 to return to the car park.

WINTER MORNING NEAR BALLATER

CENTRAL SCOTLAND

10 Clash Wood

Beyond forest and over moorland to a hilltop commanding views from the Moray Firth to the Cairngorms.

LENGTH 6½ miles (3 hours)

PARKING Car park along a minor road off the B9008, just north of Tomnavoulin

CONDITIONS Rough, muddy going in parts, with some steep stretches; exposed on high ground

REFRESHMENTS Shop in Tomnavoulin

1 Cross the stile leading from the car park into Clash Wood. Follow the signs for the Glenlivet Crown Estate Walk 9, on a forestry track that winds uphill. Many small birds, including blue tits and greenfinches, live in the woodland, though they are more often heard than seen among the dense conifers. Pass a ruined house on the right and continue to a junction with another forestry track on the right. Turn right. There are views ahead and to the right to

Ben Rinnes and the Ladder Hills. Follow the track as it bends left and goes back downhill before meeting a waymarked junction.

2 Go right at the junction, following signs for Glenlivet Crown Estate Walk 5, to reach a gate and stile across the track. Cross the stile into open grazing land, then bear to the right on a poorly defined path to reach the corner of a forestry plantation, higher up the slope. Continue along the edge of the plantation, with rough moorland rising to the right. The path bends to the right, away from the plantation, onto the shoulder of a hill, giving views over heather moorland to the Hills of Cromdale. Stay on the path, which goes gently downhill to meet a waymarked junction with the Speyside Way.

3 Turn left and follow the path along the upper boundary of a forestry plantation. The moor to the left is home to roe deer, frogs and dragonflies. Go straight on from the edge of the plantation, up a steep slope to the summit of the 570m (1,870ft) Carn Daimh, from which the Moray Firth is visible on a clear day.

4 Follow the steep track downhill to the boundary of more forestry, then continue along the edge of the plantation to a stile by a gate. Cross the stile and follow the track ahead, as it bends sharp left deep into the forest, to reach a waymarked junction.

5 Turn left and follow the signs for Tomnavoulin and Glenlivet Crown Estate Walk 5. A view over fields and moorland soon opens up to the right. Continue through a gate leading to open pasture, and carry on downhill on the waymarked farm track. To the right, the Craighead croft ruins stand by Slough Burn, which the track fords before climbing to a belt of trees. Continue through the trees to reach gorse scrub and rough pasture at the side of the Allt a' Choire burn.

6 Ford the burn, then turn right and follow it downhill, past Westertown croft. The track merges with the one from Eastertown croft to Tomnavoulin. Continue ahead across the track on a waymarked path. Cross two stiles and follow a fence between the forestry and pasture.
As the fence turns away to the right, follow the path into the plantation to meet the Clash Wood forestry track. Turn right on the track and retrace your steps to the car park.

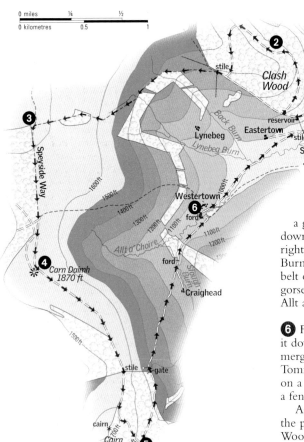

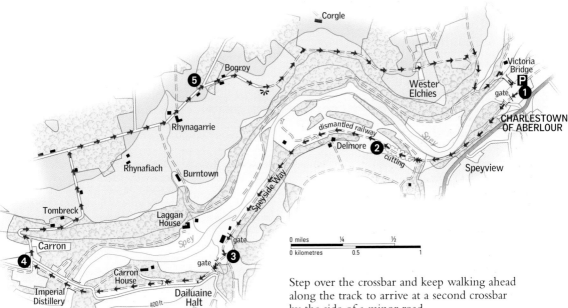

11 Aberlour

Along a disused railway beside the silvery Spey, passing distilleries, then through fields and deer woods above the river.

LENGTH 6½ miles (3 hours)

PARKING Riverside car park off High Street in Charlestown of Aberlour (called Aberlour)

CONDITIONS Mostly level tracks and lanes

REFRESHMENTS Full range in Aberlour

1 Turn left on the riverbank and walk upstream past Victoria Bridge, a suspension footbridge nicknamed 'the penny bridge' because of the toll once claimed from all who wished to cross by a local landowner. Follow the waymarked Speyside Way through a gate. The path bends slightly to the left, away from the river, to cross a footbridge over the Burn of Aberlour.

Continue along the track, which follows the route of a dismantled railway, into mixed woodland. The track bends right, to the side of the river, then passes under a road bridge and enters a cutting.

2 Continue ahead through the cutting to emerge at the far end in an open field with a view of the Spey to the right. Here buzzards can often be seen soaring high above and the aroma of malt-whisky distilling is sometimes detected on the breeze.

The track enters woodland once more, passing a whisky distillery on the right and reaching a gate with a low crossbar beside it.

Step over the crossbar and keep walking ahead along the track to arrive at a second crossbar by the side of a minor road.

3 Continue over the crossbar, keeping the road to the left. The track runs alongside the road, passing the old platform at Dailuaine Halt and going under a bridge carrying the driveway to Carron House. Descend a slight gradient to emerge at an old level crossing. Continue ahead, along a track on the far side of the road. Cross an old railway bridge over the Spey, upstream from a road bridge, and carry on parallel to the road. Pass the platform of another halt, among trees to the left, before arriving at a fork.

4 Go straight on, leaving the Speyside Way, which branches left past the Imperial Distillery. The track immediately meets the main street of Carron. Turn right and walk through the village, beyond which the road winds uphill through woodland, with a margin of copper beech trees. Continue to a T-junction. Turn right and follow the road through managed woodland, where deer can often be seen. Continue straight on, ignoring the left turning to Archiestown, for ½ mile to a fork on the edge of a conifer plantation.

5 Take the right fork. Beyond Bogroy croft, the narrow, surfaced road deteriorates into a farm track, which bends around the open hillside above the River Spey. The track runs through a belt of conifers, then follows the upper boundary of the plantation, with the fields of Corgyle croft on the left.

Continue downhill through woodland and over fields to Wester Elchies farm. Beyond the farm buildings, the track meets a narrow road. Turn right and walk downhill, around a sharp, left-hand bend, to reach Victoria Bridge. Cross the bridge and retrace your steps to the car park.

CENTRAL SCOTLAND

12 Balloch Wood

Peaceful woodland with spectacular views across Banffshire, following a burn to the Falls of Tarnash.

LENGTH 4½ or 7 miles (2½ or 4 hours)

PARKING On side of forestry track just east of Herricks water treatment works, east of Keith

CONDITIONS Well-used tracks; steep climb up Meikle Balloch Hill

REFRESHMENTS None on walk; full range in Keith

1 With the water treatment works to the left, take the higher of two forestry tracks, heading uphill through the plantation. At a junction of paths, turn right. After about 300m turn left on a narrow path marked by a small pole in the first firebreak on the left. Follow the path uphill. The path becomes steeper and emerges at the edge of a plantation near the top of heather-clad Meikle Balloch Hill. Continue half-left, aiming for a large cairn on the skyline.

2 From the cairn, walk to another cairn ahead and continue to the hill summit, from which there are glorious views. From the triangulation pillar at the summit, follow the path along the hilltop and enter the plantation again. After a slight uphill stretch, the track passes a hilltop clearing on the left. Continue to a division of tracks.

3 Fork right on the downhill track. Pass a small quarry on the left to a junction of tracks. Turn right and continue to another junction of tracks. **SHORT CUT** *Continue through the plantation, crossing two streams. The track reaches a junction met at the beginning of the walk. Continue ahead and take the next track on the left to return to the start of the walk.*

4 Turn left. At a meeting of paths on the forest edge turn right along the Old Military Road, continuing ahead at a field boundary for just over ½ mile to a gate. Go through the gate onto a farm track. At a junction of tracks turn right to Mains of Birkenburn. Follow the track through the farm, then turn left on a rough road. Follow the road to the Bridge of Tarnash.

5 Just before the bridge, turn right down steps into woodland, with a burn on the left. Follow the path; soon the Falls of Tarnash come into sight. Cross the bridge ahead and follow the path, turning sharply left along the burn. After crossing another bridge over the burn, the path bends left and uphill through birch scrub with trees to the right.

At a T-junction turn right and follow the track, bearing left. At a junction turn right on the road and continue ahead for almost 1½ miles through the woodland of Dunnyduff Wood, then through farmland, back to the parking place.

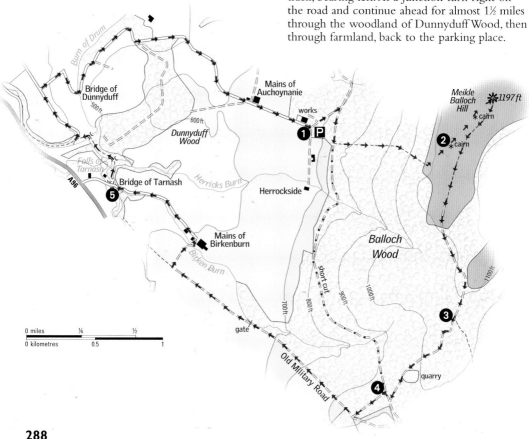

THE AUTUMN COLOURS OF DUNNYDUFF WOOD

CENTRAL SCOTLAND

13 Cullen

Past a loch and a sandy beach to the ruins of Findlater Castle, returning along the rocky shore of the Moray Firth.

LENGTH 6½ or 7 miles (3½ or 4 hours)

PARKING Small car park south of Cullen

CONDITIONS Paths near cliffs can be dangerous when wet, especially at Findlater Castle

REFRESHMENTS Cafés and hotels in Cullen

1 Walk through the gate at the end of the car park and turn left on the road, then turn right on a woodland track and climb to a stone bridge across an old railway cutting. Turn right after the bridge onto a grassy track through conifers.

2 At a fallen log carved into a bench, turn left on an uphill grassy track to Crannoch-hill Loch. Keep left of the loch, then turn right along the edge of the wood. Fields spread to the right and gorse and pasture to the left, filled with the sound of linnets, yellowhammers, whitethroats, tits and finches in summer.

3 At a junction of tracks turn left, then take the next right and pass Logie House on the left where jackdaws wander through the ruins. Go through a gate and continue along the field edge towards the sea. Near the headland, follow the path as it turns right down a gorse-fringed gully.

4 Just before the rocky shore, fork right to Sunnyside beach. Follow the grassy path, gradually rising to clifftop level, with fields on the right and gorse scrub and gullies on the left.

5 Follow the track as it winds left to the ruins of Findlater Castle, precariously placed on the cliffs below – take care on the slippery stones around the ruins. From the 16th century the castle was the seat of the Ogilvies of Findlater and Deskford, but was abandoned in favour of Cullen House in the 17th century. Return along the same track to the clifftop.

DETOUR *Turn left inland to visit a 16th-century dovecot originally associated with the castle.*

6 Retrace the route back along the shore. At the gully reached at the end of **4**, continue ahead. Beyond the next headland the path enters a bay, with fulmars and gulls nesting on the cliffs above in summer.

7 Climb steps leading around the headland. On a clear day the view stretches to the hills beyond the Moray Firth. Climbing out of a narrow gully, follow the path through another, longer bay.

8 Just before a disused salmon bothy – a shelter for salmon fishermen – fork left on a wide grassy track to clifftop level, with a caravan park on the left. Follow the path as it turns left, then continue to Seafield Street, the main street running through Cullen.

9 Turn left, walk up the hill and follow the road out of town. Beyond Seafield Farm, go through a gap in the fence on the left to join a disused road to the car park.

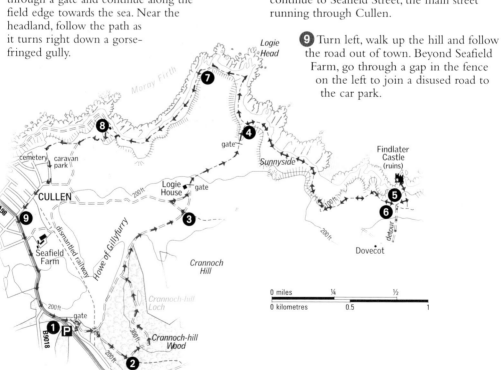

14 Glen Nevis

An energetic wander along a glen of almost Himalayan grandeur, with a magnificent gorge and a cascading river.

LENGTH **3 miles (1½ hours)**

PARKING **In car park at end of road at head of Glen Nevis, from Nevis Bridge east of Fort William**

CONDITIONS **Rocky footpaths, exposed in places and with some unstable edges; thick bracken may obscure paths. Use footwear with firm grip and good ankle support, and do not attempt walk in wet or icy conditions**

REFRESHMENTS **Café and restaurant at Glen Nevis**

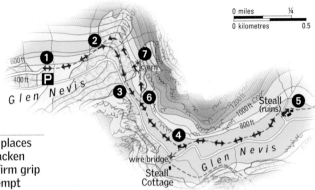

1 From the back of the car park follow the obvious path into the trees, ignoring a diversion to the right shortly after the start. The path climbs higher and crosses two streams. Soon a view is glimpsed towards the Steall waterfall.

2 Just beyond the second stream, the path climbs higher and becomes rockier; there are several scrambly sections where you may need to use your hands for balance.

The narrow, rocky footpath traces its way through the woods high above the foaming, churning waters of the River Nevis as it hurries down from the Steall meadows above to the comparatively flat lower Glen Nevis. The raging waters have gouged pots and cauldrons out of the riverbed, and the steep walls of the gorge have been hollowed and smoothed into great chambers. And all the while the rock walls echo to the sound of this aquatic thunder. Continue to where the path and river come closer together.

3 Squeeze between the rocks into upper Glen Nevis, a flat area of meadows. Suddenly the whole scene changes; instead of the tumbling, raging waters, the river takes on a stately air as it meanders across the meadowflats of Steall. Ahead, like a white slash against the cliffs of Sgurr a'Mhàim, is the 106.5m (350ft) Steall waterfall. At its foot is a tiny whitewashed house – Steall Cottage – now a mountaineering club hut, which can be reached only by crossing a three-strand wire bridge across the river.

4 Do not cross the river. Instead, continue straight ahead. After passing a gravelly area the path deteriorates and it is best to head for the riverbank. Continue for ½ mile to the ruins of a croft at Steall.

5 From Steall, retrace your steps back past the wire bridge to the entrance to the gorge.

6 Just before two giant boulders on the right, head uphill behind them; soon an overgrown path comes into view, zigzagging high up above the gorge. This was the path used by drovers with animals such as cows, mules and donkeys, which couldn't manage the track through the gorge. It has superb views up to Sgurr a'Mhàim, and down Glen Nevis towards the sweeping ridges of Mullach nan Coirean.

Follow the zigzags up to a grassy plateau crowned by a cairn. The Highlands are dotted with these piles of stone and rock. Some occur naturally, perhaps where rocks have gathered at the base of an eroding cliff, providing a den for foxes or a holt for otters. But cairns are usually man-made, and the oldest in Scotland are thought to have been built about 5,000 years ago to mark places of burial. Since then, most cairns, such as the one here, have simply been placed as waymarks on mountain paths. Others have been built as memorials to the dead in Scotland's countless battles, to honour local figures or to commemorate great public events.

7 From the cairn the path descends through pines, oaks and rowans. Follow the indistinct path as it zigzags back to the lower path at **2**, then continue to the car park.

CENTRAL SCOTLAND

15 Kinlochleven

Real high-level walking, with views of a remote fiord-like loch among imposing mountains.

LENGTH 7½ miles (4½ hours)

PARKING Car park just off B863 on south side of bridge over River Leven

CONDITIONS Generally good; some muddy sections

REFRESHMENTS Mamore Lodge Hotel

1 Leave the car park and cross the bridge over the River Leven, then take a tarmac path on the right, marked by a West Highland Way sign. Follow the path through trees to a road.

Cross the road, then cross half right over the open crescent and follow Loch Eilde Road to its junction with Lovat Road. Go straight ahead on a path that climbs gently into trees. Continue to a path on the right, just before houses, then turn right and follow the path a short distance to another path junction.

2 Fork left then, at a fence, keep straight on to follow a stony path through woods, passing a pudding-shaped hillock on the left known as Tom na Seilge. On the right, through the trees, are fine views of the river. Continue along the path for about ½ mile to a footbridge that spans Allt na h-Eilde stream.

3 Cross the bridge and continue to a division of the path. Fork left through birch scrub. The muddy path descends through a gap in a drystone wall and begins to climb a series of steep zigzags. Eventually the path begins to level off.

4 Follow the path as it bears right, high above the gorge of the Allt na h-Eilde, then begins to climb again in wide zigzags. The small grassy knoll on the right of the path makes a good viewpoint, with views across Kinlochleven to the high tops of the Mamores and south to the Aonach Eagach.

Eventually the path meets a pipeline that runs from Loch Eilde Mór to feed the Blackwater Reservoir, which is part of a huge hydroelectric power system.

5 Pass the pipeline and go left, following the path above the pipeline to a footbridge at the outflow of Loch Eilde Mór.

6 Turn left to cross the bridge and continue on a muddy path, going away from the loch, to where a track joins from the right.

7 Continue ahead, ignoring paths on the left and right, descending as the track follows the curves of the southern slopes of Na Gruagaichean.

8 At Coire na Bà the path crosses the Allt Coire na Bà by a footbridge. Keep descending and drop below a house to reach the Mamore Lodge Hotel. Keep on the track above the hotel to enjoy a wonderful view down Loch Leven, with the Pap of Glencoe on the left and Beinn na Caillich on the right. Ahead is a zigzag path that runs up the northeast slope of Beinn na Caillich. Old game stalking paths such as these are a feature of the area and are much appreciated by hill walkers.

Continue to a marker post on the left. The white thistle emblem indicates the West Highland Way, the first official long-distance trail in Scotland. The path runs from Milngavie, just north of Glasgow, for 96 miles to Fort William.

9 Turn left on the path. Soon after the path enters trees, bear left at a fork. Continue ahead, crossing a minor road, as the path makes its long descent to meet the B863. Turn left to return to the bridge over the Leven and the car park.

Map labels

Coire na Bà **8**

Na Gruagaichean

Ruigh Larach na Daraige

7

1400 ft
1200 ft
1000 ft
800 ft

Allt Coire na Bà

Allt nan Slatan

Allt a Chumhainn

Allt Seileach

Loch Eilde M'r

6

9

mast

1100 ft
1000 ft
700 ft
600 ft
500 ft
400 ft
300 ft
200 ft

West Highland Way

Mamore Lodge Hotel

Allt Coire an Eoin

Meall an Doire Dharaich

1400 ft

1300 ft

Allt Sloch...

Allt na Feàrna

Creagan Sgiathan

1200 ft
1100 ft
1000 ft
900 ft
800 ft

Kinlochmore

school

2

Tom na Seilge

KINLOCHLEVEN

P **1**

aluminium works

Leven pipeline

Tòrr Garbh

200 ft
300 ft
100 ft

100 ft

Allt na h-Eilde

400 ft
500 ft
600 ft
700 ft

water pipeline

Leitir Bo Fionn

5

3

4

0 miles   ¼   ½
0 kilometres   0.5   1

Photograph caption

LOCH LEVEN FROM THE SLOPES OF NA GRUAGAICHEAN

CENTRAL SCOTLAND

16 Inchree

Forest tracks and waterfalls, superb loch views and a military road built in the 18th century.

LENGTH 3 miles (2 hours)

PARKING Forest Enterprise car park off A82 just south of Corran

CONDITIONS Good, occasionally steep, forest tracks and paths

REFRESHMENTS Bar and restaurant at Inchree, hotels in Onich

1 Leave the car park at the sign pointing to the waterfalls and follow the path round in front of some superb ornamental gardens in one of the forestry houses. Follow the path ahead for about ¼ mile to reach a viewing platform above the falls of the Abhainn Righ, which tumble over rocky steps. The impressive waterfalls are used by an activity centre for canyonning. From here there are also superb views opening out across Inchree and the waters of Loch Linnhe to the high hills of Ardgour.

2 From the viewing platform, follow the path upwards, passing two more viewing platforms, to reach a forestry track.

3 At the junction with the track, turn left and follow the track down for about ½ mile. The walk is now waymarked with red marker posts. Eventually you reach a junction with a path.

4 Turn right and climb uphill on the path, which follows the line of an old military road. This road ran over the hill to Corrychurrachan and is believed to have been built in the 18th century by Major William Caulfield, who followed General Wade as a builder of military roads in this area. The roads were constructed with government money to enable the movement of troops and supplies for the control of the Highlands and its people.

After the path crosses a bridge over a stream, it begins to zigzag and climbs quite steeply. At the top of the steep rise there is a log seat for those wanting to enjoy the view.

Continue along the path as it now rises gently, to reach an old quarry.

5 Just beyond the quarry, at a junction, the old military road continues straight ahead as a green path. Do not follow it, but instead turn left onto the main forest track, which soon swings left and descends back to Inchree down the southeast slopes of Druim na Birlinn.

As you descend, with fine views of Loch Linnhe opening up in front, look left where the trees in a large gorge have been felled. This has been done to allow natural regeneration of broad-leaved species and native pines, to enhance the natural rock formations of the gorge, which contain marble. Over the hill immediately ahead is the dramatic double-peaked mountain of Beinn a'Bheithir, rising to over 1,005m (3,300ft) above the Loch Leven narrows.

Continue on the track to a signpost at a right-hand bend.

6 Turn left onto a path and follow it as it descends through trees to reach a footbridge over a burn.

7 Cross the bridge and follow the track below the buildings, back to the starting point of the walk.

0 miles ¼
0 kilometres 0.5

17 Benderloch

An exciting climb through forest for spectacular views from the Eagle's Eyrie and Beinn Lora.

LENGTH 4 miles (2½ hours)

PARKING Forest Enterprise car park, just south of Benderloch

CONDITIONS A fairly undemanding climb along forest paths to a bare 305m (1,000ft) summit

REFRESHMENTS None on walk; hotel and shop in Benderloch; full range in Oban

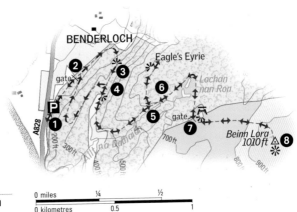

1 Take the footpath leading from the back of the car park, turning left by the information sign. Follow the red and blue marker posts along a well-made forest path, which leads past houses on the left to a gate. Go through the gate to a junction of paths immediately beyond it.

2 Turn left, still following the red and blue waymarks. The path begins to climb steadily through deciduous woodland. Beyond a sharp right-hand bend, the gradient steepens as the path approaches a viewpoint across Loch Linnhe to the mountains of Ardgour.

3 Continue from the viewpoint, climbing steeply. Beyond the top of the slope, the path levels out for a stretch, with forest on both sides, before arriving at a fork.

4 Fork left on a path with blue waymarks. It starts to climb again, skirting a clearing on the right that offers views across the Firth of Lorn to the Isle of Mull. The path twists and then climbs a particularly steep slope, to a junction signposted to Eagle's Eyrie on the left and to Beinn Lora on the right.

5 Turn left and walk up to Eagle's Eyrie, a viewpoint with a magnificent outlook across Lynn of Lorn and the broad expanse of Tralee Bay, and out beyond Lismore Island to the hills of Morvern and Ardgour. The Isle of Mull stretches away to left and beyond it are the outlines of the Garvellachs and the summits of the Paps of Jura.

Return to the signpost and take the Beinn Lora path, climbing steadily to a clearing around Lochan nan Ron, a reedy little lake where roe deer may sometimes be seen. The path divides at the edge of the clearing.

6 Fork left around the clearing that surrounds the little lake. The path then bends to the right and climbs over rough, uneven ground to reach a gate in a deer fence, with a picnic table beside it.

From the fence, which marks the upper boundary of the woods, the Moss of Achnacree – low-lying, flat land between the base of Beinn Lora and Loch Etive – can be seen to the south, and Connel airfield is also visible. The Isle of Mull lies to the west.

7 Go through the gate onto the mountainside. From here it is about ½ mile to the summit of Beinn Lora, along a path that can be very wet and boggy. The views from the top, however, repay the effort, although Beinn Lora is a relatively low peak, only just exceeding 305m (1,000ft).

Ahead lies Ardmucknish Bay; on its far shore the ramparts of Dunstaffnage Castle can be seen. Kerrera and the islands southwards are strung along the channels of Argyll's coast. To the right the narrow Sound of Mull slices between the island and the Morvern and Ardnamurchan peninsulas. The horizon behind is crowded with the hills of Lochaber and Appin, while 1,126m (3,695ft) high Ben Cruachan is distinctive among the throng of mountains spreading eastwards.

8 Retrace your steps from the top of Beinn Lora to the edge of the clearing and the path to the right that loops around Lochan nan Ron. Continue on the path, past the turning to Eagle's Eyrie, and walk on down the steep section to where the path divides at **4**.

Turn left and follow the red and blue waymarked route downhill through pine forest, which gives way to deciduous woodland. The path bends right and rejoins the outward route of the walk just above the gate at **2**. Turn left back to the car park.

SCOTLAND

CENTRAL SCOTLAND

18 Kerrera

A ferry crossing to a tranquil island, then a walk with glorious views, passing a ruined castle with a violent past.

LENGTH 6½ miles (3½ hours)

PARKING At ferry jetty on mainland, south of Oban; then cross the Sound of Kerrera by the passenger ferry (about 5 mins)

CONDITIONS Easy, on tracks and coast paths

REFRESHMENTS None on walk; full range in Oban

1 At the jetty on Kerrera, face Ferry House and turn left. Follow the track along the side of the sound, skirting the wide Horse Shoe bay. The path passes to the right of Dail Righ, the King's Field, so named because the Scottish king Alexander II died there of a fever in 1249 while fighting to assert his sovereignty – Norway was then considered the island's mother country. Continue along the level track to the Little Horse Shoe bay and its ancient fort. The track then winds away from the coast to a fork.

2 Turn left through a gate onto a track leading between hillocks towards a house called Gylen Park. A short distance before reaching it, turn right on a path down to Gylen Castle, above the twin bays of Port a'Chaisteil and Port a'Chroinn.

3 The castle was built in 1582 by the MacDougalls of Dunollie and destroyed in 1647 by Cromwellian troops who carried off the Brooch of Lorn, allegedly worn by Robert the Bruce in the 14th-century Battle of Dalrigh. The brooch was returned to the MacDougall family in 1825. Continue on the coast path, which skirts around Port a'Chaisteil then climbs through a low saddle between rocky outcrops on the far headland to reach a junction with a track.

4 Turn left and follow the track, which winds above the small inlets of Ardmore Bay and Port Dubh, separated by Eilean Orasaig – a rocky islet joined to the land by a shingle spit. Beyond Ardmore, an old house on the right, the track passes through a narrow valley, hemmed in by the rocky hills of Cnoc na Faire and Torbhain Mór.

The track follows the route of an old drovers' road leading from Port Dubh, where clansmen once drove cattle ashore from Mull before taking them to markets on the mainland. Continue downhill to a bridge at Barnabuck, where there is a view to the left of Barr-nam-boc Bay and, across the Firth of Lorn, of the Isle of Mull.

5 Cross the bridge and, a short way beyond it, cross a second bridge. Follow the track, which bends right, away from the coast and over Am Maolan, with superb views of the Firth of Lorn. On a clear day the coast north of Oban and the hills of Glencoe, Ardgour and Morvern can be seen. The track winds gently downhill to join a track from Slatrach Bay.

6 Fork right towards the Sound of Kerrera and pass a collection of houses at Balliemore, to meet the outward route of the walk close to Ferry House. Turn left back to the jetty.

SUNSET VIEW FROM OBAN TOWARDS
KERRERA, LISMORE AND MULL

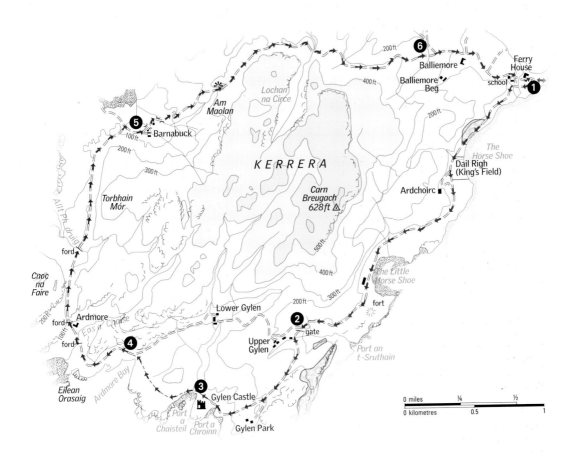

200 ft

Balliemore

6

Ferry
House

Balliemore
Beg

school

1

Am
Maolan

Lochan
na Circe

200 ft

400 ft

200 ft

Barnabuck

5

100 ft

The
Horse
Shoe

K E R R E R A

Dail Righ
(King's Field)

300 ft

Ardchoirc

Carn
Breugach
628 ft △

Torbhain
Mór

500 ft

Allt Ph druig

400 ft

ford

300 ft

The Little
Horse Shoe

Cnoc
na
Faire

200 ft

Lower Gylen

200 ft

fort

ford

Ardmore

100 ft

Eas a Chaise

4

2

gate

ford

Upper
Gylen

Port an
t-Sruthain

Ardmore Bay

Eilean
Orasaig

3

Gylen Castle

Port a
Chaisteil

Port a
Chroinn

Gylen Park

0 miles	¼	½
0 kilometres	0.5	1

Where wild means wild

The Scottish Highlands are famously untamed, but it is their remote promontories that offer the wildest walking.

Fine walking country may be found in many parts of Scotland, but it is in the Highlands that the truly rugged landscape lies. Here are sited the bulk of the mountains and glens, with their vistas of sweeping hillside and heathery brae, that are widely associated with Scotland.

Opinion varies as to where the Scottish Highlands actually begin and end, though it is generally agreed that this magnificent terrain comprises the Grampian Mountains and the mountains and glens of Easter and Wester Ross, as well as large chunks of high, hilly country further to the north and south. (In this guide, it is defined as the area north and west of a line running between Inverness and Fort William – see map, page 258.)

Far peninsulas

Some of the most amazing and uncultivated countryside, though, lies on the coastal margins of the Highlands, along the five ragged peninsulas of Morvern, Ardnamurchan, Moidart, Morar and Knoydart. These remote promontories poke out from the westward skirt of Scotland, their sea views dotted with islands – Mull, the Small Isles and Skye.

The wooded, roadless northern shore of Morvern looks across Loch Sunart to Ardnamurchan, a club-shaped peninsula whose narrow roads peter out to the west in tremendous, cliff-bounded walking country. Northeast of Ardnamurchan lies dark, deep Loch Shiel, with mountainous Moidart beyond that.

Moidart forms the southern rampart of Na Garbh Chriochan (the Rough Bounds), a tract of land devoid of roads and all but uninhabited, with scarcely a stalker's track to break the lonely miles. North again, Loch Morar divides the Morar peninsula. The A830 sweeps up to Mallaig along the western edge of Morar, but it is the one and only route through hundreds of square miles of rough terrain. You can walk a superb hill track from Bracorina on the north shore of Loch Morar across the narrow waist of North Morar, by way of the little loch of Lochan Innis Eanruig, to climb steeply down a trackless slope and reach remote Stoul with its few ruined cottages scattered along the shore. This lonely and poignant place looks across Loch Nevis to

the southern shores of Knoydart. This land is often described as 'unspoilt wilderness', and for once the hyperbole is close to the truth. A challenging 15-mile trek from the road end at Kinloch Hourn passes along the lower shore of Loch Hourn to the beautiful sandy bay of Barrisdale, then cuts in through the heart of Knoydart, down silent Gleann an Dubh-Lochain (Glen of the Little Black Lake), to reach the south coast of the peninsula.

Lesser mortals may take the ferry from Mallaig (though check winter sailings). But whether they go by land or sea, there's a fine reward at the journey's end. The Old Forge is a welcoming inn, whose proud boast is that it is the remotest pub in Britain. After a pint of Red Cuillin bitter

CAMUSDARACH BEACH, LOCH MORAR

at this award-winning establishment, slip along the shore to the Pier House restaurant for locally fished scallops and a delectable dish of Knoydart venison.

Watery haven

Up in the north of mainland Scotland, beyond the great mountain ranges and deep glens of the Grampian Mountains and Wester Ross, the landscape subsides into the million or so acres of blanket bog known as the Flow Country. Towards the west, Ben Hope (927m/3,040ft), Ben Loyal (873m/2,509ft) and Ben Klibreck (721m/2,367ft) rise up to greet the sky, while further east things level out to an undulating plateau of dun and green bogland – a seemingly

lifeless wilderness of peat and water. But appearances are deceptive. The bog, composed mainly of sphagnum moss, was created over thousands of years as new shoots grew from the mosses' dead remains. Richly acidic, it is both inedible and impervious to decay, yet it is an extraordinarily rich habitat for wildlife. In and around the water-sodden sphagnum, otters, hawks, eagles, red deer, wild cats, diving ducks, beetles, rare spiders, butterflies and dragonflies have made their home.

Walkers can strike out into the Flow Country, or take the train to Forsinard and follow the trails through the Forsinard Flows RSPB reserve, picking up information from the rangers along the way.

SCOTLAND

NORTH HIGHLANDS & ISLANDS

Deeply indented by sea lochs, Scotland's far northwest offers breathtaking vistas, while the offshore islands, with crystal-clear water and many sandy beaches, can seem almost Mediterranean on a fine summer's day.

CROMARTY

Cromarty Firth

detour

stile

stile

Sutors of Cromarty

Charlie's Seat

graveyard

tunnel

Cromarty House

200 ft

300 ft

gate

P

Sutors Stacks

coast guard station (disused)

gate

Cromarty Mains Farm

gate

gate

gate

stile

McFarquhar's Bed

0 miles ¼
0 kilometres 0.5

1 Cromarty

A clifftop walk around the coast between two firths, visiting a rocky beach and a village rich in history.

LENGTH 5 or 5½ miles (2½ or 3 hours)

PARKING Near coastguard lookout point at South Sutor, east of Cromarty

CONDITIONS Mainly good paths, but with some steep sections

REFRESHMENTS Hotels and tearooms in Cromarty

1 From the lookout point, walk along the metalled road towards the village of Cromarty. There are panoramic views over the Cromarty Firth and beyond, stretching as far north as Caithness on a clear day.

2 Where the road bends sharply to the right, continue ahead towards the farm buildings at Cromarty Mains. After a short distance, turn left, following a signpost to McFarquhar's Bed. Continue past the farm cottages and go through a gate. Continue ahead on the farm track and go through another gate into a field. Follow the track, go through the next gate and continue along an avenue of beech trees, which shade the path on sunny days. At the bottom of the field, go over a stile on the right to a clifftop area of wild flowers and bracken.

From this point on the clifftop, a steep, clearly defined path leads directly down to the shore at McFarquhar's Bed, where erosion has produced a number of natural sea arches and a sea cave, which can be found by bearing left along the rocky beach. Dolphins can sometimes be spotted in the waters of the Moray Firth. Return to the top of the cliffs.

3 Cross the stile back into the field and retrace your route uphill through the trees, continuing ahead at the gates. At the end of the track, turn right on the metalled road, then left on the road to Cromarty. Walk past the tunnel entrance to Cromarty House on the left – the staff and tradesmen's entrance. The house, an 18th-century mansion, is privately owned by the Laird of Cromarty. Concealed on the right, opposite the tunnel, is the peaceful graveyard of St Regulus. On the outskirts of Cromarty, the road continues alongside a wall.

DETOUR *Turn left and follow the road into Cromarty village, once a thriving fishing port. The birthplace of Hugh Miller, stonemason, geologist and writer, is now a museum. A tour of the old town begins from the museum at Cromarty Courthouse.*

4 Where the wall bends sharply to the left, take the path ahead to the left of a large, white house. Turn right along the coast, crossing two stiles, to join a well-marked path through woodland. The path rises steeply in places, but steps and a seat halfway up the hill make the route easier.

The Cromarty Firth stretches to the left, forming one of the largest natural harbours in Europe. The harbour was called Portus Salutis ('the harbour of safety') by ancient map-makers, and was used as an anchorage for the Royal Navy during both world wars. Follow the path back to the coastguard lookout.

2 Portmahomack

Gentle rolling farmland and two coastal villages, one facing the Sutherland coast and the other, the open sea.

LENGTH 5½ or 6 miles (3 or 3½ hours)

PARKING Village beachside car park

CONDITIONS Mostly level paths and minor roads

REFRESHMENTS Full range in Portmahomack

1 From the car park, turn right on the road, then turn right onto the road to Balnabruach. The road winds through the hamlet towards the sea, ending at a turning place by the last cottage. Take the grassy path towards the beach, skirting round a fence, to follow the shoreline. Birdlife is abundant, with oystercatchers, herons and sandpipers among the most common varieties.

2 Continue along the shoreline path, with views of the Sutherland coast and hills across the Dornoch Firth. The path can be muddy in places after rain, and it is occasionally easier to walk along the beach itself. Follow the path for about a mile to Balchladich. Just before a wooden house and outbuilding next to the shore, turn left through a gate into a field, then bear right to a gate at the top of the hill. Go through the gate and bear right to a stile by a farm track.

3 Turn left and follow the track uphill past the hamlet of Drumancroy. After a sharp bend left, the track rises gently through fields to a T-junction with a road. Turn right and follow the road as it bears right, then turn left onto a farm track, signposted to Rockfield farm. Continue to a broad path on the left, just before a pair of stone gate pillars and a wood.

4 Turn left on the path, cutting through rolling fields scattered with isolated farms, with a beech windbreak and a drystone wall on the right. In late summer, the ground is strewn with harebells. After about ½ mile the open sea comes into view. As the path nears the cliffs, it joins a narrow tarmac road, which drops down to the right to the former fishing village of Rockfield. From here, dolphins, porpoises, seals and cormorants can often be seen. Continue ahead to a sharp left bend.

DETOUR *At the bend, go through the gate ahead and continue on the track to Ballone Castle. The simple but imposing stone structure, built in the 16th century for the Earl of Ross, is now a private home.*

5 Follow the road left past Bankhead farm and Fairfield, where it zigzags through the farm buildings. Portmahomack now comes into view in the distance. Follow the road to a T-junction.

6 Turn right. Almost immediately on the right is an ancient well, still used to baptise the chiefs of the Mackenzie Earls of Cromartie. Continue uphill to the 18th-century Tarbat Old Church, with its dovecot tower. The church is now a museum, which has displays of objects found in local archaeological digs; inside are Pictish carved stones with 'vine scroll' borders, similar to those in the 8th-century Book of Kells.

Continue on the road past the old school and the golf club on the right. At a small junction, turn left downhill through Portmahomack village, past a row of cottages. At the bottom of the hill, turn left onto the main village street and walk past the small harbour, extended by the engineer Thomas Telford in the early 19th century, and along the seafront back to the car park.

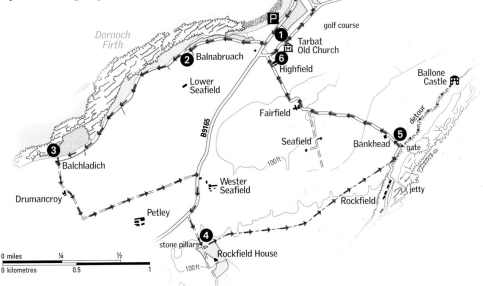

SCOTLAND

3 Littleferry

From sandy dunes and a wide beach to a trout-filled stream and the shores of Loch Fleet, teeming with wildlife.

LENGTH 4½ miles (2½ hours)

PARKING Car park on left at approach to village

CONDITIONS Mostly level paths and tracks; long sandy stretch of beach

REFRESHMENTS None on walk; full range in Golspie

1 From the car park, where an information board gives details of guided walks through the dunes – organised by the SWT – return to the road and turn left towards the former ferry pier. On the right is an old ice house, which was once used by the local estate for storing perishable foodstuffs, such as fish and meat. In winter, ice taken from local lochs or ponds was placed in the building, which would then remain cold throughout the summer months.

Just before the disused pier, turn left onto a path and walk past the old pier-master's house to the wreck of an old fishing boat. Turn left onto another path and then bear right along the grass-covered dunes. The path skirts the shoreline of the thin channel at the mouth of Loch Fleet, leading towards a spit of sand by the entrance to the loch. Numerous ducks and wading birds can be found in this area, and common seals can often be seen basking on the sandbanks.

2 Bear left and continue along the seashore. The beach, which starts out pebbly but soon becomes a mix of sand and pebbles, stretches out in front. Keep walking along the beach or follow a path on the edge of the dunes, with views ahead of the village of Golspie, Dunrobin Castle and the statue of the infamous 1st Duke of Sutherland, set high on its hill. Continue ahead for about 1¼ miles, past a go-kart track on the left, to reach a disused caravan site.

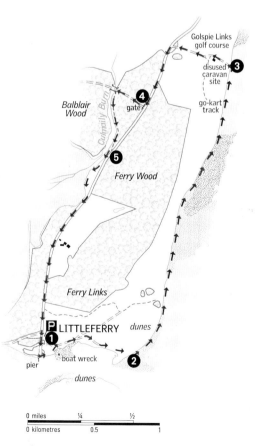

3 Turn left onto a tarmac track, passing the old site's former service building, and continue ahead across the fairways of the Golspie Links golf course, until reaching a T-junction with the road to Littleferry. Cross the road and turn left.

Follow the road for about ¼ mile to a gate on the right. This is the main entrance to Balblair Wood, which is managed by the SWT. The name 'Balblair' is common in Scotland; it is formed from two Gaelic words – *bal* or *baile*, meaning a 'town' or 'homestead' and *blair* or *blar*, meaning a 'plain'.

4 Pass through the gate and walk along the track ahead through the pine forest – home to roe deer, pine martens, red squirrels and crossbills – to Culmaily Burn, which flows into Loch Fleet. At the burn, do not cross the bridge but turn left and follow a narrow and frequently slippery path with a stream to the right. Trout can often be seen in the pools.

Continue on past a sluice gate on the right, which also forms a footbridge across the burn. Both the stream and the view now widen out unexpectedly, as the burn enters Loch Fleet, giving clear aspects of the southern and western shores of the loch.

5 Continue ahead, keeping the shore of the loch on the right, until you reach a pebbly bay. Here the shore meets the road to Littleferry. Follow the road to the right, with crofting land on the left and a plantation of conifers on the right, to return to the car park.

BEHIND THE BEACH NEAR LITTLEFERRY

NORTH HIGHLANDS & ISLANDS

4 Beinn Eighe

Through a remnant of ancient forest to the summit of a bare mountain and a glacier-carved gorge.

LENGTH 3½ miles (3½ hours)

PARKING Nature trails car park on A832 north of Kinlochewe, just past south end of Loch Maree

CONDITIONS Demanding mountain trail; walking boots and insect repellent essential

REFRESHMENTS None on walk; shop and pub in Kinlochewe, 2½ miles beyond car park

1 With your back to Loch Maree, walk to the top right-hand corner of the car park then follow the footpath through a culvert below the main road. Continue beside a burn, the Allt na h-Airighe, following the signposted mountain trail. The path passes a footbridge on the right and winds uphill through woodland, where a few Scots pines, remnants of the forest that once covered large areas of the Highlands, tower above more numerous birches.

2 Where the path and the burn diverge, fork left uphill into more open woodland. After ½ mile the path meets Alltan Mhic Eoghainn, a small burn, then winds beside it to the tree line. Once you are out of the trees there are views of rocky slopes rising from the far shore of Loch Maree, including the 981m (3,217ft) summit of Slioch.

3 At a footbridge, cross over and follow the zigzag path upwards. A few stunted trees cling to the hillside, but a ground cover of upland grasses and shrubby growth predominates – including heather, which gives cover to grouse and provides winter grazing for red deer. Eventually the path climbs less steeply, over bare country where much

THE SHORES OF LOCH MAREE, WITH SLIOCH BEHIND

of the rock is marbled with white quartzite and contains fossil evidence of primitive marine life. The gradient eases as the path climbs to a plateau ringed by mountains and reaches the highest point of the walk – marked by a cairn at 550m (1,804ft). The view ahead along the ridge is dominated by Ruadh-stac-Mór, which rises to 1,010m (3,313ft).

4 Turn right at the summit cairn, with Loch Maree lying far down the slope to the right, and follow the path downhill towards a cluster of mountain lochans. Alpine plants such as juniper, crowberry and alpine azalea lie low among rocks that may also hide ptarmigan – Britain's largest and rarest game bird, whose plumage changes from brownish grey in summer to white during winter.
Continue along the path, marked by numerous small cairns, to a small burn flowing into one of the lochans.

5 Cross the burn and follow the winding path towards Lunar Loch – the loch's name commemorates the first manned landing on the Moon. The path passes to the right of the loch, over a small burn flowing from it. Continue over a rise to An t-Allt, a bubbling mountain stream.

6 Cross the An t-Allt then follow the path towards the head of the Allt na h-Airighe gorge, marked by high bluffs rising more than 52m (170ft) from a woodland floor that is home to pine martens, Scottish wild cats, greater spotted woodpeckers and sparrowhawks. As you descend, the full length of the gorge becomes visible. Follow the path as it bends to the right along the top of the gorge and meets a stile over a fence.

7 Cross the stile into a small fenced enclosure intended to exclude grazing red deer, so that regeneration of the mountain vegetation can be studied. The view to the right emphasises the contrast between the wooded sides of the gorge and the exposed, treeless mountain above its rim.
Cross the stile at the far boundary of the enclosure and follow the path away from the edge of the gorge. Gleann Bianasdail, on the far side of Loch Maree, and Glen Docherty – to the right, beyond the head of the glen at Kinlochewe – are hanging valleys. An Ice Age glacier cut the main glen far deeper, leaving them high above the waters of Loch Maree after the ice melted 10,000 years ago. Continue downhill to a fork.

8 Fork right on a signposted woodland trail and follow it to the footbridge just before the road. Cross the bridge, turn left and retrace your steps to the car park.

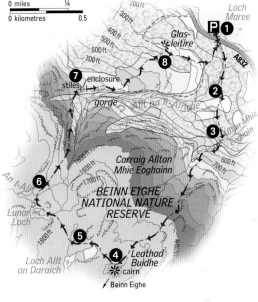

SCOTLAND

NORTH HIGHLANDS & ISLANDS

5 Poolewe

A coastal hinterland of rushing rivers, lonely lochs and gnarled rocks rolling down to the sea.

LENGTH 6 miles (3 hours)

PARKING Car park in village centre

CONDITIONS Fairly level hill walk

REFRESHMENTS Full range in Poolewe

1 Walk to the side of the River Ewe and turn left onto a minor road, which leads upstream past a church to a gate. Go through the gate and continue on the lane ahead, through deciduous woodland and past the old iron workings at Red Smiddy.

Continue through a second gate. Soon, fork left onto a track signposted to Kernsary Estate. The fork to the right leads to Inveran House, at the head of Loch Maree.

2 Continue uphill on the track, with mixed woodland of oak, birch, alder and rowan closing in on both sides. A break in the trees reveals views of Loch Maree and Inveran House and its garden. The track crosses open country at the head of the loch, before reaching a gate

that leads to a bridge over the Inveran river. From September 15 to November 15, walking beyond this point is restricted to weekends.

3 Go through the gate, where a board informs walkers that they are in a site of special scientific interest – the Letterewe Wilderness. Continue along the track, which skirts Loch an Doire Ghairbh, before bending left to run alongside a plantation of conifers. Beyond the plantation Loch Kernsary comes into view on the left and the track winds along close to the side of the loch. The area is scattered with the ruins of old crofts, and the ponies used for deerstalking can often be seen grazing. Cross the footbridge over the Kernsary river to reach a gate.

4 Go through the gate and turn sharp left, following a path beside a fence to a footbridge over a burn. Cross the bridge and follow the path along the slope above the loch, between clumps of trees and through an area of peat moor and heather, to arrive at a stile in a fence.

5 Cross the stile, then cross the burn a short distance farther on. The path continues to sidle along the side of the slope, a little above Loch Kernsary. In summer, this is a good place to see dragonflies. Cross a small burn flowing from the end of the lake and climb a low hill, before descending, past patches of gorse, towards the wide expanse of Loch Ewe.

6 Go through a gate leading into a small enclosure where the natural vegetation has been allowed to regenerate. Follow the path to a second gate at the far side of the enclosure. Pass through this gate and follow the track beyond, which leads past houses to a cattle grid and the main road. Turn left and follow the path on the sea loch side of the road back into Poolewe and the car park.

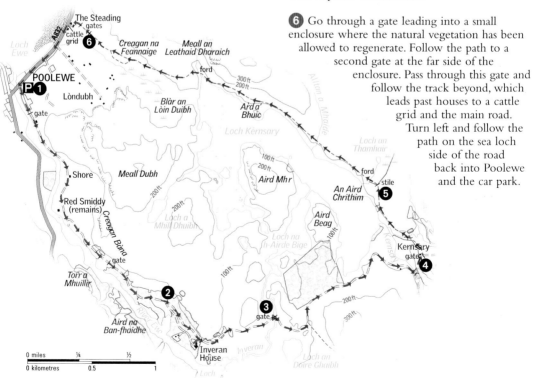

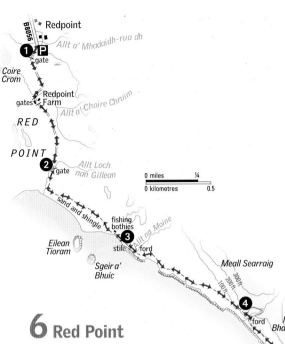

Coire Crom

RED

POINT

Redpoint Farm

gates

Allt a' Choire Chruim

Allt a' Mhadaidh-rua dh

Allt Loch nan Gillean

0 miles ¼

0 kilometres 0.5

Sand and shingle

fishing bothies

Eilean Tioram

Sgeir a' Bhuic

stile ford

Allt na Moine

Meall Searraig

Meall a' Bhaid-fhearna

Allt a' Bhaid-fhearna

ford

Allt na Criche Tuailhe

Allt na Criche Deise

ford

ford

ford

ford

ford

Craig River

Craig Youth Hostel

Lower Diabaig 3 miles

3 Cross the stile and carry straight on, over a small burn. The path shadows the rocky foreshore, before bending away from it slightly, up the lower, boulder-strewn slopes of Meall Searraig – the hill on the left – to the steep-sided Allt Serraig Burn.

4 Cross the burn and climb up the far bank to reach a broad turf-covered shelf between low rocky outcrops. Continue on through rough pasture with fewer outcrops, above a shore of rock ledges and shingle.

Several small burns flow across the path. These originate from springs and lochans higher up the slope. Continue along the boulder-strewn side of Meall na h-Uamha, a hill rising up to 288m (944ft), then descend onto the bank of the Craig River. Turn left and follow the rocky riverside path upstream for about ⅓ mile to reach a footbridge.

6 Red Point

Beside a remote strand favoured by fishermen to a long stony shore and views of the Western Isles.

LENGTH 8½ miles (4½ hours)

PARKING Car park at the end of the B8056, off the A832 south of Gairloch

CONDITIONS A long walk through undulating countryside

REFRESHMENTS None on the walk

1 Go through the gate leading from the car park and take the track signposted to Diabaig. Walk along the track to reach Redpoint Farm. Pass through the gates leading into and out of the farmyard. Walk ahead on the track, which becomes less well defined as it crosses open coastal fields. Here lapwings and skylarks are common.

2 On reaching another gate, go through it and turn right along the side of a burn to reach a sheltered sandy bay in the lee of Red Point. There are spectacular views out to sea from here to the Applecross Peninsula and beyond, to the isles of Skye, Raasay and Rona. Seabirds including oystercatchers, ringed plovers and sandpipers nest on the islets immediately off the beach, which are covered with swathes of sea pink or thrift in spring.

The path bends left just before reaching the beach, skirting a band of sand, shingle and stone, that gives way inland to dunes and rough pasture. Follow the path towards the far end of the bay, where there are three bothies (shelters), that are used during the salmon-fishing season, with poles on which the nets can be spread out. Continue to a stile in a fence.

5 Go over the footbridge and follow the path along the far bank, through rough pasture dotted with small copses, to Craig Youth Hostel. Pause here to enjoy the wildness of this remote coastal valley – a small isolated triangle of land that is cut off by rocky hills and the ocean – before walking the 4¼ miles back along the same route to the car park.

Although the walk turns back at the youth hostel, the path signposted to Lower Diabaig continues along the coast for a further 3 miles, ending at a small car park. This section of the path, which is clearly marked by cairns set amid the heather and rocky outcrops, climbs up the side of Sidhean a' Mhil, from where there are more superb views out to sea and of the Western Isles.

SCOTLAND

A SMALL LOCHAN WITH LOCH NA MEILICH BELOW

NORTH HIGHLANDS & ISLANDS

7 Raasay

Across the Sound of Raasay sea to a wooded and mountainous isle, with a flat-topped summit and wild scenery.

LENGTH 9 miles (6½ hours)

PARKING Sconser ferry terminal on the Isle of Skye; then take ferry to Raasay (20 mins)

CONDITIONS Rough paths

REFRESHMENTS Shop/post office at Inverarish

1 From East Suisnish village, turn left on the coastal road towards Inverarish. After about a mile, a road goes left to Inverarish.

2 Go straight on, following a youth hostel sign. At a junction turn left to cross a bridge over Inverarish Burn. Pass an information board and turn right, again following a youth hostel sign. The road rises through trees and emerges into open space, with a view across the Sound of Raasay.

3 At the youth hostel, continue ahead. Walk past a group of lochans over to the right, with the flat summit of Dùn Caan in the distance. Climb a short hill to reach a fork. Bear right and then into and out of a dip, crossing a burn. Continue on to a layby on the right, with a picnic table.

4 At the layby, turn sharp right onto a stony path, ascending steadily over rough ground. From the path, there are superb views of the Cuillin

Hills, over on Skye. Follow the path up to the top of the ridge, where there is another lochan. The hill of Dùn Caan is now visible in its entirety. Descend along the steep path leading to Loch na Meilich, at the foot of Dùn Caan. Bear right around the head of the loch, then climb up the track to the 443m (1,453ft) high summit.

5 Retrace your steps down from Dùn Caan. At the head of Loch na Meilich, go straight on, following the peaty and sometimes unclear moorland path towards the right-hand side of Loch na Mna.

At the head of the loch, pass between boulders and then go along the path that skirts the edge of the water. Continue over rough ground, keeping the Cuillin Hills ahead in the distance. Cairns mark the route.

The path soon joins the Inverarish Burn. Follow the burn down the glen, with the path twisting and turning over the peat, through heather and ferns, to reach a stile at the edge of a pine forest.

6 Cross the stile into the pines and descend to a forestry track. Turn left over a wooden bridge. Continue along the firm surface, cross over another wooden bridge and go through a gate. Keep following the track past the derelict buildings of a former iron-ore mine, to meet a road.

7 Cross the road to a sign, indicating the Miners Trail, which follows the line of a dismantled railway, dating from 1914. The railway once served the nearby iron-ore mine and was used to carry the ore to furnaces above the ferry jetty at East Suisnish.

Go over a stile, near to the Miners Trail sign, to enter woodland. Follow the path ahead to reach a former viaduct.

8 Turn onto the path that runs along the left of the viaduct and follow the line of viaduct pillars to reach a stream. Cross over the stream and climb up the banking onto the other side. Keep walking along the old railway trackbed up to a stile over a fence, on the border of the forestry plantation. Go over the stile and stay on the grassy path as it continues straight ahead, climbing gradually up to its highest point on this stretch of the walk. Keep following the path as it descends and leads back down into the village of East Suisnish and the ferry pier, to catch the boat back to Sconser on Skye. The old furnaces of East Suisnish's former iron-smelting works can be seen, standing close to the road on the left, just before the approach to the ferry terminal.

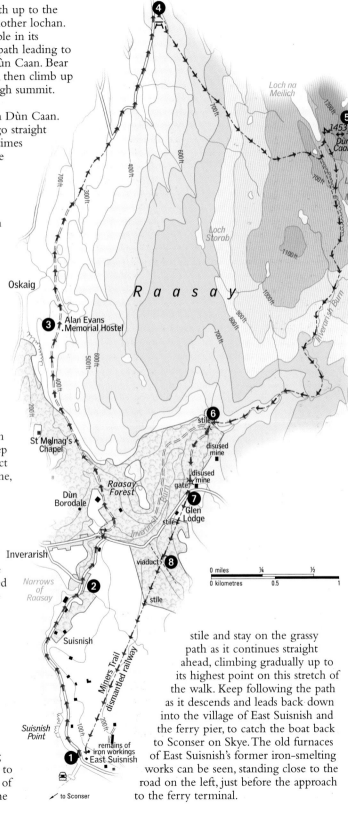

SCOTLAND

NORTH HIGHLANDS & ISLANDS

8 Sligachan

Serrated peaks and deep hollows, beside a rushing river with plunging waterfalls on the sleepy Isle of Skye.

LENGTH 5 miles (3½ hours)

PARKING In the parking bay on the south side of A863 Dunvegan road, off A87 south of Portree

CONDITIONS Rough paths with a gradual climb

REFRESHMENTS Hotel at Sligachan

1 From the parking bay, follow the gravel track, signposted to Glen Brittle on a small sign low down alongside the track. Ahead is the stunning backdrop of the Cuillin Hills, home to one of Britain's largest birds of prey – the golden eagle. Stretching south to Loch Scavaig in a continuous line of jagged peaks, the Cuillins contain no fewer than 11 Munros – summits over 914m (3,000ft). The corries and rockfaces along the ridge are the haunts of climbers who come to test their skills. Continue beside the Allt Dearg Mór river towards an isolated white cottage – Alltdearg House.

2 On the approach to the cottage, there is an obvious rough path on the right, next to an old stone gatepost with a crude waymark arrow. Take this path, which is somewhat boggy at first, with an open panorama of steep hills in front and behind. Follow the path to rejoin the river just before a waterfall, its whiteness contrasting starkly with the rocky blackness of the Cuillins.

3 Continue beside the river, with the path becoming much firmer and stonier. The group of peaks ahead is made up of Sgùrr nan Gillean, on the left, then Am Bàsteir, with its prominent 'tooth', and the steep spur of Meall Odhar completing the arc. Behind and to the left are the more rounded Red Cuillins. They are named after the reddish colour of their granite screes – quite different from the coarse-grained rock of the Black Cuillins. Continue along the path as it winds between boulders, climbing

gradually, with rowan trees clinging to the riverbanks. A cairn is reached and to the right, in the distance, the Old Man of Storr rock column is silhouetted against the sky.

4 Where the river flows through a gorge, follow the path away from the bank. The peaks of Sgùrr nan Gillean's Pinnacle Ridge become clearer on the left in a series of increasingly high steps. The path rejoins the riverbank and continues its gradual ascent, passing a beautiful gorge with a waterfall tumbling through it.

5 Where the path levels out a little, there is a superb view to the left into the bowl of Fionn Choire, dividing the peak of Meall Odhar from a ridge leading to one of the more accessible summits in the Cuillins – Bruach na Frithe ('Brae of the Forest'). In the foreground, a deep cleft carrying a watercourse splits the buttress, while high above are the serrations of the peaks.

Continue on the path to reach a small lochan, which marks the highest point on the pass of Bealach a' Mhaim.

6 Carry on past the lochan to reach a large cairn that overlooks the wooded green slopes of Glen Brittle, through which the River Brittle slowly meanders. The next section of the Cuillin Ridge towers broodingly to the left. The central peak here is Sgùrr a' Mhadaidh ('The Foxes' Peak').

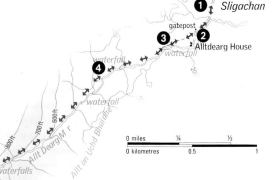

7 From the cairn, return along the outward route. This gives the walker an entirely different perspective of the surrounding landscape. It is the Red Cuillins that now dominate the view, with Loch Sligachan lying directly ahead and, in the far distance, a distinctive flat-topped summit. This is Dùn Caan, a short ferry-crossing away, on the island of Raasay.

SUNSET OVER THE CUILLIN HILLS, VIEWED FROM THE ALLT DEARG BURN

© RD indicates images that are copyright of The Reader's Digest Association Limited.

Front cover www.ntpl.org.uk/©NTPL/David Noton (Hadrian's Wall near Housesteads, Northumberland) **Back cover** Getty Images/Adie Bus (The Roaches, Derbyshire) **1** Getty Images/Axiom Photographic Agency (Brecon Beacons, Wales) **2-3** Alamy/Ed Rhodes (Losehill Pike Wards Hill, Edale, Derbyshire) **6-7** www.britainonview.com/Adam Burton (Rolling Devon farmland) **8-9** www.britainonview.com/John Miller (Cheddar Gorge, Somerset) **10** David Chapman **15** www.britainonview.com/Craig Roberts **16** Alamy/Andrew Bennett **22-23** Nature Picture Library/Ross Hoddinott **27** The Travel Library/ Derek Stone **31** Craig Joiner **34-35** Photolibrary.com/OSF/David Clapp **38-39** Derek Stone **43** The Travel Library/Tom Mackie **44-45** The Travel Library/Ben Pipe **48-49** Alamy/Derek Stone **50** Peter Booton **55** Craig Joiner **58** Alamy/Adrian Sherratt **63** Photolibrary.com/The Travel Library/Stuart Black **64** © RD **67** The Travel Library/Tom Mackie **68-69** www.britainonview.com/John Miller (Ashdown Forest, Sussex) **70** www.britainonview.com **72** © RD **76** The Travel Library/Rolf Richardson **79** Alamy/Robert Stainforth **81** Alamy/Quentin Bargate **84-85** Mike Watson **88** www.britainonview.com/Craig Roberts **91** GAP Photos/Jerry Harpur **95** Photolibrary.com/Garden Picture Library/Rex Butcher **101** The Travel Library/Chris Penn **104-105** Derek Stone **106** Alamy/Derek Payne **110-111** © RD **112-113** www.britainonview.com/ John Miller **114-115** Nature Picture Library/David Noton (Miller's Dale, Derbyshire); **116-117** Graham Uney **121** Robin Weaver **125** www.britainonview.com **126-127** www.britainonview.com/ Steve Walton **130** Craig Joiner **134-135** Alamy/Jeremy Pardoe **138** Collections/Gary Smith **142** The Travel Library/Rod Edwards **147** Axiom/Naki Kouyioumtzis **150** www.ntpl.org.uk/©NTPL/Paul Harris **155** The Travel Library/Stuart Black **158** www.britainonview.com/David Sellman **161** www.britainonview.com **164** www.britainonview.com/Jon Gibbs **167** www.britainonview.com/David Sellman **170-171** Mike Kipling (Buttermere, Cumbria); **172-173** Dreamstime/David Martyn **179** Craig Joiner **182-183** Photolibrary.com/ Robert Harding Travel/ Roy Rainford **187** David Forster **188** www.ntpl.org.uk/©NTPL/Howard Phillips **192-193** Graeme Peacock **195** www.britainonview.com/Lee Beel **196-197** The Travel Library/Tom Mackie **201** www.ntpl.org.uk/©NTPL/ Joe Cornish **202-203** Collections/Mike Kipling **204** Photolibrary.com/The Travel Library **208** Mike Kipling **212** Mike Kipling **215** www.ntpl.org.uk/ ©NTPL/Joe Cornish **219** www.britainonview.com/Rod Edwards **220-221** Dreamstime/Daniel James Armishaw (Llanberis Pass, North & mid Wales); **224-225** Photolibrary Wales/Chris Warren **228** © RD **233** © RD **237** Photolibrary.com/Robert Harding Travel/Adam Woolfitt **238** © RD **242-**www.britainonview.com/Steve Lewis **250-251** The Travel Library/ Granville Harris **252-253** www.ntpl.org.uk/©NTPL/Derek Croucher **257** Photolibrary Wales/Peter Lane **258-259** Robert Harding Travel/Patrick Dieudonné (Strathmore Valley and Ben Hope, Highlands) **260-261** South West Images Scotland **264-265** Picture Nature/Jan Holm **268** Scottish Viewpoint/D Barnes **272** Cliff Whittem **277** 4Corners/Borchi Massimo **280** The Travel Library/Tom Mackie **285** www.britainonview.com/David Noton **289** Picture Nature/Hil van der Waal **292-293** © RD **296-297** Scottish Viewpoint/P Tomkins **298-299** 4Corners/SIME/Spila Riccardo **302-303** Scottish Viewpoint/Colin McPherson **304-305** Photolibrary.com/OSF/Mark Hamblin **308** © RD **311** Scottish Viewpoint/P Tomkins

The publishers would like to thank the following people for help in checking the walks in this book:
David Bateman; Shirley Benn; Ros Blaylock; Clive Bostle; Paul Brooks; Peter Butterworth; Cynthia Chard; Jacky Cheeseman; Ray and Ann Curtis-Clarke; Derek Cooknell; Charles Davidson; Jackie Ferguson; Peter Gallagher; Graham Games; Alison Gaunt; Margaret Gibson; Pauline Goodridge; Barbara Harris; Kate Harris; Harry Hawkins; Geoff Hoggarth; Anne Hubert-Chibnall; Derrick Joanes; Joan Johnson; Michael Johnson; Mark Jones; Peter Judson; Alan and Tricia Kiddle; Marie Legg; Mark Lewis; Mary Livesey; Sarah McKeag; Phillip Mansley; Alan Moore; Harry Mycock; J.E. Noyce; David Oldfield; John Ottaway; Sylvia Penzer; Rosie Perham; Chris Playford; Mavis Rear; Ernie Robin; Sylvia Ronan; Claire Sanville; John and Jean Sheraton; Bernard Smith; Sarah Smithies; Jean Snary; Brian Spencer; Owen Star; Jacqueline Stow; Denis Taylor; Geoff Taylor; Michael Thompson; Richard Tyson; Mairi Walker; Graham Young.

The publishers have made every effort to ensure the accuracy of these acknowledgments. They will be happy to correct in any subsequent reprint any errors or omission of which they are notified.

Contributors

FOR DUNCAN PETERSEN PUBLISHING
Editorial Director Andrew Duncan
Project Manager Marion Moisy
Feature Writer Christopher Somerville
Design Paul Stradling, Keith Miller,
Kathy Gammon
Sub-editor Cécile Landau
Picture Researcher Sarah Smithies
Maps Anthony Duke
Proofreader Victoria Richards
Indexer Helen Varley

FOR READER'S DIGEST GENERAL BOOKS
Editor Jo Bourne

Editorial Director Julian Browne
Art Director Anne-Marie Bulat
Managing Editor Nina Hathway
Head of Book Development Sarah Bloxham
Picture Resource Manager Christine Hinze
Pre-press Account Manager Dean Russell
Product Production Manager
Claudette Bramble
Production Controller Sandra Fuller

Origination by Colour Systems Limited,
London
Printed in China

Every reasonable care has been taken to ensure that the information in this guide is accurate, but the routes described are undertaken at the individual's own risk. The publishers and copyright owners accept no responsibility for any consequences arising out of use of this book, including misinterpretation of the maps and directions and those arising from changes taking place after the text was finalised. The Reader's Digest Association is always pleased to hear from readers who wish to suggest corrections or improvements. Please remember that the countryside changes frequently and that landmarks, especially stiles, can disappear and be renewed in a different form to that described in the guide.

The Most Amazing Places to Walk in Britain is published by The Reader's Digest Association Limited, London. It was edited and produced for Reader's Digest by Duncan Petersen Publishing Ltd.

The Reader's Digest Association Limited,
11 Westferry Circus, Canary Wharf, London E14 4HE

The Most Amazing Places to Walk in Britain is adapted from **Country Walks and Scenic Drives**, published by The Reader's Digest Association Limited in 1998.

We are committed both to the quality of our products and the service we provide to our customers. We value your comments, so please do contact us on **08705 113366** or via our website at
www.readersdigest.co.uk

If you have any comments or suggestions about the content of our books, email us at
gbeditiorial@readersdigest.co.uk

ISBN 978 0 276 44497 5
Book Code 400-411 UP0000-1
Oracle Code 250013051S.00.24